The Public Realm

SUNY Series in Philosophy
Robert Cummings Neville, Editor

The Public Realm

Essays on Discursive Types
in Political Philosophy

edited by
Reiner Schürmann

State University of New York Press

Published by
State University of New York Press, Albany

© 1989 State University of New York

All rights reserved

Printed in the United States of America

No part of this book may be used or reproduced
in any manner whatsoever without written permission
except in the case of brief quotations embodied in
critical articles and reviews.

For information, address State University of New York
Press, State University Plaza, Albany, N.Y., 12246

Library of Congress Cataloging-in-Publication Data

The Public realm: essays on discursive types in political philosophy
 / edited by Reiner Schürmann.
   p.   cm. — (SUNY series in philosophy)
  Includes index.
ISBN 0-88706-717-4.   ISBN 0-88706-718-2 (pbk.)
  1. Political science—Philosophy.   2. Arendt, Hannah.
I. Schürmann, Reiner, 1941- .   II. Series.
JA74.P825 1988
320.01—dc19   87-20918
                                                          CIP

10 9 8 7 6 5 4 3 2 1

In memory of Hannah Arendt

Contents

Acknowledgments — ix

Introduction: *On Judging and Its Issue*
REINER SCHÜRMANN — 1

Part I. A Transcendental Philosophy of Politics

Chapter 1. *Transcendental Politics? Political Legitimacy and the Concept of Civil Society in Kant*
MANFRED RIEDEL — 25

Chapter 2. *Man's Hope*
STANLEY ROSEN — 44

Chapter 3. *Kant's Theory of Revolution*
THOMAS SEEBOHM — 60

Chapter 4. *Person and Law in Kant and Hegel*
LUDWIG SIEP — 82

Part II. A Normative Philosophy of Politics

Chapter 5. *Normative Ethics and Strategical Rationality: The Philosophical Problem of a Political Ethics*
KARL-OTTO APEL — 107

Chapter 6. *Notes for a Materialist Analysis of the Public and the Private Realms*
ROBERT PAUL WOLFF — 132

Chapter 7. *Remarks on the Ontology of "Right" and "Left"*
ROBERT SPAEMANN — 146

Chapter 8. *Ontological Grounding of a Political Ethics: On the Metaphysics of Commitment to the Future of Man*
HANS JONAS — 154

Chapter 9. *Notes on Legitimation*
JEAN-FRANÇOIS LYOTARD — 167

Part III. A Descriptive Philosophy of Politics

Chapter 10. *The Ruled and the Unruly: Functions and Limits of Institutional Regulations*
BERNHARD WALDENFELS — 183

Chapter 11.	*The Question of Life and Culture from the Perspective of a Radical Phenomenology*	
	MICHEL HENRY	193
Chapter 12.	*Contemplation in Action*	
	WILLIAM J. RICHARDSON	207
Chapter 13.	*Collective Symbolism in Political Discourse and its Share in Underlying Totalitarian Trends*	
	JÜRGEN LINK	225
Chapter 14.	*The Socialization of Human Action*	
	VINCENT DESCOMBES	239

Part IV. An Institutional Philosophy of Politics

Chapter 15.	*An Imaginary Preface to the 1984 Edition of Hannah Arendt's "The Origins of Totalitarianism"*	
	AGNES HELLER	253
Chapter 16.	*Social Movements, Revolution and Democracy*	
	ALAIN TOURAINE	268
Chapter 17.	*Toward a New Economic Style in Our Society?*	
	BERTRAM SCHEFOLD	284
Chapter 18.	*Time and Revolutionary Language*	
	REINHART KOSELLECK	297
Notes on Contributors		307

Acknowledgments

All the essays in this volume (with the exception of the Introduction) were originally delivered in the series of Hannah Arendt Memorial Symposia in Political Philosophy at the Graduate Faculty of the New School for Social Research, New York, where Arendt had been a professor of philosophy from 1967 until her death in 1975.

Some of the essays have been previously published in either *Social Research* or the *Graduate Faculty Philosophy Journal.* I thank the editors of these two journals for their permission to include these articles in the present collection.

Reiner Schürmann

Introduction

On Judging and Its Issue

"A new science of politics is needed for a new world," wrote de Tocqueville in *Democracy in America.* Taking up his call, Hannah Arendt sought to inquire anew into the realm of human affairs, into the *vita activa,* the active life. The essays collected here all develop one aspect of her inquiry inspired by the need voiced by de Tocqueville over a century ago; however, they are not essays *on* her thinking. Rather, they build freely upon the ground she has laid for that new science.

In *The Human Condition,* Arendt mapped out the method of that sought-for science—that philosophy, as it turned out. It would situate the modern age in relation to the Greek *polis;* it would mark off the public from the private realm; and it would trace the web of what she considered to be the fundamental human activities: labor, work, and action. These topics outlined a "new political philosophy."[1] It was "new" in that she wished to counter the *déformation professionnelle* of all Western philosophers, who preferred to speak of Man as a universal rather than of the human plurality. Therefore, in subsequent writings, she applied her framework to such concrete issues as totalitarianism, revolution, democracy, and republicanism. So adamant was her desire to restore the dignity of the singular that at times she denied being a philosopher—a denial she did not mind retracting in her last project. When she died in 1975, she had completed two out of the three volumes that were to complement her theory of active life by a theory of the *vita contemplativa,* "The Life of the Mind." These two volumes are entitled *Thinking* and *Willing,* respectively. The third was to deal with *Judging.* On this topic, however, we only possess posthumously published lecture notes, which I will discuss further below.

In this introduction I shall first trace, albeit critically, that attempted rehabilitation of the singular in Arendt's post-Kantian theory of judgment. Then, at my own risk, I shall look at Kant himself to see how in his critical system the singular turned into the very issue for judging. (This can best be shown by exhibiting the two senses of being in Kant, being as *Position* and being as *Setzung,* one articulating synthesis and the other dispersion). After this, I will argue that there are good reasons not to gloss over, paste up, or drown in exegetical charity the ontological rift laid bare by Kant. Finally, I shall return to this collection of essays and describe briefly the scope of its theme and the order of its composition.

"Meeting the Phenomena Head-On"

> "What if *differing* rather than consensus were the issue for thinking?"[2]
>
> —Jean-François Lyotard

To judge is to apply a law to some fact or occurrence. There can be no judgment unless the law exceeds the fact in scope and unless it somehow grounds it in depth—unless, in comparison to the fact, the law is universal in both extension and comprehension. Theories of judgment necessarily spell out a relation of subjection whereby one evaluates a particular that is the case using a universal that measures the case. We make the most modest claims to judgmental universality when we have recourse merely to some paradigmatic instance of a particular, as when we say, "As courageous as Achilles," or "As strong as Samson." A given particular, Achilles or Samson, finds itself endowed with exemplary universality as it serves to measure other particulars. The claim is modest in scope since examples apply only to selected facts, for example, phenomena of courage or strength; it is also modest in depth since it entails only comparisons, no groundings. Indeed, any exemplary standard can in turn be measured by higher standards, as when one asks, "What is better, courage or strength?" The least modest claim to judgmental universality, on the other hand, would aim at securing one standard immune to further evaluation, one supreme referent. The history of philosophy offers a supply of such ultimate representations that should satisfy even the most voracious metaphysical appetite. From Parmenides to Husserl,[3] philosophers have been the covert civil servants whose expertise has secured the (legitimating) law of (juridical, ethic, and discursive) laws. As technicians of subsumption, they have varied the *judgmental difference* between one hegemonic phantasm and the many facts or occurrences covered by its extension and anchored by its comprehension.

We say we *differ* on something whenever two (or more) conflicting claims cannot be subsumed under the same covering law. Both claims may be legitimate in their respective orders of validity, yet they may be heteronomous—falling under diverse *nomoi*—because those orders are incompatible. When two opposing parties enter a litigation, they thereby acknowledge the pertinence of one law under which they seek to be judged. Their dispute can therefore be settled. To enter a litigation is to bring one's case, as particular, under the relevant law as applicable to that case and hence as universal. No settlement can be reached between *differing* stands, that is, when the conflict amounts to a *différend*. In such a case, the mechanics of subsumption get out of gear. Lyotard, from whom I borrow the term (but only the term), cites the position of contemporary historians who deny the existence of extermination camps under National Socialism. These authors argue that they would recognize only testimony from victims—

who, by definition, can no longer give it. What common law could settle such a disagreement? From the very start, the case for grievance is robbed of all possible arguments. Lyotard also cites the French officer at Verdun who shouts "Charge!" and leaps out of the trenches; his infantry men shout back "Bravo!" and do not move. A conflict of so-called values, too, is a *différend*.

It may well be that, since Aristotle, the irreducible diversity of the sciences has entailed something like a scattergram of styles and methods, in as much as the measure-giving science remains "sought for." First principles would then govern such regions of phenomena as ethics, politics, physics, and so on, but not the constellation of these regions, not phenomena qua phenomena. Aristotle would have opened the *différend* between disciplines. No regional science is conceivable without the subsumption of particular facts under universal statements. What, then, would a radical *différend* be? It would be one in which coercion under a principle would be matched by an equal dispersion among singulars. The 'particular' is always a case of some universal, while the 'singular' merely is the case. In a radical *différend,* we stand equally exposed to laws unifying the particular and plurifying the singular.

Below I shall try to show how, in the *Critique of Judgment,* Kant not only acknowledges such a radical conflict among phenomena but also gives an ontological account of it. His discovery of reflective, as opposed to subsumptive, judgments culminates in the recognition that the singular alone—not the particular—"is." What I have called the judgmental difference between the normative one and the normed many takes on in Kant the form of two senses of being. The 'one' that serves as the law for all synthetic judgments is being as the thinking "I": the hegemonic phantasm of earlier modernity. The dispersed 'many' to be conformed to that highest unity is made up of the appearances. In reflective judgments, however, we do not determine the "existent in nature" so as to grasp it through a concept. We only mirror it. In these judgments, then, the normative force of being as one, for being as the many, breaks down. In subsuming intuitions under concepts, we constitute what is to be known and, by right, can then reach a consensus about what is to be done. No such remedy to dispersion is within our reach if 'to think being' means to reflect disparate singulars. Then, as surmised in the epigraph above, the issue for thinking may indeed be differing rather than consensus.

The strongest reading of Kant's third *Critique* as a theory of noncognitive judgments has been given in Arendt's posthumously published lectures.[4] In a homage, however critical, to her attempt to rehabilitate the singular in political philosophy, I shall discuss the affinity she claimed rather peremptorily between aesthetic and political judgments:

> The reason why I believe so much in Kant's *Critique of Judgment* is not because I am interested in aesthetics but because I believe that the way in which we say

"that is right," "that is wrong" is not very different from the way in which we say "this is beautiful," "this is ugly." That is, we are now prepared to meet the phenomena, so to speak, head-on, without any preconceived system. And, please, including my own![5]

We should certainly heed Arendt's twofold advice in these lines: to read the *Critique of Judgment* as a work of political philosophy, but also *not* to read it with what she calls her own preconceived system.

Arendt was fascinated with what she called the "rare moments of freedom" in history, the moments of interregnum when one order of rules is about to vanish and a new one has not yet entirely come into place. Such intermittent times of deep breathing are literally times of anarchy, of absence of governance. In the modern period, these were the months of the Paris Commune with its attempted revival in May 1968—when one could read on the walls of the Sorbonne, "Long live the workers' councils extended to all aspects of life"—as well as the weeks of the Russian Soviets and the German *Räte* at the end of the First World War, revived also for a moment in Budapest in 1956.

Arendt obviously never dreamt of participating in political action. She was, in Kant's terms, the enthusiastic spectator co-constituting the events, but for the reading public. It is not difficult to imagine that she would have had strong moral objections to picking up cobblestones and throwing them at various living targets, but equally evident was her aesthetic delight in the elusive meaning given to these events by another graffito at the Sorbonne: *"Dessous les pavés c'est la plage"* ("Underneath the cobblestones is the beach"). The point is that writers of wall inscriptions and editorialists, together with their readers, contribute more decisively to the public realm than those who fight battles and sign treaties. The storytellers contribute more to it than those about whom the stories are told.

Aesthetic delight is what, according to Kant, the individual beautiful object gives to the beholder. Arendt's project in her recently published lectures consists in showing Kant's discovery of judgment as an independent faculty along with understanding and willing; her project is furthermore to expand that faculty's competence to the political domain. Kant, she says, "did not recognize the political and moral implications of his discovery" (p. 107). She undertakes, then, to outline Kant's "unwritten political philosophy" (pp. 7 and 31). It is entirely a philosophy of the singular.

Knowing what is right and willing what is good are indeed insufficient credentials for entering the public realm, just as they are insufficient for appreciating works in a museum or on a stage. If what was needed for public performance, whether aesthetic or political, was merely knowledge, then intellectuals would make the best politicians. But, Kant observed, such is not the case: "It is not unusual to meet learned men who in the application of their knowledge betray an original want: . . . deficiency in judgement is just what is ordinarily called stupidity, and for such a failing there is no remedy."[6] Intellectuals are poor politicians because they make it their profession to subsume each particular occurrence under some general truth. Subsumption under universals is their occupational hazard. But politics is the art of the particular. It is, Kant says, even the paradoxical art of "thinking the particular" (quoted on p. 76)—paradoxical since we have learned from Aristotle that we can only think in concepts, that is, in universals. Only in what Kant called reflective judgments do we then "meet the phenomena head-on," that is, as *singular.*

Arendt thus shows why judgment is irreducible to cognition. She also shows why it is irreducible to will. Willing, as she understands it, is by nature single-minded, oblivious of contexts. She liked to quote Bergson in this respect: "The will acts like a *coup d'état.*"[7]

If cognition was all that was needed in the political sphere, then politics would be reduced to management, to sheer administration—the substance of which was for Arendt "the social." This prepolitical nature of social phenomena appeared most clearly to her in contemporary mass cultures: "The fundamental contradiction of the country [the United States] is political freedom coupled with social slavery."[8] If, on the other hand, the will was all that was needed in the public realm, we would be living in a world of perpetual *coups d'état*—under the "triumph of the will" she had known through first-hand experience.

The originality of Arendt's political theory after Kant lies in this topology of specifically political phenomena. They are located neither within the reach of knowledge, compelling it to true statements, nor within that of the will, impelling it to appropriation. Rather, their phenomenal site is akin to that of aesthetic objects. Just like the world of the performing arts, the world of politics *would not exist* if there were no spectators. With a predilection for overstatement that caused her trouble on more than one occasion, Arendt did not hesitate to write: "The public realm is constituted by the critics and the spectators, *not* the actors or the makers" (p. 63). The point is that the spectators alone are in a position to decide which singular act is noteworthy and which is not.

Concretely, if the French Revolution was, in Kant's words, a "phenomenon that cannot be forgotten," this is due not to such actors as Danton, Marat, Robespierre, and others, but to the "reading public" all over Europe and its "outspoken partiality." One feels partiality for this or that deed, this or that object; one cannot feel partial for universals. Kant adds, "This revolution finds in the hearts of all spectators a wishful participation that borders closely on enthusiasm." In *judgment* we cannot but approve of the storming of the Bastille, but in *moral* reasoning, Kant goes on, our disapproval has to be equally unmitigated. Right and wrong, or just and unjust, are consequences of the self-given law of freedom, hence universal. "The people may not pursue its rights by revolution, which is at all times unjust." "It is *sweet* to think up constitutions that would correspond to the demands of reason; it is *foolhardy* to put them forward seriously; and it is *punishable* to incite the people to do away with the existing constitution."[9] Kant's well-known ambivalence toward the events of 1789 illustrates most strikingly his delineation of two phenomenal regions: that where we are merely onlookers and that where we are actors. It illustrates his distinction between two faculties, that of judgment and that of the moral will. It instantiates—despite terminological fluctuations in both Kant and Arendt—the irreducibility of the singular to the particular. The singular needs to be looked at, appreciated, and judged; the particular needs to be conceived through subsumption, determined by concepts, and known.

Concerning Arendt's account, it is clearly much too partial for Kant's praise of partiality. The expanded competence she gives reflective judgments should not be taken as doctrine. We would be wise in seeking, as she did, Kant's political philosophy not only in his writings explicitly devoted to it but also in his texts on aesthetic judgment. But where we should not follow her advice to the end is in what she described as her "preconceived system": in this context, the all too sweeping disjunction between the moral and the political, as well as a certain disdain for history that pervades her thinking. Both tendencies result from her fascination with the singular.

A clear-cut disjunction between moral and political philosophy is impossible for Kant, if only because the stakes are the same in either discipline: *enlightenment* through reclaiming the subjective autonomy that had been lost under the sway of ultimate metaphysical representations. "Enlightment is man's release from his self-incurred tutelage."[10] In matters of science, to become autonomous is to prescribe transcendental laws to nature; in matters of morals, it is to submit freely under self-given imperatives; and in matters of judgment, it is to esteem things beautiful and things political for their own sake. Contrary to Arendt's repeated claim, in all these attempts at enlightenment, subsumption is indeed operative, except that judgmental standards are taken from experience—as when we say that someone is "as brave as Achilles" (p. 77)—and exercised in communication with others. Political judgments are formed through experience and persuasion just as judgments of taste are formed through education. In the absence of such exercise and education, we run the risk of life-long embarrassment in aesthetic choices and, more dangerous, of life-long mistakes in political choices. The terminological fluctuations between the 'particular' and the 'singular' stem from the peculiar status of the aesthetic and political objects: They are subsumable, not under universals, but under standards nevertheless.

Arendt's disdain for history—which she treated as one more "metaphysical fallacy" (p. 127)—results from the same fascination with singularity as she construes it from her overdrawn parallel between the aesthetic and the political judgment. The "rare moments of freedom" are unique, irretrievable. Today's superpowers may eventually relive something of the slow decline the British Empire has suffered since World War I, but we will never relive the Paris Commune or May 1968. As a consequence of her fascination with singulars, politics turns into something other than the pursuit of realizable, but common, ends. That is left to what Kant called "the mechanics of nature," by which even "a race of devils" will eventually be forced to enact a republican constitution.[11]

What remains for the public realm is one's being seen and heard by everybody in speaking about the common good. What Achilles is in respect to courage, namely, the paradigmatic instance, the revolutionary general assembly is in respect to politics. The political realm is opened up wherever participants in a community speak up: always *hic et nunc*. How strangely disembodied such a notion of the political turns out to be appears from the underlying time concept, which is more akin to the medieval "standing now" than to Kant's secularized "providence."

On the positive side, her extreme, rarified understanding of the political allows Arendt to cut through the old dilemma, whether it is an active or contemplative life that makes man happy. Had she lived to write the third volume, *Judging,* of her *Life of the Mind* she might have had to take back her earlier siding with Aristotle's *Politics* when she summed up her theory of the *polis* saying, "Acting is fun."[12] From the Kant lectures it appears inevitable that she would have had to shift her emphasis and identify *eudaimonia* neither with action nor with contemplation, but with judgment. Her Kantian revisionist reading of the Greeks might have compelled her to conclude, judging is fun.

On the negative side, however, such a shift leaves no room for the genuinely Kantian conviction that history is the locus where we emancipate ourselves from our self-incurred tutelage "over a long, perhaps incalculable series of generations, each passing its enlightenment to the next."[13] Construing a sharp either-or between Kant's trust in progress and his discovery of nonteleological judgment, Arendt concludes, "The very idea of progress . . . contradicts Kant's notion of human dignity" (p. 77). As a result, she denounces "the pseudo-divinity named History of the modern age" (p. 131). In Kant himself, no such either-or is possible, be it only because the two terms that she separates are actually held together by the ideal of the noumenal republic. This ideal generates moral imperatives that make her separation of the political from the moral look artificial as well. It is true that, at times, she does acknowledge the link between the two, but only to pull even the moral over to the side of the singular, of our choice and judgment of it: "In the last analysis . . . our decisions about right and wrong will depend upon our choice of company, with whom we wish to spend our lives" (p. 113).

The thrust toward rehabilitating the singular, as Arendt has traced it in Kant's theory of judgment, goes to the heart of his critical system. This last quotation indicates, however, most strikingly that she tried to run that rehabilitation program on impracticable tracks. To make right and wrong depend on one's choice of friends amounts to metabolizing the good into an object of chance encounter and selection, the way one encounters and selects a life companion. Such hit-or-miss morality turns the prestige of the singular against Kant's very letter and spirit.

Along which tracks, then, is one to pursue Kant's doctrine of the singular as he adumbrates it in his theory of aesthetic judgments? It is no more than an adumbration since aesthetic appreciation puts only conceptual, not paradigmatic, subsumption out of function. As the singular appears under the guise of one given particular gauged by one exemplary particular, it is not entirely set free from comprehensive measurement. Still, there exists a line of inquiry in Kant that articulates not only the judgmental difference but also the *différend* by which the one and the many impose on us their contradictory claims. This is not some argumentative strategy among others; it is the most traditional of issues in Western philosophy, a question Kant consistently shuns while answering it equally consistently: *Ti to on*; "What is being?"[14]

Synthesis and Dispersion

Kant is said to have substituted a merely formal act, apperception, for all ancient substantive referents held capable of ordering a cosmos inasmuch as they were conceived as eminently present to it. However, Kant did not quite abandon the ancients' quest for an ultimate *mensura;* he merely directed it away from the demiurge or Creator measuring his works to reason measuring its acts. He is, therefore, said to have replaced dogmatic metaphysics with critical metaphysics, the metaphysics of experience. Yet he, too, seeks an "originary" *thesis,* positing, by which we can discriminate between what is and what is not. To be sure, his transcendental egothesis cannot be "ontological" in the sense of a highest degree of being. The ultimate self-positing of thinking sought by Kant has to satisfy only the requirement of a highest condition for experience. As such, it is nothing entitative—"no thing," not a subsistent referent of which one could predicate, for instance, simplicity or eternality. Still, it has to be "originary," "an act of spontaneity," be it only as "the highest point to which all employment of the understanding must be attached."[15] Apperception is the source of mental functions, not the origin of subsistent beings. Through one of the functions emanating from it, we declare what is.

To "declare" or "accuse" is *kategorein* in Greek. In Kant, being is a category: that which tells us not *what* we experience, but *that* we experience something. As such it is one fundamental mode of synthesizing data into the unity of objective experience. Just as every other category, being is not only a law for all actual experience but also inseparably a form of all objects actually experienced. It has objective validity when gathered with the pure forms of intuition, time and space. In conjunction with these forms, the dynamic category of *Dasein* co-constitutes whatever can become a phenomenon for us. Such is Kant's doctrinal answer to the question of being. It is doctrinal inasmuch as for him anything that can be proved without recourse to appearances, anything that can be demonstrated or deduced *a priori,* is part of a doctrine. Kant's discovery of the categorial status of existence allows for a *critical doctrine* (the two terms are not mutually exclusive) of being.

A second concept of being is, however, also operative in Kant, which precedes the revolution in his way of thinking and remains operative at each major step in his critical system. It may be called his countervailing concept of being since it avails or prevails against the doctrinal notion. The 'vail'—value or worth—of this other notion equals that of the category. It pulls Kantian ontology into the direction not of the unifying one, but of the disparate singulars. It thereby opens the rift between the one and the many as equally binding for us. It opens the *différend*.

In his precritical treatise on the sole proof for a demonstration of God's existence, Kant wrote, "Being is not a predicate, nor a determination of any thing."[16] It is usually held that this early work is incompatible not only with Kant's later criticism of the ontological argument, but more generally with his transcendental method as such. That is assuredly the case—except in one respect, which is related to the understanding of being operative in the treatise. Being has nothing of a predicate since it adds no thought content to whatever we conceive. Kant's starting point is reminiscent of Leibnizian idealities (propositions in logic, mathematics, and pure geometry) among which universal and necessary connections obtain. The young Kant reasons not from 'real things', as the Scholastics did, nor from 'being' as a necessary thought content, as Descartes did, but from the universal *possibilities,* the formal presuppositions for anything real. His argument is *a priori,* based neither on observation nor on a trusted correspondence between concepts and things, but on connections among concepts. Absolute existence is attainable from that rationalist starting point— the system of rules for thinking—insofar as *that system of rules is given.* If there are any rules whatsoever for connecting concepts, be it only the opposition between "true" and "false," then material existence, too, is assured. "If all existence is cancelled, then nothing whatsoever is posited, nothing at all is given: no matter for anything thinkable, and any possibility vanishes entirely." The point is that the real and the possible can very well be negated together without any ensuing contradiction. It is, however, contradictory to hold that the real exists without the possible, or the possible without the real. *What* is being thought does not lead then, as in Descartes, to apodeicticity, but rather *that* there are thought contents ruled by necessary connections. There would be no thinking at all if these particular kinds of givens—possibles—were lacking: "That there is anything possible and yet nothing real is a contradiction since, if nothing existed, nothing thinkable would be given."[17] Being as the position of anything follows from the givenness of ideal entities.

The steps by which the early Kant argues the existence of God—stepping from any thing's givenness to absolute givenness and from existence to essence—have no direct bearing on his understanding of being. The anticipation of the transcendental method in the early treatise is, however, remarkable: without givenness as its starting point, all knowledge would remain impossible. To be sure, after the critical turn givenness is no longer that of a system of idealities. Therefore, being is then no longer understood as absolute, but only as relative positedness, that is, relative to our experience. The first feature one has to retain of the other concept of being in Kant, other than the category, is givenness as such. That concept cannot be analysed any further; it can only be determined negatively. Each major section of the *Critique of Pure Reason* contributes to such negative determination whereby givenness will appear as precognitive, precategorial and prepredicative. The most revelatory issue is that of the existing I, of how the I is given to me.

Kant claims that the Transcendental Aesthetic "establishes already of itself the objective reality of noumena" (A 249) insofar as, in experiencing, we necessarily experience something.[18] On the level of a simple encounter, what is experienced yields no knowledge yet. We cannot say what it is that we come upon. It yields however its own certitude of objective reality, namely, that something is there whereby we are affected. Contrary to some ambiguous formulations in and after Kant, this affectedness, or facticity, cannot be construed as "posited" by consciousness. It precedes all acts of the mind. Such is the very starting point of the Aesthetic: the preeminence of intuiting over thinking is due to the immediacy of the sense data. As is well known, that starting point of the *Critique* made Friedrich Jacobi complain, *"Without* that presupposition (of the noumenon) I cannot enter the *Critique,* while with that presupposition I cannot remain in it."[19] Sense affection provides obviously no knowledge of the noumenon qua noumenon; as a mere sensation, it is "blind." Nor has the being concept implied in sense affection anything to do yet with the formal constitution of objects. It is merely the concept of a datum as such, the critical descendant of the "data of possibility" in the earlier treatise. In the Transcendental Aesthetic, ontological givenness is determined negatively as precognitive.

Kant specifies his understanding of being as givenness in the Transcendental Analytic. "The 'I think' expresses the act of determining my existence" (B 158n). Affection and givenness are here self-affection and self-givenness in inner sense. "My existence" cannot be given either to intellectual intuition or to formal consciousness, since it is to be determined by the "I think." The existing

I cannot be either the noumenal or the transcendental I. But neither can it be the empirical I as observed in our mental life. For such observation—for self-experience—the intuition through inner sense would have to be joined to a pure concept of the understanding. But, Kant adds, "existence here is not yet a category" (B 422). As a mere sensation, existence precedes, he says, any experience and therefore any synthesis. In this context, then, the "I think" is turned into a proposition of existence independently of any recourse to categories. This is not, in Kant, a momentary lapse into Cartesian metaphysics. He explicitly justifies that step by describing the existing I as "indeterminately given" (B 423n), impossible to reify into a thinking thing. At this stage, it has already become impossible to maintain that existence, as the second category of modality, accuses being that is given to the senses. If such were the case, how could Kant claim that "existence here is not yet a category"?

Conversely, and for the same reason, the category cannot stand for the being *(Existenz)* of beings. If in givenness existence is not yet a category, then given beings have their being in themselves and do not receive it from the bestowing agency of the spontaneous rational subject.

How is one to construe the determinacy of the 'I think' so that it can in turn determine my existence? Obviously its *Bestimmtheit* cannot result from the pure concepts of the understanding. As the source of all determinations, the logical subject of thinking cannot itself be determined categorially. Determinacy is its very nature; it is utter spontaneity. It reigns supreme as the sole agency of configuration in experience. And yet, for it to "determine my existence," it has to be equiprimordial with givenness. The existing ego designates the as yet *indistinct* presence of an indeterminate sensation to thought. As their proto-synthesis, it lacks conceptual articulation.

The dilemma, and eventually the *différend,* is more complex than the conflict between a 'mentalist' and a 'realist' ontology. The question is not: Does being lie in the mind or in the things? The question as it arises from Kant's examination of the I, is rather: Is "my existence" the indeterminate content of sensation or the determinate act of consciousness? Kant remains perplexingly hesitant on this crucial point. He does justify the step from transcendental logic to transcendental ontology ("existence here is not yet a category"), but he does not in any way thematize the precategorial sensation of existence with which, however, in his own words, experience sets out. His hesitancy shines through when he states that, prior to any act of experience and any synthesis, there occurs the givenness of the indeterminate "something real" that is "designated as such in the proposition 'I think' " (B 423n). Could it be that the "unknown root" (B 29) of our faculties is existence as sheer presence of ourselves to ourselves? If so, this is not only a fragile root, but a fractured one. Its brokenness appears from closer scrutiny of the way such primitive self-presence comes to be determined.

In order for the existing subject to function as the stage for all beings, making them appear through representation and thereby granting them categorial being, it would have to be thoroughly determined. This is, however, not the case. Indeterminate presence proves to be a distinct moment that precedes not only knowing but also thinking and apperception. Otherwise the "I think" could not determine my existence. The originary nomothetical act, the act of legislation from which both theoretical rules and practical norms are derived, is the imposing of the I as a law unto myself: We have to "presuppose ourselves, entirely *a priori*, as legislating with regard to our own being and also as determining this existence ourselves" (B 430). Self-presence is indeterminate since in it my existence is not yet articulated. Presence precedes consciousness (apperception) as well as introspection (experience). *Being as indeterminate presence precedes being as schematized category.* The subject thus shows itself to be broken. On the one hand, there is the determinative "I think" that posits itself and unfolds into twelve categories, and on the other, "my existence" which stands in need of determination. Kant's second being-concept disrupts critical ontology inasmuch as indeterminate existence, given to inner sensation, opposes a counterpoint of ignorance to apperception as the highest point of consciousness. It opposes a counterstrategy of indistinctness to the originary strategy of supreme formal synthesis in the *cogito*.

The determinate "I think" arises from indeterminate presence and in turn determines it. Without this double strategy, there would be no subject at all. By the same token, however, determination or self-possession does not result from what Kant describes as ontologically first, "my existence." As a consequence, Kant gives two answers to the question, What is being? His doctrinal answer (existence is a category) centers being on the spontaneous I, but his countervailing answer (existence is presence) disperses being among the givens received in sensibility (of which the existing I is only the paradigmatic case). Kant's first answer to the being question follows the strategy of synthesis toward the one. His second answer hints at an undertow toward plurification or dispersion.

In these conflicting answers, something entirely different than an insufficiently worked out ontology is at stake. One has to view that break as a displacement of the old metaphysical difference between *einai* and *on*, or *esse* and *ens*, and one may speak consequently of a transcendental difference in Kant. All forms of the ontological difference, whether metaphysical, transcendental, or phenomenological, spell out an ambiguity that lies in the present participle: the English participle *being* can mean both the noun *a being* and the verb *to be*. Due to the Copernican Revolution in Kant, the transcendental difference exhibits the peculiar feature that the inherited terms of the difference are inverted. In Kant it is not the verb, not *Dasein* as a categorial act or as conceiving, that stands for indeterminacy, but the noun, the unknown something encountered in a sensation. In the transcendental difference, determination is a human doing, the act of categorizing. The verb expresses subsumption under predicates. Both in Aristotle and in Heidegger, on the contrary, the verb stands for indeterminacy and the noun, for determination. An entity determines—"forms" (Aristotle), "stops" (from *epechein,* Heidegger)—the neutral being-process. Kant's inverting the poles of determinacy and indeterminacy is the consequence for ontology of what is described today as the modern triumph of subjectivity. Determination is a subjective doing: categorizing. But the inversion is ineffectual; the subject's pretense to universal determination remains shot through with indeterminacy. Hence Kant's broken ontology, broken between verbal *kategorein* and nominal fact.

Kant's self-congratulatory comment that he has drawn up "exhaustively" the architectonic of pure reason and has solved all conflicts to "complete satisfaction" (A XII) forbids filing his broken ontology under the rubric of unsolved issues. His two answers to the being question must be taken in their *heterogeneity.* In them, Kant acknowledges the condition that makes us mortals. His analysis of the existing I shows that indeterminacy and self-determination are two equally indispensable moments of our being. Their equiprimordiality is sufficient reason to read him as articulating more than the harmonious depth-structure of *Differenz,* namely, the disharmonious surface-rupture of *différend.* As Kant subverts his doctrine of being as a category, the subject stands torn between the pull toward synthesis and the pull toward dispersion. The doctrine of being as concept (from *con-capere,* holding together, just as *Begriff* stems from *greifen,* to grasp), that is, as the act of uniting the pure sensible manifold, is subverted by his systematic need for being as givenness, as indeterminate, and as precategorial. Primitive self-presence, the starting point for experience, throws the subject's quest for self-possession out of gear. Its "ground" or "essence" (B 430) places full presence forever out of reach.

The best known formulation of Kant's countervailing concept of being occurs in the Transcendental Dialectic. The formulation is reminiscent of his precritical writings: " 'Being' *(Sein)* is obviously not a real predicate" (B 626). 'Real' does not here refer to the first category of quality any more than 'being' refers to the second category of modality. We know empirically what something is when we know its 'real' predicates or properties. In the case of the supreme being, these properties would have to be known *a priori*. If such were the case, the properties—what the medievals called 'perfections'—of that supreme being would allow for its "thorough determination." Its concept would then be rendered concrete as the "set concept *(Inbegriff)* of all reality" (B 605). But *Sein* is obviously not a real predicate once being is understood as the sensible givenness of a physical fact, to the exclusion of intellectual affection. As to the category of *Dasein,* although it is thinkable *a priori* and although it is a predicate, it does "not in the least enlarge the concept to which it [is] attached" (B 266). It is not a *real* predicate either. It gives us nothing to think. *Sein* differs from *Dasein* (or

Existenz) in that it is not thinkable *a priori* in any way, neither formally as all categories are nor materially as the supposed divine perfections would have to be. To refute all attempts at an ontological proof of the existence of God, Kant then repeats his precritical equation between being and positedness (B 626). Translated into the critical context, that equation points most decisively to being as the precognitive, precategorial, prepredicative givenness of singulars.

The being of the singular remains only hinted at in the first and the second *Critique*. It comes fully to the fore in the third *Critique,* where Kant, as Hannah Arendt had sensed, addresses it as the very issue for judging. That issue remains distorted, however, as long as one does not place it within the itinerary of the being question in Kant. The itinerary begins with the precritical assertion that being is no predicate at all; it leads to the *Critique of Pure Reason,* in which being is negated as a 'real' predicate, to be affirmed only as the copula (B 626); and it concludes with the express recognition of the two strategies in being, in the *Critique of Judgment.*

The divergent strategies toward synthesis and dispersion are expressed there through the distinction between 'position' *(Position)* and 'positing' *(Setzung).* The first addresses the possibility of things, the second, their actuality. The 'position' indicates merely the mind's ability to represent phenomena to itself, that is, to gain access to them. The term must, therefore, not be confused with the same term in the first *Critique,* where it designates the exact contrary: the "being outside my concept," for example, the actuality of a hundred thalers in my pocket (B 627). In the third *Critique,* such actuality is called *Setzung.* "The actual . . . signifies the positing of a thing in itself (outside our concept)."[20] 'Position', then, marks the relation of a representation to the understanding and 'positing' that of an existing thing to our sensibility. *Setzung* results from chance encounter. It is, as Kant adds, "contingent." Furthermore, representations are universals; 'position' denotes the strategy toward synthesis, toward the one. Contingents, on the other hand, are singulars; 'positing' denotes the strategy toward dispersion, toward the many.

Throughout his writings, Kant understands being as givenness. But only after the discovery of aesthetic judgments, by which we address the unprecedented, does givenness clearly mean for him the *there* of singulars irreducible to any representation. In calling that givenness 'positing', Kant calls attention to the act of reception in sensibility. Receptivity, as he explained already in the Transcendental Aesthetic, is an act. It does not mean passivity. 'Position' and 'positing' articulate, then, the acts of understanding and of sensibility, respectively. Kant's two ways of answering the being question result from his dualist ontology, which splits the subject into "two entirely heterogeneous pieces."[21] According to one line of argument, being is a category, a concept, the act of unifying the manifold in the understanding. According to the other line of argument, it lies "outside my concept." It is the sporadic singular, encountered by chance in sensibility and acknowledged by equally sporadic acts of compliance.

Tragic Sobriety

"That mountain there! That cloud there! What is 'real' about that? Just subtract the phantasm and the whole human *contribution* from it, my sober friends! If only you *could!*"[22] Phantasms are what Kant calls representations. Nietzsche invites his sober friends—presumably the adherents to enlightenment—to acknowledge the singular as such, without judging it as beautiful, as purposive, or as spectacular in Arendt's sense, without turning it into a particular. All phantasms subtracted, we would "meet the phenomena head-on." Judgment would be transvaluated into thinking. We would think the singular in its being. We would be entirely sober and enlightened at last. But, "If only you *could!*"

It seems that we can*not*. Aesthetic and teleological judgments are reflective. In them, the universal is not pregiven, as in determinative judgments; it is to be sought and can be retained only in the mode of an 'as if'. Neither Kant nor Nietzsche believe that we can disintoxicate ourselves from universal representations to the point of thinking no more than the singular in its being (both Kant and Nietzsche would therefore be mislabeled as 'nominalists'). But both have seen the push-and-pull that tears all human experience: the push toward unity under some representation, coupled with the pull toward dispersion among singulars. Not unlike Nietzsche's, Kant's—reluctant—statements about being arise from a deep insight into the human condition. Unlike Nietzsche, however, he shied away from what he saw. The human condition is to stand under the twofold law of collocation and dislocation, without recourse to any supreme locus from which would proceed all allocations.

As a category, concept, or phantasm, being gathers beings into one; its script is a monogram. As "outside my concept," it disperses beings into the many; its script is a scattergram. Kant never attempts to elaborate a theory of the singular. Yet throughout his writings, although mostly in passing, he recognizes that rift between being as univocal and being as plurivocal. He does more than just recognize it. By his dualism he justifies it expressly as inscribed in our very constitution. Only in one line of inquiry is there no hint, as far as I can tell, of the undertow toward plurification, and that is in his moral doctrine. There the monovalence of the law triumphs over all polyvalence. Indeed, which axiologist could sustain the fervor of an absolute value that is *prescriptive morally,* while asserting as equally *prescriptive ontologically* the counterstrategy toward "that mountain, that cloud"? Such sobriety could only deflect the subject from the orbit of implacable necessitation. It would be an exorbitant sobriety.

From the aesthetic and the teleological point of view, the counterstrategy toward the monadic appears in Kant's third *Critique* as the very issue for judging. Yet sheer compliance with monadic givens exceeds our capacity. To say how much I like that mountain, that cloud, I say, "It reminds me of . . . ," and already the singular is lost to subsumption. Already the judgmental *difference* is put to work. On the other hand, from the ontological point of view, our allegiance is as much to monadic, centrifugal dispersion as it is to centripetal synthesis. In all our activities investigated by Kant, we put to work the ontological *différend,* or rather that *différend* puts us to work. In all our endeavors it ties us in one stroke and necessarily to consolidation as well as to dissolution. The retraction toward chaos, which Kant's critical turn was meant to stem, appears as no less normative ontologically than the attraction toward order. The most enlightened insight is into that double bind. There is no greater sobriety than to recognize and live that conflict, without dreamt-up sublation.

Kant's split ontology argues an insight that is as old as Homer and the Tragics. Achilles, the most shining of all heroes, delights in his splendor, feeds his anger, savors his vengeance, is more alive than anyone else, all the while knowing his imminent death. Antigone and Oedipus are not victims 'crushed by the terrible wheel of destiny.' Rather, they enact and affirm the dissolution at the very heart of all configuration. The tragic insight does not affirm life *against* death, it affirms death *in* life. To think to its end the *différend* in being, which Kant preferred to skirt, would amount to breaking the age-old contract whereby the philosopher acts as the expert of deep anchorage and, therefore, as our most indispensable civil servant. His promotion to that worthy rank coincided with the decline of the Greek tragedy, when the noblest task came to lie in the ministry of consolidating the city and consoling the spirit. The *différend* unmasks that twofold edification as redundant hubris.

Kant with Aeschylus, then? Inceptively so, yes. In the age of Aeschylus, Greece lost once and for all its archaic smile. One century later, Democritus discovered a new pleasure. He has been called the laughing philosopher. He said he found greater joy in understanding a causal relation than he would have had in occupying the imperial throne of Persia. Nothing, indeed, protects normative edifices better than causal representations from dissolutive encroachments. In the reliability of causes, Democritus found his peace of mind and Greece, a comfort by which we have lived ever since. The *différend,* on the other hand, neither consolidates nor consoles. The inescapable, though contradictory, allegiance to both synthesis and dispersion ties us not to the edifying radiance of a cause but—like Oedipus blinded and *sophos*—to an excess of light which is the horror of night.

Discursive Types

There were strong reasons why Hannah Arendt borrowed from Malraux the title of her first major work, *The Human Condition.* In that book, she located all human experience at the conjunction of two determinants in our lives, natality and mortality. As conditions, these are not equatable with birth and death in the sense of the occurrences that open and close a life span; rather, the term *condi-*

tion has to be taken in its technical transcendental sense as designating *a priori* traits. The double-bind in which natality and mortality place us marks the *vita activa* as inescapably tragic. This starting point of her inquiries accounts for the peculiar untimeliness of her attempted new science—that is, philosophy—of politics within the contemporary types of discourse about the public realm. The present collection brings that untimeliness into relief.

Within the so-called Continental tradition, there exist, indeed, today two predominant discursive types in political philosophy. One type presents itself as prescriptive. From various quarters one hears that a theory of praxis is not worth its label unless it establishes first foundations. This claim has been put forth for some decades now from both ends of the political spectrum. On the Left, it has been couched in the discursive type of a critical theory that would secure, or rest on, some form of 'ultimate grounding'; on the Right, it has produced notorious attempts at rehabilitating the prestige of 'classical' teleology. In devoting a volume of essays to Arendt's sought-for science of politics, it seemed, therefore, indispensable to include a group of contributions on what would amount to a *normative philosophy of politics*. In that chapter, Karl-Otto Apel represents the strongest case for *Letztbegründung,* ultimate grounding, while Robert-Paul Wolff seeks normativity in the material conditions of the reproduction of life. On the opposite side, where action is viewed as grounded ontologically, both Robert Spaemann and Hans Jonas argue for pregiven ends in whatever we can undertake. Jean-François Lyotard puts subtly into question the very language of normativity and universally valid ends.

The other predominant discursive type in political philosophy today remains more modestly descriptive. Its modesty is, however, deceptive: Phenomenologists trust that a pertinent insight into the human condition suffices to assure the necessary and sufficient premises for practical intervention. They need neither ontology, nor deontology; they have no use for operations such as deriving 'ought' from 'is'; yet they are far from dismissing the question, "What is to be done?" Rather they consider that, inasmuch as they succeed in bringing into view the life-world with its given potential, this question is already being answered. In one way or another, the essays on a *descriptive philosophy of politics* all show this immanence of a practical discourse in the phenomenological one. Thus, Bernhard Waldenfels points out a potential for the unruly in every rule-governed behavior. Michel Henry traces all cultural activities to the immediately experienced, nonrepresentational, originary, utterly spontaneous subjective region called 'life'. William Richardson, focusing on Arendt's appropriation of the ancient distinction between active and contemplative life, lays bare a dimension of desire—a search for meaning—in the *vita activa;* this enables him to question Arendt's 'mentalist' conception of contemplation. The last two contributions in this chapter deal with language phenomena. Jürgen Link examines specific phrases in contemporary political discourse and spells out the inner logic that drives their symbolism. Vincent Descombes gives a description of descriptions as he looks at the ways in which we socialize our actions linguistically.

If we now look back briefly at Arendt's attempted rehabilitation of the singular, it becomes obvious why the new political philosophy for which she meant to lay the groundwork had to remain and still remains untimely: Neither the normative nor the phenomenological discourse about the public realm address the singular as *unhintergehbar,* impossible to subsume. To be sure, prescriptive and descriptive universals make for heterogeneous subsumptions—as heterogeneous as are standards imposed on action and categories read off the life-world. Still, both of these discursive types make it impossible to retain the issue for judgment she wished to hold on to, namely, the singular in its being. Not that she did not have use for either normative or phenomenological questions; in fact, she answered both, which is why these two discursive types were treated in the symposia series to begin with. But her answers to these questions could and can only infuriate the practitioners of both the prescriptive and the descriptive discourse. What did she have to say about norms? That the "rare moments of freedom" in history were those in which compelling rules for action were temporarily suspended! Such anarchism does not sit well with social scientists convinced that the heritage of the Enlightenment stands and falls with their ability to secure the one type of rationality by which communicative action would find itself necessarily placed under some universally obligatory *a priori*. And what did she have to say about descriptions? That they amount to comparing individual deeds to individual deeds: this agent X acting as bravely as that agent Y. In the private realm, "our decisions about right and wrong depend on our choice of company, with whom we wish to spend our lives"; in the public realm, they depend on persuasion. Partner-choice and rhetorics, however, do not sit well with phenomenologists looking for originative categories in the acting subject 'as such.'

It seemed advisable, then, to open the collection with a group of contributions on a *transcendental philosophy of politics*. For reasons not unlike the ones I put forth in my own criticism of Arendt's self-proclaimed affinity with Kant, all of these contributions give a reading of transcendentalism widely divergent from hers. Manfred Riedel examines the concept of civil society in the two historical contexts in which Arendt sought to anchor her own sought-for science: Aristotelian and Kantian. 'Transcendental politics' means that communication, domination, and participation are systematically indispensable elements for legitimating civic institutions. Stanley Rosen, too, seeks to confront the Kantian with the Greek heritage. His guiding question is that of the good life, which, presumably, the philosopher would have the authority to answer. Rosen follows Leo Strauss in holding that such is indeed the philosopher's task, but that due to an incompatibility between the private and the public realms, he can fulfill his mission only through a noble lie, not through "a frank public appearance." Thomas Seebohm addresses what is usually considered a blatant contradiction in Kant's political thinking, namely that, on the one hand, there can be no rightful resistance to a sovereign, but, on the other hand, Kant not only expressed his unmitigated enthusiasm toward the 1789 revolutionaries but furthermore argued that some revolutions are indeed indicators of a moral predisposition in mankind. Seebohm accounts for the systematic necessity of both claims and draws some parallels with contemporary situations. Ludwig Siep spells out the idealist ramifications of Kant's conception of person. Hegel inscribed the person into the context of reflexive self-consciousness in such a way that the universal and the singular self are identical as moments of self-referential negativity—the very specter Arendt sought to dispel.

It seemed furthermore advisable to close the collection with a few thoughts on institutions. It is true that some of the papers already mentioned mix methodical with substantive considerations; thus, Lyotard argues against Arendt's generic concept of totalitarianism and Henry, against the mediating intrusion of contemporary science upon activities in which life expresses itself immediately. Yet an *institutional philosophy of politics* does constitute an additional discursive type. On the topic of totalitarianism, Agnes Heller proposes to distinguish between totalitarian rule and totalitarian society. This version of the difference between the political and the social hinges on the role of institutions. Only in a Soviet society have all institutions come under the totalitarian sway. Alain Touraine traces historical developments in the nineteenth and twentieth centuries through which social movements—paradigmatically, labor movements—grew distant from the institutions of democracy and turned antiparliamentary. That history has directly affected our idea of progress since the widening gap has resulted in splintering the discursive continuity between social movements, democracy and revolution. In this narrative, too, the political differs from the social by virtue of institutions, but the decisive factor is dissent: social protest and political action no longer seem to share the same institutional grounds. The notions of democracy and revolution have come to seem contradictory. Bertram Schefold analyzes present and possible future economic systems. What he calls an economic style depends primarily on decision-making institutions, for example, those constituting 'the market'. Finally, Reinhart Koselleck looks at how institutions and their concepts have changed since that one historical watershed without which modern states could not have become what they are, the French Revolution. A novel understanding of historical time then translated itself into a new political language. Koselleck reconstructs their ever-changing relationship.

As the essays collected here develop Arendt's sought-for new philosophy of politics in transcendental, normative, descriptive, and institutional discursive modes, few of them are devoted directly to her work, which seems to remain untimely indeed. Each of the essays, however, whether discussing questions of method or substance, takes up an issue posed by her thinking. The section titles obviously neither exhaust the possible avenues of that possible science nor indicate some common systematic concern among the contributors. I do not see how the scope of the investigations Arendt's project calls for could be satisfied through any method other than the eclectic, which is why within any given section the topics examined many range from theoretical to macro-historical to issue-bound. This remains, then, a collection of decidedly heterogeneous pieces. It includes observations made from perspectives with which Arendt felt little affinity. While reading some of the papers, one is, therefore, tempted to imagine her reactions. All of the essays, however, suggest the fecundity of her thinking. They prove just how much she remains alive.

Reiner Schürmann

Notes

1. Hannah Arendt, *The Human Condition* (Chicago: University of Chicago Press 1958), p. 298n.
2. Jean-François Lyotard, *Le Différend* (Paris: Editions de Minuit 1983), p. 127.
3. "We are the functionaries of mankind," Edmund Husserl, *The Crisis of European Sciences and Transcendental Phenomenology,* translated by David Carr (Evanston, Ill.: Northwestern University Press 1970), p. 17.
4. Hannah Arendt, *Lectures on Kant's Political Philosophy,* edited by Ronald Beiner (Chicago: University of Chicago Press 1982). Page numbers in parentheses refer to this book.
5. Hannah Arendt in an address to the American Society for Christian Ethics, quoted in Elisabeth Young-Bruehl, *Hannah Arendt, For Love of the World* (New Haven, Conn.: Yale University Press 1982), pp. 452 f.
6. Immanuel Kant, *Critique of Pure Reason,* B 172n.
7. Hannah Arendt, *The Life of the Mind,* 2 vols. (New York: Harcourt Brace Jovanovich 1977) I: 213, and elsewhere.
8. Quoted Young-Bruehl, *Hannah Arendt, For Love of the World,* p. 166.
9. Immanuel Kant, *The Strife of the Faculties,* A 143, 148 n., and 159 n.
10. Immanuel Kant, *What is Enlightenment?* A 481.
11. Immanuel Kant, *Perpetual Peace,* A 60 f.
12. Hannah Arendt, *Crises of the Republic* (New York: Viking Press 1969), p. 203.
13. Immanuel Kant, *Idea for a Universal History,* A 389.
14. I have developed the various senses of being in Kant from a different perspective in "Legislation-Transgression: Strategies and Counter-Strategies in the Transcendental Justification of Norms," *Man and World* XVII (1984), pp. 361-398.

15. Kant, *Critique of Pure Reason,* B 132 and 134.
16. *Der einzig mögliche Beweisgrund zu einer Demonstration des Daseins Gottes* (1763). For what follows, see particularly A 1-16.
17. *Ibid.,* A 19.
18. This and all subsequent references in parentheses are to Kant, *Critique of Pure Reason.*
19. Friedrich Jacobi, *David Hume über den Glauben oder Idealismus und Realismus* (Breslau, 1787), pp. 222 f.
20. *Critique of Judgment,* B 340.
21. *Ibid.*
22. Friedrich Nietzsche, *The Gay Science,* bk. II, sec. 57.

I

A Transcendental Philosophy of Politics

MANFRED RIEDEL

1. Transcendental Politics? Political Legitimacy and the Concept of Civil Society in Kant*

The concept of civil society demands preliminary explication because it has acquired a meaning that appears hardly appropriate to the problem of political legitimacy. Indeed, it seems to repudiate it altogether. According to contemporary understanding, the meaning of civil society is relative to a particular historical period. Originating with the emancipation of Europe's urban middle classes during the sixteenth and seventeenth centuries, it designates since Hegel and Marx the historically established domination of the "bourgeoisie" over the "proletarian" class founded on the relationship of capital and labor.

The term *civil society*, however, was not first formed with the emancipation of the modern middle class. It has a prior history that points far beyond the horizon of our contemporary understanding. We find it in medieval political philosophy as well as in modern natural law. The word itself is of Greek origin and first appears as *politike koinonia* in Aristotle's political Greek city-state, the *polis*. In the first book of the *Politics*, Aristotle says that the society that dominates and contains all other societies is the so-called *polis* or "civil society."[1] In this identity, the concept enters the discourse of European political philosophy: *civitas sive societas civilis sive res publica*. This formula is, along with several variations, the conceptual theme of political philosophy that extends from Cicero to Thomas Aquinas and up to Locke and Kant. The Latin *societas civilis* is not civil society in the present-day meaning, that is, a sphere distinct from the state; rather, it is identical with it, so that the problem of political legitimacy throughout these centuries was equivalent to the problem of legitimizing civil society. The relations between human individuals are not restricted to indigenous social forms or those dependent solely on man's natural inclination.

---

*From *Social Research*, Autumn 1981.

Instead, these lead to a society based on a form of domination that in the traditional language of political philosophy has been called "civil society" ever since Aristotle. Is there a justification for the indisputable fact of such a society and the domination of men over men connected with it, and if so, what is it?

In regard to this question, the tradition in which the concept of civil society stands proposed various answers and developed different theoretical paradigms and patterns of argumentation. All of these terminate more or less in the equally famous or infamous *theory of contract*: legitimate domination is not based on the reality of subjugation or functioning institutions, but rather on conditions of civil society—the possibility of men to communicate reasonably, justly, and freely. Domination and communication are the two key concepts of the theory of contract. Respective to their correlation, distinction, or delimitation, the theoretical themes and their function of legitimation change. New difficulties, of course, present themselves here. Does not the theory of contract belong, ever since the criticism of historicism, positivism, and historical materialism, to those relics of prescientific thinking that are preserved solely in the archives of the history of philosophy where such erroneous ideas are generally kept? Doubts arise as well when we, as has become certainly unavoidable in the linguistic confusion of our time, question the linguistic presuppositions of the doctrines and theorems of the tradition. In fact, when we critically read the classical works of political philosophy, for example, those of Hobbes or even those of Rousseau and Kant, we find ourselves at the same time both attracted to and confused by the language in which they were written. We find, for example, the discussion of a political body without any explanation of how the spatial dimensions of such a body could be established. There is also the reference to a civil person, with whom we certainly can never take up relations. Furthermore, there is a general will, which is not composed of the wills of the individuals but rather is supposed to be *sui generis*. Finally, there is the use of a word taken from colloquial speech that definitely seems very unusual. We find reference to a contract that, as the authors of political philosophy assure us, has never taken place.[2] The difficulties and doubts can, however, be eliminated to a certain degree if we remember that this terminology is taken from the context of propositions that deal with politics and natural law as theoretical components of *practical philosophy* or, more precisely, that part of practical philosophy that has to do with the doctrine of principles for political action as it was developed and cultivated particularly in the modern theory of natural law. What we are dealing with here are not empirical concepts but normative ones. The principles derived from them are not statements of fact but statements of law with a claim to normative validity. In other words, they are practical principles intended to formulate rules and imperatives for political action—the action of individuals and the action of institutions—and to found and justify the "conditions of the possibility" of domination.

The legitimacy question first takes on the strict form of the theory of contract in seventeenth-century natural law. It is here—and it is only here—that the question is first raised as a question of law and that the problem of legitimate domination is solved with the conceptual means of the contract. In the following discussion of this theory, I would like to show three things: *first*, how it was at all possible to arrive at this question; *second*, why the relationship between normative and empirical-factual concepts and principles remained problematic in spite of the undeniable progress made in modern political philosophy, in particular by Kant; and *third*, whether the theory of contract is, in view of this aporia and the criticism made of it in the nineteenth century, systematically and historically obsolete, or whether it can be critically reconstructed and justified.

The Classical Paradigm: Aristotle and the Beginning of the Theory of Legitimate Domination

If one looks back to the beginnings of European political philosophy, Aristotle appears to be the first author to have seen and given positive expression to the significance of the relationship between domination and communication. At the beginning of the first book of the *Politics*, he critically discusses the opinion of his predecessors (Xenophon, Plato) that "domination" is the same everywhere: in the household as in a monarchy, in a polity as in despotism, in Greece as in Asia. This opinion is rejected by Aristotle as "not being said in the right way" and as "untrue."[3] The untruth lies in the thesis that civil domination, domination by a king, domestic and despotic domination are different only in the larger or smaller number of subjects and not in their concept or their basic nature.[4] This *eidos*, the conceptual differentiation of domination into various "kinds" and their corresponding linguistic designation, is placed by Aristotle— and this is significant for everything else that follows—not in an abstract concept of "agreement" intended to limit domination in accordance with human rights and freedom, but rather in the respective form of communication connected with the different forms of domination. Consequently, the Aristotelian approach turns toward the historically given institution of the *polis* and the forms of domination and communication existing in it. What civil domination is and what distinguishes it from all these other forms can be methodically determined only by starting with the *polis* and what it is according to its concept and its "essence."[5] The following is the Aristotelian answer: the *polis* is *politike koinonia*, civil society as a communication between citizens who are joined together as *freemen* and *equals*.[6] This does not mean that this institution is based on freedom and equality as principles of political philosophy. What it does mean, however, is that this society—in contrast to all the other societies known to exist historically at that time—has as its principle man as a freeman and as its subject the citizen as an equal.

It is in this context that Aristotle's politically normative principle, that man is by nature a *zoon politikon*, gains its historical and fundamental philosophical significance. Not only does it mean that man "actually" leads his life in the *polis*, but conversely that with the *polis* as *politike koinonia* a form of society has constituted itself historically in which the "nature" of man has become the basis of institutional domination of men over man. However, at the same time, here lies the limitation of the classical paradigm. By presupposing these institutions as already existing historically, Aristotle never even raises the question of how they would have to be legitimated in order to satisfy the demands of reasonable, just, and free communication. The relationship of the nature of man to the city-state as *civil society* remains obscure, and it does so precisely because of the doctrine peculiar to the *Politics* whereby there are two forms of domination and communication that exist "by nature": the relationship between the master and the slave and the relationship of the citizens among themselves, that is, civil society itself.

This obscurity is the reason for Aristotle's inability to legitimize the exercise of domination in the *polis* on the basis of the concept of the *polis* itself as *politike koinonia*. It also explains why in this matter he is able to draw only on the contrast with the rule of the master as a criterion of judgment. Despotic domination, belonging to the sphere of mere life and the work necessary for maintaining it, is based on compulsion and not on a law or the consent of the ruled; it amounts to unlimited, unrestricted rule over those who are by nature unfree. Civil domination is in all of these respects exactly the opposite: it is rule, restricted through law, over those who are by nature freemen; it is rule in view of the common interest of rulers and subjects, and it is proper to the sphere of the good life, that is, the virtuous and happy life, which is distinguished from the production of the necessities of life by the normative character of the "good action" peculiar to it.[7]

A theory of agreement or contract would be foreign to Aristotle. Even more so, it would be unthinkable for him given the problematical structure of his political philosophy. This aporia, which becomes apparent in the transition from the *Nicomachean Ethics* to the *Politics*, can be formulated accordingly: *If legitimate domination rests on the end of the good life, that is, the virtuous and happy life, then there is absolutely no need for the application of force in regard to those who live in accord with this end—the freemen; if on the other hand, those who are not in agreement with this end—the many—are forced to live the good life, this coercion is no longer capable of lawful legitimation.* The *polis* is necessarily a form of domination of men over men, but in regard to how this formal domination should be constituted or lawfully legitimated absolutely nothing can be determined from the Aristotelian premises. There remains a gap in political philosophy that Aristotle closes in two ways: first, through the natural theory of the *polis* as *politike koinonia*, according to which domination and communication form, so to speak, an indigenous unity; and second, through the historical and empirical interest in the existing constitutions that Aristotle, having given up all interest in a theory founding or justifying them, deals with as material politics—a kind of natural history of the forms of domination.

Theory of Agreement or Contract?

This gap in political theory determined the nature of the many answers given to the problem of legitimate domination and civil society in medieval and early modern political philosophy, periods in which Aristotelian philosophy was still very influential.

I am going to restrict myself to consideration of just a few positions and to a few comments on the way in which the problem was raised.

1. The Aristotelian tradition (from Thomas Aquinas to Suarez) presupposes the existence of civil society and thus already an authority ruling by virtue of the law of nature, even before the question of agreement as to this authority or its legitimation is raised.[8]

2. The agreement itself refers primarily, as it does in Aristotle, not to this society and its ruling authority, but rather to the laws: *nomos* and *lex*, not *arche* and *potestas* (that is, *imperium*), are interpreted first as objects of agreement (*homologia, pactum, consensus*) among the citizens, whereby *pactum* can also be considered as being synonymous with *concordia, vinculum, coetus, unio*, and so forth.[9]

3. If the concept of contract or agreement refers to society and the ruling authority derived from it—I have been unable to determine when this first happened—then it always refers to civil society as a whole and not to the individuals as its parts. We can formulate this accordingly: for the classical theory of civil society there is indeed a contract of society (*pactum societatis*), but there is no contract of agreement between individuals (*pactum singulorum*).

4. The author who first broke with these premises and uncovered the gap in Aristotelian political theory and its modern tradition was Thomas Hobbes. According to Hobbes, civil society does not exist by nature, but rather it originates through the union (*unio*) of a "number of men" in a "civil person." This union is accomplished through the contract of each individual with all other individuals, that is, the contract of the *singuli* among themselves. It is only with this step that the general problem of the philosophy of law and the state is raised, namely, the extension of the theory of contract from the partners in civil society, the citizens as freemen and equals, to the freedom and equality of men as men.

The solution that Hobbes suggests to this problem is paradoxical: Agreement (*unio civilis*) and the ruling authority do not follow *from* one another but rather stand *next* to each other in the contractual construction of civil society. It is no longer a precept of nature but of reason (*dictamen rectae rationis*) to abandon the state of nature and to seek the conditions of communicative action in a still unfounded civil society—through the agreement of every individual with all the other individuals to the restriction, valid for *all* and therefore lawful, of their natural right to everything. The state of nature, however, can no more be overcome through agreement alone than through insight into the prescriptive laws of nature (for example, that *contracts should be kept* [pacta servanda sunt]), which Hobbes derives as the rules of communicative action from the basic postulate of reason: to seek agreement and avoid conflict. Therefore, the object of the contract—possibility of communication—is at the same time the reality of domination, that is, that peculiar construction of the "state person" who actually executes the norms of reason and has, for example, the task of keeping the individuals in fear and directing their actions toward the general well-being.[10] The result is the transfer of the natural right to everything to the ruler and thus, viewed constitutionally, the establishment of absolutism—an enlightened form of absolutism, of course, which, while it concedes one natural right of freedom to the *singuli* (that of self-preservation), still falls under the Aristotelian distinction between civil and despotic domination.

5. This is exactly the view of Rousseau, who placed Hobbes and Aristotle on the same level and held the opinion that political philosophy had not moved one step forward since Aristotle.[11] The sole and irrevocable transfer of domination to the sovereign is the breakdown of all possible communication; it is the renunciation of natural human rights and freedom to an authority that can no more be legitimated on this basis than the authority of the master over the slave. The theory of agreement or contract does not fill the gap Hobbes discovered in the Aristotelian tradition of civil society; taken by itself it is a legal formalism that was also capable of being adopted by those who—like John Locke—did not seriously break with this tradition and did not see any contradiction, for example, in the assertion that civil society was based on a contract and yet at the same time, in its origin and purposes, was founded on an unchangeable law of nature that imposed its purpose on the parties to the contract.[12]

Even when Locke adopts the Aristotelian distinction between civil and despotic domination for his agreement-theory of *civil society*[13] this does not change the fact that his theory contains absolutely no criterion for the legal impossibility of a despotic domination, but indicates merely that the master-slave relationship is accepted as a historical fact—not unlike the German School Philosophy of the eighteenth century, which did not consider the statement that in the state of nature man is his own master (*sui juris*) or free to be an obstacle for the renunciation of this freedom: it merely states that subjection to domination by another requires the agreement (*consensus*) of the subject. According to the view of the German School Philosophy, such renunciation lies at the basis of all "human societies." It thereby merely follows the previously discussed Aristotelian doctrine of the indigenous unity of communication and domination ("*Imperium omne nascitur ex societate*").[14]

The Political Philosophy of Classical Liberalism: The Legitimation of Civil Society in Kant

The combination of the two concepts of communication and domination into an apparent natural unity, which Hobbes achieved in a very artificial manner by connecting the theory of contract with the theory of domination, was torn apart first by Kant. Here he was following the example of Rousseau's *Contrat social* (1762), which Kant had already recognized relatively early (between 1764 and 1768) as the "ideal" of political philosophy and which he opposed, as "civic union," to the Leviathan of Hobbes—the paradigm of the modern state.[15] This union is for Kant founded on a principle that was missing not only in the *pactum sociale* of Scholastic natural law but also in the *unio civilis* of Hobbes: the legal principle of the inalienability of man's freedom. It is only now that the conditions of possible communication between human beings—that is, their humanity, which Hobbes still conceived negatively in the doctrine of natural freedom and equality—are admitted into the concepts of politics. According to Rousseau, the right that man has by nature is not related to the *ends* which nature (the nature of things and his own nature) grants to him, but to *freedom as the basis of all rights*.[16] Hobbes had evaded this determining ground so that the essence of his constitutional law—the contract of domination necessary for the constitution of the *societas civilis*—coincided once again with the principles of the older theory of natural law. The dependency of the concept of the ruling authority as a positive and historical fact connected with renewed coincidence of constitutional law with natural law is one of the most important points Rousseau criticizes in Hobbes's theory. The *contrat social* is, according to the declared intention of the author, opposed to the legal principle of the older theory of civil society, the arbitrary renunciation of rights either to a private person (in the master-slave relationship) or to special groups (in the granting of privileges) or finally to the person of the ruler. For the individuals, according to Rousseau, can only relinquish their natural rights under the condition that they receive in return an inalienable right: to be safe from all particular (factual) forms of domination. The act of constituting civil society is equivalent to the constitution of the general will to which all are subject. As such, nobody is dependent on the will of another individual, but rather everyone is dependent on his own will.[17]

I am going to bypass the paradoxes that result from Rousseau's construction of the contract. These paradoxes concern the institutional realization of the general will in a community and finally lead Rousseau's political theory back to the ancient *polis*. Kant was able to avoid them by the method of transcendental philosophy. He conceives the social contract or contract of agreement (*pactum sociale = pactum unionis civilis*) not as a fact but rather as a norm based on *a priori* principles of reason and, therefore, the standard ("idea") of civil society as an appearance. With the help of the reflections on legal and moral philosophy written during the 1760s and 1770s and found in the posthumous works, one can follow how the concept of the contract, in connection with the concept of the general will, departs from the context of constitutional law and the orientation toward the empirical elements of natural law that sometimes dominate Rousseau's writings. Kant is able to accomplish this essentially because he does not relate the general will to the social contract, which even Rousseau still interpreted as a fact, but merely to a social principle of reason that he calls the *right of humanity*, that is, possible communication between human beings. From this right he then derives the legal possibility of the contract. This is something Rousseau had left entirely unresolved: the *Contrat social* did of course legitimate subjection and thereby established the legal possibility of a coercive power, but the question, what makes the contract itself legitimate, remained unanswered. It is at this point that Kant's introduction of transcendental method into political philosophy addresses the argument. What makes the contract obligatory for everyone is the right of humanity, the only condition of which consists in using one's freedom in conformity with possible communication, the *a priori* principle of civil society in general. Every human being has the right of restricting the freedom of every other human being to this condition that is tied to the possibility of freedom itself. The correlation of right, freedom, and the restriction of freedom to the formal condition of the agreement concerning its external use—the *a priori* principle of the possibility of communication—is also called the *law of freedom* by Kant. The objective obligation of this law corresponds to the subjective right of every individual to compel every other individual to the lawful exercise of freedom. Right is not to be regarded, however, as composed of these two different elements, for as Kant says, "the conception of right may be viewed as consisting immediately in the possibility of a universal reciprocal compulsion in harmony with the freedom of all."[18] Therein lies the fundamental problem to Kant's doctrine of right as well as the solution it offers for the problem of legitimate domination and civil society. Kant's law of freedom not only means the restriction of the free will of every individual but—and this is the decisive point—the restriction of compulsion to exactly that conditioned communication that the law itself lays down. The system of the doctrine of human right is entirely dependent on the question of how compulsion (and that also means universal communication) is possible given the presupposition of a right that belongs to man by virtue of his humanity. The contrast to the traditional manner of dealing with the problem of legitimate domination is obvious. If I had to express it in one sentence, I would say: Domination and communication on the one hand and compulsion and freedom on the other are for Kant no longer opposed to each other, but rather unified in the concept of legitimate domination (enabling everyone to exercise their freedom). Freedom, understood as the legislation of practical reason, demands for itself exercise of domination based on agreement, but in the form of legal compulsion. As such, the exercise of freedom by every individual is restricted to the conditions of its possible lawful agreement with the freedom of all other individuals "and may be thus limited in fact by others, and it [reason] lays this down as a *postulate* which is not capable of further proof."[19]

What does a postulate mean according to transcendental philosophy? It is an immediately certain practical proposition or a principle determining a *possible action* that presupposed that the nature of the action is immediately certain.[20] What is immediately certain in the field of practical judgment about communication is the necessity of a connection between freedom and compulsion in the concept of external human freedom. According to that concept, on the basis of the practical reason common to all, everyone has the right in regard to every other individual of restricting the other's freedom to the conditions of its possible lawful agreement with one's own freedom. What Kant has exposed here with this formula is nothing less than the legal obligation of the contract, which is, of course, not only immediately certain but also, as is right itself, an *idea* or a *normative practical concept*; it is the idea of the *a priori* unified will of all (Rousseau's general will), which according to Kant forms the norm for judging what is practically rational in the realm of human communication.

The legal necessity or, if you will, the legitimation of the contract through the *a priori* normative concept of right makes it impossible for Kant to interpret the contract as a fact. Kant was the first philosopher consistently to maintain the distinction between fact and norm in the theory of contract or, formulated in modern terms, the distinction between descriptive and prescriptive statements. The idea of the original contract, according to the appendix to the first part of the *Doctrine of Right*, is a concept of practical reason to which no empirical example can adequately correspond, but which, as a norm, no case may contradict. *Fact* is defined here by Kant as an object of appearance (to the senses)—and this was the way the French revolutionaries understood the *contrat social*: as a real act and the historical foundation of the new constitution based on the declaration of human and civil rights. A norm, on the other hand, is a mere idea of reason, but one possessing objective-practical reality, that is, obligation and universal validity for the formation of public opinion and will and for the rational determination of communicative action as well as for the institutions within which this action takes place.

The Aporia of Norm and Fact on the Classical Liberal Theory of Legitimation

Whereas new empirical and normative concepts are no longer intermixed in the *theory of contract*, as they were with Hobbes, Kant tacitly reintroduces empirical concepts into the normative approach in the subsequent *construction of the contract of civil society*. He thereby contradicts the underlying premises of the transcendental construction. For a philosopher of Kant's stature this is an unusual procedure and one that deserves closer examination and analysis. Having conceived of the contract as a norm and not as a fact, it becomes—that is the premise of the transcendental construction—the standard by which civil society is judged in its historical manifestation. Civil society, understood as the appearance of the *a priori* will of all unified in the idea, is not now the cause of the contract of agreement *but the result of it*: "The civil constitution is not arbitrary, but according to reasons of right necessary for the security of the other [individual]. Society is not the cause of this condition either, but rather the result of it. The practical sovereign ground of right makes society."[21] So it appears that domination itself thus merges completely with agreement—in the "sovereign" ground of right, which allows only legal compulsion and that according to Kant originates solely in the concept of freedom in its external use.

The construction of the lawful civil society, however, deviates somewhat from this picture. This construction, which referred to the declaration of human and civil rights by the French National Assembly (1791), was first presented by Kant in an essay that appeared at the beginning of the 1790s: "On the Common Saying: This May Be True in Theory, but It Does Not Apply in Practice" (1793). It was later adopted without any changes in the second part of the *Doctrine of Right* (1797). It is based on three "*a priori* principles" that claim to represent pure rational principles of external human right:

1. The *freedom* of every member of society as a *human being*.
2. The *equality* of each with all the others as a *subject*.
3. The *independence* of each member of a commonwealth as a *citizen*.[22]

The first and second principles are, as are the principles of the *Déclaration des droits de l'homme et du citoyen*, diametrically opposed to the legal principle of the traditional civil society that was hierarchically structured and conceived only in terms of nature and natural law. The right of freedom that every member of the *societät* has negates the rights and freedoms of the corporations, the cities and communities, landowners and classes. It is the right of the emancipated and free man who, having eliminated the privileges of the traditional civil society, is concerned with himself, pursues his own happiness, and acts according to his own private free will. Kant expresses it in the following "formula":

> For each may seek his happiness in whatever way he sees fit, so long as he does not infringe upon the freedom of others to pursue a similar end which can be reconciled with the freedom of everyone else within a workable general law—i.e., he must accord to others the same right as he enjoys himself.[23]

The right of freedom includes legal equality, the equality of men as "subjects." It designates the uniformity of human beings as subjects in the realm of civil domination—the legal equality of all as equally subject to the universal laws that the modern constitutional state has codified. The same thing is expressed in Kant's formula of right, whereby right presupposes the restriction of the freedom of every individual to the condition of its agreement with the freedom of every other individual.

Considered from the point of view of the first and second principles, the only legal consequence would have been for Kant, in conformity with the extension of the status of "citizenship" to "every human being in the state," to use the concept of civil society in the sense of "civic union," that is, the totality of persons free and equal before the law. He is prevented from doing this, however, by the peculiar conception of the third principle, the "independence of each member of a commonwealth as a citizen." Due to the formulation of this principle the transcendental method of practical argumentation shifts to the empirical and social realm. As a result, the constitution of civil society breaks down in the medium of the traditional *societas civilis* of natural law. I am not going to discuss in detail the reasons for this conspicuous failure of the Kantian theory. Rather, I will summarize them in a few theses.

The *first thesis* is that the aporia of norm and fact, which thus enters into the concept of civil society, is caused essentially by Kant's introduction of the predicate "independence" (*sibisufficientia*). As an *a priori* principle, unproven and as such unprovable, it stands above the transcendentally and legally founded principles of freedom and equality; instead of them it forms the *differentia specifica* of the concept of citizenship. It is not the legal principle of freedom, which is equally valid for everyone, but the fact of independence, which cannot be determined by formal legal means, that qualifies an individual for participation in the right of civil society, *the right of "colegislation"*:

> The *independence* [*sibisufficientia*] of a member of the commonwealth as a citizen, i.e., as a colegislator, may be defined as follows. In the question of actual legislation, all who are free and equal under existing public laws may be considered equal, but not as regards the right to make these laws.[24]

The right to legislate is undoubtedly the most important right in the "original contract" that Kant had cleansed of the traditional premises of natural law and placed at the basis of his idea of an *a priori* lawful constitution of civil society. If it is restricted, then the purification was either incomplete or merely pretense.

The *second thesis* is that the incompleteness of the critical purification corresponds to the dependence of the conception of contract in natural law on empirically given features of civil society. The original contract, which according to its own idea is supposed to substitute universal legislation based on the *a priori* unified will of all for all particular dominating authorities, incorporates domination into itself in such a way that it becomes immanent to the original legislation. What is reintroduced in the original contract, as in modern natural law in general, is the paradigm of civil society (*societas civilis*) found in classical political philosophy. The difference is that the foundation of civil society on a contract conceals the exercise of domination behind the universality of compulsion without succeeding in making it "universal." Qualification as a party to the contract, as a citizen, presupposes "the independence of whoever in a nation wants to be not merely a part of the commonwealth, but also a member of it, i.e., whoever, of his own free will, wants to be in association with others the active part of the commonwealth."[25] Thus the pure spontaneity of civic action, whose expression is the legislation of the *a priori* unified will of all (the *pactum civile sive sociale*), is restricted to this condition. The ability to participate in legislation is, together with the original contract, preceded by independence as a restricting condition. What is supposed to be valid for the mere "idea of reason" (the original contract) draws its validity from the sphere of appearances. In the preliminary work to *Theory and Practice*, Kant noted:

> One must already have citizens, however, before one can have subjects of the state. Thus, in respect to the community, the *pactum civile* is a preceding condition, only that individuals whose existence is dependent upon the will of another and who therefore do not enjoy a free existence have no vote.[26]

While it is supposed to legitimate civic domination according to *a priori* principles, the original contract is, with respect to the "right to vote," justified according to an *a posteriori* principle that under closer examination turns out to be the political principle of the classical paradigm of civil society.[27] The normative and legal consequences of the contract are obstructed, as it were, by this recourse to the sphere of appearances.

The *third thesis* is that Kant, in theory, tacitly assumes communication without domination because his concept of citizenship conforms to the model of the citizen established by Aristotle and the Aristotelian tradition. In the sphere of appearances, the society that the contract is supposed to schematize is based on the concept of the economically and legally independent citizen, whose only quality is that he "must in the true sense of the word *serve* no one but the commonwealth."[28]

In this respect he differs from the person who earns his living "by allowing others to make use of him," who is merely a "helper in the commonwealth"[29]—the farm hand, domestic servant, laborer, in short, the class of the "dependent," which has, according to Kant, no lawful public position within civil society. This is drastically underscored by a comment on the relationship between the citizen and servant that is also found in the preliminary work to *Theory and Practice*:

> A Citizen is a human being in society who has his lawful independence, that is, someone who can be considered as a member of the universal public authority of legislation. Consequently, a servant is a human being who is merely rooted in other citizens as a parasitic plant.[30]

For those who depend on the substance of the "household" the proposition of the legal impossibility of "dependence from domination" has only limited validity, for they are "helpers" of the commonwealth only because their "economic" dependency corresponds to the appropriation of political power on the part of the citizens—because they "must be commanded or protected by other individuals and therefore possess no civic independence."[31]

Not without reason has it been said that here, and throughout all modern natural law, the idea of right is still clothed in what seems to be a "feudal" garment.[32]

One has to disregard, of course, the somewhat inappropriate word "feudal," not only in respect to Kant but also in regard to other authors, because it unduly shortens the historical horizon we are dealing with here. Kant did occasionally consider the idea, only subsequently to reject it, however, in the concern with

> . . . whether only an individual who is a landowner can be a citizen, i.e., whether the quality of a citizen and therefore member of the public legislation must precede the possession of land or must be established solely on it.[33]

As opposed to all efforts of the romantic and conservative theories of state in reaction to the French Revolution to explain society simply from the point of view of a theory of the legal ("feudal") consequences of the ownership of land, Kant's political philosophy belongs to the larger paradigm of a "civic" oriented philosophy of institutions in Europe that stretches from the period of high Scholasticism to the eighteenth century.[34]

Nonetheless, in several passages of the text under consideration, it becomes clear that the representation of "civil society" in Kant's transcendental politics already stands at the close of this era.[35] Confronted with the principles of freedom and equality, the principle of independence causes a number of difficulties in the definition of the concept of a citizen, which did not exist for the traditional political theories.

My *fourth thesis* is that the reason for these difficulties lies in the confrontation of the first and second principles with the third, which can in no way be justified on a normative basis. It is noteworthy that, in regard to the foundation of his own political philosophy, Kant himself points out the contradiction that results from the introduction of this category from the traditional paradigm of civil society. Not only does he "admit that it is somewhat difficult to define the qualifications that entitle anyone to claim the status of being his own master," but he also notes that the distinction between the "active and passive citizen of the state" derived from this category "appears," when we consider the latter, "to stand in contradiction to the explanation of the concept of a citizen of the state in general."[36] The difficulties also expressed explicitly in the presentation of Kant's theory result from the fact that on the one hand the "quality of man to be his own master [*sui juris*]" is contained *a priori* in the one innate right, the human right of freedom, which forms the basis of the first and second principles in the construction of the contract of civil society.[37] The introduction of independence as the third principle compels Kant to use this concept differently.[38]

For now the quality of man as *sui juris* is given a meaning that is taken from the characteristic of the *paterfamilias*. The systematic location of the principle of independence within the *Doctrine of Right* is the "Right of the Household Society," which Kant deals with under the revealing title of a "personal right in respect to things."[39] Seen from here, the "examples" Kant uses in his effort to eliminate the "difficulty" presented by the definition of the concept of a citizen become understandable. They belong to the conception of the "household" as the manorial and economic sphere of civil society, from which the laborers, as dependent on the master's power of disposition over the material and means of production, are excluded:

> The journeyman to a merchant or tradesman; the domestic servant . . . all females and in general everyone who does not obtain the means of his existence (sustenance and protection) through his own trade, but rather is necessitated to acquire them by being at the disposal of others, is not a civil personality and his existence is, as it were, merely an accident.[40]

Such individuals are mere *operarii* (laborers) for whom only the *praestatio operae* (the guarantee of their labor) is possible, not the production and disposal of an *opus* (work). The question arises, however, why the connection, which is unquestionably there, between the third principle in the construction of the contract and the "Right of the Household Society" does not become more apparent systematically in Kant's transcendental politics.

My answer to this is contained in a *fifth thesis*: Because as a consequence of the predominance of public right over private right, the traditional foundation of the right of civil society in "domestic society," the domination of a freeman over a household and its members, is entirely foreign to the Kantian doctrine of right. Only the scheme of the concepts remains; the concepts themselves have changed. One will have to look here to find the actual source of the "difficulties" Kant speaks of and the solution provided for them. Domination over a household is not required in order to be, as a citizen, one's own master (*sui juris*); it is sufficient just to have "any piece of property" and to sell it, whereby it is presupposed, according to the principles of freedom and equality, that "everybody" can acquire or sell property and so "work their way up from the passive status to the active one."[41]

In this way the first and second principles of Kant's construction of the contract for a lawfully constituted "civil society" could be aligned with the third, at the cost, however, of the *a priori* status of "independence." The subsumption of independence under the category of "property" indicates that it has been introduced by Kant into the contingent sphere of commodity exchange in society. The *a priori* legal construction of the original contract *prescribing* communicative action free of domination describes at the same time a society that no longer coincides with its own name ("civil society" in the sense of a pure society of right). It is clear that here we are dealing with the liberal ideal of emancipation, which Kant is advocating in opposition to the social and class constraints in regard to property and the legal restrictions to its acquisition. This means, however, that the model is incompatible precisely with those elements that constituted "independence" as a legal principle in the traditional paradigm of civil society. This would explain the ambivalence of the transcendental construction of the original social contract. The same concept, which it retains and normatively justifies as an *a priori* principle, is abandoned *a posteriori* at its foundation, the ownership of the property. Independence as a privilege of the "citizen" becomes the right of "man," a right that "everybody" can acquire. The transcendental construction presupposes a social sphere of unobstructed exchange of property and commodities that would free the formalism of the contract while lacking the capacity, however, to represent and delimit it conceptually. For Kant this sphere is only a secondary consequence of the *a priori* legal construction of civil society, and this is why he does not realize that this society suddenly assumes a new form—that the concept of right that merely seems to imply mutual freedom and equality has as its consequence one-sided dependency and renewed inequality.

This is the fundamental aporia of Kant's transcendental politics which he bequeathed to nineteenth-century liberalism. On the basis of my deliberations, I think I can rightfully conclude that the impossibility of solving this aporia in terms of classical liberal philosophy is due in no small part to the metaphysical presuppositions of the classical paradigm of civil society that Kant adopted, along with the concept of legitimate domination underlying them, from the prevailing theory of natural law, and which he attempted—contrary to the implications of the theory of contract—to justify normatively. In contrast to the liberal philosophy of the constitutional state, the social theory of the nineteenth century was more perceptive and realized that the *a priori* unified will of all contained in the theory of contract, the *universal will*, is not universal at all, but rather is violated in its formal *a priori* universality by material suppositions. The state, as we can read in Marx, does not exist through a universal ruling will but rather emerges out of the material forms of existence of individuals and takes on "the form of a dominating will,"[42] which makes the state an illusionary community for the dependent class. Marx's criticism sagaciously uncovered the deficiencies of the liberal theory of legitimation, but at the same time it sacrificed the merits and usefulness of the contract theory as a formal standard for the judgment and practical regulation of the material and social living forms. Consequently, in the paradigm of sociality that Marx substituted for the contract of natural law in the *German Ideology* (1845) and in the *Communist Manifesto* (1848), in the *paradigm of association* in which the *free development of every individual is the condition for the free development of all*, the idea of right and of the *a priori* unified will of all disappears as a reference for the practical and normative judgment of such "development." This can only mean: the disappearance of the possibilities of communication and participation for individuals in a society. The aporia of the societal paradigm is that it provides no means of avoiding the overthrow of reason and the irrationality of the factual becoming normative, the process that caused the demise of liberal theory and since then has become the common ground of the otherwise so divergent schools of historicism, positivism, and historical materialism.

In this situation, which is essentially the one confronting us, it will be necessary once again to guide our thinking concerning the relationship between communication, domination, and participation according to the point of view and methodical possibilities of practical philosophy—a discipline that, significantly enough, died in the same era in which natural-law concepts and forms of argumentation were also abandoned and forgotten. The fundamental concepts of natural law, such as the *state of nature* and the *contract*, were considered to be erroneous simply because they were unhistorical and nonsociological, foreign to real living conditions and social processes or merely distorted reflections of them. In truth, they are the elements of an *a priori* normative construction that has as its task the *methodical construction of legitimate domination in reference to the possibility of communication* about as well as *participation in civic institutions* and the *modes of action* appropriate to them. The elements of the contract were not introduced to explain the beginning and origin of the state, but rather to establish its ideal norms, their gradual formation, and the basis of their validity.

In any event, the thesis that historical origin and normative conceptual construction are to be thrown together indiscriminately definitely contains a dogmatic assertion that has yet to be proven. The tools of the philosophical analysis of language, the history of concepts, and the methods of practical argumentation, however, permit us to examine these elements. It is conceivable that after this examination and a critical inquiry into the tradition of the political theory of natural law, we will be able to rehabilitate such paradigms as the contract and use them as the foundation for a philosophy of civic institutions.

NOTES

1. *Politics* I 1, 1252 a 6-7.
2. See Margaret Macdonald, "The Language of Political Theory," in Anthony Flew, ed., *Logic and Language* (Oxford: Blackwell, 1963), p. 167.
3. *Politics* I 1, 1251 a 9-16.
4. *Politics* I 1, 1252 a 10.
5. *Politics* III 1, 1274 b 33-34.
6. *Politics* III 6, 1279 a 27; VII 8, 1328 a 35-37.
7. *Politics* I 5, 1254 b 2-14; I 7, 1255 b 16-37; III 4, 1277 a 33-b 77; VII 14, 1355 a 5-7, b 27-28.
8. Cf. Thomas Aquinas, *De reg. princip.* 1, I, c. I; *S. th.* I/II, qu. XXI, art. 4 ad. 3; Suarez, *Tract. de legibus* III, c. II 4.6
9. Cf. the ancient evidence in Alfred Voigt, ed., *Der Herrschaftsvertrag* (Neuwied: Luchterhand, 1965), pp. 37-52, which can be associated neither with the scheme for the contract of rule nor with the one for the contract of society. Representatives of the analytical school of thought in political philosophy correctly speak of a "contract of citizenship," which is to be distinguished from the modern scheme of contract ("contract of government" and "contract of community"). Cf. D. D. Raphael, *Problems of Political Philosophy* (New York: Praeger Publishers, 1970), pp. 86-93.
10. *Leviathan* 1. II, c. XVIII.
11. Cf. J.-J. Rousseau, *The Social Contract, or Principles of Political Right*, edited by Charles M. Sherover (New York: New American Library, 1974), pp. 7, 13-15.
12. John Locke, *Second Treatise of Government*, in *Two Treatises of Government*, edited by Peter Laslett (New York: New American Library, 1977), pp. 366-67.
13. Locke, *Second Treatise of Government*, c. XV, sec. 174.
14. Christian Wolff, *Jus naturae* (1751), 1. VII, c. I, secs. 195-96.
15. Immanuel Kant, *Gesammelte Schriften* [hereinafter *GS*], the Prussian Academy of Sciences Edition, 22 vols. (Berlin: G. Reimer, 1902-38), 19: 98, Reflection 6593.
16. Rousseau, *Contrat social* 1. I, c. IV; *Emile* 1. II.
17. Rousseau, *Contrat social* 1. I, c. VI-VIII; 1. II, c. II-III.
18. *Introduction to the Doctrine of Right*, sec. E, in *GS* 6:232. In regard to this, see Julius Ebbinghaus, *Gesammelte Aufsätze, Vorträge und Reden* (Hildesheim: G.

Olms, 1968), pp. 274ff as well as K.-H. Volkmann-Schluck, "Der Ursprung des Rechtsstaats aus der Idee der Freiheit," in his *Politische Philosophie* (Frankfurt: Klostermann, 1974), pp. 96–128.
19. *Introduction to the Doctrine of Law*, sec. C.
20. *Logic*, sec. 38.
21. *GS* 19: 533, Reflection 7847.
22. *GS* 8: 290; 6:314; cf. the preliminary work to the *Doctrine of Right*, *GS* 23: 293 ("Three Principles of Universal Human Rights") and the preliminary work to *Theory and Practice*, *GS* 23:136 ("Every member of a nation has a threefold quality in relation to the government").
23. *GS* 8: 290.
24. *GS* 8: 294. The principle of independence also refers thematically to the traditional distinction between "despotic" and "civic" domination; cf. the preliminary work to *Theory and Practice*, *GS* 23: 136–37, the "Explanation: Against Despotic Government."
25. *Doctrine of Right*, II, sec. 46, in *GS* 6: 314.
26. *GS* 22: 137; cf. *GS* 8: 295. The same restriction can be found, by the way, in Rousseau as well as the French Encyclopedists as has been correctly pointed out by Iring Fetscher, *Rousseaus politische Philosophie* (Neuwied: Luchterhand, 1960), pp. 261ff; cf. Diderot, "Art Représentants," in *Oeuvres* (Lyon, 1792), 10: 108; D'Holbach, *Systeme Social* (1773), 1. II, c. IV..
27. *Doctrine of Right*, II, sec. 46, *GS 6: 314: Theory and Practice, GS* 8:295.
28. *GS* 8: 295. Cf. the following thesis: "Those who are not entitled to this right [of legislation] are nonetheless obliged, as members of the commonwealth, to comply with these laws, and they thus likewise enjoy their protection" (*GS* 7: 294).
29. *GS* 7: 295.
30. *GS* 23: 137.
31. *GS* 6: 315.
32. Cf. Wilhelm Metzger, *Gesellschaft, Recht und Staat in der Ethik des deutschen Idealismus* (Heidelberg: Winter, 1917), pp. 98–99.
33. Cf. the preliminary work to *Theory and Practice*, *GS* 23: 137. This is a direct consequence of the idea of the *a priori* unified will as a condition of the possible acquisition of property in general; cf. Gerhard Lehmann, *Kants Besitzlehre* (Berlin: Akademie-Verlag, 1956), p. 10.
34. This misconception already begins with the pseudo-Kantian Schmalz, who misunderstood Kant in this point as well; cf. *Das Recht der Natur* (1795), vol. 2: only the "landowners" are citizens, all the other parts of the population are "cohabitants." See also L. H. Jakob, *Philosophische Rechtslehre* (Halle, 1795), pp. 472–73.
35. *GS* 23: 136.
36. *GS* 8: 295n; 6: 314.
37. Introduction to the *Doctrine of Right*, *GS* 6: 237–38. Cf. Kurt Borries, *Kant als Politiker* (Leipzig: Meiner, 1928), pp. 95–96, who maintains that for Kant himself what "logically" results from this innate right is that the civil constitution rests "merely on the ability of the individuals in their relations with one another to behave

toward one another in conformity with external laws" (*GS* 23: 137). Borries, however, quotes only half of the sentence; Kant adds: "and there one has first to be a citizen."

38. Cf. the divergent construction in *Perpetual Peace* (1795), Second Section, First Definitive Article, according to which a civil constitution is founded on: "firstly, the principle of *freedom* for all members of a society (as men); secondly, the principle of the *dependence* of everyone upon a single common legislation (as subjects); and thirdly, the principle of *legal equality* for everyone (*as citizens*)" (*GS* 8: 349). Recently, J. Ebbinghaus, "Das Kantische System der Rechte der Menschen und Bürger," *Archiv für Rechts- und Sozialphilosophie* 50/1 (1964): 48ff, has once again made the effort to save "independence" as an *a priori* principle of law. Apart from the fact that his interpretation that here we are dealing with something that is "specific to Kant" is historically wrong, even Ebbinghaus is unable to retain the meaning that Kant actually connected with this concept. The limitations which he sees himself compelled to make ("conditional participation of dependents in legislation") are plainly irreconcilable with Kant's construction.

39. Cf. *Doctrine of Right*, I, secs. 22ff, in *GS* 6: 276ff; cf. also *GS* 20: 240ff, which was provoked by the reviewer from the *Göttingischen Gelehrten Anzeigen*, 28th copy, Feb. 18, 1797, who rejected this section as "the new phenomenon in the juristic heavens."

40. *GS* 6: 314; 8: 295. The connection to the "Right of the Household Society" does not, of course, prevent Kant from conceiving only of those who are the "domestic servants" as "integral parts of the household" (*GS* 12: 180-81; 6: 361). What is decisive is the domestic and patriarchal form of the processes of production that gives the examples an unmistakable metaeconomic character and the consequences drawn from them in regard to civil law the curious unintelligibility which interpreters of Kant so often lament. Cf. Hermann Cohen, *Kants Begründung der Ethik*, 2nd ed. (Berlin: B. Cassirer, 1910), p. 527; Borries, *Kant als Politiker*, pp. 99-100.

41. *GS* 6: 375.

42. *Deutsche Ideologie*, in Karl Marx and Friedrich Engels, *Werke*, 39 vols. (Berlin: Dietz, 1958-68), 3: 312.

Stanley Rosen

2. Man's Hope*

Possibly in violation of the categorical imperative, my hosts have invited and indeed encouraged me to act as *advocatus diaboli* in the case of Kant's political philosophy. I am extremely grateful for the invitation, but I must disown all responsibility for the immoral implications of what I am about to say. Let me begin with a general sketch of my intention and strategy. I want to consider Kant's teaching in terms of the following problem: To what extent, if any, can philosophy exist in public? I can restate this problem in a somewhat more explicit manner. Is there a philosophical doctrine of justice, virtue, or the common good that provides us with a theoretical resolution to the question of the best regime? Or is political philosophy rather the accommodation of philosophy to politics, an accommodation designed for the different and only partly compatible ends of each? The alternatives embedded in these questions are at odds with one another, although they are not quite mutually exclusive. I hope to show that the unsatisfactoriness of Kant's complex teaching stems from his attempt to reconcile the conflicting implications of the alternatives just noted. The difficulty is rather easy to state in a provisional manner and has been identified by others, most recently Y. Yovel. There is no rational connection between Kant's political teaching and his moral philosophy.

Before I turn to the details of my own elaboration of this difficulty, a word is in order concerning its overall structure. My lecture is not intended as a "refutation" of Kant for two closely connected reasons. The first is that I am concerned this afternoon with Kant's fundamental insight and only secondarily with the specific arguments he provides to support this insight. Insights of this kind are neither proven nor refuted by arguments; they rather determine what one regards as pertinent or irrelevant in the way of argumentation. The second reason is the nature of my own insight into the relation of philosophy and politics. I shall be as brief as possible in describing this insight, but I must allude to it in order to make evident my motivation in criticizing Kant. It should go without emphasis that I claim no originality for what I am about to say. Such confidence as I may possess with respect to this insight stems from its rather obvious nature. I regard it as trivial, and it is hard for me to see how anyone could

---

*From *Social Research*, Autumn 1981.

disagree with it. The insight is this: Philosophy is by its nature a revolutionary activity in both the theoretical and practical senses. To think is inevitably to determine one's conduct. Unfortunately, the farther we carry out the implications of thinking, the more we interfere with successful practice; most important, the more we suppress those practical conditions that are essential for philosophy. Philosophers differ as they are resigned to this situation or not. Those who refuse to accept the conflict between theory and practice usually persuade themselves that justice is enlightenment and that to enlighten is to suppress the darkness, but also those who dwell and think within that darkness. Those who accept the conflict between theory and practice devote themselves to the task of devising a politically salutary presentation of the revolutionary nature of philosophy. There is no altogether satisfactory way in which to do this, or at least no doctrinal formulation of how to do it. Philosophers of this second kind must therefore, so to speak, live by their wits. They must accommodate the needs of philosophy to the political circumstances of the time, rather than attempt to change the time or bring history to its fulfillment. In some ages, and perhaps in most, this will lead them to present elaborate doctrines to the politically influential representatives of the public. In other ages, and perhaps in our own, a different rhetorical stance may be desirable, perhaps even the rhetoric of frankness. Whatever approach one takes, whether of the first or second kind, great and unavoidable dangers are involved. Since whatever I might have to say in my own voice about the relation of philosophy and politics would share in these dangers, I am in no position to refute Kant. The most I can do is to criticize him, and in so doing I honor the spirit of the father of critical philosophy.

History the Dimension of Human Perfection

The following remarks constitute a conjecture, not on the beginnings of the human race but perhaps on its end or purpose. Like Kant, I hope for the best. Unlike Kant, however, I do not look to history for the fulfillment of that hope. Kant's political philosophy is intertwined with his philosophy of history. As I understand it, this has two main characteristics. *First:* philosophy is transformed by way of "criticism" (in the technical sense of the term) into science and morality. Since science is subordinate to morality, and since, despite the distinction between the two, morality is fulfilled within a political context, the result is that philosophy is assimilated into praxis or "politics" in the extended sense of the term. *Second:* nature is amoral, and therefore immoral, in the sense that it frustrates moral ends. But politics, and so too political perfection, occurs within nature. Therefore, nature must be amenable to moral suasion if our hope for moral perfection is reasonable. The middle term between nature and politics is history. Let me add directly the main difficulties associated with these two main characteristics of Kant's doctrine of politics and history. First, philosophy is gradually transformed into ideology by way of its assimilation into praxis. This is accompanied by the gradual transformation of criticism into meta-ideology. Second, history is either natural or supernatural. If it is natural, it cannot be the principle of moral perfection. If it is supernatural, it cannot be rational or a consequence of human freedom and spontaneity.

Kant's insistence that moral perfection is higher than theoretical perfection, or his doctrine of the primacy of practice, has led him to be described as a revolutionary thinker, not just in critical or epistemological terms, but as the grandfather of the nineteenth-and twentieth-century senses of praxis. In this view, Kant liberates man from the restrictions of classical nature and thereby prepares the rise of man the self-creator. The Copernican revolution is then seen as the guarantee of human freedom, but also as the basis of man's infinite self-discovery and perfectibility. To misuse somewhat a Leibnizian term, on this interpretation Kant is an optimist. I must disagree. It would be something of an exaggeration, but one which points us in the right direction, to call Kant an extreme conservative and a pessimist, for whom the main function of the Copernican revolution is to suppress revolution, that is, to eliminate the dangers, existential and political as well as moral, of philosophy. In other words, I put forward the following suggestion: Kant wishes to suppress philosophy in the "classical" sense (or in what I shall shortly call its "Platonist" form), and basically for practical reasons. The price he pays for this act of suppression, however, is a "commitment" to history as the dimension of human perfection. The value of timeless truth is thus transferred to the domain of temporality, but without any justification, whether from nature, history, or critical philosophy. As Yovel puts this point, there is no bridge within Kant's system between empirical history in time, bound by natural laws, and nonempirical history of reason. So Kant postulates God, which postulate asserts and finally presupposes, but does not explain, the synthesis.[1] The unsupported character of the postulate of God is soon the cause of its rejection, or as I would put it, the demise of this postulate creates a vacuum within Kant's system which is soon to be filled by historicist ideologies.

Let these paragraphs suffice as an introductory statement of my conjecture. I want to consider Kant today as a Neoplatonist in the following sense. Kant breaks with the philosophical tradition instituted by Plato, but for an essentially Platonic reason, namely, not to initiate a new epoch of free self-production but in order to guarantee the moral safety of the community. Since my intentions are not philological, I will use the term *Platonism* as a convenient name for the dominant pre-Kantian tradition. Platonism starts with a fundamental distinction, rooted in nature, between the philosophical and the nonphilosophical aspects of the soul. Life, expressed brutally but accurately, is a war between these two aspects for the domination of man. The Platonist believes that philosophy cannot win this war. Hence, he promulgates a "conservative" public doctrine, theoretical as well as practical, in order to achieve, or to contribute to the achievement of, a compromise between the philosophical and nonphilosophical elements. The feature of the compromise I want to emphasize here is that philosophy never makes a public appearance. As Socrates says playfully but truthfully at the beginning of the *Sophist,* by way of a quotation from Homer: genuine philosophers are as hard to recognize as gods, for they move about the cities of mortals disguised by fantasms, thanks to the ignorance of the nonphilosophers.[2] "Fantasms," incidentally, is the Eleatic Stranger's technical term for images in which the proportions of the original are distorted to accommodate human vision. The Stranger associates the art of making fantasms with sophistry. The deepest problem of the *Sophist* is how to distinguish between the philosopher and the sophist. For Platonism in the sense of this example, political philosophy is the accommodation of philosophy to the public; it therefore consists of fantasms of philosophy. The Platonist conceives of philosophy as restricted by, yet as essentially unharmed from, this accommodation. Since philosophy is for the Platonist inseparable from science, science itself is, or ought to be, distinct from politics. Whatever other reasons might be given for making this distinction, the most visible reason is that of justice or morality. Science detached from philosophy will destroy the human race or reduce it to barbarism. But philosophy cannot enter into the political domain in an unaccommodated manner. Hence, the Platonist subjects science to severe restrictions, and specifically in the domain of practical application or what we now call technology. No such restrictions are made by Kant, nor are they compatible with his teaching, despite the submission of science to morality. Kant believes, or seems to believe, that this submission can be carried out precisely because science has been detached from philosophy or from metaphysics. The suppression of metaphysics is also the suppression of nature in the Platonist sense. The amoralism of the new nature allows for the subordination of the new science to a moral doctrine that at least allows us to hope for moral perfection. However, I am getting ahead of myself.

To continue with the Platonist, philosophy can hope at the most for the private perfection of isolated individuals. He does, however, admit tacitly (sometimes not so tacitly) that this perfection is inferior to what would have been the case in a genuinely philosophical community. Nevertheless, the inferiority of private to public perfection, in the sense of a philosophical public, is irrelevant, since the philosophical community is impossible in the world of deed. The rise of modern science presents a radical challenge to Platonism for two reasons. First, it casts a fundamental doubt upon the Platonist conception of philosophy and science. The new conception, to be as brief as possible, is connected to the reinterpretation of formal structure, which is no longer regarded as actuality but as possibility. Form is thus submitted to the agency of two closely related powers: temporality or history and the human will. Second, the new conception provides a basis for optimism concerning the outcome of the war between the philosophical and the nonphilosophical elements in the human soul. Whereas for the Platonist the chief weapon of the philosophical element in this war is rhetoric, for the new science it is the satisfaction of desire. I mean this latter in two senses. First, the desire of the philosophical element for truth is satisfied, if only by means of a promissory note for the infinitely distant future, by a new conception of truth. Second, the desires of the nonphilosophical element of the soul are satisfied by the transformation or conquest of nature. When for instance Kant says that we may infer our capacity to accomplish the highest good from the fact that it is our duty to do so, he is tacitly employing the thesis that the true is the possible.

However, this point holds good in a humbler and more comprehensive sense. Nonphilosophical desires, despite Platonist rhetoric to the contrary, can be satisfied much, not to say infinitely, more easily than can philosophical desires. Philosophers, whether Platonists, Kantians, or what we may for the moment call post-Kantians, are *dreamers,* that is, men who are satisfied by the hope of satifaction. But the non-philosophical element in each of us demands immediate satisfaction in the form of food, drink, sex, property, security, praise, and so on. to put this in a slightly different way, modern political philosophy begins with the rejection of what Machiavelli calls the "imagined republics and principalities that have never been seen or known to exist in realty,"[3] or the dreams of the ancients, in favor of "something useful." Machiavelli's conception of the useful is derived from his recognition that "there is no room for the few while the many have a place to lean on."[4] In accord with the exigencies of the world as it is, virtue is reinterpreted as the capacity to achieve order through the satisfaction of basic human desires. From our present standpoint, Machiavelli remains within the Platonist tradition despite his rejection of Platonist rhetoric. Machiavelli's failure to mention philosophy in *The Prince* does not alter the fact that his "new" morality is motivated by the conviction that philosophy has no place in the public world. Machiavelli's political philosophy, especially as formulated in *The Prince,* amounts to the assertion that the nonphilosophical element in the soul has won the war with the philosophical element.

Nevertheless, *The Prince* takes certain steps that are assimilated into the antiPlatonist revolution instituted by the new science. The emphasis upon *fortuna* and the efficacy of relying upon one's own arms, or the independence of the great founder of a new state, anticipates what is subsequently to be called freedom and even spontaneity. And the radical revision of the classical conception of virtue grounds the achievement of justice in the satisfaction of nonphilosophical desire. In the post-Machiavellian or scientific stage, *fortuna* and the satisfaction of desire reappear in what I regard as a fundamentally incoherent synthesis of form as possibility (hence of truth as defined by the will) and of matter as the manifest basis of certitude. This produces a schizophrenic condition in the human soul that replaces, or is the transformed version of, the earlier war between the philosophical and the nonphilosophical elements. Nonphilosophical desires are made the constitutive principle of human life, whereas philosophical desire is made the regulative principle.

Kant's Copernican Revolution

I suggest that Kant's philosophy can be understood as the last effort to preserve Platonism, albeit now as *aufgehoben* into the new science. Kant understands knowledge not as Greek *epistēmē* but essentially as mathematical physics in the Newtonian sense. Not only is knowledge to be conceived in accord with the Newtonian paradigm, but it is also the case that, at least with respect to the comprehensive theoretical framework, the desire for knowledge has been satisfied. As one might express this, the categories and concepts, as well as the regulative ideas, of critical philosophy are an ambiguous blend of actuality and possibility. The conditions for the possibility of scientific thought are neither sharply actual nor sharply possible. The subsequent deterioration of Kant's doctrine, or the rejection of the transcendental domain, or the revision of this domain in terms of Fichtean and Hegelian doctrines of spiritual productivity, prepares the way for the triumph of will over intellect, possibility over actuality, and subjectivity over objectivity.

To stay with Kant for the moment, in principle, and in something more than principle, Kant believes himself to have satisfied the theoretical component of philosophical desire. In other words, we now know, thanks to critical philosophy, that theory is science. Metaphysical desire is satisfied in a different sense, namely, by the transcendental dialectic, which shows not only that there is no metaphysical knowledge in the traditional sense but also no metaphysical satisfaction. In my opinion, this last point has always been understood by all Platonists. However, in Kant's Neoplatonism, a transcendental demonstration of the impossibility of such satisfaction, together with the separation of science from metaphysics, and the claim to have completed the *critical* task, is intended to divert what Kant assumes to be the dissatisfaction inherent in Platonist metaphysics into critical and scientific satisfaction.

Nevertheless, Kant, like every philosopher with the possible exception of Hegel, could not be satisfied by satisfaction. Kant retains the moral dissatisfaction of Platonism. But he either believes or hopes that he is in a position to provide an unsatisfied satisfaction even of this desire, if only in belief or hope. The main point is this: philosophy has now been transformed into science and criticism. As freed from what I am calling "metaphysics," which has been, so to speak, dialectically bracketed, philosophy is now politically safe in the most important sense. It can present itself publicly as at once the guarantor of the satisfaction of nonphilosophical desires and as neutral toward—that is, leaving room for—the nonphilosophical hope concerning God, freedom, and immortality. But a serious difficulty remains for Kant. The quasi-virtuous expression of science and criticism is the surface of the ambiguous features of moral and teleological neutrality. Science and criticism are *indifferent* to morality. The conditions for the possibility of scientific thought carry with them no deductively demonstrable basis for the categorical imperative, or for the ultimate achievability of a community of virtuous persons.

At this step, Kant attempts to synthesize the conservative and radical elements in his nature. As we have seen, he reassures us that our desire for justice or morality will be satisfied by a well-founded or reasonable hope. However, this hope is now rooted in history and so to the spatio-temporal world, the world of deed and not the world in speech, however distant in time. Plato's hope is satisfied only in speech, not in deed; it is a daydream of virtuous men. Kant's hope, for others if not also for himself, is, in a manner reminiscent of Nietzsche, a self-induced delusion for the sake of good health. Since we cannot be morally satisfied unless our hope of moral satisfaction is reasonable, we are *therefore* to hope that our hope is reasonable. We hope, not because it is absurd to do so, but because it is absurd not to do so. Unfortunately, this does not make hope rational.

"Theory," now understood as science and perhaps criticism, is rendered subordinate to praxis or morality, not on theoretical grounds, but on the basis of the peculiarly philosophical hope for the unity of theory and practice. As a result, philosophy in Kant's teaching undergoes a double concealment. First, it is replaced by a bracketed or sanitized metaphysics and a publicly safe (or supposedly safe) science and criticism. But second, even in its new form, philosophy is concealed by the moralizing teleology of the philosophy of history. Kant wishes to persuade us that natural science and natural history or phenomenal experience are receptive to the teleological and moral regulation of reason. We are to be persuaded to conceive of science and criticism as *morally salutary even though amoral.* Science and criticism are to be regarded as the instruments by which man's hope may be fulfilled, but we must hope that they are instruments of the right sort.

In Platonism, philosophy attempts to preserve its freedom (not the same thing as human freedom in the modern sense) by the production of a rhetorical intermediate between itself and politics. We now refer to this intermediate as "the history of philosophy," which is already a sign of the failure of Platonist rhetoric, since the main purpose of that rhetoric, one might say, was to prevent the rise of history or historicity. The new science, looked at philosophically rather than in terms of its methods, produces or prepares for the advent of historicity by transforming formal structures into possibilities. This transformation, of course, does not take place overnight. It will be helpful to turn now to a brief discussion of Descartes as a pivotal figure in the revolution against Platonism, hence, in the transition from Platonism to Kant's version of Neo-platonism. This will also enable us to bring out somewhat more sharply the link between science and hope in the career of political philosophy.

In the *Regulae,* Descartes says that we may express formally the ratios of things without taking into account their specific natures.[5] I use the term *ratios* to express the "orders and measures" of both simple elements and geometrical shapes. The Cartesian method is a generalization of mathematics, whose objects contain nothing of experience. They "consist of nothing but rationally deduced consequences."[6] They are, so to speak, a pure crystallization of reason. This purity or lack of empirical content has been interpreted, wrongly in my opinion, as *metaphysical* neutrality. If mathematics, or *mathesis universalis,* is a pure crystallization of reason, then Cartesianism is Idealism. This thesis is supported by the fact that what counts as simple and complex (or absolute and relative) elements depends upon the investigator's intention. In other words, the order and enumeration of the elements is a function of the problem the investigator sets himself. Whereas problems may arise initially from practical experience or from non-philosophical desire, there is no reason why this should always be the case. The Cartesian method is not metaphysically neutral, but it is compatible with both finite and infinite progress. The crucial point here is how we define human intentions, or whether they can be defined at all. In all this, we see a striking anticipation of Kant's Copernican revolution. Nature reveals her secrets to us if *we* formulate the proper questions. But even more, "nature" is now reconstituted as the ostensibly nonmetaphysical dimension of extension or matter in the void, subject to man's will through the instrument of *mathesis universalis.*[7]

I shall not discuss here what I regard as Descartes' rhetorical accommodation of his scientific reconstitution of nature to the religious and popular philosophical views of his day. Suffice it to say that, within that rhetorical presentation, the main point emerges in the claim that God's will is prior to his intellect. I have introduced Descartes as a crucial transition figure in our conjecture concerning man's hope. Descartes is a radical anti-Platonist who envisions the satisfaction of human desires, or the fulfillment of human hope, through the replacement of philosophy by mathematical physics, a replacement that is temporarily camouflaged by an accommodating rhetoric of metaphysical theology. If we disregard this rhetoric, bequeathing it to the professors, the mainspring of Cartesian strategy is immediately clear. The arithmetical and geometrical properties of everyday life are to be detached from their "phenomenal" representations and made the basis for the reconstitution of phenomena in accord with the human will.

That is, man's hope is to be transformed into man's intention. The Platonist conception of nature as both constitutive and regulative, hence as both temporal and external or sempiternal, is rejected. The new nature, as arithmetico-geometrical, may or may not be eternal; this is a problem depending upon the exact relation between cognition or will and formal structure. This much is clear, I think. Since the configurations of natural elements within human experience are at the disposition of human will, nature is at least potentially contingent, temporal, or protohistorical. In addition, Descartes (or "Cartesianism" in a sense analogous to "Platonism") wrongly assumes the metaphysical neutrality of nature. Metaphysics is "bracketed" or transformed into rhetorical reassurances that scientific philosophy will not only not harm society but will in fact achieve its salvation. Cartesian rhetoric prepares the transition from Platonist rhetoric into the rhetoric of the modern scientific epoch. At bottom, this rhetoric is common to Husserl and to Carnap, to mention two pivotal figures from our own time. Instead of a doctrine that mediates between the privacy of philosophy and the publicity of politics, we are introduced to a "politicized" version of philosophy, presented as a politically salutary science.

However, with all its public accommodations, Descartes' revolutionary anti-Platonism was too radical for philosophers like Leibniz and Kant. I am not here concerned with defects intrinsic to Cartesian mathematical physics, such as the analysis of motion, change, or force. Our subject today is political philosophy. Given the topic of our symposium, we restrict ourselves to Kant. It was obvious to Kant that modern Newtonian science threatened the very foundations of political and moral health. Nevertheless, he took for granted the soundness of the Cartesian reconstitution of nature and the truth of Newtonian science. To a certain extent, he took for granted Hobbes's analysis of human nature as a special case of the natural motion studied by physicists; that is, he accepted Hobbes's interpretation of human existence as war. Whereas for Hobbes the fear of violent death checks human vanity, which would otherwise lead to an infinite series of desires, for Kant there is a somewhat analogous reliance upon the cunning of self-interest. Both fear and self-interest lead to political order and peace. But they do not lead to moral virtue, a failure of no interest to Hobbes but of crucial importance to Kant. Kant's goal was then to overcome the defects of a Hobbesian interpretation of human nature, a task in which he was assisted by his reading of Rousseau, but to reconcile nature, whether in its human or nonhuman manifestations, with reason or spirit (if I may use that term without invoking Hegelian echoes). The Cartesian doctrine of the will is obviously unsatisfactory for this purpose. In the first place, it is amoral; secondly, it promotes possibility over actuality in such a way as to endanger the stability of the eternal structures of mathematical physics itself. Kant turned instead to a mathematicized version of Rousseau's doctrine of the general will as the crucial feature of the noumenal domain. In other words, whereas critique has no direct moral consequences, it leaves room for the domain of morality and freedom.

To state the results, or the intended results, of Kant's Copernican revolution in one sentence, the Cartesian effort to free man from superstition and powerlessness was transformed into a morally regulated version of scientific progress. For Descartes, freedom is power. For Hobbes, power is a function of freedom from fear, whether of ghosts or violent death. For Rousseau, freedom is a consequence of the general will. In each of these thinkers, man is encouraged to rely upon himself. Whereas Descartes is still close to Machiavelli's individual of outstanding virtue, Hobbes and Rousseau assimilate the autonomy of the individual into the self-regulation of the political community. Kant extends self-regulation to the theoretical as well as the practical domains. Freedom is thus the synthesis of spontaneity and reason. However, freedom is not yet morality. If we put to one side his obviously prudential provisional morality, we may assume that, for Descartes, morality is a trivial consequence of scientific enlightenment. In Hobbes, morality is replaced by fear, which produces peace and order. Rousseau claims to ground morality in sentiment or conscience. Kant is considerably more cautious than his predecessors. As I understand him, he accepts Rousseau's argument, directed against Cartesianism, that scientific progress is not automatically accompanied by moral progress. On the contrary, the truth of science, if allowed to apply to the spiritual domain, would eliminate the very basis of morality. But Kant cannot accept Rousseau's doctrine of sentiment, which renders morality irrational. To be moral, one must be free. But freedom is self-regulation, and rules must be rational if human existence is to possess significance and value. In my opinion, Kant's reasoning is circular at this point. Morality is rational, but rationality is either amoral or anti-moral. That is, Rousseau's sentiment is assimilated into the sense of dignity appropriate to a rational being. However, in order to sustain this sense of dignity, Kant must turn to the domain of purposes, ends, and the highest good. In the last analysis, he must turn away from nature toward history. But the evidence of history is sufficiently controversial, to say the least, as to preclude a rational foundation for morality, whether in a deductive or a juridical sense. Kant must therefore invoke hope with respect to the future. But the hope of good men is not the same as the hope of bad men. The hope of good men is thus sustained by morality, and we have described a circle.

Circles apart, Kant's intentions are relatively plain. Science is detached from morality, and the two are to be reunited by teleology. The turn from nature to history is dictated by the nonteleological character of science. The rejection of Platonic in favor of Newtonian science thus dictates the emergence of the philosophy of history, at least to moralists and political philosophers. As I see it, then, this is the basis for Kant's resolution of the war between the philosophical and the non-philosophical elements in the human soul. In Platonism, the soul is natural. There is no dualism of nature and spirit, but rather a dualism within nature. The soul is thus the "showplace" of the rational and nonrational dimensions of nature. For this reason, the war within the soul can be terminated only by the destruction of the soul. In a sense, Kant accepts this doctrine; that is, he dissolves the "nature" of Platonism into what we may provisionally call extension and thought or self-consciousness. Whatever the character of Kant's religious convictions, there can be no doubt that this is the point of contact between modern science and the Judaeo-Christian tradition. The soul is distinct from, even as a resident of, nature. The ambiguous status of this residency is apparent in Kant even before any question of morality, namely, in the phenomenal world. This world cannot be explained solely in terms of cognition and mathematical structure. It is rooted not merely in spontaneity but also in receptivity, hence in *Empfindungen*. The phenomenal world is not a pure creation of the ego, whether absolute or finite. It status *as* a world is thus relative to the nonrational as well as to the rational principles of Kant's teaching. The phenomenal world exhibits the rational and the nonrational, just as does the nature of Platonism. But in Platonism, the conception of rationality as *phronēsis* or a mixture of intuition and sound judgment allows us to bridge the gap between the rational and nonrational sides of nature in a reasonable—that is, plausible—way. Kant's conception of rationality allows for no such bridge.

Perhaps I can bring this point out more sharply by means of a Husserlian criticism of Kant. In the *Krisis,* Husserl notes that, for Kant, inner sense is temporalized or phenomenal.[8] But transcendental concepts are formed within inner experience. It is therefore necessary to acquire apodictic certainty about inner experience as the ground of scientific objectivity. This would amount to the derivation of the sense and validity of transcendental concepts from an apodictically purified *doxa* or science of the *Lesbenswelt,* which Kant does not and cannot supply. In other words, phenomenal experience, hence political and historical life in the broadest sense, is not constituted transcendentally. It is therefore not accessible to rational understanding in the strict or scientific sense. Kant emphasizes what he takes to be the merits of this situation, namely, that morality, for him the most important aspect of phenomenal life, is freed from science. Unfortunately, as he does not emphasize, this reduces *phronēsis* or everyday intelligence and judgment to the level of the subrational. Worldly wisdom is no substitute for a transcendentally constituted rational understanding of phenomenal human existence. I will not here debate the issue of whether Kant's many writings on everyday life are prudent or foolish. The crucial point is that there is no constitutive bond between practical and theoretical intelligence. In order to make sense out of practice, Kant must turn away from practice as it is lived. Since he cannot turn to reason in any of its diverse senses, his only recourse is to *hope.* In one last formulation, what Kant calls "practical reason" has nothing to do with phenomenal experience, practical intelligence, or sound judgment.

The Fact of Morality

We have now reached what I take to be the sharpest formulation of the dilemma faced by Kant. There is no epistemic basis for moral hope. Knowledge is of nature, the domain of mechanism. Worldly wisdom is phenomenal in an ambiguous if not self-contradictory sense. That is, it is not knowledge of nature, since that would be scientific knowledge. But neither is it knowledge of the noumenal domain. As a result, it seems to be a kind of phantom knowledge of a phantom world, and so a dream. To awaken from this dream would be to disappear as human beings. Even as dreamers, we cannot hope to be awakened in the next world by a just God who rewards us with personal immortality. Such a hope is unworthy of rational men, since it is a hope for miracles. In somewhat different terms, to hope in this manner is to subordinate spontaneity to receptivity, or to give up self-regulation, and so too religion within the bounds of reason alone. But if we reject this hope, we are left with phantoms.

In addition to its insubstantial character, phenomenal experience, strictly speaking, cannot be moral, since morality is rooted in the transcendental. The closest we can come to an empirical understanding of morality is by deducing political order from self-interest and, as Kant observes, this might result in a society of cunning devils. In other words, even history is unreliable. Since we have no knowledge of the noumenal, and hence none of the ostensible significance of history, what we take to be the signs of moral progress may actually be the punishment of false hope imposed upon us by a malevolent deity. For all we know to the contrary, our phantom existence is residence in Hell. Suppose that we put ourselves into a Cartesian mood and ask: Is there any evidence within phenomenal experience that justifies the hope of good men, despite all that a malevolent deity might arrange to delude us?

The only evidence I can find in Kant's writings is what he calls the fact of morality. Kant claims, in my opinion rightly, that human beings perceive the difference between right and wrong, or what in Platonic language may be called the noble and the base, in their everyday lives. In other words, he claims that we perceive moral obligation, but not a guarantee of the rewards associated with moral conduct. I want to suggest that the perception of nobility and baseness reveals the defect in Kant's distinction between the noumenal and the phenomenal. On the basis of this distinction, there cannot be a genuine perception of righteousness, justice, or nobility, but only the appearance of such a perception. In the domain of human affairs, we are restricted to a noncognitive or phantom *doxa*. But such a restriction goes directly contrary to our deepest perceptions, as these are granted even by Kant. Deductive and juridical arguments alike rest necessarily upon undemonstrated premises or axioms. If morality is a fact, then it must, so to speak, be an axiom; that is, it must provide direct evidence either for religious faith or for what I am calling Platonism, namely, the view that nature is regulative as well as constitutive. I cannot engage in a detailed discussion of the point here, but I would claim that the evidence of everyday life, while it is itself the distinction between nobility and baseness, offers no support whatsoever for hope of reward, whether in heaven or in a future stage of history. Kant was enough of a Platonist to recognize that the sharp distinction between obligation and reward is politically disastrous. This at least is how I understand his turn to hope *qua* philosophy of history. But the unsatisfactory aspects of historical hope are themselves rooted in the rejection of the Platonist conception of nature.

I have already noted that this rejection is ostensibly justified by the triumph of modern science. Whether the justification is more than ostensible would depend upon a very deep understanding of Platonism and modern science, neither of which I possess. Fortunately for me, one thing is sufficiently clear to be asserted with reasonable confidence. The Platonist conception of nature, whatever its other difficulties, is more compatible with our experience than the Newtonian or Kantian conception. I should like to go one step farther. The modern scientific conception of nature, as it continues to function in twentieth-century thought, suffers from a vitiating circularity. Science begins from, and purports to explain, everyday, pretheoretical experience. But it also rejects pretheoretical experience as misleading, contradictory, or insufficiently explicit. Science therefore attempts to explain the pretheoretical by de- and reconstructing it, namely, by the production of a theory. But that theory also produces the pretheoretical world, to the extent that it is regarded as rational or intelligible. One could say that the pretheoretical world is an ambiguous and shifting amalgam of the secondary effects of past theories. In other words, the task of constructing a new and ostensibly more adequate theoretical explanation of the pretheoretical world actually begins with a historical artifact: the refuse of past theories. This is the post-Kantian version of the phantom of phenomenal experience in Kant.

One of the ironies of the history of philosophy is the thesis that Platonism is the doctrine of two worlds, whereas modern philosophy is the gradual development of the doctrine of one world. I would of course not deny the dualistic character of Platonism; on the contrary, I have emphasized it. But this dualism has nothing to do with two worlds. On the contrary, it is modern philosophy and modern science that dissolve the one world of Platonism into two distinct domains of primary and secondary qualities, the phenomenal and the noumenal, or the historical and the posthistorical. As the greatest figure in modern philosophy, Kant looks both to the past and the future. Like all Platonists, Kant sees the danger posed by philosophy to morality. Yet his attempt to save morality produces the philosophy of history, which either dissolves morality or renders it forever inaccessible. Let me emphasize that my own criticism of Kant is not moral. If Kant's teaching leads to the dissolution of morality, that is a serious immanent defect. My objection to Kant is rather that his teaching leads also to the dissolution or at least suppression of philosophy. I would make the same claim against Platonism. Kant is a Neoplatonist because he suppresses philosophy on fundamentally moral or political grounds. Of course, Kant believes that this suppression is actually a redefinition of philosophy on the reliable basis of modern science. I have tried to show today that this belief is false, primarily in terms of Kant's own explanation of praxis, that is, of morality, politics, and history. Summarily stated, modern science offers no reliable basis whatsoever for understanding human existence. I believe that Kant would accept this claim. Unfortunately, his allegiance to modern science leads him to deprive us of *any* basis for the rational understanding of human existence. One does not need to be a Platonist to see that Kant's teaching is unsuccessful. And one does not need to repudiate modern science in order to suggest that the main defect in Kant's teaching is his doctrine, essentially Newtonian, of nature.

Scientism and Historicism

I come now to the conclusion of my conjecture about the history of philosophy. My consideration of Kant was motivated by my interest in the following question: To what extent is it possible for philosophy to exist in public? For the sake of covenience, let us define philosophy as a comprehensive reflection on the structures and purposes of human experience. We might also call it an enduring exhibition of the unity of theory and practice. The Platonist denies that this reflection or exhibition can be conducted in full public view. Kant makes philosophy publicly respectable by purging it of metaphysics in any but a dialectical context and subordinating it to morality. His revision of Platonism produces two main consequences that, again for the sake of brevity, I shall call scientism and historicism. By scientism, I mean nothing other than the thesis that philosophy is the philosophy of science, or metascience. It follows from Kant by the single step of rejecting the transcendental trappings of criticism along with metaphysics. Since this thesis amounts to the rejection of philosophy as understood by both Platonism and Kantianism, it is of no further interest to us. For it grants, or rather asserts, that philosophy, in the older sense, must not be permitted to make a public appearance. This assertion is just moralism carried to the extreme degree.

Of the various forms of what I am calling "historicism," the most interesting is that represented by Nietzsche and Heidegger, whom I take together in disregard of Heidegger's contention that they are to be sharply distinguished. If a distinction is necessary, let it be this: Nietzsche emphasizes the practical dimension of the unity of theory and practice, whereas Heidegger emphasizes the theoretical aspect. For our purposes, the main difference between Platonism and historicism, in the variant I am considering, is this: The Platonist preserves the privacy of philosophy beneath the rhetorical mantle of a publicly salutary doctrine having little to do with philosophy as it is actually practiced. In the Nietzsche-Heidegger variant of historicism, the rhetoric is transformed into a demand that philosophy come into the open. At the same time, this demand is compromised, or attenuated, by the intermittent admission that it is *impossible* for philosophy to come into the open. In Nietzsche, the public assertion of the principle of esotericism is covered over by epigram, and more comprehensively by a patently incoherent doctrine or revelation of liberation within the bonds of necessity. This is Nietzsche's version of Kant's historicist hope. In Heidegger, the public manifestation of philosophical thinking is veiled over by the assertion that uncovering is also concealing. Heidegger does not mention it, so far as I am aware, but what is true of Being must also be true, *a fortiori,* of the philosopher or postphilosophical thinker. The Heideggerean public appearance of philosophy is therefore at once and as such a disappearance of philosophy from the public view. What was in Kant the phantom quality of phenomenal existence is extended by Heidegger to cover philosophical existence as well, while, in a characteristically Kantian mode, the genuine thinker awaits a liberating gift from the future.

With every apology for the haste of this sketch, I want nevertheless to suggest, if only in a conjectural manner, that with all the differences among philosophers, they seem to agree on one crucial point. Philosophy cannot exist in public, in the full view of the public, and perhaps not even in its own full view. The rhetoric of historicism is no doubt more appropriate to our own epoch, since it creates the illusion that philosophy has cast off its ironical reserve, in keeping with the insistence of the time upon sincerity and honesty. Even post Heideggerian irony á la Derrida and his associates is presumably sincere, since it does not pretend to be what it is not and it accepts public honors for presenting itself as what it is. However, an ironical wink at irony is not quite the same as the public appearance of philosophy. The deconstruction of metaphysics is again Kantianism carried to the extreme, with the net result that dialectic replaces metaphysics instead of bracketing it.

I do not wish to leave you with the impression that, in my view, scientism and historicism are direct consequences of Kant. The most one could say is that Kant's peculiar and unsuccessful resolution of the quarrel between the philosophical and nonphilosophical elements in the soul begins a process, accelerated by Hegel, that produces scientism and historicism. Kant's intentions were honorable; he hoped for the best. My disagreement with Kant comes down to a single issue. I deny the efficacy of history, whether as a genuine or rhetorical solution to the problem of man's hope. But this is just another way of admitting that philosophy can never exist in public, and so there are no solutions to man's political problems. To say this, however, is not the same as to deny the public perception of the distinction between the noble and the base. It is rather to repudiate philosophical justifications as well as refutations of that perception.

I accept the thesis that philosophy cannot make a full and frank public appearance. It does not follow from this that philosophy can make no public appearance at all. In my opinion, however, necessity and morality combine in the following way: What we require is a frank admission of the incompatibility of the private and the public domains. In practical terms, we require as little political philosophy as possible. The public appearance of philosophy is always in the interests of justice. However, as was first demonstrated by Plato's *Republic,* and as is unconsciously being demonstrated today by the new school of analytical political philosophy, an unrestrained desire for justice leads to a radical disregard of the fundamental facts of political life. Such a disregard can culminate in nothing other than the destruction of both philosophy and justice. The extraordinary view that there are rational arguments in support of just acts is a tacit denial of the intuition of the noble and the base. To deny this, however, is to deny the very experience that our theories of justice are supposed to preserve. It is therefore to destroy philosophy, which, in the deepest and most comprehensive sense, is as the unfolding of the perception of the distinction between the noble and the base, the good, and as such, man's hope.

Notes

1. Yirmiahu Yovel, *Kant and the Philosophy of History* (Princeton: Princeton University Press, 1979), p. 21.
2. Plato, *Sophist* 216C.
3. Niccolò Machiavelli, *The Prince,* ch. 15.
4. *Ibid.,* ch. 18.
5. René Descartes, *Regulae ad directionem ingenii,* edited by Giovanni Crapulli (The Hague: Nijhoff, 1966), p. 16
6. *Ibid.,* p. 6
7. *Ibid.,* pp. 19, 25.
8. Edmund Husserl, *Die Krisis der europäischen Wissenschaften und die transzendentale Phänomenologie,* edited by Walter Biemel (The Hague: Nijhoff, 1954), pp. 116–117.

Thomas Seebohm

3. *Kant's Theory of Revolution**

Kant has received praise for his ideas on eternal peace and for his ethical opposition to war. However, what he says about subjects' rights of resistance against the sovereign and about revolution does not please the liberal and socialist intellectuals of the nineteenth and twentieth century. Moreover, his views seem to be inconsistent.

One line of thought on this subject is developed in his systematic writings, especially the *Metaphysical Principles of Justice,* and in his popular writings, especially in *On the Old Saw.* Another one can be found only in the popular writings, especially in *Perpetual Peace* and the *Strife of the Faculties.* It will be the task of the following considerations to show (a) that both lines of thought are complementary and consistent with each other and (b) that Kant's theory of revolution and the problems connected with it are of more than historical interest. They are of significance especially in light of current concerns. Accordingly, (1) I will give a brief summary of the consequences of the line of thought developed in the systematic writings and a more extensive outline of the second group. (2) I will reject some attempts to "explain" their inconsistencies psychologically and/or sociologically. I will suggest that Kant's critics would have a hard time trying to solve the dilemmas he faced. (3) I will attempt to explain the complementary character of the two lines of thought in the framework of the architectonic of Kant's practical philosophy. This attempt will focus on the *double* function of anthropology in practical philosophy.

No Rightful Resistance

According to Kant's philosophy of law, the sovereign—that is, the legislative power—is irreproachable; the ruler—that is, the executive—cannot be resisted and there is no appeal beyond the highest judge. The subjects have no rights of coercion against the sovereign, only duties toward him. The sovereign alone has the right of coercion but no duties. A defective constitution can be changed only by the sovereign through reforms. Such reforms can affect only the executive power, not the lawgiving power. *Prima facie* it seems to be the case that Kant

---

*From *Social Research* (Autumn 1981).

recognizes in the *Metaphysical Principles of Justice* at least a right of necessity that can justify resistance, but a careful reading shows that Kant denies in the *Principles* themselves that such a right exists at all. In the *Old Saw* he is explicit about this point: It is not possible to justify resistance against the sovereign by a right of necessity. There is no rightful resistance at all, in "works or in *words*." If there is no rightful resistance even in words, one can ask the questions: What is the practical significance of the right of the people to complain publicly about violations of their rights by the ruler and the sovereign? In what does the right of free speech, mentioned elsewhere, consist? If it pleases the sovereign he can introduce censorship, and if some subjects protest against it "in words," the sovereign has the right to punish them. No other consequence can be drawn from the principles mentioned above.

Kant derived these principles from the categorical imperative via the principle of law, which will be analyzed later. Though the theoretical background is different because of its idealistic character, the practical political consequences can be called Hobbesian in every respect. This holds even for the further principle that, after a successful revolution, the new sovereign has the same rights and the subjects have the same duties as under the old sovereign. Such principles seem to be acceptable only for those who are willing to defend the morality of the bureaucracy of Prussian Germany. It is worth noticing that the inconsistency of claiming the right of free public discussion while simultaneously denying the right to challenge the sovereign even verbally if he denies that right was an inconsistency characteristic of the Prussian-German state as well. In that state, the subjects' political impotence and intellectual liberty were connected in a syndrome that always appeared bizarre and dangerous to the neighboring countries in the West.[1]

The second line of thought occurs first in *Religion Within the Limits of Reason Alone*. Kant mentions that it is impossible to determine the outcome of a revolution. Revolutions are dangerous—they cannot be planned rationally and the situation after the revolution might be worse than it was previously. Hence, it is only by "providence" that a revolution can lead to progress in the development of mankind. He adds a peculiar warning against revolutions. It might be that a revolution which is not guided by providence would lead to a constitution with shortcomings that can be eliminated only by another revolution, which in turn would be outside rational control. This is a purely *pragmatic* consideration—that is, it is an observation about what happens and has happened to mankind. Principles of the philosophy of law as such are not discussed. Kant is saying that, although it is imprudent to begin revolutions, there are certain shortcomings in constitutions that can be changed only by revolutions and that it is not inconceivable that some revolutions would lead to progress.[2]

We find further development of these types of pragmatic-anthropological considerations in *An Old Question Raised Again*. In addition, some viewpoints are mentioned here that pertain to the philosophy of law and can be connected with similar points made in *Perpetual Peace*. It is essential to keep in mind that *An Old Question Raised Again: Is the Human Race Constantly Progressing?* is the subtitle of section II of the *Strife of the Faculties* that has the heading *Strife of the Philosophical Faculty with the Faculty of Law*. The "philosophical faculty" should not be misread as "philosophy," especially not as Kant's systematic philosophy. The philosophical faculty is the faculty of the liberal arts, including the sciences and all empirical disciplines as well as mathematics, logic, and metaphysics—that is, all disciplines not oriented toward a profession such as medicine, jurisprudence, or theology. In the third section, for instance, Kant demands that forensic medicine should be replaced by forensic psychology, representing the philosophical faculty. The *Strife* in the second section is hence not between philosophy in the strict sense and the faculty of the law. It includes viewpoints taken from our—and Kant's—empirical knowledge about the human race and the human character. What Kant raises again in 1798 is the old question he had dealt with already in 1784 in *Ideas Toward a Universal History*. In the *Strife* he raises the question again in connection with observations about a phenomenon he has not yet dealt with in the *Ideas*, namely, the French Revolution. He treats this revolution as an instance of the type mentioned in the *Religion*, namely, one which can lead to human progress.

The main point is that a revolution which can never be judged positively from the standpoint of the law can be considered positively on extralegal considerations. First, Kant analyzes the reaction of the spectators to the French Revolution. He characterizes the key term he uses in his description as anthropological. The French Revolution had a very peculiar effect on its spectators. This effect is independent of such questions as whether the revolution was considered to be a success or a miscarriage. This effect is present in the spectators even if they admit that the atrocities and miseries of the revolution are a motive for every sensible man to avoid such an experiment in the future. Kant describes this effect as follows: The spectators (a) develop a strong sympathy for one group of the parties in the struggle, the revolutionaries. (b) Without having intended to enter into revolutionary activity themselves, they develop a strong wish to participate in the struggle, an attitude that borders on enthusiasm. (c) They are willing to express this enthusiasm even under circumstances which are, or might be, dangerous—that is, the will to express it is not guided by self-interest. Kant defines enthusiasm, which is, according to him, an anthropological concept, as follows: "Genuine enthusiasm always moves to what is purely moral, such as the concept of right, and it cannot be grafted onto self-interest." Enthusiasm is *"the participation in the good with affect."* As an affect, enthusiasm is not good without qualification and the qualification is that the affect should be under the control of reason. The object of the affect, the idea of right, is of course good without qualification. In this sense the attitude of the spectators is morally good.

Kant goes one step further in ascribing the same affect—and hence moral goodness—to the revolutionaries:

> Monetary awards could not elevate the adversaries of the revolution to the zeal and grandeur of the soul which the pure concept of right produced in the revolutionaries; and even the concept of honour among the old martial nobility (an analogue of enthusiasm) vanished before the weapons of those who kept in view the right of the nation to which they belonged and of which they considered themselves to be the guardians.[3]

Two comments are in order. (1) If there is anything wrong with the enthusiasm of the revolutionaries, it cannot be attributed to the affective nature of their enthusiasm. Kant observes the same enthusiasm in the spectators and does not criticize it. It should be kept in mind that Kant does not teach that actions guided by maxims that have an admixture of affect are immoral. Such an assumption about his teaching results from a misreading of the *Groundwork of the Metaphysics of Morals* and the second *Critique*, which deals with the transcendental grounding of the principles of morality. It cannot even be said that such actions are merely legal. As the *Metaphysics of Morals* shows, the categorical imperative commands that one cultivate the affects that make it easy to be guided by maxims that correspond to the categorical imperative; moreover, one should employ them to fight those affects that do not have this very property. The free moral act, which can never be proven empirically, is in this case the decision to educate one's character toward attaining a system of habitual inclinations and affects.[4] If, therefore, genuine enthusiasm occurs, it can be taken as an indicator of such a moral education and self-education and hence as a sign of the "moral predisposition" of the human race. Kant considers the enthusiasm of the spectators as well as of the revolutionaries to be such a sign. (2) According to Kant, this is genuine enthusiasm, as passionate participation in the good, because it has as its moral cause in the idea of right, the right that a nation must not be hindered in providing itself with a civil constitution that appears good to the people themselves. Furthermore, it is genuine because the end pursued by the revolutionaries is at the same time a duty, namely, the duty to realize the republican constitution, the only one that provides the conditions whereby war can be avoided in the future. The spectators are correct in judging that any attempt to stop revolutions from within or without must be morally condemned. Such an intervention would be directed against the natural right of man to develop a constitution in which all citizens participate in legislative activity—that is, giving themselves the laws that they have to obey. The idea of such a constitution is a Platonic ideal, the *respublica noumenon*. Every state insofar as it is a state at all participates in this idea, and it is a duty in a *respublica phaenomenon* to strive for a full realization of the *respublica noumenon*. A critical attitude is necessary. There is a tendency in every state to pretend that this goal has already been reached or that nothing more can be achieved than what has been realized in a certain constitution. Such pretensions have to be criticized. The inadequacies of every constitution have to be shown in each case.

The development of a perfect republic begins with the evolution of mankind from the natural to the civil state. This evolution leads mankind through the fiercest battles. War, both civil and foreign, destroys all forms of statutory constitutions. War alone cannot lead to the republic and to eternal peace, but it destroys all imperfect constitutions, leaving only two, the republic and monarchy. Before investigating the interrelation of these two with the further aid of some passages from *Perpetual Peace,* it is necessary to clarify the background of the idea of an evolution of mankind and its moving forces in the *Ideas Towards a Universal History.*

According to the *Ideas,* the greatest problem for mankind, one that seems almost insoluble, is the institution of a just civil constitution. In the state of nature man has two tendencies, the tendency to isolate himself and the tendency to enter social relations. The tendency to isolate himself is not primarily the tendency to retreat and live as a Robinson, though this might be one of the forms in which it expresses itself. Rather it is the tendency to have things ordered according to the precepts of one's own mind— in the language of Kant's philosophy of right, to determine according to one's own mind what one's own rights are and what the rights of others are. As a consequence, we have the inclination to use coercion wherever possible against others with whom we disagree in this respect. Since such an attitude is supposed to be held by everybody, the result is universal antagonism. If it functions as the leading maxim, the tendency to enter social relations will be to enter a just civil constitution. Both tendencies are themselves in antagonism in the *constructed* state of nature but they determine as *well* the whole development of the civil state.

The tendency to enter social relations will be the tendency to obey the sovereign, but only a sovereign who is just, because this tendency also fosters a respect for the rights of others. It holds, however, that whoever is chosen to be the sovereign or declares himself to be the sovereign will be human, of course, and if he follows the first tendency, he will be unwilling to respect what others think to be their right; he will be inclined to use coercion to shape things according to his own mind. Thus, he will be in a state of natural antagonism not only toward other sovereigns and nations but also, to a certain degree, toward his own subjects.[5] In the *Ideas,* Kant considers war to be the attempt of nature— that is, providence—to push development in the direction of the destruction of old, imperfect constitutions (perhaps including rebellions and revolutions as specific kinds of war). In the *Strife of the Faculties* he explicitly adds civil war (doubtless thinking of the French Revolution) as a special factor after indicating in the *Religion* that revolutions might be useful in some cases for the progress of mankind. The *Strife* adds that the French Revolution is an instance of a revolution in which sympathizing spectators and the revolutionaries themselves are defending the idea of a just civil constitution. It should be kept in mind that such a case is, for Kant, a special case. Not every rebellion and revolution in history has this character.

Kant makes the further observation in the *Strife* that revolution leads to the elimination of all constitutions except two, monarchy and republic. This remark should be taken as exactly what it is: an observation that, after the French Revolution, is empirically true for Kant. According to *Perpetual Peace*, the monarchy is in a peculiar situation. The monarch is supposed to give only the laws that the people would give to themselves and has to treat the people according to the laws of freedom. In the language of the *Ideas*, the monarch has to consider what the *people* think about their rights and not what *he* considers in his mind to be their rights. The people, however, in accordance with their reason, would introduce the republic, and hence it is the duty of the monarch to introduce the *true* republic via reforms. He ought to consider revolutions, which have been produced by nature, as an admonition of nature to perform his duty.[6] A monarch not acting in this direction violates the right of the people and cannot claim that injustice is done to him if he is deposed in a revolution that occurs as a natural event.

Revolution a Natural Catastrophe

The thesis that there is no right of resistance against the sovereign was deduced by Kant from the principle of right and so, in the last instance from the categorical imperative. Is such a principle compatible with the above evaluation of the moral character of revolutionaries and of those who sympathize with a certain type of revolution? Before trying to answer this question we must examine (a) all attempts to understand this problem as an inconsistency that can be explained with psychosociological tools and (b) the fact that the problem is a genuinely systematic problem—not only for Kant but also for us.

The first attempt to explain psychologically why Kant is "inconsistent" in this respect goes back to Heinrich Heine and is repeatedly mentioned in more recent literature. It is assumed that Kant at first applauded the French Revolution, as did the German bourgeoisie in general, and was then horrified by the terror and the atrocities that occurred when plebeian elements took over in the last phase.[7] This explanation might be true of the German bourgeoisie, given the emphasis their representatives in the Prussian-German state in the nineteenth century gave to Kant's treatment of the right of resistance. It does not, however, work for Kant himself. The philological evidence reveals that Kant's most sympathetic remarks about the French Revolution are his *last* published words about it in 1798.[8] The legal theory of resistance occurs for the first time in 1793.[9]

A second attempt assumes that the reverse is the case: here it is assumed that there is a general development in Kant's practical philosophy in which metaphysical and religious remnants such as the postulates of practical reason, which are inconsistent with the real spirit of critical philosophy, lose their significance. Kant's position at the end of his life is the position of a radical democrat in the Marxist sense. His varying positions toward the French Revolution provide further evidence for this line of development.[10]

There can be no doubt that Kant's practical philosophy underwent a steady development which had not yet come to an end even in his last years. The same holds for his theory of revolution. The problem is, however, whether this development is smooth or whether it has the character of an inconsistent patchwork. It is obvious that he himself must have thought that both aspects of his theory of revolution are compatible. The final formulation of the legal theory was published in 1797,[11] and the writings that deal with the positive aspects of the French Revolution, published in 1795 and 1798,[12] do not mention restrictions regarding the legal theory. On the contrary, Kant is adamant in his rejection of a right of resistance that could serve as a justification for a revolution.

Since the chronology of the publications does not leave any space for assumptions about a course of development, the last recourse for psychological explanation is the assumption that we can distinguish between an esoteric and an exoteric treatment of the problem of revolution in Kant.[13] The formulations of the exoteric treatment are influenced by censorship, which is responsible for Kant's more reactionary statements about revolutions.

There can be no doubt that Kant's activity was subject to some pressure after the Woellner affair in 1793. It is true, furthermore, that the *Strife of the Faculties* as a whole marks the end of that period and that Kant, assuming a change in the censorship policy of the Prussian government, felt free to be more outspoken in several respects.[14] It is, however, doubtful that this fact can explain incompatibilities in Kant's remarks about revolutions. The following facts must be kept in mind: (1) The two theses that (a) sovereigns ought to consider revolutions as nature's punishments for not fulfilling their duty and that (b) it is the monarch's duty to introduce a republican constitution via reforms, that is, to abolish monarchy itself, were published by Kant in 1795, in the middle of the epoch dominated by Woellner.[15] (2) Kant promised to avoid public statements in matters of religion. In political matters he was never asked nor did he promise to suppress his thoughts.[16] Though the *Strife* adds new anthropological viewpoints, it cannot be said that they are more radical than those already mentioned by 1795. (3) Kant's more reactionary position is corroborated in writings that are esoteric in the sense that they were not written for the public but for professional philosophers. Hence, if a possible difference between the esoteric and the exoteric exists, it is in the exoteric writings, that is, in those written for the public. As mentioned in (2), it is doubtful that such a difference can be substantiated regarding these publications. The main difficulty in explaining the incompatibility by this esoteric/exoteric distinction is that the more reactionary aspect of his thoughts on revolution are developed in his systematic—that is, esoteric—writings, in the *Metaphysical Elements of Justice*. Though they occur for the first time in public writings in 1793, it is absurd to assume that Kant presented them there and in the *Elements* to please the censor. The *Elements* was not written for the public and Kant never gave up the right to express himself freely in professional writings. Furthermore, it was his principle always to tell the truth but not always to state the whole truth. Hence, if he suppressed something in the *Elements* there is no justification for the conclusion that what he stated there explicitly was not unconditionally valid for him. Finally, the *Elements* was published in 1797, but *Perpetual Peace* was published in 1795; hence, both were published under the reign of Woellner. In other words, Kant published both aspects of his theory of revolution at a time when he had good reason to believe that he was under the watchful eye of the censor. (*4*) The *Strife,* written at a time in which Kant thought that the situation had improved, again confirms the conclusions concerning the right of resistance drawn in the *Elements* in 1797. Hence, though it can be admitted that censorship might have had a certain influence on the way in which Kant presented the positive aspects of his theory of revolution in 1795, there is no possibility of explaining the *prima facie* incompatibility between his two approaches to the phenomenon of revolutions by the distinction of an exoteric and an esoteric teaching or by the fact of censorship.

The only conclusion that can be drawn is that Kant himself did not see these apparently conflicting viewpoints as incompatible. Before explaining Kant's view in this matter, it should be noted that the problem of reconciling these two approaches in dealing with the phenomena of revolution and resistance was not confined to Kant. It has existed as a problem of morality in the nineteenth and twentieth centuries. If one considers the attitude of intellectuals toward some variants of political resistance against the state—for example, the activity of anarchists of the Bakunin-Netchajev and Baader-Meinhof groups—one can find certain parallels to the attitude which Kant observed in the French Revolution's sympathizers. There is a sharing of certain social and political ideals, an enthusiasm for the realization of these ideas, sometimes a wish to participate that in most cases is not transformed into a genuine intention to participate. Confronted with the question of why they refused to take this last step—and this question was asked by the activists as well as by conservative critics of their social ideals—these intellectuals have usually answered that they were in disagreement with the activists regarding the means but not the ends of revolutionary activity. One can ask here: What are the means? The answer is: Violence. But what does this mean in Kantian terms if not the use of coercion against the sovereign? Hence, the same dilemma that is characteristic for the Kantian approach occurs in such an argument, without, however, presupposing the framework of his theory. Today's "sympathizers" attempt to back their position with the sly remark that the activists' use of violence is not justifiable because they act in isolation from the masses and disregard economic conditions and other real factors. This observation does not escape the Kantian framework. Mass movements and economic realities are natural factors that cause revolutions and force men into revolutionary activity. The question whether such activity is morally justifiable should be directed in this case to the masses themselves since it was claimed that acts of violence are justifiable if the revolutionary acts in concert with the masses. The question has two aspects: (a) "Why do you do it?" and, given the answer "Because I am forced to do it," a further question arises, which is often forgotten but ought to be asked in moral matters, namely, (b) "Is it morally good that you are forced to do it?" A positive answer to the latter question is tantamount to an endorsement of the thesis that social and political progress ought to be brought forth by revolution, that is, that the only morally justifiable means for producing such progress is revolution. It is not to be expected that you and I, as members of the masses following the call of conscience, would give such an answer. Who wants to be in a situation in which he has to turn against the powers of the state with violence? Who would not prefer a situation different from the natural social situation that, as a brute situation, forces him to react as a natural brute? It seems to be a command of the categorical imperative to give a preference to all other means of gaining social and political progress and to condemn morally every situation in which the masses are forced to initiate revolutionary activity. The reason is that the situations in which they are forced by nature to act immorally are situations in which they feel themselves deprived of their human dignity. Nobody can justify a revolution morally. It can be justified theoretically only as an inevitable natural process, that is, as a catastrophe in which reason and morality have no role, except for the hope that by chance the result might be an improved state of affairs—that means first of all a state of affairs in which revolutions would no longer be necessary. The general principle of moral judgment that one must observe is that the moral quality of an action performed by somebody under the force of circumstances can be positive only if a further question—whether it is good that he was forced to do it—can be answered positively as well, because only in that case would it hold that he ought to do it even without being forced to do it. The fact that one is forced to do something as such is in itself always immoral, because to admit that one is forced to do it is to admit that one does it whether one considers it to be right or wrong.

Hence, those sympathetic to the modern revolutions and revolutionary activities are, in principle, in exactly the situation Kant describes, and their attitude is *prima facie* as contradictory as Kant's. From a moral point of view, they can admire the enthusiasm for the good in some revolutionaries, but they can never provide a moral justification for the act of revolution itself. It is possible for them to justify this act naturally, that is, perhaps to explain it theoretically, which would enable them to blame the governing powers and the sovereign for the situation. But again that means blaming these powers morally for having forced their subjects into a situation in which they have to act immorally. Hence, instead of criticizing Kant for inconsistencies, it would be better to ask why he was not bothered by the inconsistency. It might be that he has a clue that could help us to solve the antinomy between the inability to find a moral justification for the revolutionary act as such and the enthusiastic feeling of sympathy for some revolutionaries and revolutions.

Virtuous Revolutionaries

Kant's solution to this dilemma is special because he rejects the usual approach in which some cases of coercion against the sovereign are justifiable and others not. As will be shown below, such a distinction is itself inconsistent according to Kant. No act of coercion directed against the sovereign is possible, yet it is possible to consider *some* revolutions as indicators of a "moral predisposition in mankind." A correct understanding of this thesis must first take into account that it belongs to the realm of pragmatic anthropology, whereas the other thesis, which excludes resistance against the sovereign, belongs to a derivation of moral principles *a priori,* that is, to the metaphysics of morals. All the essays that deal with the positive aspects of Kant's judgments about the French Revolution can be considered as belonging to section E of the second part of the *Anthropology from a Pragmatic Point of View.*[17] They are further corroborations of the general viewpoints mentioned in this section, which is entitled the *Character of the Species.* The transcendental justification for such considerations is given in the final parts and especially in the appendix of the *Critique of Judgment.*[18] Hence, the incompatibility in question is rooted in the difficulty of connecting a transcendental and metaphysical treatment of moral principles with pragmatic anthropology. Therefore, the difficulty comes under the general heading of the problem of the applicability of the categorical imperative.

This problem can be solved only if the function of anthropology in Kant's moral philosophy is grasped properly. Anthropology is not excluded from the realm of metaphysical investigations about morals. As Kant says in the introduction to the *Metaphysics of Morals,* though anthropology can never be used in order to ground the principles of morality—that is, the categorical imperative—it is nevertheless presupposed in the metaphysics of morals as the realm to which the principles have to be applied.[19]

It is the specific nature of man that has to be subsumed under the categorical imperative in order to derive the more concrete conclusions from the formal principles. A pragmatic anthropology must, in addition, investigate the subjective conditions of human nature that might help or hinder the development of morality. It is pragmatic because the principles of morality can be grafted onto the findings of this anthropology. Such grafting reveals the second-order duties, those concerning the cultivation of affects and emotions—that is, duties to strengthen those affects and emotions that help, and to weaken the ones that hinder, moral progress.[20] The denial of the right of resistance clearly belongs to the application of the principle of justice to anthropology, while the considerations about the possibility of a positive function of revolutions and the genuine enthusiasm of those sympathetic to revolution and of the revolutionaries themselves belong to pragmatic anthropology.

First we have to consider the denial of the right of resistance. The problem of resistance belongs to the philosophy of law. Practical laws of reason are ethical if duty alone is the incentive. In addition, they can be juridical if other incentives are possible.[21] *Jus* refers to all ethical laws that (a) are external, that is, refer to relations between persons, and (b) justify coercion if violated. Coercion is the additional external incentive. The following principle of justice that is derivable from the categorical imperative: "Every action is right, through which or according to whose maxim, the freedom of volition (liberty) of everybody can coexist with the freedom of volition (liberty) of everybody else according to a universal law."[22] It is essential for a correct understanding of the freedom of voliton to keep in mind that this freedom is not transcendental freedom. The latter is implied in the categorical imperative as shown in the deduction of the second *Critique*.[23] Freedom of volition corresponds to the right of all sensible, finite, rational, and practical beings to direct their will to an external object, such that they have the liberty to do so. This principle is derived from the categorical imperative, because its denial is tantamount to the denial of an operating will in such beings. They can have only external objects as objects of their will.[24] Freedom of volition is therefore implied in the concept of a finite, sensible, rational, and practical being. It is, however, a right in the proper sense only if practical activity is subsumed under, the categorical imperative and if the result of this subsumption is the principle of right. The object of the will, which is only a "possession" if not related to the principle of right, becomes, if acquired under the principle of right, a *possessio noumenon* or "property," that is, an object that belongs to somebody whether it is in his actual possession or not.

A violation of the principle of right is the successful attempt to bring into one's possession someone else's possession by violence or coercion. To use coercion against such an attempt is to restore the principle of right and, hence, is rightful. In a state of nature—that is, outside civil society—the universal law mentioned in the principle of right has the character only of an idea, which can be interpreted differently by different individuals. This is the source of the struggle over rights in the state of nature; that is, it is not necessary, according to Kant, that everyone is everyone's enemy and tries to deprive him of his property. The problem is rather that even people who intend to act justly can get involved in struggles over their mutual rights. The state of nature is not a state of war but a state in which war cannot be avoided.[25]

A struggle over rights is the indicator that a universally valid law, recognized by all, does not exist. Since the principle of right, derived from the categorical imperative, demands that such laws exist, it is the moral and legal duty of everyone to enter the state in which such laws do exist, the civil state.[26] In the natural state every individual as a rational being has three functions regarding the principle of right: the function of determining what the law is, the function of using rightful coercion whenever the law is violated, and the function of judging whether a certain action conforms to law or not. All these functions must be represented properly in the civil state. There must be a lawgiver, the sovereign.[27] Whatever laws he promulgates must guarantee the principle of right. That means first of all that they have to fulfill the negative criterion that the people could have given these laws to themselves and hence that these laws do not violate their rights. What laws are given depends necessarily on the concrete situation. There is no positive criterion for just laws *a priori*. It is the free discussion of the citizens and the sovereign's duty to take this free discussion into account that provide the only criterion for just lawgiving and for a sovereign's fulfillment of his duty.[28] Rightful coercion is rightful in relation to a law; hence, the lawgiving sovereign has the right of rightful coercion in the civil state. The people *have to give up that right* and let it be represented by an executive power, that has to be separated from the legislative because it is *under the law*. The separation is necessary since what the executive does has to be lawful, and the executive, as well as everybody else under the law, has to be judged in this respect. The function of passing such judgments must also be represented in the civil state as the judicial power. This power has to be separated from the legislative and executive powers because one of its functions is to decide whether the executive acts properly under the law. Such decisions cannot be reached in acts of lawgiving *per se,* because given laws are presupposed in such decisions. Nor can such a decision be made by the executive because in this case the members of the executive would violate the general principle of representation that is characteristic of the civil state.

What has been sketched has the character of a formal ideal, a Platonic ideal, as Kant says. It is the ideal of a *respublica noumenon,* which corresponds to the idea of the *possessio noumenon.*[29] The realization of this ideal requires that the task of finding the forms of proper representation be perfectly solved. Disregarding this question, we can ask, *with respect to this ideal,* whether there can be any right of resistance. The answer has to be no because resistance has to be understood in this case as the use of coercion against the sovereign. Right can be realized only in the civil state. To enter the civil state means, however, to let oneself be represented by the sovereign and the executive regarding the right of rightful coercion. To use coercion against them means, consequently, to leave the civil state again and to step back into the state of nature. Such a step (1) is contrary to the command of practical reason to enter the civil state, and hence is against duty, and (2) is a step back into a state without realized right, *status justitia vacuus,* in which there is necessarily a struggle over right, *ius controversum.* Hence, there is no right of resistance of the people against the sovereign; such resistance always happens in a *status justitia vacuus.* There is, according to Kant, no such right in the civil state.[30] It doesn't even make sense to appeal to a right of necessity that could support such a right of resistance. There is no right of resistance in the state of nature because in that state right is always controversial and therefore also a right of necessity. Unlawful actions done in cases of extreme need remain unlawful as such. It is questionable whether such actions are punishable if refraining from action would have caused more damage to the defendant than the punishment he can expect for the action. However, this viewpoint is meaningful only if the civil state as such is not called into question. It is not applicable as an endorsement of the use of coercion against the sovereign. Though Kant never contemplates such a case, it follows from his principles that resistance against the executive could, in certain cases of extreme need, be considered to be an instance in which a judge can apply the "right" of necessity. A rebellion or revolution, however, whose goal is to take away the right of coercion from the sovereign can never constitute such an instance. By implication it is directed against the legitimation of the judicial power, which is bound to the laws given by the sovereign. The sovereign has, on the other hand, the right to use coercion against everybody who tries to resist him by force. The first consequence of the principle of right is that everybody must enter the civil state. Whoever refuses to enter or leave the civil state violates the principle of right and, given that principle, rightful coercion can be used against him. Therefore, the sovereign alone has the right of coercion and the subjects have no rights of coercion against him.[31]

This construction, which is the consequence of the application of the categorical imperative to human beings as finite, sensible, practical, rational, and moral beings, can be considered from two perspectives. The first perspective is that of the ideal state, the *respublica noumenon.* The sovereign of a realized *respublica noumenon* never violates his duty; that is, he never violates the rights of his subjects. In such a state, there is neither a right nor a motive to resist the sovereign. One may ask, however, if what is correct in theory is also applicable in praxis. It is undeniable that in praxis sovereigns violate the rights of the people. As a matter of fact, anthropological observation teaches us that, while they do not admit it to be their maxim, sovereigns often act as if people had no rights. The reason behind the sovereigns' hypocritical attitude is their fear of resistance. The people know that they have rights and will be inclined to use coercion against a sovereign who denies these rights in principle. Such a consideration takes us from the metaphysics of morals and justice to anthropology. As mentioned above, Kant holds that (1) no anthropological fact can determine what ought to be according to the moral law, (2) moral laws are the result of the application of the categorical imperative to anthropology, and (3) a meaningful *pragmatic* anthropology needs the moral law as the guiding thread for its investigations. The anthropological fact that sovereigns do violate their duty and that people are inclined to react to such violations with acts of rebellion has to be considered first from the viewpoint of the moral law. The moral law applies to something much more concrete than the ideal of a civil state for finite, sensible, rational, and practical beings. It is actual human behavior in the civil state, an anthropological fact known by experience—in this case, an historical experience—that has to be subsumed under the principle of right. Such a subsumption reveals the specific shortcomings of the sovereigns and subjects. The sovereign is mistaken in the assumption that rights in general can be reduced to the right of coercion. He makes the invalid conclusion that the people have no rights because they have no rights of coercion against him. The people initiating a rebellion make exactly the same mistake. Correctly assuming that they have rights, they conclude that they also have a right of coercion to defend those rights against the sovereign. From a moral point of view, both the sovereign's denial of the rights of the people and the people's claim of a right of rebellion against the sovereign are equally wrong. Both destroy the possibility of justice by implicitly denying the conditions of the existence of universal laws. The sovereign does so directly in refusing to give laws that the people would give themselves; the people do so indirectly if they enter a rebellion. They claim a right of coercion for themselves against the sovereign, thus destroying the very presupposition of universal laws. It follows that the element of injustice in a rebellion is not unjust toward a sovereign who acts as a tyrant in violating the rights of the people.[32] As a tyrant he himself has left the civil state and entered the state of nature. The act of injustice in a rebellion is directed against the duty of entering and remaining in the civil state. Hence, after a successful rebellion, the obligation of obedience to the sovereign immediately becomes an obligation to the new sovereign.[33]

Since anthropological facts are not principles of moral judgments but must be judged morally themselves, Kant is adamant in pointing out the element of injustice in every revolutionary act, even in cases in which, to some extent, he praises revolutionaries and the outcome of a revolution on moral grounds. However, these facts are subject to considerations of pragmatic anthropology. The task of such considerations is to discover which inclinations guiding human behavior are contrary to the realization of the moral law and which are not or are even potentially favorable. Such a consideration is by no means inconsistent with the transcendental grounds of morality. These have as their moral consequence the duty to discipline inclinations contrary to the moral law and to cultivate those that are in accordance with it. To do so is an act of transcendental freedom.

Considerations concerning the principle of right have a peculiar status in pragmatic anthropology. Justice, as external duty, has two incentives: the obligation to obey the moral law and rightful coercion. External, natural factors that force human beings to be just—first of all, to enter the civil state and to work for its perfection—are legitimate objects of such investigations because they can be considered from a pragmatic and teleological viewpoint as rightful coercion by nature. The whole realm of the so-called real factors can be taken into account.[34]

An initial observation shows that the interplay of these factors is responsible for mankind's never completely having left the state of nature—neither in some beginning phase nor in the course of its development. Rather, leaving the state of nature seems to be an insoluble task.[35] The chosen sovereign can represent the rights of the people only if he is just himself. But in the optimal case he will have the same moral qualification as the best of his subjects, and in most cases he will have worse qualifications for the simple reason that enjoyment of the exclusive right of coercion will attract those who want to determine what is right according to their own minds. On the other hand, people will always enter the civil state with a *reservatio mentalis,* insisting on a right of resistance against the sovereign because they know about his very human nature. The states and constitutions that have emerged in history are nothing but attempts to enter the civil state. They are not only islands surrounded by an external realm in which right is controversial and is consequently governed by war; sovereigns who act as tyrants, as well as rebellions by groups defending their rights and interests against the sovereign, represent the state of nature within the civil state. Such actions within civil states have to be considered as *natural* events governed by natural self-interest.[36]

Practical reason demands that mankind ought to enter the civil state. The question is whether there is a factor that forces mankind to do this. As mentioned above, the history of mankind is governed by antagonisms. The mere attempt to enter a civil state can be considered to be caused by nature through the antagonisms that would force even a herd of devils (provided they are rational) into a civil society and into the development of a perfect civil society.[37] The natural factors presupposed in this anthropological thesis are twofold. First, these devils have to be humans in their biological constitution, that is, not determined by instinct and plagued by antagonisms in their social relations. Second, they have to be rational, that is, have technical-practical reason. It has been said that Kant's "cunning of nature" is an imperfect forerunner of Hegel's cunning of reason.³⁸ Depending on one's viewpoint, this either honors him too much or too little. Practical reason, as well as understanding and practical-technical rationality, lies within the minds of concrete human beings. Nature provides antagonisms and the human ability to deal with them rationally—that is, with the aid of all of its faculties except practical reason, which, as the source of morality, is supranatural. The point of the anthropological thought experiment is that human nature without moral predisposition does not contradict the command of the moral law that man enter into the civil state. On the contrary, it forces mankind to enter it, provided mankind is able to calculate its own interests rationally. Hence, on a higher level, it is a moral task to develop one's ability to recognize the real factors determining human actions.

Kant's treatment of rebellions and revolutions from this point of view is a good example of this general principle. From the standpoint of pure self-interest, it is not reasonable to enter into revolutionary activities against the sovereign because the immediate consequence is to fall back into a state of nature in which antagonisms are completely unchecked and no rational planning is possible. Whether the new lord who emerges after the rebellion will be better than the old is at least doubtful. If he is better, then he would be better by chance or providence, which is really beyond the control of human reason. According to historical experience, in many cases he will probably be worse. It should be kept in mind that this observation refers to past revolutions and rebellions, which do not exhibit what is, in Kant's view, characteristic of the French Revolution. The rights defended against the sovereign have always been understood in such rebellions as rights of specific groups of society—certain estates, the church, religious minorities. They are rebellions for the sake of one group's self-interest. If the participants understand them as justifying a use of force against the sovereign, then such a self-understanding can indicate that the state of nature has not yet been left behind. This partisan nature of rebellions shows that the judgment of practical reason that no right of coercion exists that can be directed against the sovereign does not contradict the careful calculation of self-interest. What is correct in moral theory is applicable in practice.

According to Kant, the French Revolution reveals a new anthropological fact that must be treated differently. All other revolutions and rebellions, considered closely, defended specific rights of groups against the sovereign and/or replaced the sovereign with another one who promised to respect those rights. Since all parties involved in such revolutions could easily be identified as defenders of certain interests, no general sympathy could develop for one of the parties. It is noteworthy that one of the parties in the French Revolution, however, defends the right of the people (a) to give themselves a constitution and (b) to design this constitution according to the principle of a *respublica noumenon,* that is, according to the principle of representation of the people as the only source of legitimation and also according to the principle of the proper division of the legislative, executive, and judicial powers. The goals pursued here with genuine enthusiasm *eo ipso* transcend all interests of specific groups and corresponding "rights."

It has to be acknowledged that the goal of the French revolutionaries is morally justifiable and that enthusiastically striving for the realization of this goal provokes the enthusiastic sympathy—equally justifiable morally—of those not involved in the revolution. The question is whether any rightful use of coercion against the sovereign can be justified as a general principle of law. The answer has to be no! The reason for this is that the new republic cannot be built on a constitution that implies the right to revolution because such a right would function as a possible justification for counterrevolutionary activities. The new sovereign's acts, while designed to inaugurate the rights of the people, will necessarily violate all sorts of rights and interests of specific groups, which have of course no right to resistance in this case. To claim any right of partisan coercion over the sovereign would entail an ever greater contradiction because the constitution is designed to allow all citizens to participate in the process of lawmaking. Therefore, for the subjects of a state, no general principle of a right to coercion can be derived from the French Revolution.

Is it possible to claim a right of coercion over the sovereign for the French Revolution and all other revolutions of the same type? Again the answer has to be negative. One has to distinguish between (a) the act of using coercion against the sovereign and (b) the activities of the revolutionaries toward the introduction of the new constitution once the first act has taken place. Only (b) indicates a moral predisposition of mankind, whereas (a) represents a step back into the state of nature and cannot be justified morally. It indicates that the civil state it abolishes is only a coverup for the state of nature, which is not abandoned at all, and that the sovereign himself behaves as if he were in a state of nature. Hence, no injustice is done to him. The whole aspect (a) of revolution cannot be interpreted morally in a positive way because it occurs as an event of nature, whereas (b), on the other hand, has its moral qualities only insofar as it can be understood as an overcoming of the state of nature, guided at least in part by practical reason. The terrible consequences of (a) prove that it is in no one's interest to reach what obtains in (b) by the morally good intentions of the revolutionaries. This proves again that, on the one hand, the technical-practical judgment guided by self-interest and, on the other hand, the judgment of practical reason do not contradict each other. It is in everyone's self-interest that if (b) can be reached without (a), it ought to be reached that way.

The new anthropological fact revealed in the French Revolution as well as its result—the emergence of a true republic—entail, in addition, new pragmatic consequences. The actual existence of a republic is the proof that the realizations of a *respublica noumenon* cannot be considered to be a practical impossibility. Since it is the duty of all rulers to give only the laws people can give to themselves and since the constitution, which is as close to the *respublica noumenon* as possible, is the only one that a people can give to itself, monarchs, if they are to fulfill their duty, have to introduce this constitution via reform. They themselves leave the civil state and enter the state of nature if they do not fulfill their duty; therefore, they have to consider revolutions in general as natural events that warn them about what might happen to them if they remain in the natural state too long, that is, if they wait too long to fulfil their duty by introducing the republic. Kant is misunderstood if this part of his doctrine is taken to be an expression of an unjustifiable optimism about reforms.[39] His pragmatical anthropology allows us neither a speculative construction of past and future events nor predictions about what will happen. It teaches us what we ought to do and how we ought to do it given our specific anthropological situation. Given the French Revolution, the morally optimal solution is the introduction through reforms of a perfect republic by the existing sovereigns. Such a development would also be in their interest and everybody else's calculated self-interest since, if they do not move in this direction, revolutions with all their atrocities will occur again and again as natural events. A reform can be planned, but revolution cannot be planned. The hope that in some of these revolutions some revolutionaries will participate who have the moral qualities and cultivation of character exhibited by the French revolutionaries is, from a Kantian point of view, even less justifiable than the hope that a sovereign, provided he permits free public discussion of the lawgiving process, will move in the correct direction.

The seeming inconsistencies in Kant's theory of revolution vanish if one keeps in mind (1) the difference between a metaphysical theory of justice and corresponding considerations pertaining to pragmatic anthropology and (2) the French case as a representative for Kant of a set of new anthropological facts that need specific interpretation. The French Revolution confronts us with human beings who fight *in* a revolution, but apparently not for rights based on self-interest. The goal of their fight is the realization of the *respublica noumenon* in a *respublica phenomenon*. Their fight and the sympathy others have for it are indications of a moral predisposition in mankind because their goal is nothing but a perfect and conscious transition from the state of nature to the civil state. This interpretation is in conflict neither with the metaphysical theory of justice nor with the corresponding observations of pragmatic anthropology. The principle that a revolution is unjust insofar as it is a return to the state of nature remains unchanged, and the observation that an overthrow is always contrary to a correct calculation of everybody's interests remains unchanged. A revolution does not reveal any moral predisposition. It is a natural event that can be explained only naturally and is not connected with any moral interest. The moral predisposition is revealed by the behavior of the revolutionaries and their sympathizers *after* a revolution has occurred as a natural event leading back to the state of nature and in the state of nature. There is no just revolution, but there are revolutionaries who are virtuous. Their virtue and moral predisposition are not revealed by their behavior in the step back to the state of nature and in the state of nature, but in their struggle to leave it again with the goal of introducing a constitution that corresponds to a true civil state. This is consistent with Kant's view of the state of nature. Although there is no justice in this state, there may be virtuous and justice-loving human beings in it. The French Revolution shows that this is indeed the case. From the viewpoint of the moral law, a revolution is the step back to the state of nature; it indicates that mankind in general has not yet left that state. Mankind failed to solve its most difficult task. This failure cannot be justified morally, just as war cannot be justified morally. Both can be explained naturally, but it is a perversion of moral judgment to consider it a moral achievement if we are not able to steer the course of nature according to moral principles. It is always hypocrisy that leads us to the judgment that there are just wars and just revolutions. It is a duty incumbent on all, the sovereign as well as the people, to avoid them as long as possible. If they occur, the only possible moral question is, which of the involved parties is more to blame? Moral praise can be given only for the goals pursued by the parties after entering a war or a revolution. No moral praise is possible if the goal is not determined throughout by the principle that wars as well as revolutions ought not to occur. I think that this Kantian approach deserves some careful reconsideration at a time when terrorism, revolutions, and wars converge in a worrisome syndrome. It gives us some *consistent* hints about the distinctions we have to make in our moral judgments about such events.

Notes

1. The main sources concerning the right of resistance are: Immanuel Kant, *On the Old Saw: That May Be Right in Theory but It Won't Work in Practice* (1793), translated by E. B. Ashton (Philadelphia: University of Pennsylvania Press, 1974), pp. 65–66; cf. Immanuel Kant, *Gesammelte Schriften* [hereinafter *GS*], the Prussian Academy of Sciences Edition, 22 vols. (Berlin: G. Reimer, 1902–38), 8: 297–98; Immanuel Kant, *The Metaphysical Elements of Justice* (1797), translated by John Ladd (Indianapolis; Bobbs-Merrill, 1965), pp. 81ff (*GS* 6:318).

    Regarding the remark about Prussia, cf. Dick Howard, "Kant's Political Theory: The Virtue of His Vices," *"Review of Metaphysics* 34 (December 1980): 325–350, at 337, n. 24. Though this essay was published after I wrote this paper, the latter has been influenced by discussions I had with Professor Howard after a lecture he gave at Penn State. It can be considered as a partial fulfillment of the general program which I think I share with Professor Howard.

2. Immanuel Kant, *Religion Within the Limits of Reason Alone* (1793), translated by T. M. Greene and H. H. Hudson (New York; Harper & Row, 1960), pp. 112–113 (*GS* 6: 122).

3. Immanuel Kant, "An Old Question Raised Again: Is the Human Race Constantly Progressing?" (1798), in Immanuel Kant, *On History,* edited by Lewis W. Beck (Indianapolis: Bobbs-Merrill, 1963), pp. 143ff (*GS* 7: 85ff).
4. Immanuel Kant, *The Metaphysical Principles of Virtue* (1797), translated by James Ellington (Indianapolis: Bobbs-Merrill, 1964), p. 122 (*GS* 6: 457).
5. Immanuel Kant, "Idea for a Universal History from a Cosmopolitan Point of View" (1784), in Kant, *On History,* pp. 15–20 (*GS* 8: 21–28).
6. Immanuel Kant, "Perpetual Peace" (1795), in Kant, *On History,* pp. 130, 119–120 (*GS* 8: 382, 372–373; cf. Kant, "An Old Question," pp. 150–153 (*GS* 7: 91–93).
7. Such remarks are in the meantime not acceptable even for Marxist authors, though Heine was of influence in this tradition. Close to it, though not mentioning Heine, is A. A. Piontkovskij, "Teorija prava i godsudarstva Kanta," in T. I. Ojzerman, ed., *Kant i sovremennost* (Moscow, 1974), pp. 154, 161ff. A. Gulyga, Kant (Moscow, 1977), rejects the interpretation of Heine in almost all its aspects; cf., e.g., p. 203.
8. Kant, "An Old Question."
9. Kant, *On the Old Saw.*
10. This approach seems now to dominate Marxist as well as other approaches. Cf. Yirmiahu Yovel, *Kant and the Philosophy of History* (Princeton: Princeton University Press, 1980), pp. 125–126, 154–155; E. Ju Solov'ev, "Teorija 'obščestvennogo dogovara' i kantovskoe moral'noe obosnovanie prava," in *Filosofiia Kanta* (Moscow, 1974), pp. 204–205, 230ff; Gulyga, Kant, p. 244.
11. Kant, *The Metaphysical Elements of Justice.*
12. Kant, "Perpetual Peace" and "An Old Question."
13. Suggestions in this direction are often made in connection with the thesis mentioned above: cf. Yovel, *Kant and the Philosophy of History,* pp. 215ff; Solov'ev, "Teorija 'obščestvennogo dogovora,' " p. 186; Gulyga, Kant, p. 203.
14. Cf, the preface to *Strife of the Faculties* in *GS* 7: 10–11.
15. Kant, "Perpetual Peace."
16. Cf. Kant's letter to Wöllner, *GS* 7: 7–8.
17. Immanuel Kant, *Anthropology from a Pragmatic Point of View,* translated by Victor L. Dowdell (Carbondale: University of Southern Illinois Press, 1978), pp. 237–238 (*GS* 7: 321–2).
18. Immanuel Kant, *Critique of Judgment,* translated by James C. Meredith (Oxford; Clarendon Press, 1952), pt. II, pp. 92ff (*GS* 5: 429ff).
19. Kant, *The Metaphysical Elements of Justice,* pp. 16–17 (*GS* 6: 216–217).
20. Kant, *The Metaphysical Principles of Virtue,*#35, p. 122; cf. pp. 50, 59–60, 69 (*GS* 6: 457; cf. 392, 401, 409).
21. Kant, *The Metaphysical Elements of Justice,* p. 19 (*GS* 6: 219).
22. *Ibid.,* p. 35 (*GS* 6: 230).
23. Immanuel Kant, *Critique of Practical Reason,* translated by Lewis W. Beck (Indianapolis: Bobbs-Merrill, 1956), pp. 48–49 (*GS* 5: 47).
24. "Freedom of volition" and "liberty" are both used to translate Kant's term *freie Willkür,* which he uses as a German term for the Latin expression *liberum arbitrium sensitivum. Freie Willkür* is the *Willkür* of a being that has a free will and freedom in

the transcendental sense, i.e., the freedom of practical reason. It is a *Willkür* under the possible double determination of sensibility and practical reason. The passage that deals with the relation of *Wille and Willkür* in the most extensive way is in *The Metaphysical Elements of Justice,* pp. 11-14 (*GS* 6: 212-214). For the further application, cf. *ibid.* ##2-9.

25. *Ibid.,* #44, p. 76 (*GS* 6: 312).
26. Since it is a duty of justice, everybody can be rightfully forced to fulfill this duty. Cf. *ibid.,* p. 65 (*GS* 6: 256).
27. Cf. *ibid.,* ##45-49 for what follows.
28. Cf. Kant, *On the Old Saw,* p. 65 (*GS* 8: 297); "Perpetual Peace," pp. 129-130 (*GS* 8: 381); "An Old Question," pp. 148-149 (*GS* 7: 89-90); "What is Enlightenment," in Kant, *On History,* pp. 7-8 (*GS* 8: 39-40).
29. Kant, *The Metaphysical Elements of Justice,* pp. 64-65 (*GS* 6: 255). My interpretation assumes that Kant understands by *respublica noumenon* exactly that which is developed in ##45-49.
30. The note, *ibid.,* p. 87 (*GS* 6: 321), seems to tolerate a *jus necessitatis* and hence to be inconsistent with *On the Old Saw,* p. 68 (*GS* 8: 300). Kant, however, rules out this possibility in the *Elements* themselves, p. 41 (*GS* 6: 235). It is impossible to interpret a *causa necessitatis as a jus.*
31. Kant, *The Metaphysical Elements of Justice,* pp. 84-85 (*GS* 6: 319).
32. Kant, "Perpetual Peace," p. 85 (*GS* 8: 382).
33. Kant, *The Metaphysical Elements of Justice,* pp. 88-89 (*GS* 6: 323).
34. Pragmatical considerations concerning virtue have a primarily psychological-anthropological character and require self-experience. Considerations concerning law and justice have a sociological-anthropological character because they refer in addition to external social relations. Kant's so-called "philosophy of history" does not refer to individual historical events and epochs as does, e.g., Hegel's philosophy of history. It deals with the character of the species. Like modern sociology it uses historical events only as instances and examples for general theorems about the species.
35. Kant, "Idea for a Universal History," pp. 15-17 (*GS* 8: 21-23); cf. Kant, "Perpetual Peace," pp. 111-112 (*GS* 8: 366).
36. Kant, "Perpetual Peace," p. 120n (*GS* 8: 373n).
37. *Ibid.,* pp. 111-112 (*GS* 8: 366).
38. Cf. Yovel, *Kant and the Philosophy of History,* pp. 301ff, 140n., 149. To base one's interpretation of Kant on the term "cunning of reason" indicates that Kant is read from an external, Hegelian point of view. The same holds for an interpretation of Kant's term "antagonism" as "dialectical." Dialectics is for Kant a logic of illusion. Paralogisms are characteristic of such a logic, and so are antinomies, their very basis. Antagonisms, on the other hand, are real, external relations in social drives and interactions. They are anthropological facts discovered by experience. As such they lack the character of dialectical opposition based in the nature of reason as reason. They have a function in the empirical explanation of the course of human development which is restricted to the analysis of human interests and their clashes

as well as to the question of what kind of behavior would be rational, i.e., appropriate for the solution of the problems of the human race. They serve sociological explanations via ideal types in the sense of Max Weber. If Kant speaks of "providence" regarding such explanations, this term implies that nature in general can be understood from a teleological point of view, i.e., as supportive of, and not in contradiction with, the development of morality. There is, however, another use of "providence." At times, Kant refers to real and possible individual events which have significance for the moral progress of the human race and which indicate its moral predisposition. Such events cannot be explained empirically. His observations regarding the French Revolution belong to this second category. The two approaches are methodologically different but consistent throughout. They are inconsistent only from the Hegelian point of view, i.e., under the requirement that essence and individual are one and can both be grasped by pure thinking alone beyond the conditions of experience.

39. The following is an answer to a remark made in the discussion of this paper. The same point has been made, however, also in the literature; cf. Solov'ev, "Teorija 'obščestvennogo dogovora,' " p. 229.

Ludwig Siep

4. *Person and Law in Kant and Hegel**

There are two reasons why it seems important to me to discuss the concept of a person and its relationship to the concept of law in the philosophies of Kant and Hegel: The first reason is that the concept of a person is especially suited to establish the connection between first philosophy as transcendental philosophy or speculative logic and practical or political philosophy;[1] the second reason is that in my opinion the current theory of the person in analytical philosophy is deficient in this regard.[2]

The concept of a person proposed by Kant and Hegel (as well as by Fichte and Schelling) is based on a theory of self-consciousness. With a few exceptions such as Thomas Nagel or Harry Frankfurt, this is not the case in analytical theories of the person. Their primary concern is the problem of identifying a person "externally" as an observer does. They therefore seek criteria for the distinction between persons and other objects and for the identification of individual persons. Self-consciousness is usually reduced to a kind of privileged access to mental states and at best to the source of the epistemic "asymmetry" between self-ascription and the ascription made by others with regard to such states. I doubt that the criticism voiced from these positions is adequate to the theory of self-consciousness proposed by Kant and German Idealism.

The following remarks may serve to characterize the basic tenets of that theory:

1. In self-consciousness each person is given in two distinct respects: as determinate and as universal. This means that I am this or that determinate person "for myself," for a self that can abstract from any of these specific determinacies, that can imagine itself as being other than it is, and within certain limits can actively change itself.[3] But at the same time each person must be something determinate and specific. I cannot be the self for which I am this

---

*Translated by Thomas Nenon. The author would like to thank D. Scheffel, G. Geismann, H. Oberer, M.J. Gregor, and W.H. Walsh for their suggestions and comments on the section dealing with Kant. From *Graduate Faculty Philosophy Journal*, Vol. 10, No. 1 (Spring 1984).

specific person without being some specific person and without being *this* specific person.

2. The universal consciousness for which I am this specific person includes my essential characteristics. The first of these is spontaneity, an activity that is not externally determined. In every "I think," in every "I want," and in every "I am aware of an obligation," the "I" denotes a self-producing activity. The basic traits emphasized in the philosophical tradition's highest concept of activity apply to this activity: it is the *energeia* of theory and praxis at the same time; it is an activity that cannot be conceived of as being other than existent; it is the activity of thought directed toward itself; and it is an activity that has itself as its own goal.

3. A further basic characteristic of this activity illustrates its relevance for practical philosophy: it is the activity of legislation. The way that the self prescribes laws is different for the realms of nature, ethics, and legal justice. Furthermore, Kant conceives of law differently from Hegel. But the basic fact that the universal self prescribes laws implies that these laws apply to all persons in the same way, that they oblige all persons unconditionally, that all persons are simultaneously legislators of and subject to them, and that they are "autonomous."

In this essay I will try to elucidate these basic traits further and to indicate the consequences they have for practical philosophy. I prefer to speak of practical instead of political philosophy because for Kant at least the latter is basically concerned only with the historical realization of practical philosophy, which encompasses moral philosophy as well as the philosophy of law and state.

I.

There are no extensive passages dealing with the concept of a person in Kant's philosophy.[4] This is surprising given the importance this concept has both for his theoretical and for his practical philosophy. An indication of just how important it is for him can be gained from his *Anthropology from a Pragmatic Point of View:* "The fact that man can have the idea 'I' raises him infinitely above all the other beings living on earth. By this he is a *person;* and by virtue of his unity of consciousness through all the changes he may undergo, he is one and the same person—that is, a being altogether different in rank and dignity from *things,* such as irrational animals, which we can dispose of as we please. This holds even if he cannot yet say 'I' . . ." (AA VII, 127; 9).[5] Though this passage is not a central one, there are three things that should be noted here: First, that personhood is based upon the ego's capability of being conscious; second, that the person remains the same due to the unity of consciousness throughout all fluctuations; and third, that the person thereby distinguishes himself from things, which are objects of arbitrary choice and can be mere means to ends. And this implies that persons cannot conduct themselves toward other persons as they please.

The significance of the consciousness of self and identity—how these are related to each other is still unclear at this point—is illustrated more clearly in another definition of person taken from the *Introduction to the Metaphysics of Morals:*

> Person is that subject whose actions can be *imputed* to him. *Moral* personhood is then nothing other than the freedom of a rational being under moral laws (psychological personhood is by contrast merely the capability to become conscious of one's own identity in various states of existence). The consequence is that a person is subject to no laws other than those which he gives himself (either alone or at least jointly with others). (AA VI, 223; *24*)

Though I do not intend to give a complete interpretation of this central passage here, I would like to point out the following: persons are characterized by the accountability of their actions and this implies the possibility that they can relate their own actions to laws. The difference between a person and a thing is implied in this possibility of "accounting," whether it be performed by the agent himself or by others: "A thing is that which cannot be held accountable" (ibid.). The concept of accountability provides the link between psychological and moral personhood in Kant. But psychological personhood itself is based on the "logical" unity of self-consciousness. As Kant states in another passage from the *Anthropology:*

> Given the various changes within a man's mind (of his memory or of the principles he accepts), when he is conscious of these changes can he still say that he remains the very *same* (as far as his soul is concerned)? The question is absurd. For it is only because he thinks of himself in these various states as one and the same *subject* that he can be conscious of these changes; and man's "I" is indeed twofold in terms of form (manner of representation), but not in terms of matter (content). (AA VII, 134; *15*)[6]

This twofold aspect of the ego is explained in the sentence which precedes it:

> It looks to us, here, as if the "I" were doubled (which would be contradictory): 1) the "I" as subject of thinking (in logic), which signifies pure apperception (the merely reflecting "I"), and about which there is no more to be said than that it is a perfectly simple idea; 2) the "I" as *object* of perception and so of inner sense, which contains a manifold of determinations that make an inner *experience* possible. (ibid.)

Apparently there is a "double aspect" theory of self-consciousness at the basis of Kant's theory of person: a pure, logical subject constitutes an empirical "I-object" perceived by the inner sense. But unfortunately he never explained in detail how the logical identity of the thinking subject and the temporal form of the inner sense "contribute" to the concept and consciousness of personal identity over time. According to the third paralogism of the *Critique of Pure Reason*, this identity does *not* follow directly from the identity of pure apperception. Thus, Kant scholars came to the conclusion that Kant either leaves the question of personal identity over time open or explicitly claims that it is unsolvable, since the identity of a person requires a permanent noumenal ego which is inaccessible to our empirical knowledge.[7] But there can be no doubt that for Kant persons cannot think of themselves other than as remaining the same throughout the temporal change of their states—although he did not accept that this "sameness" was that of an atemporal substance, an unchangeable and indestructible soul. The fact that we have to regard ourselves as possessing immortal souls cannot be proved in theoretical philosophy, it follows instead only from the correct explanation of our moral consciousness, as the second postulate of the *Critique of Practical Reason* demonstrates. I am convinced that the outlines of a theory of personal identity within the limits of theoretical philosophy can be drawn by looking at the *Critique of Pure Reason* as a whole and at some "Reflections" from Kant's *Nachlass*.

The passages quoted from the Anthropology are a clear indication that we have to start with the doctrine of transcendental apperception—which Kant in a "Reflection" from the 1770s (5049) even calls "transcendental, logical personhood" (AA XVIII, 72). In the first Critique, however, it turns out that the "perfectly simple idea" of the ego that Kant speaks of in the *Anthropology* (AA VII, 134; *15*) must be further distinguished from the consciousness of the ego's identity in all its representations, upon which the identity of the person is based. Thus, we must follow the steps that lead from the former to the latter. The simple self-relation of cognizant activity is, as Kant formulates it in the *Metaphysical Foundations of Natural Science*, the "mere preface" or "general correlate" (AA IV, 542; *103*) to apperception. In itself it does not contain the differentiation of representations, but rather only the consciousness of a spontaneity that is not determined by something outside itself and can think whatever it pleases. This spontaneity itself is, of course, not arbitrary, not a mere possibility: it cannot be thought of as being other than "actual" or "existent."[8] In his analysis of the "original-synthetic unity of apperception" *(Critique of Pure Reason*, B 132 ff; *152*), Kant proceeds from this pure consciousness of spontaneity to the consciousness of this activity's general (or possible) relationship to representations that it does not produce on its own but that "can be given prior to all thought" (B 132; *153*). Kant's general term for representations of this kind is "intuition." With regard to this relationship, I am inevitably conscious that in each representation of something I must also be able to become conscious of my "I think." Otherwise the content of these representations would be unthinkable or at least "nothing at all for me" (ibid.). This relation of "any representation" to one and the same subject involves or presupposes for Kant yet another moment of apperception: the consciousness of an activity of synthesizing. The consciousness of the ego as the spontaneous synthesis of representations—which qua synthesis and furthermore as kinds of synthesis (categories) are not determined by anything external—is the *synthetic* unity of apperception. This synthesis then makes it possible for me to become conscious that I am the *same* thinking being in all of the *different* representations united by me in my consciousness. This consciousness is the "identity of apperception" or that self-consciousness that Kant calls the *"analytic* unity of apperception" (B 133; *154*). And it is this consciousness that "forms out of all possible appearances, which can stand alongside each other in one experience, a connection of all these representations according to laws. For this unity of consciousness would be impossible if the mind in knowledge of the manifold could not become conscious of the identity of function whereby it synthetically combines it in one knowledge" (A 108; *136* f.).

So much for the "logical" structure of self-consciousness. It seems that we can discover all of the fundamental traits mentioned above in this with the exception of the twofold self-reference. The fact that this one aspect is lacking is not surprising because here we are concerned only with the pure universal "logical" self. Nevertheless, the general structure of the self's relationship to givenness has at least been demonstrated, and it has been shown that self-consciousness would be "empty" without synthesizing and determining its given representations or intuitions. Moreover, this relationship to something given to it characterizes not only the "logical" but also the self-intuiting I. The ego's self-intuition is only possible given inner sense and the conditions for its possibility. These are, on the one hand, the temporal fluctuation of inner intuitions and of our own states which are given in these intuitions; and, on the other hand, the impossibility of distinguishing the ego from its states and representations (a clear contrast to apperception as an act of understanding). In his famous letter to Marcus Herz on February 21, 1772, Kant writes: "With regard to the inner sense, however, thinking or the existence of the thought is one and the same as I myself" (AA 129). It is nonetheless impossible that I could be completely identical with the existence of my thought even in inner self-intuition, for then no *self*-intuition would be possible.

The general form of self-intuition in inner sense then, must be as follows: as an object of my self-intuition I am always a determinate state, which is in the process of passing away; as the subject, however, I am the person to whom this state and its transition into the past is present. As the "oneness" between the subject and its states, I can grasp myself only in the unity of my past and present states. And this holds necessarily for every fluctuation of my states in time. The unity of those states intuited in the past and my intuiting them at present is certainly not the same as the unity of the thinking subject in its thoughts. Kant himself points this out in another reflection from the 1770s: "If subsequently someone were to become conscious of himself and all of his actions just as we recall them, then he would consequently be me. Therefore, the identity of the person is *not* based on a concurrence in apperception, but rather upon its continuation, even if it entails obscure representations" (AA XVII, 594, Refl. 4562). One could call this continuation of the person in time a "schematization" of apperception's pure identity of understanding in time—if it were not a form of inner receptivity rather than an activity of transcendental imagination like the transcendental schematism. But one can say that the temporal identity of the person understood in this manner makes it possible for Kant to maintain consistently that the self must necessarily be determinate *and* free from every particular determinacy: I am aware of my continuation beyond any intuited state of myself. However, even this identity is not yet something public, objective, and unmistakably recognizable for everyone. It can become so only if one can point to some temporal duration—for instance from my birth until now—that is determinate in the sense of being measurable or measured. In order to do this, one must relate the fluctuations of one's inner states to lasting and mobile objects in space, with regard to which objective temporal occurrences can be measured. For a self-conscious being that is presented in its outer senses not only *in* a body but *as* a body, this is no problem: The "permanence during life is, of course, evident *per se,* since the thinking being (as man) is itself likewise an object of the outer senses" (B 415; *373*). But this presupposes persistence *(Beharrlichkeit)* as a temporally "schematized" category (category of substance), which in turn presupposes the pure self-consciousness of apperception.

This may suffice as a sketch of the connection between the psychological and the transcendental identity of the person as depicted in the *Critique of Pure Reason.* But what have we gained? Is the definition of the practical or moral concept of the person not concerned with a very different, higher level of personhood? Doesn't Kant speak of the person, of freedom, and of the law in the moral sphere as rational ideas in the strict sense of *"Vernunftideen"?* In his work on religion, for instance, Kant calls the person the "idea of the law." What can the identity of self-consciousness in the understanding mean for such rational ideas?

It is indeed false to say that the practical concept of the person follows from its theoretical concept. Nevertheless, the practical concept of the person is inconceivable without self-consciousness and its structure, as the concept of accountability shows. The concept of the person in practical philosophy does not render the theory of self-consciousness superfluous but rather completes it. Since practical reason "commands" laws that are not restricted to or conditioned by sense-intuitions or inclinations, the moral person participates in a different sort of legislation. However, one might argue that even the pure consciousness of practical reason is not separated from the determinate person: the moral law is for its part "formal," and thus for the human person it requires content which results from his maxims of conduct. The need for determinacy contained in the formality of the moral law is "less direct" than that contained in the concept of self-consciousness within theoretical philosophy; it is not simply a specific empirically determinate person that is given to my practical reason, but rather my free choice to imagine a whole range of purposes and my capacity to produce motives for acting. And in turn, my choice is free due to the fact that it can be determined by the laws of reason. The structure of practical personhood is not essentially different from that of theoretical consciousness. Pure practical reason is also in me and actual for me. Just as the "I think" is no mere possibility, but instead "exists" within me, moral personhood is also no mere possibility. It is rather the "fact" that I am conscious of the moral law, i.e., that I am conscious that I can and ought to act according to rules and reasons that are comprehensible and unconditionally binding for every person. The analysis and explanation of this inescapable fact is indeed the "proof" of pure practical reason or moral freedom. That moral freedom and consciousness of oneself are necessarily connected is most clearly stated in the following reflection: "The question whether or not freedom is possible is perhaps identical with the question whether or not man is a true person and whether the ego is possible in a being with external determinacies" (AA VII, 464 f. Rfl. 4225).

It should now be possible to define the "practical" sense of accountability more precisely. This sense implies more than that I simply ascribe my past states to myself as the same person. Whenever I hold myself practically accountable for something, I am aware of myself as the "free cause" of my actions. In order to do so I must presuppose that I can determine my "faculty to desire something" *(Begehrungsvermögen)* by means of arbitrary purposes and that I can adapt these purposes to the framework of the laws given by reason. According to Kant, the *Critique of Pure Reason* demonstrates that freedom is not inconceivable and that it cannot be empirically refuted; at least as a cosmological concept, freedom is consistent with the law of causality, which holds for all objects of experience.

Finally, the last component of the definition of persons as accountable beings, the fact that I as a person relate my actions to the laws of practical reason, means that I know them to be commanded, forbidden, or allowed by the moral law in general and by the specific ethical and juridical laws. To speak generally, what these laws demand is a totality of persons *("totum personarum"* cf. AA XIX, 446, Refl. 7524) who, without impairing their personhood, can reconcile their inner purposes and external actions according to universal laws. These laws demand that persons have an interest of the highest order in their own moral personhood and that of all other persons—or in the case of juridicial laws, at least respect for the personhood of others. In the latter case this implies that I respect their freedom to decide upon and pursue their own purposes and to prescribe laws for themselves as well as—together with them—for others.

II.

In order to clarify the consequences of this Kantian concept of the person for his political philosophy, we must address ourselves to Kant's philosophy of right. It is the foundation for all political philosophy in-so-far as all rational politics, according to a quotation from the work *Perpetual Peace,* is nothing other than "the exercise of the doctrine of right" (AA VIII, 370; *161*).

It is obvious that the concept of the person is central to Kant's philosophy of right. "The concept of rights," states Kant in § B of the Introduction to the *Metaphysical Elements of Justice,* "applies only to a person's external and practical relationship to other persons, insofar as their actions as facts can influence each other (either directly or indirectly)" (AA VI, 230; *34*). "Facts" or "deeds" (cf. 227) refer here to actions for which—and for the consequences of which—a person is accountable. Right is the condition of the possibility that persons can at all be persons in their external actions directed toward objects. It makes it possible for them to be free in their choice of purposes and means and free in their capability of relating their actions to a law concerned with the consistency of various persons' free external actions. In its structure, the universal principle of law *(das allgemeine Rechtsgesetz),* corresponds to the moral law, even though it is not directly deducible from the latter. It is a principle demanding the legal regulation of our external leeway: "In your external actions conduct yourself such that the free exercise of your volition can exist together with everyone else's freedom according to a universal law" (AA VI, 231; *35*). It is a categorical imperative, however, which I do not have to adopt as a maxim. To do that is an ethical obligation, but it is not legally binding. Legal obligation demands a certain type of external conduct, to which everyone may be induced "by others perhaps even by force" (cf. ibid.). At the same time, the universal principle of law is the origin of rights that Kant divides into innate rights, the "internal mine and yours" (AA VI, 237; *43*), and into rights that can and must be acquired, the external mine and yours.[9] Since this internal "right that belongs to every human being due to his humanity" (ibid.) is but one, namely, the right to be undisturbed and unimpaired in acts and states that are in accord with the laws of justice ("independence from the forcible volition of others"), it is not a principle that would allow the deduction of particular rights. This is possible only with regard to that which is externally mine and yours; the freedom of a legal person can be systematically determined only in view of its utilization of the objects of action (things as well as deeds and states of other persons). In order to attain a legal securing of one's right's—both internal and external—that would not be dependent upon empirical contingencies, it is necessary to have intersubjective, public legislation and juridication; it is necessary to have a state. In Kant's philosophy of right, the internal mine and yours is dealt with only in the *Prolegomena* (AA VI, 238; *45*). External mine and yours, insofar as it can be conceived and validly established without the concept of a state, is the subject of private law; the principles of a public state of justice are discussed in public law. In the following, I would like to sketch the role that the concept of the person plays in private and public law.

For Kant the area of private law concerns the rational relationship of persons to objects of their external free choice: it is the person's right to have or obtain something as "mine." Similar to ascription and accountability, the legally valid "having" of something is a kind of self-relationship whose basic structure corresponds to that of self-consciousness as depicted above: the person is aware of himself as one who, in harmony with other persons, prescribes formal laws for his free volition, which must in turn be concretized in his dealings with objects. Kant claims to have provided a transcendental deduction of the right to property by referring to this structure. In the *Metaphysical Elements of Justice*, a "transcendental deduction" signifies the attainment of concepts of understanding that are universal as well as independent of space and time and are gained by "ignoring the empirical conditions" (AA VI, 253; *62*) of the relationship between volition and things as well as between volition and the deeds and states of other persons. In a second step, the capability of subsuming these concepts under the law of reason with regard to right is demonstrated. Concerning the relationship between persons and things, this means that one must proceed from persons' physical seizure of things onward to an "intelligible possession," that is to a legal claim independent of the factual circumstances of disposition. This possession must conform to the universal principle of law. In § 2 of the section on private law, Kant utilizes an *argumentum e contrario* in order to show that this is possible; if external objects were not generally objects of free volition, the realization of purpose through external means would be impossible. If someone could dispose of objects only so long as he had them in his actual possession, the free external disposition of them would be completely dependent upon contingencies and the "coercive and arbitrary volition" of others, and these cannot be regulated by universal laws of justice. Objects themselves, however, cannot legally bind me, for a legal obligation is according to its very concept mutual. One can obligate oneself to limit the arbitrary use of something in view of one's own conscience or the moral law or in view of others, but not in view of a being that has no will and therefore cannot in turn obligate itself. According to Kant, legal obligation is always reciprocal obligation (cf. AA VI, 237; *44*).

This basic idea, together with the division of external objects according to the categories of relation in Kant's theoretical philosophy (substance = bodily thing outside of myself in space, causality = another person's volition to perform a certain action, community = the state of another in relationship to me) provides the basis for the whole content of private law. It is well-known that by his application of the category of community to the relationship between persons, Kant deduces a right to deal with persons "in the same manner as objects" so that persons can temporarily become "belongings" and objects of asymmetrical coercive laws, for instance, the right to "retrieve" a runaway servant. This aspect of Kant's personal law is certainly problematic and in the end cannot be reconciled with his concept of the person, especially since this—albeit temporary—reduction of a person to "inherence" (AA VI, 314; *79*) excludes him from the fundamental civil right to participate in legislation. In private law the participation of persons in legislation— which, according to the general introduction, is part of the very definition of a moral person—consists in the fact that only such laws can be considered obligatory that can also be viewed as an instance of a universal, cooperatively established law. According to Kant, this requires "a mutual will that is not contingent but rather *a priori,* thus necessarily unified and therefore universally legislating" (AA VI, 263). This universally legislating will must be presupposed in purely rational private law as the basis for all forms of property and acquisition rights. It must, however, also be constituted as a guarantee of the "security of the mutual bindingness" of these rights as "the collectively universal (common) and ruling will." Obligation in the legal sphere entails not only demonstrable validity, but also enforceability, because otherwise a violent "restriction of freedom" (cf. AA VI, 230 f; *35–36*) would not be removed by legal means. Such a common will is a "civil constitution." The *a priori* demonstrable rights and institutions of such a constitution are the subject of Kant's public law.

Regarding Kant's public law, I would like to concentrate upon two questions:

1. What is the significance of Kant's use of the concept of person for the authorities of a state?
2. How can Kant distinguish between active and passive citizenship given his definition of moral persons as colegislators?

Kant's doctrine of the social contract, like Hobbes's and Rousseau's, deals with the idea of the constitution of a collective "person" with a will that is not merely composed of the particular wills of individuals, but is instead a truly "common and public" will *(On the Old Saw: That May Be Right in Theory But It Won't Work in Practice,* AA VIII; *297*). By the social contract a self-subsistent "state will" is constituted that is independent of the individuals' empirical interests. According to its "idea" (AA VI, 313), this will, as a kind of general resolution and decision, must have the form of a practical rational inference: it must have three authorities, which Kant in turn calls "persons" or "personalities." If this terminology is to be more than a mere metaphor, then the authorities in the state must be accountable in some manner or other. The physical persons who "represent" them must act in their commission, so to speak. Especially if we proceed from the theory of personhood that I have sketched out, it may seem that the moral person of the authorities can "abstract" from the individual person. On the other hand, the inviolability of the "internal mine and yours" of one's body, one's life, and one's freedom of mobility is the "right of mankind" in every person, a right that the state must secure and, of course, respect. The state as legislator is the "irreprehensible" author of laws only "with regard to that which concerns the external mine and yours" (AA VI, 316; *81*). The principles of those laws are demonstrated in Kant's doctrine of private law. Thus, the laws of the state which can be justified by Kant's idea of an original contract must aim at protecting every person's freedom of action. The "personhood" of the administrative powers—the legislature, the executive, which is subordinate to it, and the judiciary—therefore implies only that the existence and function of these powers is unconditionally demanded and that they must be independent of the interests of any individual and of everyone together *(omnes et singuli,* AA VI, 315; *80).* Applying the structure of self-conscious personhood to administrative power—whether Kant explicitly means to do that or not—does not require giving those powers the right to abstract from the rights of individual persons. So much for the first question.

But what about the person's right "to be subject to no other laws than those he (either alone or at least jointly with others) has given himself (AA V, 223; *24*)? What happens to this right within a state? The idea of a social contract constituting a justifiable state includes unanimous consent. And regarding the introduction of a majority rule for legislature composed of delegates, Kant also prescribes unanimous agreement upon this contract (*On the Old Saw* . . . AA VIII, 296). The problematic point in Kant's governmental law, however, is well-known. It is the fact that he makes the right to participate in legislation dependent upon the ability to support oneself—either through property, art, craftsmanship, or scholarship insofar as these are not exercised in personal dependence upon a "household" *(oikos)* (AA VI, 314 f.; *79* and *On the Old Saw* . . . AA VIII, 295 f.). The apparent intention of this restriction is to guarantee the correspondence between the will of the legislators and the universally common will of the people—a point overlooked by many critics. The elimination of the particular will, which in its vote distorts the resolution of the common will, is not attained by Kant—as it is by Rousseau—through the prohibition of delegations and political parties, but rather by attempting to secure the independence of those who legislate. The demand that each person be self-sustaining within the naturally necessary realm of practice (self-preservation) is, so to speak, the manifestation and concretization of pure spontaneity in man's empirical activity. But if this demand, which is derived from the idea of the state (AA VI, 313; *77*) is an essential condition of civil freedom in the sense of one's being obligated only by a law in whose legislation one participates—either directly or by the right to vote in an election of delegates—then the institution of "the right of domestic authority" established in private law becomes even more problematic. For it is this very right that is responsible for a temporary exclusion from civil freedom. One could even say that the right of domestic authority and the norm that demands self-sustenance as the condition of active citizenship conflict with each other insofar as the latter at least excludes laws that restrict the possibilities of attaining self-sustenance—which the protection of the former might require. It seems to me that the concept of the person as essentially legislating established in the Introduction to the *Metaphysics of Morals* does not allow for laws that prevent any adult and mentally accountable being from exercising the right to participate—either directly or indirectly—in public legislation.[10]

III.

Hegel's concept of the person is, like Kant's, comprehensible only if one proceeds from his theory of self-consciousness. For Hegel, however, self-consciousness does not refer only to individual self-consciousness. No mere metaphor should be inferred when Hegel speaks about the self-consciousness of groups, nations, epochs, and the like. Self-consciousness for Hegel is a structure of self-distinction or of self-determination, and since Hegel shares Spinoza's view that determination is negation, this means that it is self-negation. But self-negation is also the conceptual structure of reality in general that discloses itself in its various moments by means of self-negation and thus exhibits itself as the totality of the moments thereby developed. The development of self-consciousness differs from that of the concept in that individual self-consciousness is one essential component of self-consciousness in general, and that each supra-individual self-consciousness must therefore be "realized" in some individual's self-awareness. Basically, this unity of universal and individual self-consciousness is what Hegel calls "person." However, there are degrees of personhood according to the generality or comprehensiveness of that universal self-consciousness which is represented by the individual. An understanding of Hegel's theory of the person is further complicated by the fact that higher degrees of personhood are not defined in terms of the concept "person," but rather in more complex and differentiated terms (subject, spirit, and so on). Moreover the term *person* is also used in a one-sided sense that is subject to criticism; it is used as a concept in which the unity of the universal and the individual self are understood under the predominance of the latter, in that the person is reduced to the subject's self-reflection upon a universality accessible to it.

As one moment in the concept of self-consciousness, the concept of a person is also characterized by the structure of self-referential negativity. In the following I shall try to explain what this means by interpreting the important note on self-consciousness and personhood found in the *Science of Logic* at the beginning of the chapter on the "Concept."

> The *ego* ("I") is first of all the pure unity which refers to itself. This does not occur directly, but by means of the process in which the ego abstracts from all determinacy and content and thus reverts into the freedom of unlimited self-sameness. It thereby becomes universality: unity which only by the *negative* act of abstraction is a unity with itself and thus contains all determinate being dissolved in itself. *Second,* the ego in its self-referential negativity is just as immediately *singularity,* it is *absolute determinacy* which sets itself in opposition to that which is other than itself and thus excludes it—individual personhood *(Logic* II, p. 220).[11]

According to this passage, the twofold self-relation, in which the ego is aware of itself as something both universal and free of all determinations and simultaneously as something determinate and singular, is also characteristic of Hegel's theory of self-consciousness and personhood. Two important differences from Kant are nevertheless obvious here:

1. For Hegel, the unity of self-consciousness is not based upon the pure self-relatedness of thinking, but rather upon the identity of universality and complete individual determinacy. The ego is "just as immediately" one as the other. It is—as is stated later—the "complete unification" of "both of these moments." The negation of all determinacy and absolute determinacy, however, are mutually exclusive. If the identity of the ego has to be conceived as the unity of both moments, it must be a self-contradictory identity. And the person is not just one moment in this contradiction—as it might seem according to the passage quoted—but rather the whole contradiction. It is, according to another passage in the *Logic,* the "absolute dialectic" (ibid., p. 502).

2. The second difference from Kant consists in the fact that the ego's pure self-consciousness—which is *one* moment of self-consciousness—is not an immediate notion that can be separated from all cognitive content and presupposed, but is instead already the result of an "abstraction" and the ego's "retrogression" into itself (ibid., p. 220). The ego's freedom from its determinations must therefore be understood as a process of emancipation in which one's given determinacies are relativized by one's consciousness of them, called into question, and finally appropriated. The liberated self is not only able to abstract from all determinacy; it can also maintain all determinacy as "dissolved within it." For Hegel, universality does not signify the common denominator that remains after the abstraction from everything not commonly shared, but is

rather—as it is in Rousseau's concept of the *volonté générale*—a totality of differences that come to coincide with one another without being reduced. To what extent the individual person is capable of such universality is a question I will deal with later.

First, however, I would like to examine the first point of difference between Kant and Hegel. Is the thesis that the identity of the person consists in the contradictory unification of universality and singularity anything other than the absurd assertion of an incorrigible dialectician? Can we discern a rational meaning in this assertion? How can the pure universality of an ego's being free from all determinacies be *the same* as the person's individuality, that is, the relationship in which it excludes from itself everything other than itself? In the following passages, I suggest two approaches to an explanation, the first of which refers to arguments from Hegel's philosophy of spirit, the second to logical structures in Hegel's sense without attempting to discuss the general conception involved in his science of "pure ontological forms."

In the perspective of my first approach, universality also entails singularity insofar as I am aware of myself as an individual self only by abstracting from all my external determinations. The thesis, then, is that one's individuality is not based on public criteria of identity but rather upon the ability to abstract from all public determinacies. I am the determinate self that I am because my thought can free me from all determinacy. One is tempted to add: I am so *for myself.* But in the *Philosophy of Right* Hegel attempts to demonstrate that the pure self-consciousness that individualizes me is capable of finding a public, intersubjective expression. The inversion of this first formulation of identity must then be that the relationship toward others in which I exclude them *is* my universal self-consciousness. Hegel's thoughts on the genesis of the self as expressed in the philosophy of subjective spirit may serve as an illustration of this formulation.[12] Here also, the fact that self-consciousness is a result is emphasized. One finds oneself, as it were, only by dissolving one's emotional and customary unity with others. What is originally present is not the independent ego that is free in its own thought, but rather the member of a "collective," be it a collective of language, family, or labor. According to Hegel, the first step from this "external being" *(Aussersichsein)* back to oneself is that one finds oneself through others, either by being loved or in some other form of recognition. In short, I become a cognitive self free from all of these relationships in my consciousness by my separation from this unity with others and by my excluding them from my "personal sphere." Keeping both sides of the identity thesis in view, one can summarize my first proposal for explanation as follows: Only by means of my pure, cognitive self-consciousness do I separate myself from others, individualize myself—and it is only by means of such separation that I am a cognitive free self. Kant's *"sapere aude"* as the demand for a conscious cognitive emancipation from servitude still forms the background for this thesis.[13]

I would express my second proposal as follows: According to the passage on which I am basing my interpretation, the identity of the universal and the singular self consists in the fact that both of them are moments of "self-referential negativity." According to Hegel's philosophy, this not only implies a negative activity which is aware of itself as such, but also a self-referential negativity which negates itself. What does this mean for the abstraction from all determinacies? Abstraction appears to negate otherness, but in the case of self-consciousness, the determinacies are conscious representations or thoughts. Determinate thoughts, however, are in themselves already negations: distinctions within indeterminate complexes of representations or undeveloped thoughts. Every determination implies a negative judgment (an "is not" statement). Thus, the abstraction or dissolution of determinacies within the ego is not just a negation of otherness but rather a negation of one's own negativity. And conversely, it must be stated that self-distinction from others in the sense of individualization is a self-referential negation. This is true not only because of the unity between the self and others mentioned above, but also in the more formal sense of negation from one's own indeterminacy, from one's not having yet committed oneself. Both self-determination and abstraction from one's own determinacy are thus negations directed toward their own negativity.

I am not sure that my approaches have been successful in alleviating the abstruseness of Hegel's thesis concerning the "dialectical identity" of the person. At the very least the expression "self-referential identity" still sounds odd. For, in the first place, identity here is quite obviously not a relationship between various entities or between temporally distinct states or stages of some entity. Just as for Kant and for Fichte, for Hegel this kind of identity is based on the identity of thought in its relationship to itself. However, in contrast to Kant or Fichte, Hegel does not allow the identity of self-relatedness to be separated from the relationship to otherness, to givenness, to the contents of thought, to non-thought or whatever one might like to call it. In that case cognition would be interpreted as a synthesis between act and content, and the act of thought itself would always remain the same; it would be impossible to grasp the meaning of thinking as a process that together with its contents is subject to change, that develops itself but is never completely exhausted in any of its contents. And it would be just as impossible to grasp the identity of the person who "persists" throughout a constant development of consciousness, and that means through a succession of reflections and reversals in consciousness. According to Hegel, another concept of identity is called for in order to grasp such "mental" processes.

This new concept must be an identity which establishes itself by means of a radical self-alteration. It cannot be the unity of a lasting substance nor that of a subject that distinguishes itself from everything else, nor can it be the mere activity of negation or of self-alteration itself. In a certain sense, it must be the whole process, not as an aggregate of all stages, but instead as the unity that "dissolves" them. However, since this unity itself is again a determinate stage, it appears that we have at best a temporal succession of increasingly complete stages which express the person in a more "concentrated" way. At worst, it appears that we have nothing other than a continual self-denial, self-negation, self-dissolution. If the unity of the person is a kind of composition—even if this is understood in the sense of growth or development—then there must be a sameness that persists throughout the mutual negation of the various stages, a sameness subject neither to temporal fluctuations nor to arbitrary changes in the person's ideas and decisions. For Hegel also, the identity of the person must be something stable and indissoluble in the succession of changes. But such a stability can only be derived from a totality that develops distinctions within itself according to atemporal criteria and merely exhibits them in time. Hegel's practical philosophy seeks to demonstrate that the individual person cannot develop such a totality on his own.

IV.

Hegel's theory of the practical, active person cannot be considered an expansion of the concept of theoretical self-consciousness in the same sense that Kant's can. The fact that the logical-ontological structure of personhood also serves as the basis for the philosophical doctrine of right is illustrated in § 35 of *Philosophy of Right:* "Personality implies that as *this* person: (1) I am completely determined on every side (in my inner caprice, impulse, and desire, as well as by immediate external facts) and so finite; yet (2) nonetheless I am simply and solely self-relation, and therefore in finitude I am aware of myself as something *infinite, universal,* and *free.*" On the other hand, the concept of the person in the *Philosophy of Right* is indeed an expansion beyond the mere structure of individual-universal self-consciousness, inasfar as in the *Philosophy of Right,* the person appears as a form of free will. The free will that—according to Hegel's preceding theory of the will—wills itself, is aware that it "fulfills itself from within itself" *(Enc.* § 469) and endows its determinations with intersubjectively identifiable "existence." Its inability to do so as an individual will or person becomes apparent only after a succession of stages in which it partially succeeds and fails, as it were, only "in the final instance." In Hegel's *Philosophy of Right* these preliminary stages are "abstract right" and "morality."

In abstract right we have a system of forms and norms of conduct that can indeed be viewed as systematic consequences of the concept of the person. To a great extent, Hegel is in substantial agreement with Kant's doctrine of private law. The first inadequacy pertaining to this systematic concretion or self-determination of the concept of the person—and also to Hegel's presentation of personal consciousness—is that it follows from a relation between the person and something other than persons, namely, impersonal things. It is not a self-distinction and for this reason the concept of the person remains the same in all forms of private law. It does not develop. Private law is concerned rather with a manifestation of the various moments of personhood—the acquisition of property as a free determination of the "external sphere of freedom" (PR § 41) and the alienation of property as a sign of one's independence from any determinate thing. It is a manifestation related to "that which is other than oneself," things, and other persons. In contractual law, the second stage of abstract right, the person already attains the "identity" (PR § 74 ff.) of a common will together with other persons. Nevertheless—and this is the second inadequacy of abstract right—the way in which the totality of personal rights and the universal will directed toward them are made conscious by individuals and groups (contractual persons) is not a lasting "identity." It is not independent of time and arbitrary volition. Outside of the realm of state, one's *opinion* of right and *valid* right are not definitely distinguishable. This is Hegel's subject in the section on "wrong" *("Unrecht")*. What is at issue here is less the Kantian problem regarding the uncertainty in deciding about conflicting claims without public jurisdiction than the latent possibility for each individual qua self-conscious person to elevate his personal claim to the "true" right that overrides the commonly accepted law— this is the "rational" aspect at the heart of every crime.

Its reverse side, punishment, is a first experience of the fact that the person must find his rational identity not in an absolutely independent singular will, but rather as a moment within the totality of a universal will. If this self-negation is to take place by means of the dialectical character of the person itself, if the person is not to be dissolved, but rather integrated into a kind of identity more suited to his essence, then it is decisive that there must be "morality." This chapter does not contain Hegel's ethics. Nor does it contain either a justification or a refutation of moral conduct in general. The issue here is rather the increasing development of autonomous personhood in a series of historical views concerning right and morality.[14] Gradually the person sees himself accountable for his deed and recognizes his responsibility, he performs actions with consciousness and interest, he desires to further his own welfare as well as that of others and to realize the good he sees as unconditionally necessary. Hegel himself does not speak of moral persons because the "exclusive singularity" that distinguishes a person from all others is not the dominant moment in this form of the will. The moral will wants that which is justifiable, that which is universal and valid for all. At the same time, however, it seeks instructions for its particular deeds. If it were possible to proceed from moral subjectivity—or in Kant's terms, from moral personality—and thereby develop a system of duties in relation to which every agent could attain the identity of a moral "character," then the concept and consciousness of the person would indeed suffice for the mental identity of self-conscious individuals.

This cannot succeed, however, because the concept of the "unconditionally good" originating in the mere consciousness of the individualized subject turns out in the end to contain nothing but the "dissolving" character of that subject. No objective good can meet the subject's requirements for being unconditionally good. The unconditionally good, which according to its very claim is supposed to be independent of the individual's subjective and arbitrary will, can only be rendered determinate and concrete by the subject's autonomous decisions, determinations, and purposes. But with regard to the capability and the will to subjective distinction and decision, the difference between autonomy of conscience and moral cynicism disappears. The self-referential negativity of the singular person as such, which is posited as the absolute source of morality, cannot be maintained in the face of the demand that a system of unconditionally valid rules for a community of autonomous persons must be developed. The concept and consciousness of a singular person as such must therefore be granted a limited right within a comprehensive totality in which one's identity can be secured.

As we all know, Hegel discovers this totality in the state. To be more precise, he finds it in that state, that includes and stabilizes the family and civil society and that has a constitution according to which the various governmental powers—royalty, administration, and legislation—are separate but coordinated with one another.[15]

The forms of ethical life (the family, and so forth) and the various governmental powers of the state correspond to the conceptual moments of universality, particularity, and singularity. Thus, for Hegel they can be demonstrated as the conceptually necessary ways in which the universal will particularizes itself and is brought into correspondence with particular wills. Hegel does not conceive of the state as a contract between persons, nor of legislation as the supreme power that must be exercised by everyone who possesses the characteristics of an independent personal will. Are these essential differences from Kant's philosophy of state also based upon Hegel's concept of the person?

They are, indeed, in two respects: First, the totality that is differentiated into a system of necessary determinations, the totality in which the person gains his identity by surrendering his spiritual autarchy, cannot be dependent upon the willful negativity of persons. A contract, however, always depends upon a contingent harmony of interests. Reason requires the institution of contracts only with respect to the mutual alienation of objects because the particular object at issue in a contract rightly depends only upon the arbitrary will of the contract's partners. But if the common will has a necessary purpose, then its establishment cannot be conceived of as a contract. Life in a state organized according to rational principles is absolutely necessary even for the identity of every person if the person is not to be subject to the whims of forces inside or outside himself, including his own subjective freedom to dissolve all determinacies. Only in the state do persons participate in a "substantiality" that is conceptually necessary and that in social reality exists on its own power—in this sense, is a "causa sui." Such a state is established as a rational state through the process in which the individual gradually appropriates the customs, emotional ties, social roles, and so on that have dominated it all along and confronts them with the rights of persons to an external sphere of freedom as well as with the internal moral authority to subject all standards to criticism. The "Idea" of the state thereby becomes accessible to consciousness and gains a new form of reality. In this state, personal freedom is taken into account as well as the individuals' right to forms of unification in which a greater stability of consciousness can be gained than the persons could achieve on their own.

It is the way in which the "spirit" of a rational state permeates the "relationship" between its citizens as well as their "ethical life and consciousness" that Hegel calls "Law" (PR § 274). This concept of law is obviously much closer to the Greek notion of "nomos" than to the modern concept of a law as a strictly general rule commanded by a rational will. Correspondingly, the relationship between person and law is not thought of as a common legislation undertaken by unified persons, as it is in Kant. It instead resembles the pure notion of the ego: the latter is not an autonomous origin in which concepts and rules are posited; the notion of the ego originates rather in the ego's appropriation of rules. Just as the person attains his free self-consciousness by appropriating and dissolving the rules that determine it, so, too, does the person contribute to the establishment of rules "suited to persons" by his appropriation of them and, at the same time, by renouncing the establishment of rules through subjective reason alone. Persons and laws for Hegel are necessarily interrelated. To put it pointedly, the mutual "dissolution" of persons and laws establishes both the identity of the person and the rational state.

However, Hegel is also familiar with the usual modern concept of law as the obligatory, enforceable establishment of rules by governmental legislation. And he seems to take for granted that the state's "objective" acts are laws or can be traced back to laws (PR § 280 App.). Nevertheless, his doctrine of governmental powers substantially reduces the importance of legislature as compared to the theories of the legislative state from Locke to Kant, and this occurs to the advantage of royal power. Even this reduction can be traced back to his theory of the person: just as universal self-consciousness must necessarily be identical with some individual consciousness, so, too, must the universal will be "concentrated" in a personal individual will. In a set of student's notes from Hegel's lecture on the *Philosophy of Right* in 1819–20, it is stated: "Subjectivity as such is immediate in the subject. Subject can only be as *this* subject. This negativity, which infinitely relates itself to itself is nothing other than personhood. Subjectivity is therefore exclusive Oneness, an exclusive person. In that sovereignty is a "this," it is the sovereign, the monarch."[16] This means that the state's universal will, which is objectified in a system of institutions and is concerned with the rights of persons, must in turn be "singularized" in a natural person.

This theory of the personalized state will implies not only that states must be legally represented by persons, but also that the "final decision" with regard to alternative actions in a state cannot be deduced from laws or from criteria of a universal rationality. The decision must indeed be based on the "spirit" of the constitution and the culture of the state, but it cannot be determined or controlled by appeal to them. It is possible simply to understand this thesis as an echo of the Aristotelian concept of prudence and to regard it as well proven by political experience. But one can also regard it as evidence for a voluntarism in political philosophy that has had fatal consequences especially in the German philosophy of the state—one need merely recall the example of Carl Schmitt. At least on this point, viewed from the perspective of political philosophy and our historical experiences in this realm, Kant's conception of the relationship between person and law must be recognized as superior to Hegel's.

What, on the other hand, is convincing in Hegel's conception is his attempt to grasp the mutual relationship between personal and cultural self-comprehension. For Hegel, the identity of a person cannot be separated from the stability of a character that constitutes itself by appropriating and further developing the forms of common conduct and common self-comprehension. For Kant, at least in his later doctrines concerning the "character of the person" in the *Anthropology* (AA VII, 285 ff.; *151* ff.) character emerges by means of the appropriation of moral principles that are identical for all mankind (cf. AA VII, 293; *158*). Character is "the property of will by which he binds himself to definite practical principles that he has prescribed to himself irrevocably by his own reason" (AA VII 252; *157*). Kant excludes the imitation of existing customs or a gradual mediation by means of education or instruction as elements in the constitution of such a character.[17] Character is attained by an "explosion" or a "revolution" that pertains to the way of thinking (cf. AA VII, 294; *159*). Whether or not such a revolution has occurred is something that even the individual himself cannot know with certainty.[18] For Hegal also, "revolutionary" changes in consciousness fulfill a necessary function in the constitution and further development of the character of individuals and whole cultures. However, these are not mere preparations for stability in one's character: rather, such stability can itself only be understood as the development of a self by means of such changes. Even in a culture based upon a system of rational rights and institutions, a person's character is still taken as something that develops. Hegel's insight into the mutual interdependence between cultural and personal "stability" seems to me to be as important as his attempt to understand "identity" in terms of developments with radical changes. But I am not convinced that he succeeded in his efforts toward a new conception of the logical forms necessary for this task.

Notes

1. In contrast to Hannah Arendt, I am not seeking the foundations of a political philosophy in Kant's theory of judgment. Cf. Hannah Arendt, *Lectures on Kant's Political Philosophy*, ed. and with an interpretive essay by Ronald Beiner (Chicago, 1982). I instead consider Kant's philosophy of right to be the proper foundation. According to Kant, politics is concerned with the realization of rational justice within and among states. I agree with Hannah Arendt's opinion that in Kant's practical philosophy "man is understood as a legislative being" (ibid., p. 8). The value which a rigid proof of that conception would have for the foundation of human rights and democracy, should not be underestimated.
2. One exception is of course John Rawls, but he explicitly distinguishes between the concept of a person in theoretical and in moral philosophy, and his theory of morals is founded upon the analysis of the concept of a person as implicit in the norms of a particular culture. Cf. J. Rawls, "Kantian Constructivism in Moral Theory," *The Journal of Philosophy* LXXVII (Sept. 1980), pp. 571, 517 f.
3. In my view there is more than a vague analogy between this conception of a universal self and Thomas Nagel's "Objective Self" (see Nagel's *The View From Nowhere* (New York: Oxford University Press, 1986).
4. There are few investigations which attempt to reconstruct Kant's doctrine of the person from his scattered statements on this subject. Cf., for example, H. Heimsoeth, "Persönlichkeitsbewusstsein und Ding an sich in der kantischen Philosophie," in *Studien zur Philosophie Immanuel Kants I, Kant-Studien*, Erg. Heft 71 (Bonn, 1971; 1st ed. 1924); J. Schwartländer, *Der Mensch ist Person* (Stuttgart, 1968); K. Ameriks *Kant's Theory of Mind* (Oxford, 1982), especially Chapter IV. Particular aspects are discussed in P. Kitcher, "Kant on Self-Identity," *The Philosophical Review*, vol. XCI, no. 1 (January 1982) p. 41–72; W. Sellars, *Metaphysics and the Concept of a Person*. In K. Lambert, ed., *The Logical Way of Doing Things*. New Haven: Yale University Press, 1969; A. Haardt, "Die Stellung des Personalitätsprinzips in der "Grundlegung der Metaphysik der Sitten" und in der "Kritik der praktischen Vernunft," Kant-Studien 73 (1982) 157–68. G. Mohr, "Personalité et liberté dans la Critique de la raison pratique." *Revue Internationale de Philosophie* (forthcoming).
5. Kant's *Critique of Pure Reason* is quoted according to the first (A) and second (B) editions. All other works are quoted according to the Akademie-Ausgabe (AA). Wherever English translations were available, the quotations were compared with the English translations listed below and the page number of the translation listed in italics. The translations of Kant found in this paper, however, are not necessarily those of the translation editions; English translation page numbers are given only as an aid to readers. The English translations consulted were:
Critique of Pure Reason, Trans. Norman Kemp Smith, New York/Toronto, 1965.
Anthropology from a Pragmatic Point of View, Trans. with an introduction and notes by Mary J. Gregor, The Hague, 1974.
Perpetual Peace, Trans. M. Campbell Smith, New York/London, 1972.

The Metaphysical Elements of Justice, Trans. John Ladd, Indianapolis, 1965.
Metaphysical Foundations of Natural Science, Trans. James Ellington, Indianapolis/ New York, 1970.

6. For an interpretation of these passages, see also W.H. Walsh, "Self-Knowledge," in *Kant on Pure Reason,* ed. R.C.S. Walker (Oxford, 1982) pp. 153 ff.
7. Karl Ameriks, *Kant's Theory of Mind* summarizes his interpretation of the "Kantian view" of personal identity in the following manner: "Such identity is not *a priori* or merely inwardly knowable, but ordinarily speaking it is in a sense empirically determinable (even by the person himself) although ultimately speaking, it is not thus certainly knowable and it is this unknown identity (or non-identity) that matters most" (p. 149). In contrast to Ameriks' view, it seems to me that the question of the diachronic identity of the person is resolvable within the framework of Kant's theoretical philosophy without recourse to the supratemporal identity of a noumenal ego. We must not think of ourselves only as identical logical subjects but also as continual persons throughout the fluctuations of our psychic states—not on account of the contents of inner sense, but rather due to its form. Which particular states are indeed mine is, however, a question which cannot be decided by the form of the inner sense; it requires external perception and an objective location of events in time. Regarding the question "what matters most," one might indeed say that for Kant in the end everything depends upon the certitude of our immortal souls as a supratemporal noumenal identity of the ego; but one cannot employ this identity, which is only demonstrable in moral philosophy, in order to found the inner-temporal identity of our "psychological" personhood without falling into the very paralogism which Kant criticizes.
8. Cf. H. Heimsoeth, "Persönlichkeitsbewusstsein . . . ," pp.244 f.
9. In order to establish the *external* "mine and yours" as rational right, more however is required than just the principle of law: namely the "legal postulate of practical reason" which allows one "to view and to deal with any object of my volition as objectively possible 'mine or yours' " (AA VI, 246; *53*). Regarding the relationship between internal and external "mine and yours," cf. Mary Gregor, *The Laws of Freedom* (Oxford, 1963), p. 50. In his preparatory studies to the *Metaphysical Elements of Justice,* Kant compares the relationship between internal and external mine and yours with that between internal and external perception according to the "Refutation of Idealism" in the *Critique of Pure Reason* (cf. M.J. Gregor, ibid., and AA XXIII, 309 f., 426).
10. I do not see much support in Kant's texts for the interpretation that Kant uses the principle of self-sustenance to delegate to the state the task of insuring the economic independence of all its adult citizens. Such considerations have a systematic location only in the philosophies of Fichte and Hegel.
11. I quote Hegel's *Science of Logic* according to the Lasson edition (G.W.F. Hegel, *Wissenschaft der Logik,* ed. G. Lasson, Hamburg, 1963). The *Philosophy of Right* and the *Encyclopedia* are quoted by the paragraph number (abbreviated Enc. and PR). I have used T.M. Knox's translation of the *Philosophy of Right* (Hegel's *Philosophy of Right,* trans. with notes by T.M. Knox, Oxford, 1975).

12. Cf. my more extensive treatment of this point in *Anerkennung als Prinzip der praktischen Philosophie, Untersuchungen zu Hegels Jenaer Philosophie des Geistes* (Freiburg/München, 1979).
13. Kant was not, however, the first representative of the German Enlightenment to adopt Horace's *"sapere aude."* Regarding his predecessors, see H. Wuttke's essay on Christian Wolff in *Christian Wolff's eigene Lebensbeschreibung,* ed. H. Wuttke, (Leipzig, 1841).
14. I deal with this point more extensively in "The *'Aufhebung'* of Morality in Ethical Life," in L.S. Stepelevich and D. Lamb, *Hegel's Philosophy of Action* (Brighton, 1984).
15. In his doctrine of the division of powers, Hegel is more concerned with the forms of interaction and mutual participation than with a strict separation and mutual control of powers. Compare my "Hegel's Theorie der Gewaltenteilung" in H. Ch. Lucas and O. Pöggeler eds., *Hegel's Rechtsphilosophie im Zusammenhang der europäischen Verfassungsgeschichte,* (Stuttgart:Bad Cannstadt 1986) p. 387–420.
16. G.W.F. Hegel, *Philosophie des Rechts. Die Vorlesung von 1819//20 in einer Nachschrift,* ed. D. Henrich (Frankfurt, 1983), pp. 240 f.
17. It is well known that, in addition to "character taken absolutely," Kant also deals with other characteristic properties of man, such as those expressed in his physiognomy or his habits. On this level, a mutual interaction with the "character of one's nation" is apparently also possible. All this is, however, irrelevant with regard to the true character, the "absolute unity of the inner principle of our conduct generally" (AA VII, 295; *159*). Furthermore, Kant comprehends the character of nations primarily as natural, innate properties which can be traced back to an original people and are "unchangeable" for relatively "unmixed" nations such as the English and the French (cf. AA VII, 312; *174* f.)
18. Cf. AA VII, 295; *160* "the sole proof a man's consciousness affords him that he has character is his having made it his supreme maxim to be truthful, both in his admissions to himself and in his conduct toward every other man."

II

A Normative Philosophy of Politics

Karl-Otto Apel

5. Normative Ethics and Strategical Rationality: The Philosophical Problem of a Political Ethics*

The Project of Inquiry

In what follows I shall try to contribute to the solution of two old problems. The first is the question as to what makes up the specific problem of a political ethics. This question will constitute my chief concern because I suspect that there is a certain tendency—especially today—to disguise the specific character and difficulty of the problem of a political ethics. The second is the question whether a rational solution to the problem of a political ethics is conceivable, that is whether there is an ethics conceivable that is at the same time philosophically satisfactory and suggestible to a politician. With regard to this second question, I shall only propose some regulative ideas at the end of my paper since I happen to think that, up to now, there has been no philosophically satisfactory ethics that, at the same time, could really help or serve a politician.

In the main part of my paper I shall deal with my two problems in terms of a theory of types of rationality of action, namely, *technical rationality, strategical rationality,* and *consensual-communicative rationality.* I shall not proceed systematically, but rather try to approach my problem historically by a reconstructive sketch of the modern situation or constellation with regard to ethics and the three mentioned types of rationality. I shall begin by introducing two famous comments on political ethics. Both of them are certainly not satisfactory philosophically, in my opinion, but they are nonetheless very appropriate for an illumination of the problems I have to deal with. What I have in mind are the positions of St. Augustine or Martin Luther on the one hand and Nicolo Machiavelli on the other.

---

*From *Graduate Faculty Philosophy Journal* (Winter 1982).

Political Ethics in the Light of Christianity and the Emancipation of Value-Neutral Types of Rationality at the Beginning of Modern Times

Augustine, the Christian saint and father of the church, has the merit, it seems to me, of having exposed the problem of political ethics in a radical way by depriving the ancient attitude toward the use of political power of its innocence. He performed this, for example, by his famous comparison of secular states with gangs of brigands, that is "groups of men, led by the will of the leader, which are held together by a social contract and share the booty according to a fixed agreement."[1] Augustine has qualified his verdict by speaking of "states without justice," but since his comparison has to be considered against the background of his doctrine of the two realms or states, the *civitas dei* and the *civitas diaboli,* there is no doubt that the wordly state (the *civitas terrena*) must be equated with the *civitas diaboli*; that is, it cannot realize justice, on Augustine's account, since it is based on "self-love," whereas only the *civitas dei* is based on the love of God and hence on justice.[2]

Thus, it becomes clear that there is no real chance of an ethics of secular politics left by Augustine. Only as citizens of the invisible church that make up the *civitas dei* may politicians hope to participate in the mercy of God in spite of their worldly business, so to speak. This dualistic perspective is reconfirmed and even sharpened by Martin Luther's version of the two-realms doctrine at the beginning of modern times. For now the Christian ethics of love is contraposed as a matter of pure belief to the secular reason that for Luther is merely a prostitute in the service of self-love. And in his different writings on different political occasions Luther even suggests a kind of double-entry bookkeeping with regard to the practical behavior of politicians and military persons who have to maintain order and obedience also by "stinging, and strangling."[3] Thus, political ethics according to Luther's doctrine of the two rules sometimes seems to be reduced to the famous suggestion: *pecca fortiter et crede fortius.*

Hence, it is not difficult to make the transition from Luther's views concerning the worldly rule of politics to the purely secular analysis of the conditions of power politics by his contemporary Nicolo Machiavelli, although, to be sure, Machiavelli no longer speaks as a theological advocate of a patriarchal order but rather as a spokesman of the purely secular *ratio* with regard to the conditions of conquering and maintaining the political power.[4]

In order to have at hand some illustrative arguments for my later discussion of the problems, let me quote some characteristic passages of Machiavelli's with regard to the so-called *necessità,* that is, the compulsion or coercion of the situation to be faced by a politician. In this context, his most principled and provocative argument with regard to ethics can read as follows: "There is such a vast difference between life as it is and life as it ought to be that he who gives up doing as one does in favor of doing as one should do would rather bring about his ruin, than his maintenance. A man who in every respect would only do the good would by necessity perish among so many who don't do good. Hence, a prince who wants to hold his own must be able not to do the good . . . according to the coercion of the situation."[5]

Or, in other words: "One has to know that there are two modes of fighting: one by laws, the other by force. The first is peculiar to men, the second to the brutes. Since, however, the first often does not suffice, one has to make use of the second. Therefore, a prince must know well to appear sometimes the brute and sometimes the man."[6] Thus, according to Machiavelli, "the organizer of a state or legislator has always to proceed from the assumption that all men are bad and will always follow their bad mentality as soon as they have an opportunity of doing so."[7]

Considering as a whole Machiavelli's suggestions to the politician—especially in his *Principe*—one may still today come to the same ambivalent opinion as obviously was held by the discreet readers of his works in the period of "absolutism" when the doctrine of *raison d' état* was advanced. On the one hand, his suggestions had to be refused or even scandalized in public from the moral point of view; on the other hand, one could not deny that Machiavelli in his conception of *necessità* had pointed out some features of the politician's situation that no one could avoid facing.

With regard to our problem of political ethics one may perhaps be inclined to say that Machiavelli's suggestions are not satisfactory from the point of view of ethical reason, for—to mention only one point—in his *Principe* he does not even ask the question as to the humane purpose of conquering and maintaining political power. But precisely for this reason one may state as well that Machiavelli for the first time has analyzed politics from the abstract point of view of *instrumental-technical rationality*, or rather, more precisely, from the point of view of *strategical rationality*; for strategical rationality may be defined, I suggest, as application of instrumental-technical rationality under the conditions of reciprocity of human interaction, that is, as application to persons of instrumental-technical rationality under the presupposition that the other persons will try as well to instrumentalize one's own actions or even intentions for their own purposes.

Even more precisely one may perhaps say that the political type of strategical rationality uncovered and analyzed by Machiavelli is that of friend-enemy relationships, to speak along with Carl Schmitt.[8] On this occasion one should recall that at the time when this type of strategical rationality was released on the stage of an untraditional politics in the Italian Renaissance, another type of strategical interaction between people began to emancipate itself from the restrictions that were imposed on it by traditional religious morals. What I mean is, of course, the strategical rationality of economic behavior, especially banking business, for example, charging interest in early capitalism.

Whereas the strategical behavior in politics stands under the regulative principle of maximizing one's power, possibly by alliances with friends as against enemies, the strategical behavior in economics follows, one might say, the regulative principle of maximizing profit, possibly by cooperation and sharing of profits with business partners. Yet both of these types of strategical rationality of action are constituted by an abstraction from ethical aims or purposes beyond the specific maximization rules, and, in addition, they also do not provide from their own *ratio* those restrictive rules of the game—for example, norms of law or fairness rules, even with respect to the game of warfare—by which strategical behavior always was confined in the course of human history.

I should complete my survey of the abstract types of rationality that were released at the beginning of modern times by mentioning the instrumental-technical rationality in the narrow sense that displayed itself in close connection with the rationality of experimental physics, as for example, hydrostatics, cinematics, and mechanics. These types of rationality may be distinguished from strategical rationality by the fact that they may be defined by a complete abstraction from human interaction. Thus, they may be conceived as types of regulating solitary actions or cognitive operations within the frame of the so-called subject-object-relation as it was thematized by modern philosophy from Descartes to Kant. Nevertheless, these types of strictly monological rationality were to become significant for the occidental problematic of political ethics for two reasons.

First, in a very fundamental respect, the scientific-technological rationality of the subject-object-relation has molded modern philosophy to such an extent that modern epistemology in general did not even explicitly introduce the "subject-cosubject relation" of human interaction and communication as a condition of the possibility of knowledge—for example, sharing intersubjectively valid meanings of language and hence also intersubjectively valid truth. This is ethically relevant because in reflecting on the communicative preconditions of cognition one could have detected fundamental ethical norms as conditions of the possibility of valid arguments of science and philosophy, in brief, as being ethical conditions of all serious thinking. Instead, "methodical solipsism" became a presupposition of modern philosophy from Descartes through Husserl; hence, ethics had to be grounded, even by Kant, without explicitly presupposing a transcendental subject-cosubject relation. But this point is an anticipation which I will take up and explicate later.

The second reason why the scientific-technological rationality of the subject-object-relation has become relevant for the occidental problematic of political ethics is that this monological type of rationality has concealed to some extent even the communicative structure of strategical action. Thus, up to now it has never become quite clear, I think, that there is an important structural difference between strategical interaction between people, say in politics or economics, and so-called social technology based on explanations and predictions of behavioral science. And for this reason alone, not to mention the ethics of communication, the so-called paradoxes of self-fulfilling and self-destroying prophecy have hardly ever been analyzed in an adequate way.

Instead, in the political program of technocracy—from Bacon on or from Saint-Simon to Marx and Lenin, and even in Popper's restricted program of "piecemeal social engineering"—responsible planning in politics has been based on the assumption of repeatable social experiments performed by the "subjects" of social technology with regard to human "objects" of its operations. That is, the fact that human beings as objects of behavioral science and social technology keep their status as partners and/or antagonists of interaction and communication has thus far not been taken into account by a systematic theory of understanding human rationality of action. But this also is an anticipation of a problematic to be taken up and explicated later.

At present, I want first to summarize the results of my historical introduction of the more or less abstract types of human rationality as a contraposition to the supra-natural or metaphysical positions of Christian ethics. First, it becomes immediately clear, from this point of view, that all mentioned types of rationality are value-neutral or "value-free," to speak with Max Weber. This means, with regard to traditional metaphysics, that the modern conceptions of rationality do not thematize, let alone prescribe, an ultimate aim or purpose of human life; they rather suppose purposes that are immanent in the pertinent operations—as, for example, a certain type of experimentally controllable knowledge and its application by instrumental technology and certain aims of strategical behavior as may be formulated by rules of maximization of profit or power.

From a Christian point of view, as it was expressed, for example, by Luther, this means that they all represent a type of *ratio* that in the last resort may be imposed in the service of self-interest without providing any anti-egotistic motive or norm of action of its own. This is why Luther calls secular reason a prostitute and it is also why all mentioned types of abstract rationality appear to be unsatisfactory from the viewpoint of ethical reason. But then, of course, the question arises as to what ethical reason could be or even the more radical question as to whether there is such a thing as ethical reason or, in other words, a type of rationality that would not be value-neutral but would rather ground a fundamental norm of moral action or value of a good life.

This question of the possibility of rational grounding of ethics in general has to be answered, it seems to me, before discussing the actual specific question of the possibility of a political ethics. Therefore, let us consider in some detail the first question that, I suggest, makes up the characteristic problem of practical philosophy in the modern age after the dissolution of the medieval *ordo* in favor of a dichotomy of nonrational Protestant ethics on the one hand, and value-neutral types of rationality on the other.

The Failure of Grounding Ethics by Instrumental-Strategical Reason

Strictly speaking, both a methodical distinction between, and a hierarchy of successive answers to, the questions of rational ethics in general, philosophy of law, and political ethics may only be found in Kant. And he indeed has delivered the first paradigmatic conception of an ethical legislation by an autonomous reason that is independent of religious belief as well as of the service of rationality to self-interest. But before examining Kant's solution, I shall consider modern natural law in its Anglo-Saxon version, initiated by Thomas Hobbes, and leave the discussion of the neo-Aristotelian versions of natural law and of practical philosophy in general for later. My reason for proceeding in this way is provided by the following preconceptions:

1. All neo-Aristotelian conceptions of practical philosophy and especially of political ethics up to our day—which in a certain sense comprise even the Hegelian philosophy of the state—may be considered as attempts at a renewal, after the dissolution of the medieval *ordo,* of that substantial unity of reasonable *praxis* that was presupposed as the "good life" of Man in the *polis*. Now the question whether such a renewal of "substantial morality" (*substantielle Sittlichkeit* in the sense of Hegel) may suffice in answering the questions of a political ethics may best be answered in respect to the present situation of mankind. So I leave it to that discussion.

2. On the other hand, the Hobbesian type of practical philosophy may be considered as the immediate answer of modern rationality to the dualistic dilemma that I tried to display at the beginning by quoting Augustine and Luther. For the answer of Hobbes and his many successors up to the modern game-theorists of strategical behavior may be reduced, I suggest, to the following thesis: There is no need for substituting a nonvalue-neutral type of ethical reason for modern abstract rationality. Value-neutral, instrumental, or rather strategical rationality, put in the service of well understood self-interest, may in fact solve the problems of ethics in general and especially those of political ethics. Now this is a deeply challenging thesis that I would like to refute first in this paper before showing that a Kantian type of ethical reason without strategical rationality will not do either, and a neo-Aristotelian type of "substantial morals" of the *polis* even serves to veil those problems that were exposed by the Christian thinkers and by the modern types of practical philosophy from Hobbes to Kant.

Turning to Hobbes's answer first, one could analyze his approach as being based on a combination of three elementary presuppositions: (1) the presupposition of a nominalistic conception of the free will in the sense of arbitrariness; (2) the presupposition of affects, like greed, pride, and fear of death as a natural basis for human self-interest; (3) the presupposition of reason or rationality in the sense of a value-free faculty of calculating, with the aid of signs, all kinds of consequences of given premises.

By combining these presuppositions, Hobbes derives his so-called natural laws, which he equates with the principles of Moral Philosophy: (1) to seek peace and keep it; (2) to restrict one's natural right to all things, if others are also prepared to do so, and insofar as it is necessary for the sake of peace and self-defense; and (3) to keep concluded contracts.[9] As is well known, it is on the basis of these natural laws grounded by a rationally calculated self-interest that, according to Hobbes, the social contract and thereby the constitutional state may be morally grounded as well as explained with regard to its emergence.

Now, as a consequence of Hobbes' presuppositions, it is quite clear that his principles of morality or natural laws are nothing but "hypothetical imperatives" or "advices of prudence" in the sense of Kant; that is, their validity is always dependent on the preservation of self-interest as the last normative instance. This is in fact clearly expressed in Hobbes's qualifications of the second law (which he equates with the "golden rule" of the Holy Scripture), and it is explicitly formulated by his definition of a natural law as being a "general rule found out by reason, according to which a man is forbidden to do that, which is destructive of his life, or taketh away the means of preserving the same, and to omit that by which he thinketh it may be best preserved."[10]

Thus, the crucial question in our context is whether Hobbes's rational grounding of his natural laws is sufficient to secure the intersubjective validity of norms of actions as a minimal demand of a constitutional state that is based on social contract.

Hobbes's answer initially could be that the intersubjective validity of his natural laws is guaranteed insofar as one may suppose an equality of human beings with regard to his three suppositions: arbitrariness, affects, and reason as a faculty of calculating consequences. Of course, reason could be defective in the single case and, precisely for this reason, which may also be calculated in advance, the social contract must include a contract of subjection to a sovereign who guarantees that the norms of the law are followed by everybody. But we can not be satisfied by this answer and should narrow our question as follows:

Even if we suppose a perfect rationality of human beings in the sense of Hobbes's faculty of calculating, would it suffice to ground the validity of Hobbes's "moral principles"? For example, is it rational, in Hobbes's sense, to conclude and keep contracts? In my opinion the answer to this question could only be that it is indeed rational on Hobbes's premises to be interested in concluding contracts in general and in other people's keeping them; furthermore, it is rational to keep contracts oneself as long as one's interest is satisfied by an existing contract and a breach could be followed by sanctions. But it is not rational, on Hobbes's premises, to keep contracts in those situations where one could break them without running the risk of negative consequences and where one could, by breaking a contract, draw a parasitic surplus-advantage from other people's keeping the contract. Rather it is rational, from a purely *strategical* point of view, to enter into all contracts with a "criminal reservation" (*proviso*) for eventualities of the latter type. In addition, it is not rational either, on Hobbes's premises, to abstain from concluding favorable contracts that happen to be agreements at the cost of other people who are not participating in but affected by these agreements.

Now these two negative examples suffice, I think, to show that Hobbes's natural laws, insofar as they can be rationally grounded on his premises, are not at all principles of morality. They are instead principles of a strategical rationality that could be followed by criminals or members of a Mafia as well as by virtual or actual members of a constitutional state. In brief, Hobbes's principles of well understood, rationally calculated, self-interest seem to reconfirm Augustine's and Luther's judgments on secular states or, similarly, secular reason.

But in reflecting on this latter suggestion, I hasten to add that it must be a precipitous conclusion, for Hobbes's premises are not even apt to explain the coming about and functioning of a constitutional secular state. Every commonwealth would break down for lack of legitimation, I think, if its citizens were motivated *only* by a calculated self-interest in the sense of Hobbes's premises, that is, if the norms of positive law had not only to discourage parasitic motives and to encourage moral ones but also to replace the moral dispositions by gratifications and sanctions. Thus far I would also consider it extremely implausible that the problem of the establishment of a constitutional state or commonwealth could be solved for a people of intelligent devils, as even Kant, along with Hobbes, postulates in the naturalistic perspective of his political philosophy.[11] In short, I would like to claim that self-interest plus strategical rationality is not enough to ground morals and hence not enough to explain the coming about and functioning of constitutional law since legality may be distinguished, but cannot be completely separated, from morality.

In order to corroborate this thesis, let me supplement my discussion of Hobbes by a comment on a characteristic neo-Hobbesian proposal of grounding political ethics—a proposal that was advanced in our day especially with regard to international relations. I think of Hermann Lübbe's thesis that the philosophical problem of the rational grounding of moral and individual norms is trivial, whereas the real problem is that of providing social validity for rationally grounded norms. The neo-Hobbesian justification for this tenet is provided by

Lübbe's model of grounding norms that, as he explicitly claims, reduces the whole problem to one of instrumental-technical rationality.[12]

Lübbe's reductive claim rests on the following consideration: Norms of action may be understood as a response to conflicts of interests between people, groups, or even states. This becomes obvious, for example, in the case of fixing contested quotas for catching fish—say whales or herring—among the interested nations. In order to find out which norms are rationally justified in fixing the quotas, it is necessary only to consider the contested norms as means of reaching the next higher purpose that is common to the conflicting parties. For by this consideration, it may be shown that the norms are indeed means or instruments to be used to serve a common interest of life. Of course, this procedure should be repeated, according to Lübbe, in case the common purposes become contested themselves.

The crucial point of this model, in my opinion, is the procedure of agreement about common purposes or, respectively, "super-purposes." And precisely this aspect of the model is ambivalent with regard to the presupposed type of rationality. On Lübbe's account, it is important to reach an agreement as quickly as possible by focusing on the interests of the conflicting parties and by leaving aside all ideological or esoteric implications. Now if this principle is followed, then the whole model is one of a strategical rationality of negotiating that has nothing to do with morals. For in this case the model may also be applied by the members of two gangs who have problems with organizing, say, the drug trade. Hence, we are again led back to Augustine's or Luther's verdict against secular rationality. If, on the other hand, the procedure of agreement had to be a *moral* one, then it would have to consider and observe from the beginning some principle that would at least forbid a quick agreement of merely the conflicting parties at the cost of all other affected people.

Moreover, even if all affected people were actually to agree on some purpose, this purpose might not be identical with the "good life," as Lübbe supposes, for it could be that incidentally all affected people are actually interested in something harmful, say drugs.

This critical analysis of Lübbe's model of grounding norms may be reconfirmed, I think, by a closer analysis of his thesis that the real problem of morals and law is that of providing "social validity" to the norms. For this part of the general thesis is ambivalent. On Lübbe's account, the problem of providing social validity to norms is identical with the problem of the procedures of providing legal force or validity to those norms that are rationally grounded. Now this assumption of the identity of legal and social validity is plausible only, in my opinion, if there is a constitutional state whose laws are sufficiently grounded by a consensus of the whole people. If this is not the case, as actually must be supposed for many states in our day, then the problem of providing social force to the norms is very different from the problem of providing legal force or validity. And the reason for this difference may then be sought in the fact that the norms that are legally put into force are not sufficiently grounded rationally. In other words, even legally valid norms need not be legitimate morally, and for this reason they may not be capable of being put into force socially.

This shows, I would claim, that the problem of *grounding norms rationally* is by no means philosophically trivial, as Lübbe supposes, since it can*not* be reduced to an instrumental-technical or strategical problem. This may also be shown with regard to modern "game-theory" if it is used as a foundation of ethics together with contract theory, as is the case, for example, in John Rawls's *Theory of Justice*.

The theory of strategical games, to be sure, may show that the natural state of men must not be just a state of *bellum omnium contra omnes*. Cooperative games or rather cooperative phases of games are possible and even probable on the presupposition of purely strategical interaction. Nevertheless, the tacit conventions of the natural state must be replaced by the idea of an explicit social contract, if norms of justice are to be grounded rationally. For it is only on this level of a contract that the rational decisions or choices of the individuals who are presupposed by the game theory may be made explicit. Thus, the problem of justice or fairness is posed by Rawls through a combination of the presuppositions of strategical game theory and contract theory. But precisely on these preconditions the problem arises whether a rational choice in the sense of the theory of strategical games, that is, on the presuppositions of arbitrariness of the will, self-interest, and value-neutral rationality, may be thought of as a sufficient foundation of justice.

Rawls tries to solve this problem by an ingenious trick.[13] In order to show that reasonable human beings could or would choose a state of justice on the presuppositions of strategical rationality, he supposes an artificial, so-called original, situation where the "moral point of view"—that is, the reciprocal acknowledgment of human beings as having equal rights—would be identical with the point of view of everybody's self-interest. This is reached chiefly by the supposition of the so-called "veil of ignorance" with regard to one's own position in the commonwealth to be established by the social contract; for in such a situation, according to Rawls, everybody would calculate his risks and, hence, would choose from his or her self-interest a social order that is oriented toward a compensation of individual disadvantages rather than toward reconfirming the natural and social inequality of starting chances. In short, everybody would choose a social order of justice. Thus, Rawls tries to make congruent, so to speak, Hobbes's foundation of the social contract with that of Kant.

I do not think, however, that Rawls has succeeded in doing so. More precisely, he has not shown that in the "original situation" everybody must choose (from his or her self-interest) a social order of justice in such a sense that he himself must give up, in principle, the "tacit criminal reservation" with regard to the chosen order. This at least cannot be achieved, in principle, I would claim, by the fiction of external boundary-conditions of the situation of choice. It could only be conceived by the supposition of an internal determination or motivation of the will toward negating or at least restricting the principle of calculated self-interest by another principle of reason. But in this case reason would not be a value-neutral faculty of calculation in the service of self-interest but rather a faculty of a trans-subjective motivation and valuation. Is such a faculty of reason conceivable? This question seems to be the most radical one of modern practical philosophy, after Luther and Hobbes and all their successors together denied the possibility of a noninstrumental reason.

Kant's Idea of a Morally Legislative Reason and Its Shortcomings: The Aporetic Emergence of the Specific Problem of Political Ethics

Now it is well known that Kant answered in the affirmative precisely this question, for he postulated a morally legislative faculty of autonomous reason that would be an alternative or counterinstance with regard to all heteronomous determinations of the will, such as the determination of divine commands on the one hand and the determination by Hobbes's affective self-interest on the other. Kant also showed that the autonomous legislation of reason can in fact be conceived in terms of a principle that provides a criterion of trans-subjectivity. For this is what the "categorical imperative" means by postulating a maxim of the will that could serve as a universal law for all rational beings (who would constitute the "realm of purposes," that is, the realm of a community of beings that are ends in themselves and must be respected as such by one another).

Kant also provided a foundation for the social contract and thereby for the constitutional state of law. This foundation postulates, similar to Hobbes's conception, a reciprocal restriction of arbitrariness but, contrary to Hobbes, it does not justify this postulate by the calculated self-interest of the arbitrary will but by the autonomous legislation of the free will *qua* reason. Reason itself, according to Kant, demands the social contract, i.e., the reciprocal restriction of self-interest, as a regulative principle of justice. The significance of this conception becomes clear from considering the fact that neither a contract itself nor—as I tried to show—the self-interest that may lead to entering a contract can provide a rational justification for keeping a contract.

It is from the point of view of his foundation of the constitutional state of law that Kant also approached the problem of a political ethics in his shorter writings where he also deals with the problem of a philosophy of history. The connection between these two topics—political ethics and philosophy of history—is given for Kant by the fact that the constitutional state of law—in his terminology: the "republican state"—has by no means been realized as yet but is itself only a "regulative idea." Thus, already at this point a long-range duty and task of political ethics with regard to the future arises. But the internal connection between this task of political ethics and philosophy of history becomes entirely clear if we consider the Kantian tenet that justice in the sense of the republican state cannot be realized within single countries if it is not simultaneously realized on the international level by the establishment of a cosmopolitan society or union of states on the basis of law.[14] This task of international politics is especially treated by Kant in terms of his project of establishing "eternal peace", and it is at this point that Kant's idea of historical progress shows its ethical foundation. For supposing the possibility of historical progress, trying to reconstruct history in such a way as if it could be continued in a progressive way is for Kant not primarily a matter of scientific knowledge or metaphysical speculation but above all a postulate of practical reason and hence a duty.[15]

Thus far Kant indeed has delivered a paradigm for the hierarchic conception of an ethics of reason that provides a foundation for the constitutional state and for a long-range perspective of political *praxis* and reconstruction of history. Therefore, let us ask the question whether this conception provides a satisfactory solution for the problems of ethics in general and of political ethics in particular.

In a sense I am prepared to answer this question in the affirmative, but this affirmation would only refer to a transformed version of the abstract foundation-scheme of the Kantian hierarchy of ethics of reason, philosophy of law, and political ethics. But before I can explain what I mean by that, I must say some words on the shortcomings of Kant's conception, especially with regard to political ethics.[16]

First, I would note that the crucial problem of grounding normative ethics by reason, or, in other words, the question whether there is such a thing as a non-value-neutral but morally legislative reason, has not been answered satisfactorily by Kant, although he raises this problem explicitly.[17] The reason why Kant could not solve this problem may ultimately be found in his dualistic metaphysics, which I think prevented him from working out a radical conception of a *transcendental* philosophy based on the unity of theoretical and practical reason. What I mean is the distinction between "noumena" and "phenomena," according to which man is a "citizen of two worlds," such that he may be thought of as *free* only in the "intelligible world," whereas in the world of possible experience he must be conceived as being determined by natural causes with regard to all his perceptible actions. From this metaphysical dualism the following aporetic consequence may be derived with regard to the problem of grounding ethics on practical reason.

Since Kant conceived of the autonomous legislation of practical reason as identical with the free will, he could not prove the existence of practical reason because the existence of the free will cannot be recognised but only thought of as possible in the world of noumena. Thus, he could not ultimately ground the binding validity of the "categorical imperative," but had to presuppose it as an evident "fact of reason" that, on its part, is a practical reason for supposing the existence of a free will. (*Du kannst, denn du sollst*[18]). This doctrine of the "fact of reason" could of course not be acknowledged as a foundation of normative ethics by modern metaethics. For on the one hand, it appears as a replacement of a foundation by a dogmatic assertion; on the other hand it is, even as an axiom, exposed to the reproach of suggesting the possibility of deriving ethical norms from a fact and thus committing the "naturalistic fallacy."[19]

Another consequence of Kant's metaphysical dualism is the fact that he cannot conceive of an intervention of the free will and thus of moral action in the realm of possible experience, since in his world of nature there are no possible phenomena of "intentional actions," not to speak of "moral intentions," but only phenomena of events determined by natural causes. This implication of Kant's metaphysical dualism has in turn two precarious consequences.

First, with regard to normative ethics in the narrow sense, it follows that Kant cannot really conceive of man's responsibility for the effects and side effects of his actions, for these effects are supposed to be determined independently of man's intentional intervention, such that the difference between moral and immoral actions cannot even be detected, on Kant's premises, in the world of experience. This is at least one of the reasons why Kant defines the morally good solely by the "form of the will," that is, by explicit abstraction from the question of the consequences of actions. (Another reason for this is the fact that Kant, so to speak, takes the quasi-divine perspective of judging the good or bad will of a man rather than the perspective of a man who, being of good will, poses to himself the question of which action—and that means which initiative action together with its effects and side effects—would be a good one. At least in his *Groundwork*, Kant does not even think of the consequences of actions for other people that are to be answered for by the agent, but he thinks only of the good or bad consequences for the agent himself, which, as he plausibly argues, should not be taken into consideration by an agent of good will.)

It seems understandable that this peculiarity of Kant's ethics of the good will, which is close to protestant ethics, has later given rise to Max Weber's distinction between "ethics of (the form of) mind" (*Gesinnungsethik*) and "ethics of responsibility" (*Verantwortungsethik*). This distinction, in my opinion, points indeed to one of the most serious shortcomings of Kant's approach with regard to the problem of political ethics. (This becomes immediately clear in the notorious example of *Gesinnungsethik* that was delivered by the old Kant. With regard to the question of whether one should speak truthfully or lie in case one should be asked by a murderer for the hiding place of his virtual victim in one's house, Kant in fact insisted on the priority of the "perfect" duty of speaking truthfully over the "imperfect" duty of saving the life of a fellow human being.[20] We shall later see that this example points to the crucial problem of political ethics: the necessity of a mediation between consensual-communicative rationality and strategical rationality.)

The other precarious consequence of Kant's separation between man as "noumenon" and man as "phenomenon" refers to the relationship between ethics and the socio-historical sciences. On the presupposition of his metaphysical dualism, Kant cannot really cope with the problem of the identity of the addressees of his ethics with the human objects of socio-historical science. This may be shown especially with regard to the concept of action. On Kantian premises, one may, strictly speaking, only conceive of imperceptible actions of understanding or will on the one hand and perceptible actions as cases of causally determined behavior on the other. What is completely lacking in this dualistic picture—as it is, by the way, in modern scientism—is the world of communicative experience, experience of the intentional actions of human beings as virtual partners of interaction and as addressees of speech.

This world of experience, which later became the subject matter of the so-called *Geisteswissenschaften,* is of course presupposed by Kant—on a a level of common sense—in his political writings. Thus, he explicitly states that the "reasoning public" (*räsonierende Öffentlichkeit*) is the addressee of philosophical ethics as well as of enlightenment in general.[21] Still he does not take this sphere of communicative experience as the paradigm case for a scientific understanding of human actions in history, but he reconstructs history essentially on the presupposition that action of free will and hence moral intentions cannot be experienced as phenomena and hence must not even be presupposed as motives of people's action in history.

This is the background from which it becomes understandable that Kant poses himself the task of explaining the establishment of a constitutional state even for a people of intelligent devils.[22] I intimated already that this super-Hobbesian supposition is by no means realistic but rather a paradoxical overstatement in the spirit of a metaphysical dualism that combines ethical idealism with empirical naturalism. In any case, this dualism prevented Kant from accounting for the fact that the human subjects of history must after all (notwithstanding their selfish motives) have been identical with the addressees of his ethical writings who are called upon as responsible subjects of a progress towards a cosmopolitan society of law and peace.

Thus, Kant in his philosophy of history did not arrive at a perspective of critical reconstruction of history that would take into account *both* the possibility of an understandable internal history of moral progress and, at the same time, of an external history of actions to be explained by the natural mechanism of selfish motives.[23] Instead, with regard to empirical history, he extrapolated and generalized his example of the establishment of a constitutional state by intelligent devils. In order to reconcile this naturalistic view with his ethics, he introduced the speculative assumption that the divine providence or the cunning of nature will use the natural mechanism of human selfish motives in such a way as is necessary in order to reach those aims of progress (as, for example, a cosmopolitan society or union of nations) that are at the same time set as a long range task of moral striving.[24]

I do not wish to deny that even this speculative device—which was taken up by Hegel—may be heuristically fruitful in that it points to the *possibility* of putting selfish interests in the service of moral purposes. From Adam Smith to the modern economical theory of strategical games, these possibilities have been studied carefully. But if this device should not lead to leaving all responsibility to a divine providence, then it presupposes, in principle, that there are or may be also human political instances within history that may responsibly judge and make use of the quasi-natural mechanisms in politics and economics in the service of justice.

But it is not only Kant's metaphysical dualism that prevents him from adequately mediating his ethical postulates with the reality of history but also the peculiar rigorism of his *Gesinnungsethik*. This becomes evident, I think, at the only place where he in fact raises explicitly the problem of the morality of a politician. I mean the passage in the appendix of the treatise *On Perpetual Peace,* where Kant discusses the problem of a possible conflict between morals and politics.[25]

The interesting thing in this context is that Kant forbids to the "moral politician" precisely all those practices that he presupposes as those of the divine providence in all philosophy of history. Thus, the "moral politician" should not use the empirical mechanism of human selfish motivations in order to reach even the best aims—as, for example, an order of eternal peace—but he should always follow the categorical imperative in treating other people on principles of justice. And as a necessary criterion of justice Kant formulates in this political context the "transcendental" principle of "publicity": "All actions related to the right of other people whose maxim is not compatible with (the) publicity are unjust."[26]

In defending the priority of this principle of rightness over any principle of utiltiy, Kant goes so far as to affirm the sentence: *"fiat justitia, pereat mundus."* And he comments on this sentence as follows: "The political maxims must not suppose as supreme principles of political wisdom the wealth and happiness of a state to be expected as consequence of observing the maxims, hence they must not be oriented toward the purpose or will as it is set up by every single state, but they must proceed from the pure concept of the right duty (i.e., from the "ought" whose principle is given *a priori* by pure reason) whatever the physical consequences of this may be."[27]

Thus, Kant may conclude his consideration by the statement: "Hence there is objectively (i.e., on the level of theory) no conflict between morals and politics."[28]

Contrary to Kant's opinion, it seems to me that we have at this point reached a stage of consideration where the problem of a political ethics is by no means settled but rather exposed as a challenge to reason. For this much seems immediately clear: Kant, in his attempted settlement of the conflict between morals and politics, arrives at the same kind of implausible solution as in the case of his example of the murderer who must not be deceived. And the reason for the implausibility of Kant's suggestion obviously hangs together with problems of reciprocity and problems of responsibility.

To put it quite simply and provisionally: If we lived in a world where the generalized reciprocity of rights and duties, as it is postulated by the "categorical imperative," were acknowledged and generally observed, then Kant would surely be right with regard to all his suggestions of truthfulness as a perfect duty; and especially his principle of "publicity" would indeed be the best warrant for justice, as it is already today within the limits of well-functioning democratic states. But the specific problem of political ethics is made up of the fact that we do not (or not yet) live in a world as it is morally postulated by Kant. And at this point the problem of responsibility comes into play in a way that is at least pointed to by Max Weber's distinction between *Gesinnungsethik* and *Verantwortungsethik*.[29] For there the politician is not allowed *morally* to disregard the probable consequences of his actions because he must not consider them from a Kantian perspective as good or bad consequences just for himself but as consequences for those people who are put in his hands.

As a consequence of this perspective of responsibility, the politician—and this is, in a sense, every human being—is confronted with the following, apparently paradoxical, situation of human reciprocity: On the one hand, he must, from a moral point of view, suppose (consider if possible in principle) that his political opponents also acknowledge and follow the categorical imperative. But this does not mean that they will share his assessment of the situation and hence of the practical decisions about concrete norms or actions to be taken. On the other hand, in a situation where two political adversaries, for example, representatives of antagonistic systems of self-interest, would both acknowledge in principle the validity of the categorical imperative and, furthermore, would even share the assessment of the situation and the practical decisions to be taken, they still cannot know this with certainty with regard to each other and therefore are not allowed to completely trust each other. This latter situation seems to make up, for example, the paradoxical character of disarmament negotiations.

One may put this whole problem into a clearer light, I suggest, by introducing general systems theory at this point. I think we cannot but recognize that life on all levels—and thus on the level of human culture—must organize itself by setting up functional systems that must preserve their identity through maintaining themselves against their environments. These systems of self-maintenance, I suppose, are the very subjects of self-interest and of strategical rationality of actions. If we grant this as a fact of life, then the specific problem of a political ethics (this term taken in a broad sense) seems to be the following: Should it be possible to take into account the right and even the duty of self-maintenance of social systems in a world of possible conflicts between systems without reducing ethical reason to instrumental-strategical rationality in the service of self-interest?

Having thus vaguely pointed out what I consider the specific problem of political ethics, I shall at the end of my paper present a very rough sketch of what I, for a long time now, have tried to work out as a "transcendental-pragmatic foundation of an ethic of consensual communication and of strategical responsibility."[30]

The Problem of Ethical Reason as a Problem of Consensual Communication and Strategical Responsibility

In what follows I shall first try to show how Kantian ethics might be reconstructed and transformed in terms of an ethics of consensual communication. In a second step I shall then try to suggest that the fundamental norm of consensual communication also provides a regulative principle of a moral strategy for dealing with those situations where the conditions of consensual communication cannot be supposed to exist.

I think that transcendental philosophy in general and ethics in particular may be grounded in a radical way by avoiding all metaphysical implications of the Kantian system—as, for example, Kant's unsolvable problem of a "transcendental deduction" of the reality of the free will and hence of autonomous reason—and, moreover, by also avoiding the well-known aporias of all attempts at a deductive procedure of ultimate grounding, say, of axioms.[31]

Instead I shall begin by reflecting on the situation of argumentative discourse that, I want to emphasize, cannot be circumvented or transcended by arguments. I would emphasize, moreover, that this situation is structurally identical with that of every serious attempt at thinking solitarily, but by valid arguments. Now in this situation—which I suppose is our present situation right now—we can convince ourselves by strict reflection[32] on the implicit meaning of our argumentative acts that in order to argue seriously we must have acknowledged a "normative principle of trans-subjectivity" (to use this term in the first place).

This principle may easily be distinguished from that of strategical rationality of human interaction. For we must have excluded from the beginning any intention to realize perlocutionary effects by rhetorical tricks or to reach our aims of argumentation by means of diplomatic negotiation or by threats of violence, and so on. Instead, we must have acknowledged *a priori* that it is possible, in principle, to *share* the intersubjective validity of meaning and truth with our communication partners, or rather, strictly speaking, with all possible competent members of an indefinite community of argumentation. For if we have entered serious arguing we cannot be satisfied by the message—say of modern paradigm-relativism—that the possible redeemableness of our validity claims is confined, in principle, to a certain culture or form of life. We would rather immediately unmask this statement of the relativist as a pragmatical self-contradiction in light of his own universal validity claim.

I am, of course, not talking now of the factual difficulties of intercultural understanding or even of the factual expectation of a consensus by arguments that one could have even in our civilization, for example, at this conference. I am talking only of those transcendental presuppositions of argumentation that cannot be denied without committing a pragmatic self-contradiction, or, in other words, without rendering the whole enterprise of argumentation meaningless.

Now the principle of trans-subjectivity that we must have acknowledged in serious arguing implies also a fundamental ethical norm, namely, the "principle of generalized reciprocity of rights and duties." For in the situation of argumentative discourse we must suppose an "ideal speech situation"[33] and thereby adjudicate equal rights and duties of asking and answering all kinds of questions concerning any conceivable topic to all possible members of the argumentation-community. (It may be noted at this point that, from our present viewpoint, the usual pragmatical restrictions with regard to the time of the discussion, the participants and relevant topics must of course be conceived of as being already the result of a consensus and thus presuppose the above outlined fundamental ethical norm.)

One could think that the ethical norm that must be acknowledged in every serious argumentative discourse is that which comprises all the pertinent rules of this type of language game. Thus, we would have acknowledged just a special ethics of argumentative discourse that has no internal relationship at all to the other language games or forms of life. But this, I think, would be the worst misunderstanding of the whole approach. For those who seriously engage in an argumentative discourse—say in the way Socrates did—must also presuppose that real problems of life can be solved by reasonable arguments and that this is the only way to redeem those validity claims as may be inherent in all forms of human communication; hence, it is the only alternative to settling differences of opinion or conflicts of interest strategically—say by negotiations or by open fight. Therefore, one may say that the institution of argumentative discourse, being the very institution of thinking or of intergral reason, is the "meta-institution" with regard to all social institutions since it is the only conceivable instance of a reasonable legitimation of institutions.

At this point one might ask, how it should be possible that the fundamental ethical norm that is presupposed by an argumentative discourse could have a function of grounding or legitimating with respect to practical conflicts of interest outside the argumentative discourse. The answer is that our fundamental norm is not a material norm to be related to a special type of situation, but rather a "meta-norm" that prescribes the ideal procedure of grounding or legitimating material norms, namely, that it should be performed by seeking a consensus of all affected people by an argumentative mediation of their interests. In short, the fundamental norm that we must have acknowledged in a serious argumentative discourse is the "rationale of consensual-communicative interaction."

As such, it seems to me to be the integral rationale of human action and thus far to be superior to the rationales of the value-neutral types of technical and strategical rationality of action. And since it is itself only an implication of the principle of trans-subjectivity that is the normative rationale of practical and theoretical discourse, one may claim that this principle is the result of a transcendental-pragmatic decoding of the Kantian "fact of reason." As such our principle shows up two methodical advantages in comparison with the Kantian principle.

First, it is immediately clear that it is a normative principle that we must have acknowledged and not just an "evident fact," as Kant suggests in his rather unfortunate formulation. Thus, Moore's criticism of Kant's committing the "naturalistic fallacy" loses its object.[34] Second, our principle is nothing but a reflective explication of those validity claims and rules of their possible redemption that must have always been inherent in human communication by speech. For it can be shown, I would claim, that sharing of meaning and truth, which is a condition of the possibility of a genuine communication by speech, cannot be reduced to some kind of strategical interaction—say of reaching perlocutionary effects without needing illocutionary effects, namely, the mediating stage of sharing conventional meanings by the communication partners.[35]

Now since the rationale of consensual communication must always have been inherent in human interaction, we may claim the existence of an anthropological counterpart or analogue to the transcendental-pragmatic foundation of ethics. And this provides us with a framework for grounding and integrating a developmental logic of stages of moral consciousness as stages of the internal awareness of the principle of generalizable reciprocity up to the stage of an ethics of consensual discourse. (I am of course relating to the "developmental logic" of Piaget and Kohlberg and its reception by Habermas.[36])

So much for the envisaged transformation of Kantian ethics by a transcendental-pragmatic conception of an ethics of consensual-communication. What about the special problem of a political ethics that we have claimed to be unsolvable on the basis of a Kantian *Gesinnungsethik*?

First, one may show indeed that many of Kant's shortcomings with regard to the special problem of political ethics, namely, the problem of responsibility for systems of self-maintenance as against antagonists, rest on the fact that Kant did not sufficiently consider that the categorical imperative must imply the principle of generalized reciprocity in an ideal communication community.[37] Had he considered this fact sufficiently, he would not have needed to oppose Benjamin Constant who told him that the duty of speaking truthfully is based on the reciprocity of rights and duties and therefore should not be applied in speaking to a man who obviously has the intention to murder.[38] It is easy to extrapolate this situation in order to realize that all the characteristic problems and difficulties of a politician of good will hang together with the problem of facing the situation of insufficiently realized reciprocity between individuals, groups, or even states.

At this point, however, one should think that our ethics of consensual communication is in no better position than that of Kant. For it is an ethics of the *ideal* communication-community, to speak by abbreviation, and the first thing a responsible politician has to consider is the fact that we never live in an ideal communication-community. One may also express this fact in terms of my differentiation between types of rationality of interaction in the following way: It is a distinguishing feature of the ideal argumentative discourse that it is unburdened, so to speak, by strategical interaction, for this is, as we said, the precondition of a rational redemption of human validity claims. Now the politician, because he has to pass responsible decisions, is never in such a situation. The real situations of his communications with other people are rather characterized by a mixture of consensual-communicative and strategical interaction. (The second ingredient may be further analyzed with the aid of game-theory.)

However, what does follow from this ascertainment? Is the ethics of consensual communication plainly not binding for him? Are we thrown back to Machiavelli or to the irrationalism of Max Weber's ultimate value-decisions? Or—to mention a currently fashionable suggestion—is it just Aristotelian *phronesis*, that is prudence, circumspection, and sensibility for the right measure, that must make up his ethics?

Now to answer this question first with regard to domestic politics, I could point to the following fact: If the idea of democracy has a normative-ethical quality, as I think it has, then it is nothing else than the idea of an approximate realization of the fundamental norm of consensual communication, namely, of mediating the ground of legitimation of norms or laws through a procedure of consensus formation. Of course, the affected individuals are only *represented* (in the parliament) and the discussions are terminated by "decision-procedures," as, for example, majority votes. But these pragmatic restrictions that may be modified again and again do not reduce the idea of democracy to that of just a decision procedure, as is maintained by many "politologists" today. For it seems clear to me that the difference between the decision procedures in a democracy and, say, a dictatorship is constituted precisely by the fact that only in the first case the procedures are themselves a result of those procedures of consensus formation that stand under the regulative idea of maximizing the consensus of all affected persons.

Thus, I dare to defend the thesis that, at least with regard to domestic politics, modern democracies have already acknowledged the regulative principle of progressively realizing standards of an ethics of consensual communication.

But what about foreign politics and international relations, which are the classical fields of reflected strategical interaction since Machiavelli and that, according to Leopold von Ranke, must hold the primacy of politics in general? Is there any good reason, philosophically, to maintain the thesis that even with regard to this field a politician of good will is bound in some way by the ethics of consensual communication vis-à-vis the interests of all affected people? Or is it true that with regard to this field a kind of Hobbesian or rather Darwinian natural state must always continue to exist and would even provide in the last instance normative criteria for a responsible politician, as some sociobiologists seem to suggest.

One could of course argue from my perspective that, strictly speaking, there is no Hobbesian or Darwinian natural state possible on the level of human existence, simply for the reason that human thought is based not only on the strategy of the proliferation of genes,[39] which rules animal behavior, but also necessarily on sharing meaning and truth and hence on sharing consensual communication. But this (correct) argument would not help us very much since the principle of consensual communication may be restricted to just one political system of self-maintenance or to an alliance of those systems at the cost of other parts of mankind. This is of course a very topical argument in our age of the ecological crisis, especially in face of the threatening overpopulation of the earth. And indeed a Nobel Prize winner in economics has recently suggested that an adequate solution to the problem of restoring the ecological equilibrium may be provided by leaving to starvation those peoples of the third world that could not help themselves.

I think this suggestion might not be very far from what many prominent people in the rich industrial nations tacitly hold these days. In most cases, I suspect, the real problem is veiled by the neo-Aristotelian talk of political prudence and responsibility that leaves it open as to whether the responsibility is related to the fate of humankind or only to the maintenance of the standard of life in one's own political system, or rather in those systems that are economically dependent on each other. For at this point it becomes relevant that Aristotle's ethics of *phronesis* is based on the distinction between prudent political *praxis* and skillful technical *poesis* but has not yet analyzed the difference between strategical praxis and consensual-communicative praxis. This point, of course, results from the confinement of this ethics to the self-maintenance system of a *polis* (in contradistinction, for example, to the cosmopolitan ethics of Antisthenes and the Stoa).

However, should it really be left to politicians of good will to mediate the imperatives of strategical rationality and hence the responsibility for their special systems of self-maintenance through the fundamental norm of an ethics of universal consensus-formation?

At the conclusion of my paper, I would like to point to the Kantian perspective of the *factual* development of the international relations in this century. Kant called it a "philosophical chiliasm" to hope that some day a federal union of states based on law would make it possible to guarantee at least a state of peace;[40] beyond that he trusted that the "reasoning public" inspired by philosophy would help to propagate republican principles, that is, the regulative idea of constitutional law based on the consensus of all affected persons, on a cosmopolitan scale. Now I think that this vision is going to be realized to a certain extent. I will mention only one interesting point:

At present there is not only such an organization as the UN but there is even a kind of public coercion toward dealing with all kinds of international problems—as, for example, problems of the ecological crisis or of disarmament—by way of dialogues and conferences. And these conferences must at least *pretend* publicly to follow the rule of mediating by rational arguments the interests of all affected people. it is of course not allowed to any realistic politician to confuse these conferences with argumentative discourses as they are postulated by philosophical ethics. (Those people who are inclined to fall victim to such a confusion and to overlook the strategical features of the international conferences are called "starry eyed" in a now fashionable jargon.) Nevertheless, the public compulsion, which underlies the pretention of fiction that these conferences are means of consensus-formation through rational discourse, is not only an occasion for the cool smiling of the so-called realists; it is also a hint of what practical philosophy today has to demand as a "regulative principle" of a political ethics.

Let me try finally to formulate this regulative principle in terms of a pedantic ethics of consensual communication. I think an educated politician of today who is of good will, but who also stands for a contingent system of self-maintenance, has to follow the fundamental norm of an ethics of consensual communication in the following way: he has to follow a long-range moral strategy of helping to realize the political conditions of consensual communication that are demanded by the fundamental norm of ethics. But the fact that he must follow a *strategy* means that he has to mediate the demand of ethics in concrete situations through the demand of defending the justifiable interests of the system he stands for. This is a vague rule, to be sure, but it demands a bit more than just crisis-management or profiteering for the next election.

Notes

1. Aurelius Augustinus, *De Civitate Dei*, IV, 4.
2. *Ibid.*, XIV, 28. Cf. also G. Ritter, "Politische Ethik. Vom historischen Ursprung ihrer Problematik," in H. -D. Wendland, ed., *Politik und Ethik* (Darmstadt: Wissenschaftl. Buchgemeinschaft, 1969).
3. See especially M. Luther, *Ob Kriegsleute auch in seligem Stande sein können*. Cf. also R. Niebuhr, *The Nature and Destiny of Man II* (1943), 194 ff.; and E. Troeltsch, *Die Soziallehren der christlichen Kirchen und Gruppen* (3d. ed., Tübingen, 1923), 473 ff., 486 ff., 500 ff.; and Joh. Heckel, *Im Irrgarten der Zwei-Reiche-Lehre* (München, 1937).
4. With regard to Machiavelli cf. G. Ritter, *Die Dämonie der Macht* (Stuttgart: Hausmann, 1947).
5. N. Machiavelli, *Principe*, chap. 15.
6. Ibid., Ch. 18.
7. Ibid., Ch. 18.
8. Cf. Carl Schmitt, *Der Begriff des Politischen* (1932).
9. See *Leviathan*, I, chaps. 14 and 15, (London/New York: J. M. Dent & Sons, E. P. Dutton, 1944, repr. 1957), pp. 67, 74, 83.
10. *Leviathan*, I, chap. 14, p. 66.
11. I. Kant, *Zum ewigen Frieden* (Akademie-Textausgabe; Berlin: W. de Gruyter, 1968), vol. 8, p. 366.
12. H. Lübbe, *Philosophie nach der Aufklärung* (Düsseldorf, 1980), p. 194 ff.
13. J. Rawls, *A Theory of Justice* (Harvard University Press, 1971), chap. 3. For a different interpretation of Rawls' work, one which starts from a transcendental-pragmatic reconstruction of his foundation of the "fairness" principle, see K.-O. Apel, "Diskursethik als Verantwortungsethik und das Problem der ökonomischen Rationalität," in B. Bieroest and J. Wieland, eds., *Sozialphilosophische Grundlagen ökonomischen Handelns* (forthcoming).
14. Cf. I. Kant, "Idee zu einer allgemeingen Geschichte in weltbürgerlicher Absicht," 7th sentence, Akad.-Ausg., vol. 8, p. 24.
15. Cf. *Zum ewigen Frieden, loc. cit.*, p. 386.
16. With regard to what follows, cf. my paper, "Kant, Hegel und das aktuelle Problem der normativen Grundlagen von Moral und Recht," *Akten der Stuttgarter Hegel-Tagung 1981* (forthcoming).
17. See, e.g., *Grundlegung zur Metaphysik der Sitten*, Akad.-Ausg., vol. 4, pp. 392, 425, 444 f., 447 f., 449 f.
18. Cf. *kritik der praktischen Vernunft*, Akad.-Ausg., vol. 5, pp. 46 f.
19. Cf. K.-H. Ilting: "Der naturalistische Fehlschluss bei Kant," in M. Riedel, ed., *Rehabilitierung der praktischen Philosophie*, Bd. 1 (Freiburg: Rombach, 1972), pp. 113-32.
20. See "Über ein vermeintes Recht aus Menschenliebe zu lügen," Akad.-Ausg., vol. 8, pp. 423-29.

21. Cf., e.g., "Was ist Aufklärung?" Akad.-Ausg., vol. 8, pp. 33-42.
22. Cf. note 11.
23. The distinction between "internal" and an "external history" was introduced by I. Lakatos in his essay "History of Science and its Rational Reconstruction," in R. Buck/R. S. Cohen, eds., *Boston-Studies in the Philosophy of Science* (Dordrecht: Reidel, 1971), pp. 91-36. But this distinction may and must be extrapolated with regard to any rationally understandable dimension of human history.
24. Cf. "Idee zu einer allgemeingen Geschichte in weltbürgerlichter Absicht," (see note 14).
25. See Akad.-Ausg., vol. 8, pp. 370 ff.
26. Ibid., p. 381.
27. Ibid., p. 378 f.
28. Ibid., p. 379.
29. Cf. G. Roth/W. Schluchter, *Max Weber's Version of History, Ethics and Methods* (Berkeley: The University of California Press, 1979).
30. Cf. the following of my papers: "Das Apriori der Kommunikationsgemeinschaft und die Grundlagen der Ethik," in *Transformation der Philosophie* (Frankfurt a.M.: Suhrkamp, 1973), vol. 2, pp. 358-436. English trans. in *Towards a Transformation of Philosophy* (London: Routledge & Kegan Paul, 1980); "The Conflicts of Our Time and the Problem of Political Ethics," in Fred R. Dallmayr, ed., *From Contract to Community* (New York: Marcel Dekker, 1978), pp. 81-102; "Types of Rationality Today," in Th. Geraets, ed., *Rationality Today* (Ottawa: University Press, 1979), pp. 307-39. Cf. also the contributions of K.-O. Apel, D. Böhler, and W. Kuhlmann in K.-O. Apel et al. *Funkkolleg "Praktische Philosophie/Ethik,"* (Weinheim/Basel: Beltz, 1980/81).
31. Cf. my argument with Popperian "Critical Rationalism" in "The Problem of Philosophical Fundamental Grounding in Light of a Transcendental Pragmatic of Language," *Man and World*, vol. 8, no. 3 (1975), pp. 239-75.
32. On this concept which is directed against the current assumption that there are no transcendental presuppositions of the concept of theory that are not themselves theory-dependent, cf. W. Kuhlmann, "Reflexive Letztbegründung," in *Zeitschrift für Philosophische Forschung* 35 (1981), pp. 3-26.
33. Cf. J. Habermas, "Towards a Theory of Communicative Competence," in *Inquiry* 13 (1970), pp. 360-75.
34. Cf. G. E. Moore, *Principia Ethica* (Cambridge, 1966), pp. 114, 126 ff.
35. Cf. my argument with Paul Grice's intentionalist theory of meaning in "Intentions, Conventions, and Reference to Things," in H. Parret and J. Bouveresse, eds.; *Meaning and Understanding* (Berlin/New York: W. de Gruyter, 1981), pp. 79-111.
36. Cf. J. Habermas, "Moral Development and Ego Identity," in *Telos* 24 (1975), pp. 41-55; and *Telos* 26 (1976), pp. 176-82. An attempt at an application of the "developmental logic" to the history of ethics was made by the author in Apel et al. *Funkkolleg "Praktische Philosophie/Ethik,"* 1981/82, loc. cit.
37. In fact there are hints in Kant's texts, especially in connection with the "realm of purposes" that the moral law or principle of generalization implies the principle of

generalized reciprocity. But Kant draws no consequence from this in those cases where he deduces *moral duties* from the categorical imperative but only considers reciprocity as a principle of justice on the level of "legality."
38. See "Über ein vermeintes Recht aus Menschenliebe zu lügen," Akad.-Ausg., vol. 8, pp. 423–30.
39. Cf., e.g., R. Dawkins, *The Selfish Gene* (Oxford University Press, 1976).
40. Kant, "Idee zu einer allgemeinen Geschichte in weltbürgerlicher Absicht," 8th sentence, Akad.-Ausg., vol. 8, p. 27.

Robert Paul Wolff

6. Notes for a Materialist Analysis of the Public and the Private Realms*

I take as the text for my reflections today Hannah Arendt's well-known essay on "The Public and the Private Realm" in *The Human Condition*. Arendt's thesis, you will recall, is that the ancient and necessary distinction between the public and the private, successfully and fruitfully sustained in classical Athenian life and thought, has been undermined and all but destroyed by the rise of the social, which substitutes behavior for activity and thereby makes a genuine politics impossible. Arendt sees Karl Marx as the central chronicler and celebrator of the tendencies she deplores. I think that Arendt's approach to this subject is fundamentally misguided, and though my remarks will not rise to the level of a coherent focussed argument, for I do not see my subject clearly enough for that, I hope that you will find them of value and that by their means I can contribute to the remembering and honoring of Hannah Arendt.

*Some Literary Critical Observations, By Way of a Beginning***

The world of a novel or romance is brought into existence by the storyteller's words and has its existence only in and through those words. It would not be quite correct to say that the world is created by the storyteller's words, for that would suggest that once created, it could continue to exist after the words had died away. The truth is that a fictional world exists in and is constituted by the words of the fiction. Only what the novelist calls into existence by his or her words exists in that fictional world, and it exists only *as* it is thereby conjured up.

---

*From *Graduate Faculty Philosophy Journal*, vol. 9, no. 1 (Winter 1982).
**My discussion of the nature of a fictional world is taken from Cynthia Griffin Wolff, who is, to the best of my knowledge, the first critic to analyse the ontological status of fictional worlds in this way.

Because a fictional world exists through the narration of the fiction of which it is the world, two things are true of it. First, a fictional world *exists from a point of view*, namely, the point of view of the author of the fiction. When I say that fictional worlds exist from a point of view, I do not mean simply that they embody a certain attitude toward life, although that is true and significant, as we shall see. Rather, I mean quite literally that fictional worlds are inherently, or essentially, perspectival. Their ontological status is such that they are spatially and temporally anisotropic. There is a privileged or distinguished place in the world—that of the narrator of the fiction or, in more complex fictions, that of the author—from which the events and objects of the fiction occur or exist. In this way, fictional worlds are ontologically distinguishable from the real world, for the real world is ontically prior to the various perspectives or standpoints from which narrative accounts of it can be composed. From this ontological asymmetry there follows an epistemological asymmetry: the perspective of the author is necessarily the correct perspective from which to apprehend the fictional world. When I read an historical account of the Terror, it makes perfectly good methodological sense to ask whether I can achieve a better knowledge of the events by adopting a narrative standpoint other than that of the account. It even makes sense to ask whether I can retell the very account itself from a different perspective and thereby achieve a deeper insight than the author of the account himself or herself was able to achieve. But it would be a thoroughgoing confusion to ask whether I could achieve a deeper insight into the fictional world of *A Tale of Two Cities* by supplementing the narrative with Donald Greer's statistical analysis of the incidence of the Terror.

The space and time of a fictional world obey rules decreed by the author. In *Bleak House*, for example, events take place in locales of a fictional London that fluctuate in their distance from one another throughout the novel. The changing spatial relationships are a metaphor for shifting moral relationships, and space thus carries a *meaning* that is objectively inherent in the fictional world.

The second peculiarity of fictional worlds is that because fictions are constituted by, and exist through, language, the idiosyncratic connotations of the heightened language of the fiction—connotations that distinguish one author from another and serve, in part, to define the literary style of that author—become constituent features of the fictional world itself. Certain words, phrases, syntactical constructions, or tropes have a significance for the author that is thereby embedded in the fictional world. In *War and Peace*, Tolstoy makes his aristocratic characters speak French when they encounter one another in polite society. This stylistic maneuver carries a freight of meaning—the contrast between the westernized aristocrats and the peasants springing autochthonously from the soil of Mother Russia, the inner division of convention from native sentiment, and so forth. In the real world of Napoleonic Russia, the habitual use of French as a language of aristocratic conversation might or might not in any particular instance have these significances, but in the fictional world of *War and Peace* it *must* have this meaning, for Tolstoy has constituted his world thus.

The real world can be construed as inherently perspectival or fraught with meaning only insofar as we conceive it in religious terms to be the object of a continuous divine creating. Thus understood, space becomes the field on which God's story unfolds, and time takes on the anisotropic structure of a narrative, with a beginning, a middle, and an end. A fictional world can be in and of itself metaphorical, some things objectively standing for others, so long as the author has constituted it in that way. But in the real world, the moon's reflection of light from the sun does not *of itself* refer to the relationship between lover and beloved, or pope and emperor, unless God tells the story of the world in that way.

A divinely created world is indeed inherently perspectival. Heavenly bodies, men and women, kings and nations, exist from God's point of view. They exist in order to exemplify or fulfill God's purposes. They have an objective *telos*. Certain words—sin, faith, grace, salvation—have objectively heightened meanings, corresponding to the shape and meaning of certain decisive events in the fictional world of the divine Narrator—the creation, the fall, the exodus, the covenant, the incarnation, and so forth.

Once we decisively give up the fantasies of religion and acknowledge the absence of mystery in the world, we must put behind us as well the notion of a narrative shape to history and nature. There will be no objective metaphors—no childhood, adolescence, and maturity of civilization. Nor will there be places and times rich with objective meaning, pivotal places on which the human story turns. There will simply be time and space and the seamless flow of events. In particular, we shall have to give up the fantasy of classical Greece, which substitutes, in the sophisticated adult mental lives of many richly cultivated European and American intellectuals, for the never-never land of "once upon a time" fairy tales.

Hannah Arendt, like so many learned thinkers of the Western tradition, construes the past two millennia of the cultural and political history of the European peninsula of the Eurasian continent as having the structure of a fictional world. Her narrative perspective is that of a cultivated and alienated member of the continental upper middle classes, and the dominant tonality is nostalgia for the lost glories of Classical Athens. That time and place occupy a privileged position in the perspectival fiction conjured by Arendt, and their invocation consequently carries a moral and aesthetic weight in her discourse utterly incompatible with the ontological status of the historical actuality. A cluster of small agricultural and trading communities in the eastern Mediterranean is accorded the same heightened resonance and pendulosity (to use Auerbach's lovely word) that other communicants in other frames of mind have imputed to Calvary, to Mecca, to the Paris of the 1790s, to St. Petersburg in October 1917, or to the Constitutional Convention in Philadelphia in 1787.

A Materialist Analysis

This is not to suggest that Arendt's account of classical Greece is factually inaccurate, any more than to suggest that Tolstoy has misrepresented the Napoleonic Wars. An historical novel written with meticulous attention to the latest historical scholarship is no less a fiction for all the learning of its author. In the real world, we can be nostalgic for ancient Athens, just as we can be nostalgic for medieval Paris, or for the court of Genghis Khan, or for Hoboken in the 1940s. But only in a fictional world can a place and time be in and of themselves objectively nostalgic.

Because Arendt writes from within a fictional world in which ancient Greece shines as the golden age toward which we longingly yearn, rather than from within the real world in which the affairs of fifth century B. C. Greece are merely one among many examples of human collective behavior—because she persistently confuses the two in her writings—it is nearly impossible to come to grips realistically and objectively with her theses. The richness of her learning and the depth of her philosophical penetration merely complicate the task, for she intertwines the real world and the fictional in a manner difficult to dissect.

It is characteristic of this way of approaching the analysis of Western civilization (which, needless to say, is in no way peculiar to Arendt) that the etymologies of words are made to carry an enormous freight of meaning, as though by a logical reversal the world itself were constituted by the words with which we describe it (a reversal, of course, that is literally true of fictional worlds). Consider, for example, the following extraordinarily effective and evocative "argument by etymology," as we might characterize it. Speaking of the household realm, which is the sphere of the private, Arendt says:

> Not the interior of this realm, which remains hidden and of no public significance, but its exterior appearance is important for the city as well, and it appears in the realm of the city through the boundaries between one household and the other. The law originally was identified with this boundary line [footnote: The Greek word for law, *nomos*, derives from *nemein*, which means to distribute, to possess (what has been distributed), and to dwell. The combination of law and hedge in the word *nomos* is quite manifest in a fragment of Heraclitus: *machesthai chre ton demon hyper tou nomou hokosper teichos* ("the people should fight for the law as for a wall"). The Roman word for law, *lex*, has an entirely different meaning; it indicates a formal relationship between people rather than the wall that separates them from others. But the boundary and its god, Terminus, who separated the *agrum publicum a privato* (Livius) was more highly revered than the corresponding *theoi horoi* in Greece.] which in ancient times was still actually a space, a kind of no-man's land [footnote: Coulanges reports an ancient Greek law according to which two buildings were never permitted to touch] between the private and the public, sheltering and protecting both realms while, at the same time, separating them from each other. The law of the *polis*, to be sure, transcended this ancient understanding from which, however, it retained its original spatial

significance. The law of the city-state was neither the content of political action (the idea that political action is primarily legislating, though Roman in origin, is essentially modern and found its greatest expression in Kant's political philosophy) nor was it a catalogue of prohibitions, resting, as all modern laws still do, upon the Thou Shalt Nots of the Decalogue. It was quite literally a wall, without which there might have been an agglomeration of houses, a town (*asty*), but not a city, a political community. This wall-like city was sacred, but only the inclosure was political. [footnote: The word *polis* originally connoted something like "ring-wall," and it seems the Latin *urbs* also expressed the notion of a "circle" and was derived from the same root as *orbis*. We find the same connection in our word "town," which originally, like the German *Zaun*, meant a surrounding fence. See R. B. Onian, *The Origins of European Thought*, 1954, p. 444, n. 1] Without it a public realm could no more exist than a piece of property without a fence to hedge it in; the one harbored and inclosed political life as the other sheltered and protected the biological life process of the family. [The legislator therefore did not need to be a citizen and frequently was called in from the outside. His work was not political; political life, however, could begin only after he had finished his legislation.]

This is Arendt at her best, weaving together historical materials, etymological tracings, evocative tag-lines from ancient authors, all in the service of a dominant vision of modern Western society as a disastrous falling-away from the antique city, with its clear demarcations of the private and the public realms embedded in law, in philosophy, in architecture, in religious ritual, even in the landscaping, and all serving to make possible a politics of rational discourse among equal participants in the public space.

The inhabitants of this antique city seem not, in Arendt's account, to be real people who enact roles and interact with one another in all the ambiguous, complex, mechanical ways that characterize human life everywhere. A permanent rosy glow tinges the lineaments of the portrayal of this happy place and time, where true political discourse flourished in public places, and the sacred rituals, language, geography, and art reinforced one another to constitute and sustain an aesthetic/intellectual whole of great beauty, power, and profundity. It is all powerfully affecting, and thoroughly unreal. It is a literary construction, existing from the perspective of a modern narrator, imbued with the nostalgic longing of its author, or indeed many authors, and quite unlike the actual day-to-day existence of real people.

Contrast this with Arendt's characterization of modern society.

The emergence of society—the rise of housekeeping, its activities, problems and organizational devices—from the shadowy interior of the household and into the light of the public sphere, has not only blurred the old border line between private and political, it has also changed almost beyond recognition the meaning of the two terms and their significance for the life of the individual and the citizen. Not only would we not agree with the Greeks that a life spent in the privacy of "one's own" (*idion*), outside the world of the common, is "idiotic" by definition, or with the Romans to whom privacy offered but a temporary refuge from the business of the *res publica*; we call private today a sphere of intimacy whose beginnings we may be able to trace back to late Roman, though hardly to any period of Greek antiquity, but whose peculiar manifoldness and variety were certainly unknown to any period prior to the modern age.

It is decisive that society, on all its levels, excludes the possibility of action, which formerly was excluded from the household. Instead, society expects from each of its members a certain kind of behavior, imposing innumerable and various rules, all of which tend to "normalize" its members, to make them behave, to exclude spontaneous action or outstanding achievement.

(and finally): behavior has replaced action as the foremost mode of human relationship.

What are we in fact to make of this extraordinary claim that behavior has replaced action as the foremost mode of human relationship? Arendt does not say, at least in the essay we are discussing, but by action she presumably means autonomous, rationally guided deliberation and choice, what Kant would characterize as the agency of a noumenal being. Behavior, by contrast, consists of phenomenally determined events in space and time, subsumable under descriptive laws and explainable by inclusion in a temporal sequence of empirical causes.

Does it make the slightest sense to claim that in the good old days, men acted, whereas now they only behave? Certainly not according to Kant, who argued that every bit of human behavior must at one and the same time be understood as the appearance of rational agency. If Arendt merely means to lament that there were intellectual giants in the earth in those days, then we may enjoy her dirge, but can scarcely treat it as a scientific diagnosis of the modern age. Are we to imagine that the political maneuverings of Charlemagne, Henry the Eighth of England, Robespierre, Lenin, or the members of the United States Congress are *behavior*, but when Athenians encountered one another in the marketplace, their gossip, their political deals, their musings about public affairs took on the elevated metaphysical status of action? This is romance, an intellectual version of Hemingway's adolescent fantasy that when the hero and heroine of *For Whom The Bell Tolls* make love, the earth moves.

Any useful distinction between action and behavior must be grounded in an objective analysis of human nature and development, not in an essentially literary tradition that identifies certain places and times as having special weight or valence, and that orients us toward those places and times in a nostalgic, elegaic, or celebratory mood. This injunction, let me say, holds with equal force against those romantic political thinkers whose orientation is forward to a future event called "the revolution," which is invested with a heightened significance that can be rationalized only in a fiction or in a divinely created world. The invocation of "the revolution" rests on the same fatal misconceptions as the invocation of classical Greece.

The Genetic Underdetermination of Human Personality

The normal growth and development of even the higher mammals proceeds according to genetically determined pathways that fully determine the nature of the mature individual instance of the species. The young may need adults of the species in order to complete their growth to maturity—to teach them how to hunt, perhaps—but within a given species, the process of normal maturation is everywhere the same. Consequently, although one can observe variations among adult wolves, or apes, or dogs, these variations do not constitute culture. Hence, we cannot meaningfully speak of the cultural component in the development, or life-cycle, of any of the animal species. A wolf, left to grow to maturity in the wild, grows up to be a healthy, normally functioning adult wolf; a bear, left alone to grow to maturity, grows up to be a healthy, functioning adult bear.

Human beings, however, are different. Our genetic inheritance radically underdetermines our healthy, normal growth. A human child, deprived of the interactions, relationships, experiences, constraints, introjections, and meanings that we call culture, grows up to be a subnormal, unhealthy, dysfunctional animal.

In his writings, Erik Erikson gives us an account of the complex patterns and processes by which a mature, functional ego develops in the growing child. Leaving to one side the details of Erikson's theory of the emergence of a coherent personality through the staged development of libidinally activated bodily zones, what is clear in his theory, and in virtually all other modern accounts of personality development as well, is the central and essential role played in the development of a healthy ego by the human culture and society in which the infant grows up.

The language, bodily styles, emotional interactions, roles, expectations, prohibitions, and enticements by which the plastic libidinal energy of the infant is shaped into a focussed personality play an essential role in the development of the ego. They must not be thought of as supererogatory additions, available perhaps only to advantaged babies from culturally rich upper-middle-class families. Nor must they be thought of as corrupting and perverting intrusions into the normal, autarchic growth processes of the natural human being. Jean-Jacques Rousseau has done us all a great disservice by making so entrancingly plausible the absurd notion that the healthy child, preserved by an appropriate pastoral environment from the corruptions of civilization, will grow naturally and spontaneously into a vivacious, moral, active, appealing Frenchman. Rousseau's modern disciples, such as the poet, philosopher, and social critic Paul Goodman, have substituted formal education for city life as the corrupter of natural innocence, but their mistake is as great as Rousseau's. Culture is an essential element in the formation of a healthy, coherent ego. In speaking of culture, needless to say, I am referring to the totality of patterns of meaning-laden interaction, ritual, body style, religion, technology, kinship relations, and productive activities that form the subject matter of cultural anthropology. I am not speaking of the "high culture," so-called, of our or any other society. Indeed, I am referring to what Arendt disparagingly calls *the social*, but which she construes as having arisen in Western history at a specific, relatively recent time, rather than as forming an indispensable component of all distinctively human life.

Erikson's analytic models and also his detailed accounts of the child-rearing patterns of a number of Western and non-Western societies show how our genetic inheritance places limits or constraints on what sorts of experiences and interactions can serve as the developmental matrix for the emergence of a healthy ego. But these limits so radically underdetermine healthy growth that a wide variety of very different cultural patterns seem equally well to complete the determining structure of personality development. Despite Erikson's own efforts, in *Gandhi's Truth* and elsewhere, to extract substantive moral conclusions from his clinical explorations of healthy and pathological child development, no sound conclusions can be drawn about the relative superiority of one culture over others merely from a consideration of the objective determinants and requirements of healthy human growth. We can conclude that the social is an essential precondition for the formation of adult personalities having the characteristic coherence, organization, and functioning that we recognize as human; but that no society and culture is, in *this* regard, superior to any other.

The implications for our present topic are reasonably straightforward, I think. It is a fantasy to suppose that in the heady youth of Western civilization, autonomous individuals flourished who were capable of a form of agency metaphysically distinct from the debased behavior to which we have latterly sunk, that we are now victims and products of the social, of behavior that is habitual, banausic, vulgar. "It is decisive," Arendt says, "that society, on all its levels, excludes the possibility of action, which formerly was excluded from the household. Instead, society expects from each of its members a certain kind of behavior, imposing innumerable and various rules, all of which tend to 'normalize' its members, to make them behave, to exclude spontaneous action or outstanding achievement." But society always and everywhere imposes innumerable and various rules that tend to normalize its members. Indeed, as we have just seen, in the absence of some such network of rules, patterns, habitual expectations, traditions, and social norms, we would not have spontaneous action or outstanding achievement but pathology of the most elemental and inchoate sort—not even interestingly twisted human beings, like Iago or Smerdyakov or Lady Macbeth, but institutional cases with malformed egos, lacking affect or focussed rationality.

Material Reproduction and Social Reproduction

"Men can be distinguished from animals by consciousness, by religion or by anything else you like," Marx writes in one of the best known passages of the early writings. "They themselves begin to distinguish themselves from animals as soon as they begin to *produce* their means of subsistence, a step which is conditioned by their physical organization. By producing their means of subsistence men are indirectly producing their actual material life" (*German Ideology*). I take this insight to be not only fundamental to Marx's entire theoretical enterprise but also true and fundamental to any attempt to understand the human condition.

The central concept of a science of society is not strictly *production* but *reproduction*, for the finite, temporal character of human existence dictates that the conditions of that existence be endlessly reproduced through time. The central analytical feature of reproduction, as opposed merely to production, is that the product or output of one cycle of production becomes the material or input for the next cycle. In this way, a circular flow of inputs and outputs is endlessly established and reestablished, forming the context and basis of human existence.

There are three species or modes of reproduction, inseparably intertwined with one another in actuality, but distinguishable for purposes of theoretical analysis. The first mode of reproduction is material reproduction, the subject of the political economy that formed the central activity of Marx's mature years. In the process of material reproduction, the coal, iron, linen, and corn that emerge from this cycle of production serve as the material inputs into the next cycle. Out of this conception of material reproduction emerges the concept of a physical surplus, the distribution and employment of which is thus the focus of theoretical investigation and practical decision. By contrast with neo-classical marginalist political economy, with its emphasis on the problem of efficient allocation of scarce resources, the classical political economy culminating in Marx's *Capital* takes as its two central issues the distribution of the social surplus and the conditions of economic growth. The concept of reproduction serves to concentrate attention on the class conflicts that dominate the processes of distribution and the internal systemic contradictions that impede or entirely frustrate the growth of the annual product.

The second mode of reproduction is human reproduction, by which I mean both the replacement of the old generation of men and women with the new and also the daily replenishing of human capacities and energies that are depleted by laboring and must be recreated in order for the processes of material reproduction to go forward. Human reproduction has the same cyclical structure as material reproduction, for today's children are tomorrow's parents. The inclusion of human reproduction within the circle of material reproduction, by means of the analytical concept of the subsistence wage as the natural price of labor-power determined by the cost of its reproduction, is one of the major theoretical achievements of classical political economy.

Finally, because human nature is, as we saw, radically underdetermined by its genetic material base, and because human beings are therefore social and historical beings, we must complete the analysis of reproduction with the concept of social or historical reproduction. By social reproduction I mean the unending recreation of society itself as a largely unintended collective human product and also as the historical transformation and transmission of culture. This social reproduction is carried out in and through language, kinship relationships, patterns of interpersonal interactions, customary and explicit practices of child-rearing, religion, mores, laws—and also, as we shall shortly wish to emphasize, through the reproduction of the social relationships of material reproduction.

Because of the underdetermination of human personality, the process of social reproduction is not an activity carried out by independently completed human beings who transmit an external and supererogatory culture from generation to generation. The social that is reproduced is constitutive of human being. It completes and specifies the matrix of determinable, but indeterminate, potentiality grounded in the physical nature of the human species. History is thus not a story told by a narrator who has his or her being separately from the tale. In this sense, Louis Althusser is quite correct that there is no *subject* of history, meaning by that, I take it, that there is no narrator whose tale history is.

Since this notion of the social constitution of human being is central to such conclusions as I shall try to draw concerning the distinction between the public and private realms, let me take a few moments to try to clarify it a bit. There is a familiar methodological presupposition underlying a good deal of the political theory, economic theory, and moral philosophy of the past several centuries, according to which the ontological structure of desire, deliberation, choice, and action is prior to and independent of the social context of these purposive activities. Both Kant and Bentham, for example, despite their dramatic opposition on so many fundamental issues of moral philosophy, suppose that the structures of goal-identification, goal-orientation, rational deliberation, choice, and implementation of choice in action, can be analyzed independently of the particular material context in which they occur. The utilitarians sometimes write as though the new-born infant, to put the matter facetiously, differs from the mature adult only in being completely ignorant and as yet not in control of its voluntary nervous system. Not merely the content of desire but also and more importantly the structure of desire is treated as given exogenously. The infant's problem is then construed as three-fold: first, to obtain knowledge of causes and effects in order to be able to predict the consequences of its actions; second, to carry through a rational deliberation guided by canons of prudential calculation, in order to determine the most efficient way to satisfy its desires; and third, to obtain some measure of control over its environment so as to be able to put the results of its deliberations into operation. This conception of human action is then embodied in the moral philosophy of utilitarianism, the political theory of classical liberalism, and the economic theory of free-market political economy.

The truth is totally different from this fantasy, which, I suggest, remains methodologically operative despite the fact that few if any theorists of the human condition would subscribe to it in the simplified sketch I have given of it. The process by which the infant develops into a coherent, effective adult is a process of enculturation whereby specific, determinate modes of desiring, willing, choosing, and acting take form as the characteristic ways in which the adult *is* a person. This framework of coherent purposiveness is at once the product of, the substance of, and the producer of human society. In the personality of each individual this structure of cyclical reproduction is reinstated.

It may be, as Erikson suggests at various places in his writings, that from a transcultural perspective we can perceive certain deep similarities in the outcomes of culturally specific but diverse processes of personality formation. He says, for example, in an often-quoted passage from *Childhood and Society*, that "Each individual, to become a mature adult, must to a sufficient degree develop all the ego qualities mentioned [in the preceding characterization of the stages of the life-cycle], so that a wise Indian, a true gentleman, and a mature peasant share and recognize in one another the final stage of integrity." But it would be a thorough confusion—not one made by Erikson—to conclude that we could abstract from these and other cases of ego-integrity a framework or formal structure of healthy—or, in Erikson's own Platonic usage, virtuous—choice and action that could then serve as the basis for an independent theory of action. The cultural context is primary, and only through an understanding of it can we arrive at an insight into the social reproduction of distinctively human being.

If I understand Marx correctly, his espousal of a materialist theory of society consists essentially in the claim that the patterns, processes, and institutionalizations of material reproduction constitute the major determinants of human and social reproduction. I take this to mean that the way in which a society cyclically reproduces its food supply, its housing, its transportation, its technology, and so forth shapes and specifies its kinship patterns, its religious rituals, its personal relationships, its legal institutions—and, of course, its politics as well. Needless to say, there is an interaction here, and the transmission of the forms of material reproduction from generation to generation must proceed through the reproduction of society. Nevertheless, I understand Marx to be asserting that we can only understand the historical processes of change and the cultural specificity of any given society by beginning, in our analysis, with the forms of material reproduction.

It follows from this assumption, and also from the arguments of the first two parts of this paper, that any objectively grounded distinction between the public and the private realms must be drawn *within* the social, and rooted in the processes of material reproduction, not drawn in *contrast* with the social. For the social is the matrix within which specifically human being develops and is actualized, and the processes of material reproduction—if Marx is correct—are the primary determinants of the social.

Arendt imputes to Marx, and to political economists in general, the view that "politics is nothing but a function of society" and that "action, speech, and thought are primarily superstructures upon social interest." But in fact politics *is* a function of the social, as indeed is everything that is distinctively human. The Kantian conception of a kingdom of ends—a community of rational agents engaged in rational discourse about the objectively right—is arrived at not by a legitimate process of philosophical analysis but by an illegitimate process of abstraction. It is, indeed, precisely the sort of illegitimate abstraction that Kant elsewhere shows us leads to the vacuities and contradictions of rational psychology and theology.

Let us ask instead what could constitute a materialist basis for a legitimate distinction between the public and the private, keeping in mind the remarks that have been made about the nature of material, human, and social reproduction and the genetic underdetermination of human personality, and trying, insofar as possible, to avoid the substitution of a narrative within a fictional world for a description of the real world.

When I speak of the public realm, I intend two different meanings, depending on whether I am speaking of form or of content. From the standpoint of *form*, the public realm is that system of mutual recognitions, ritual performances, shared acknowledgements, and institutional arrangements within which, and by means of which, a society of men and women self-consciously recognize their collective existence and set themselves to make and carry out collective decisions. In Arendt's evocative image, it is a *space* in which men and women meet one another. From the standpoint of *content*, the public realm is the totality of those substantive matters of major social importance that are the objects of collective decision.

The central matter of major social importance in any society is the reproduction of society itself—material, human, and social. If Marx is right, then the determinant mode of reproduction is material reproduction. Hence, the central matter of major social importance must be the cyclical reproduction of the means of subsistence and production, their distribution to the several classes defined by these processes of reproduction, and the allocation of the physical surplus generated in each cycle of production. In many societies, of course, these matters of major social importance have not yet become the object of anyone's decision. The allocation of the physical surplus either for immediate consumption or for productive investment, although possibly the single most important matter of major social importance, only becomes an object of someone's decision at a relatively advanced state of social and economic development.

Even after many matters of importance concerning material reproduction have become objects of decision, they may as yet not be objects of collective decision, and hence may not have entered the public realm. This, I take it, is the central insight of Marx's critique of capitalism as a society in which the processes of production become increasingly socialized while the processes of distribution, allocation, and control over the social surplus remain private. The rate of economic growth, the composition of capital investment, the structure of relative prices, the pattern of wage payments, the social rate of unemployment— all those are matters of major social importance that are either not at all objects of collective decision in a capitalist society or else have only very imperfectly become objects of collective decision and therefore subjects for discourse in the public realm. It is a striking fact, for example, not sufficiently recognized in discussion of politics in societies like ours that even so vitally important a matter as the terms of the contract negotiated by the auto manufacturers and the auto workers cannot become an issue in the discourse of public life, whereas the administration's policy with regard to such relatively unimportant matters as the disposition of several islands off the shore of mainland China can be the focus of a presidential campaign.

So long as the determination of the processes of material reproduction is excluded from the public realm, a species of false consciousness will infect the public life of a society, rather like the self-delusion that afflicts those persons who deny and repress the libidinal basis of rational thought processes. In our society, the exclusion of the work world, in which the labor of material reproduction is performed, from the public sphere encourages the delusion that democratic political procedures constitute substantive political liberty. Citizens whose work world is dominated by the canons of labor discipline suppose themselves free because periodically, on election day, they can share in the determination of matters of secondary social importance.

Arendt, I suggest, cooperates in and endorses this misconception of the nature and appropriate content of the public realm. She writes in a deliberately anachronistic vein that communicates a sense of dismay, indeed of contempt, asserting, for example, that "since the rise of society, since the admission of household and housekeeping activities to the public realm, an irresistable tendency to grow, to devour the older realms of the political and the private as well as the more recently established sphere of intimacy, has been one of the outstanding characteristics of the new realm." She concludes this paragraph, apocalyptically, with the claim that "the monolithic character of every type of society, its conformism which allows for only one interest and one opinion, is ultimately rooted in the one-ness of mankind. It is because this one-ness of mankind is not fantasy and not even merely a scientific hypothesis, as in the 'communistic fiction' of classical economics, that mass society, where man as a social animal rules supreme and where apparently the survival of the species could be guaranteed on a world-wide scale, can at the same time threaten humanity with extinction."

The truth, I suggest, is that in every era and every society the processes of reproduction—material, human, and social—constitute the major determinants of human being in general and of the form and content of the public realm in particular. As these processes of reproduction develop, and in particular as the processes of material reproduction develop, the control, direction, and shaping of reproduction becomes an object of conscious collective decision. It becomes possible, in short, for the matters of the greatest social importance to enter the public realm. When this happens, the result is not at all the loss of a golden age, nor the dying away of reason, nor the disappearance of opportunities for "spontaneous action" and "outstanding achievement." Quite to the contrary, the reception into the public realm of the processes of material reproduction as objects of collective decision makes possible for the first time the achievement of self-conscious rational deliberation about and control over the fundamental conditions of human being.

Robert Spaemann

7. Remarks on the Ontology of "Right" and "Left"*

I would like to propose a hypothesis to explain three historical developments: First, since the eighteenth century political awareness has been marked fundamentally by a dichotomy that has long been characterized, for contingent reasons, by the concepts of "right" and "left." Second, both these positions are subject to a certain inner contradiction: in political reality, they tend to bring about the opposite of what they originally intend. As concerns the radicalism of the "right" and the "left," their similarity is surprising in view of their mutual animosity. Third, the concepts of "left" and "right" have since ceased to express the fundamental political alternatives of our times.

My hypothesis is the following: Classical political philosophy revolved around the concept of nature and the natural. After Plato and Aristotle overcame the antithesis *physis-nomos* with a finalistic conception of nature, according to which man is a speaking and political being "by nature," political philosophy became a theory of natural right, which prevailed until the sixteenth century. After the renunciation of teleology in the conception of nature from the fifteenth century on, political theory runs into an inevitable antinomy. The *physis-nomos* antithesis of the Presocratic thinkers breaks out again.

Perhaps the simplest formulation of this antinomy is the one Freud proposed: the pleasure principle and the reality principle. At first, an infant is determined exclusively by libido, by the desire for physical well-being. But soon the child meets with an indifferent reality, which resists his desires. The child must adapt to this by learning to discipline his or her desires for the sake of survival. The reality principle is identical with the survival principle. According to Freud, the *conditio humana* can never be a happy one because man submits himself to the conditions for his preservation only *nolens volens* and for lack of something better. Deep down in his nature he will always remain libido and therefore will accept the restraints of reality only by force.

---

*From *Graduate Faculty Philosophy Journal*, vol. 10, no. 1 (Spring 1984).

Everyone knows the thesis of the radical left of the sixties, which seemed victorious until the oil crisis, the thesis of Marcuse that we already live in the period of transition to the society of surfeit, which in principle permits diminishing the weight of the reality principle and freeing the realization of libidinous subjectivity in a more complete unfolding. Marx's eschatological maxim, "to each according to his needs," was interpreted in Freudian categories. The antithesis of libido and self-preservation, of the pleasure principle and the reality principle, is the exact and inevitable result of abandoning the idea of finality in nature in general and in human nature in particular. Viewed as a teleological structure, nature is at the same time a principle of perfection, the principle of the movement proper to a being on the one hand, and on the other, the principle that restricts that movement by the inner goal of an optimum. This optimum, this state of perfection, is both the state of well-being of a being's happiness, as well as the state of its optimal preservation. The principle of perfection and the preservation principle are ultimately one and the same: the good.

What were the reasons that led to dropping the teleologically oriented question "why"? It is clear that the phenomena did not compel the abandonment of the teleological view of nature. We know today that changes of paradigm are never compelled by the phenomena. The reasons are metascientific. The constitution of modern science has nonscientific grounds. This path cannot be retraced here. It is a long way from the knowledge of the meaning of the Hebrew word *Yadah* to the Cartesian concept of *certa cognitio*. "The Lord knows the way of the just," it is said in the first Psalm. "I know thee not," says the judge to the evil one on the last day. "Adam knew his wife and she bore his son." It was Franz von Baader who last referred to the connection between knowledge and cohabitation. Here, knowledge signifies becoming one with the other, the absorption of consciousness of the self. At the end of this road, on the other hand, is the windowless brightness of the consciousness-remaining-by-itself, for which nature has become absolute foreignness.

The most important stage along the way was that of the theology of creation. It did not let nature stand as something final, as did all of antiquity, but rather inquired further into its genesis. And this genesis was understood as the result of an action. Aristotle had said, art is in nature. But how does art come into anything? How does it come to the flutist? The answer: by practice. And this is the consequence of methodical intentional steps. So how does art come into nature? Again, only by plan and intention. This was the argument with which medieval Aristotelianism joined teleology and theology together. The intention that guides the arrow is not in the arrow but rather in the archer, writes Thomas Aquinas in employing natural teleology as the basis for a proof of God. Thomas still understood the analogy *mutatis mutandis*. The earthly maker can subject only external causal processes to his goal. The creator really endows the things with teleological "art". The example of the archer, however, made history in a paradoxical way. In the late Middle Ages, Ockham and Johannes Buridan turn it against teleology: finality exists only for conscious action. If the goal of natural processes lies outside them in the divine consciousness, then we can see the processes themselves only from a causal viewpoint. We can admire the world as the machine of the divine constructor; in the world itself, we can discover only the mechanical laws He used.

Natural teleology is idolatry and the mechanical view of nature *vindicatio divini numinis,* writes the Renaissance natural philosopher Sturmius. Francis Bacon adds that teleology is useless. If we want to do something with nature, it is of no use to us to think about where nature wants to go in and of itself. Knowledge of nature is now at the service of making. To know a thing means to "imagine what we can do with it when we have it," writes Thomas Hobbes. Teleology was, on the contrary, sympathetic knowledge of nature, the attempt to understand nature somehow as our equal. Such understanding was not at the service of man, but was an element in man's self-comprehension in the whole of the world. The theological and practical inquiry further into nature means a simultaneous distancing from it. Man transcends nature and conspires directly with the creator. Thus, nature becomes a mere object of use, *uti*. The relation of enjoying devotion, *frui,* that is, knowing in the archaic sense, is restricted to the relationship God-man, according to Augustine. The consequences of this were drawn only by the modern bourgeois world. Science entered the service of praxis; no longer is science, as theoria, the goal of praxis. The contemplative relation to the world appears immoral. Since nature comes to be the domain of human making, of human pursuit of goals, the consideration of any immanent goals in nature itself must be disregarded. The earlier understanding of man's mastery over nature did not see this rule as a despotic one, but as a hierarchy, in which the lower purposes could not simply be ignored; rather, they stood in a pre-established harmony with the higher purposes. Human purposes were also natural purposes and the theory of the human soul a part of "physics." A discussion conducted by Socrates with Thrasymachus at the beginning of the Platonic *Politeia* is characteristic. Socrates had used the image of the shepherd to characterize the ruler in a state. Thrasymachus points out that the shepherd delivers the sheep to the butcher and therefore doesn't have the well-being of the sheep in view. Socrates replies that this end is accidental to the shepherd's art. As a shepherd the shepherd provides for the well-being of the sheep. At the bottom of this is the fact that the best sheep for people are the ones that have also best been able to develop as sheep during their lives. The art of the butcher does not define the art of the shepherd. Precisely this changes in the modern world. Here, the market dictates to the breeder how he is to keep the animals, and in no way is the keeping attuned to the animals' well-being. The viewpoints of the animal protector are external to those of the animal keeper and must be asserted "from without."

The classical idea of a hierarchy of purposes presupposed something like an objective teleology: things are not only purposes *for themselves* but are *in themselves* natural purposes. Modern ontology, however, knows purposes only as tendencies to self-preservation, that is, the preservation of that which is. The definition of teleology as a tendency to self-preservation can be called an inversion of teleology. Whenever teleology is mentioned in modern biology and when teleological structures are simulated by cybernetic models, then *telos* is understood merely as the *telos for* that system. Functionality is always defined by self-preservation. Aristotle, on the contrary, had interpreted self-preservation as a lowermost form of the striving of all that is finite for participation in the eternal. The tendency toward duration in time is, so to speak, the imitation of an unattainable identity with the eternal. Medieval philosophy tried to conceive of "objective" teleology with the concept of *repraesentatio*. In the fifteenth century, philosophy paved the way for the destruction of teleology. Leibniz and Kant, however, noticed that this destruction is itself only comprehensible as the expression of definite but necessary purposes of reason.

I should like to define the two purposes, the two interests, that guide us in an ateleological and a teleological interpretation of nature as follows: the interest in the control of nature on the one hand, and, on the other, the interest in feeling at home in nature, in being able to understand ourselves as a part of nature with nature as our equal. Classical finalistic philosophy of nature is determined by this latter interest. When Aristotle says, the stone falls downward because it seeks its *oikeios topos,* its home, we consider that an anthropomorphic way of speaking. But when we say, "the dog is hungry"—is that also an anthropomorphism? Plato and Aristotle defend the view that the finalistic way of speaking about natural processes is not just a *façon de parler.* Aristotle says of Anaxagoras, who had spoken of reason in the cosmos, "He was the first sober man in contrast with the random talk of his predecessors." This sounds strange to our ears. The predicate "sober" would not occur to us in describing teleological language. Yet what Aristotle means is clear: the scientific attempt to interpret the dog's barking upon his master's return without the word happiness is somewhat fantastic. The fundamental idea in the program of a nonfinalistic reconstruction of Socrates from the Big Bang is indeed comprehensible. But it is impossible to keep this idea in mind when reading the Platonic *Apology* of Socrates. Moreover, it remains a mere program because it would only be attainable in an infinite number of steps. It strays out into the *apeiron,* and to Aristotle that means it is excessive. Thus, the talk of Empedocles is "random" when he considers directionless mutation and selection of what is conducive to survival to be sufficient for explaining the phenomenon of purposively organized beings. If man discards the teleological view of nature, he must cease understanding himself as a natural being, as a part of nature.

I do not wish to discuss here the reasons why the idea of a teleology of nature was given up at the end of the Middle Ages. Undoubtedly, it was, above all, the interest in the progressive control of nature that led to the abandonment of teleology. In order that we might subject nature to our aims, we must avert our eyes from the purposes that could be immanent in nature's beings themselves. But now, if man forgoes the teleological view of nature, he must also forgo understanding himself as a natural being, as a part of nature. That is the situation of Descartes. Should he nevertheless still wish to understand himself as a natural being, he can no longer understand himself as a being who is concerned with the good. That is the situation of Hobbes. Hobbes makes out human desire to be blind and limitless desire. No longer is there a greatest good which could set an intrinsic limit to striving. There is only a greatest evil, namely, violent death. Only fear, this mother of wisdom, limits the appetite, the desires that in themselves are infinite. So too does the reality principle of Freud. This principle of preservation is represented by the state. Since human libido in itself knows no limit, the power suppressing it must also be limitless. The position of the "right" is defined by taking sides with the preservation principle, with the reality principle or the rationality principle, where "rational" is opposed to the unlimited pursuit of pleasure. The position of the "left" is defined by taking sides with libido, pleasure, imagination, and utopia. "Self-preservation" and "self-realization" are the two leading viewpoints. What is common to both is the absence of an idea of natural finality in man and society. The concept of the *telos* splits apart, but the *disjecta membra* release energies like the splitting of an atom.

It was Rousseau's singular role in modern history to simultaneously represent both antagonistic principles in his person. He writes: "I see no tolerable mean between the strictest democracy and the most thoroughgoing Hobbesism." Rousseau denies the possibility of being a human being and a citizen at the same time. Therefore, education can rear either a human being *or* a citizen, but not both. "By nature" man is neither a speaking and rational nor a political being. Rousseau drew up educational programs for both, for the human being and for the citizen.

The antiauthoritarian upbringing of Emile is the education of the human being. The totalitarian education in the essay on "The Government of Poland" is the education of the citizen. What Rousseau abhorred was the idea of a mixed education, which produced a "double-person." Since nature is no longer understood teleologically, entering the state means leaving nature. In the second *Discourse,* Rousseau speaks of the "divine voice" that bids man to leave the state of nature. Whoever does not hear this voice, however, need not be alarmed: he may stay in the forests without falling short of any inner finality of human nature.

As Leo Strauss rightly observed, there are inevitably revolutionary consequences when the natural man—in this sense of "natural"—asserts his claims within a political order. Rousseau did not foresee that. His political writings did not have such a goal. It was not his political writings, but rather his "nature" writings that paved the way for the revolutionary sensibility of 1789. Only after the revolution did his "civil" writings, above all the *Social Contract,* begin to serve as documents legitimizing the established new order. *"Volonté générale"* is after all a "rightist" concept. It represents the preservation principle of a state's political unity. Rousseau himself writes that the *volonté générale* has been destroyed by the modern emancipation. This destruction, he says, began with Christianity, which is a "human religion," a natural religion, and not a civil religion.

The Vicomte de Bonald understood all this very well. His critique of the revolution centers on the concept of *volonté générale.* He sees in the revolution the revolt of man against the *volonté générale.* He accuses Rousseau—contrary to Rousseau's own assertions—of surrendering the *volonté générale* to the *volonté de tous,* that is, to a "will of man," which works unremittingly at destroying the *volonté générale.* Moreover, Bonald was alone in seeing the connection between this schism in modern political consciousness and the ambiguity of the word *nature.* He attempted to rehabilitate a teleological interpretation of this concept, and, with this in mind, distinguished between the concepts *"naturel"* and *"natif."* In Bonald's terms, Rousseau's *homme naturel* is merely an *homme natif.* He writes, "The bourgeois is a primitive man (an *homme natif*); Bossuet, Fénelon, Leibniz are natural men (*hommes naturels*)." Yet Bonald's attempt at reestablishing a teleological concept of nature only leads to an "inverted teleology."

Classical finalism was a transcendent and dynamic finalism. Its formulas were *"omne ens est propter suam propriam operationem"* (all being is for the sake of its own activity) and *"omne agens agit propter finem"* (all agency acts for the sake of the goal). The ultimate goal of all finite beings however was to represent God. Thomas Aquinas writes that by nature all beings love God more than they love themselves, whereas the inverted teleology receives its precise formulations from Spinoza: "*Conatus sese conservandi est essentia rerum*" (the striving for preservation is the essence of things). Bonald writes, "Man is on earth for nothing other than perfecting the means to his physical and moral self-preservation"; thus understood, the good is synonymous with subjecting the whole of life to the conditions for its preservation. The social function of preservation comes to be the highest criterion for metaphysical and religious truth. This kind of pragmatism distinguishes Bonald as a forerunner of Auguste Comte and the most important theoreticians of the right. Charles Maurras called the *"Action française" "Le parti de Bonald."* Péguy was probably the first to see the hidden nihilism of the modern right, which defends the preservation of its concerns without being able to guarantee their value. In defending the revolution against students of Comte, against the Maurassians, against the "intellectuals," Péguy understood himself to be a defender of the traditional values of France.

For it was the people of the *ancien régime* who carried out the revolution. The nonfunctional concept of truth also enabled a man like G. K. Chesterton to plead on behalf of the Jacobins. Péguy's battle for truth in the Dreyfus affair was a battle against the nihilism of the left and the right, a battle against instrumentalizing truth to serve the preservation or destruction of the established order. That is why he wrote, "Where the Dreyfus affair begins, politics ends, and where politics begins, the Dreyfus affair is over."

Truth is a purpose in itself, and all non-nihilistic politics must ultimately be subordinated to nonpolitical goals. Yet for the antiteleological functionalism of the left and the right such a truth is "abstract."

In reality, as a world-view, the positions of the left and the right are abstract positions. Politics will always be a domain of conflict, and therefore there will always be a more leftist and a more rightist mentality in politics. In a given situation, a person can place more emphasis either on the rights of man or the reason of state, which can alone guarantee these rights. Since every established order contains a certain imbalance in the distribution of burdens and compensations, there will always be some who are above all interested in increasing the opportunities and freedoms of certain groups and others who above all do not want to risk the degree of freedom and constitutional rights already attained. It is only natural that the perspective of the better situated differs from the perspective of the underprivileged. All of that is normal. Political nihilism begins where right and left are espoused as world-views, as total theories of the world and the state. Hegel demonstrated that every abstract position becomes dialectical when understood as the whole: it turns into its opposite. Marxism illustrates this in our age. It is the left par excellence: man against citizen, *homme* against *citoyen*. With the negation of Hegelian teleology as a point of departure, Marx explicitly refers to Rousseauian dualism. The political superstructure is no longer the perfection of human nature, but rather its alienation from itself. Humanity's liberator is therefore the class that has no share in any of the historical forms of human perfection, not in the family, not in civil society, not in religion. The revolution sets in motion a process of collective emancipation of natural man, of man as a species. This process is in essence unlimited, which is to say it is without goal. The unfolding of human energies and abilities is not directed toward "perfection", but is a purpose in itself. The person in the Marxist future society will be a dilettante, who does not take seriously the things he does. He will fish, he will hunt, he will criticize, without being a fisherman, a hunter, or a writer since any professional occupation would be alienation. One might recall Plato's thesis that all activities in all well constituted states take on a professional form, or Hegel's thesis that finds the alienation of man to be a necessary state in coming to one's self. For the antifinalism of Marx, all transcendence of man is only the loss of his identity. The future classless society without rule will no longer have an immanent *telos*. Its purpose will only be the progressive subjugation of external and internal nature. In order to organize this progressive subjugation of external and internal nature, however, a totalitarian order and absolute power must first be established. Where the left does not want to stand still in helplessly protesting against reality, it becomes technocratic and adopts ideas of the right in such a way that the advocates of the right now become the defenders of human freedom, which at bottom has no specifiable meaning for them, no "what for". In the first half of our century we have learned that the real result of Marx is always Comte. The real social theoretician of our age is not Marx, but Comte, only he did not succeed as a Father of the Church. The catechism of the Comteian states is the Communist Manifesto.

Progressive control of nature, "the struggle against nature," has been the leading idea of European society for the past three centuries. The classical idea, on the other hand, was that there is a final and hierarchic order of natural beings in nature with man at the summit—not, however, unlimited progress in man's subjugating nature. Human mastery of nature should, rationally, not be despotism. The idea of progressive and unlimited control of nature was an idea of the European bourgeoisie and was taken by Marx to its culmination. It is just this idea that is meeting its limits today. Ecology is the epochal event in contemporary awareness. Man, we have discovered, must again understand himself as a part of nature and nature as a final structure. If he dismisses this view as an anthropomorphism, "man" himself becomes an anthropomorphism. The idea of progressive control of nature is accompanied in Marx by another idea that replaces the idea of perfection as a purpose: the society of glut. It is evident that all repression can disappear if there is an excess of all goods. But this idea is also dead. We know today that man's material resources are limited. Therefore W. Harich recommends communism today with the argument that it better manages deficiency than expansive Western capitalism. Management of deficiency is the traditional task of the right. If Harich is right concerning socialism, then with such a recommendation he is no longer a man of the left.

Faced with ecological problems, the categories of the right and the left have become obsolete. The decisive question is whether the ecological problem is understood as a teleological problem or merely as a new technological problem. The men of the left and the right are above all technocrats. To them, the great task of curbing human need as well as organizing production and distribution is a problem of organization and police. It is decisive whether or not we succeed in grasping the limits to the control of nature as an opportunity, that is, whether we are able to rediscover the double sense of *telos* as "limit" and "meaning". The ecologically qualified new scarcity can be overcome in a spirit of justice, freedom, and human dignity, only if in public discussion we take teleological viewpoints into consideration again.

Hans Jonas

8. Ontological Grounding of a Political Ethics: On the Metaphysics of Commitment to the Future of Man*

That there are indeed duties to posterity, and that people in general are obligated by them, has been taken for granted at all times and to my knowledge is contested by no one. At the same time, the reach of these duties into the future used to be short, fading off into the distant unknown. Insofar as posterity is already with us in the persons of our children, practically everyone acknowledges and for his part implements such duties to them by rearing them, providing for them, preparing them for life, and perhaps leaving property to them. Beyond one's own offspring, posterity can be the object of care by individuals in the form of philanthropic and other bequests for the public good, intended and endowed for the long term. To the politician and statesman, whose concern is the whole, the duty to posterity naturally has a wider span in terms of the numbers, space, and time over which this whole extends. The object of such a duty can succinctly be described as insuring—and in the first place not jeopardizing—a secure, viable, morally sound and physically satisfactory commonwealth for the foreseeable future. But in the past that "foreseeable" was necessarily of a modest range and likewise the power to shape events ahead of one's own time. Beyond a certain stretch, hardly exceeding the lifetime of the newborn, future generations were expected to look after themselves. They could be trusted to be in a position to do so, as environing nature was trusted to go on yielding the wherewithal for their doing so. The problems of their day, though beyond present anticipation, were assumed to be no different in kind from our own and thus as manageable in future terms as ours are in present terms. Least of all was it a question whether there *will* be future generations and whether there *will* be a natural environment supportive of civilized human life. Thus, the

---

*From *Graduate Faculty Philosophy Journal*, vol. 10, no. 1 (Spring 1984).

much more far-fetched question whether there *ought* to be future generations at all went unasked and, as utterly redundant, could sleep its untroubled sleep in the certainty that there would be anyway.

None of this is certain anymore, none of it can still be taken for granted. A new factor has entered the human and planetary equation. It is called modern technology. Its impact on things terrestrial is such, in magnitude, time range, and quality, that our duty to posterity assumes entirely new dimensions, embraces entirely new objects, and now even includes the responsibility for there going to *be*—and for there *not failing* to be—an indefinite posterity for man on earth. Thus, the far-fetched question whether there *ought to be* is no longer redundant.

Let us consider first the *kind of obligation* toward posterity that this stern, new dispensation lays upon us. Pursuing this line of inquiry will lead of itself one step further back to the more elusive question of *whence,* from what intelligible, sanctioning ground, that obligation might draw its prescriptive force.

At the outset we must realize that the obligation involved here is not covered by the traditional idea of rights and duties—the idea grounded upon reciprocity, according to which *my* duty is the counterpart of *another's* right, which in turn is seen in the likeness of my own right: once certain rights of another are established, then my corresponding duty to respect them and, where possible, to further them, is also established. The premise here is mutuality: what goes for me also goes for the other and is indeed predicated on his observing the duty equally with regard to me. His violating my rights to that extent suspends my duty to observe his. This mutuality holds even for my duties to the larger whole, my country, my polity, my nation, as Socrates so eloquently argued in the *Crito*.

This whole scheme fails for our purpose. Obviously, posterity cannot reciprocate my observation of rights. Even the concept of a unilateral right of posterity over me is invalid when the issue is posterity's coming to exist in the first place. For only that which *makes* claims *has* a claim—and to make claims it must first of all *exist*. Everything alive makes a claim to life, and perhaps this is a right to be respected. The nonexistent makes no demands and can therefore not suffer violation of its rights. It may have rights when it exists, but it does not have them by virtue of the mere possibility that it will one day exist. The claim to existence begins only with existence. But the ethic we seek is concerned with just this not-yet-existent, and its principle of responsibility must be independent of any idea of a right and therefore also of a reciprocity—so that within the framework of this sought-after ethic, the question jokingly invented for the situation, "What has the future ever done for me? Does it respect my rights?", cannot possibly be asked.

Now it is easy to see that the duty toward children and the duty toward later generations are not the same. The duty to care for the currently existing child produced by us can, even without the incentive of feeling, readily be based upon the responsibility of the *cause* for its effect, that is, upon our having *originated* the child's existence, and then, in consequence, upon the *right* that henceforth pertains to this existent and issues from its being. Thus, despite nonreciprocity, the obligation here rests on the classical principle of rights and duties, albeit both unilateral in this case (the suckling has no complementary duty, the parent no complementary right). But something other than the duty arising *from* procreation, which already corresponds to a right arising from existence, would be the duty *to* such procreation, to the generating of children, to reproduction in general. This duty, if it exists, is far more difficult to prove, if at all, and then surely not from the same principle; and a *right* of the unborn to be born (more precisely: of the ungenerated to generation) is simply not arguable from any principle whatsoever. Thus, here we would deal with a duty that is not the counterpart of another's right—unless it be the right of the Creator God over his creatures, to whom, with the bestowal of existence, he has entrusted this continuation of his work.

It is this sort of duty that is involved in a responsibility for future mankind. It charges us, in the first place, with ensuring that there *be* a future mankind—even if no descendants of ours are among them—and second, with a duty toward their *condition,* the "quality" of their lives. The first duty involves the duty of procreation (though not necessarily everyone's) and as such is not deducible, by extension, from the duty of the begetter toward the life already begotten. If that more general and prior duty—to their *being* a posterity—does exist, as we would like to suppose, we have yet to show its sanctioning ground, one that it needs all the more, the less it is supported by a natural urge of feeling. That grounding will be our speculative task. The very setting of the task implies that any duties toward the *quality* of future life are predicated on this presumptive duty to ensure that there *be* future life and with it future subjects of possible rights—and this duty answers to no right whatsoever, but rather gives *us* in the first place the (otherwise dubious) right to bring beings like ourselves into the world without their choice. The individual right to procreation follows from the general duty to continued human existence, and not vice versa. That primary duty, totally one-sided, empowers us vis-à-vis all those who succeed us, not so much to grant them the gift of their existence (which ill agrees with forcing it upon them) as to *tax* them with it—namely, with the very sort of existence that is capable of the burden that is the true object of our duty to bestow that existence.

Thus, the first rule for the mandatory "quality of life" of our descendants is gained from the *imperative* of their existence, and all further rules are subject to its criterion. The first rule is, therefore, that no condition of future descendants of humankind should be permitted to arise that contradicts the reason why the existence of mankind is mandatory at all. The imperative that there be a mankind comes first.

With this imperative we are, strictly speaking, not responsible to future human individuals but to the *idea* of Man, which is such that it demands the presence of its embodiment in the world. It is, in other words, an *ontological* idea, which does not, however, (as the "ontological proof" alleges to do with the concept of God) guarantee the existence by the very essence of its subject—far from it! Instead it entails that such a presence *ought* to be and be watched over, thus making that presence a duty for us who can endanger it. It is this ontological imperative, emanating from the idea of Man, that stands behind the prohibition of a *banco* gamble with mankind. Only the idea of Man, by telling us *why* there should be men, also tells us *how* they should be. The truly categorical imperative, which thus arises out of the novel dangers to the continued human presence in the world, commands nothing but this: *that* there be *human beings,* with the accent equally on the *that* and the *what* of obligatory existence. Since the principle of this imperative is not an idea of *action* (of how to behave), but rather the idea of possible agents in general, claiming that they *ought to exist* (fallible as they must be), it is "ontological," that is, an idea of *being*. It follows that the first principle of an "ethic of futurity", committing us to the future of man as such, does not itself lie *within* ethics as a doctrine of action (within which thereafter all duties toward future beings belong) but within *metaphysics* as a doctrine of being, of which the idea of Man is a part. Can we provide such a reasoned, metaphysical principle? At least we must make the attempt, so as not to leave the asserted commitment to the mercies of its immediate emotional appeal. Let us, then, try our hand at the needed ontological underpinning.

At the very outset it must be clear to anyone even fleetingly aware of the current consensus in philosophy that an attempt of this kind runs head-on against the stone wall of two of the most firmly entrenched theoretical dogmas of our time: that there is no metaphysical truth, and that no "ought" can be derived from "being." I refuse to be intimidated by either. To take the second first—asserting an unbridgeable gulf between "is" and "ought"—this result of a previous epoch-making critique, formative of the modern mind, has never been seriously questioned. Plainly, it is true only of a concept of being that has been suitably neutralized beforehand as "value free"—so that the nonderivability of an "ought" from it follows tautologically. To expand this trivial conclusion into a general axiom is equivalent to asserting that no other concept of being is possible, or that the one serving as the premise here and ultimately borrowed from the natural sciences is the true and complete concept of being. Thus, with the very assumption of such a concept of being, the rigid separation of "is" and "ought" itself already reflects a definite *metaphysics*, one that can only boast the critical (Occamistic) advantage that it makes the most parsimonious assumption about being, and therefore the one most meager for the purpose of explaining the phenomena—hence, at the price of their impoverishment.

But if the dogma that no path leads from "is" to "ought" is, by reason if its ontological presupposition, a metaphysical proposition, then it falls under the interdict of the first and more fundamental dogma: that there is no metaphysical truth. *This* contention has its own presupposition to which *its* validity is tied.

Just as the dogma of "is" and "ought" presupposes a definite concept of being, so the denial of metaphysical truth presupposes a definite concept of knowledge, for which it is indeed true: "scientific" truth is not to be had about metaphysical objects—once again a tautological conclusion since science is just concerned with physical objects. So long as it is not indisputably shown that this exhausts the whole concept of knowledge, the last word on the possibility of metaphysics has not yet been spoken. It is indeed the arrogated or too readily accorded epistemological monopoly of modern science, expanded into an ontological monopoly, that has created the deadlock in which ethical theory finds itself. For the very same movement that put us in possession of the powers that now have to be regulated by norms—the movement of modern knowledge called natural science—has by a necessary complementarity eroded the foundations from which norms could be derived. It has destroyed the very idea of norm as such. First it was nature that was "neutralized" with respect to value, then man himself. Now we shiver in the nakedness of a nihilism in which near-omnipotence is paired with near-emptiness, greatest capacity with knowing least what for.

In any case, for the sake of our required first ethical principle (which should tell us why future men matter by showing that "Man" matters), we cannot avoid taking the imprudent plunge into ontology, even if the only ground we can ever hope to reach there should prove no more secure than any at which pure theory must come to a halt. It may well be forever suspended above an abyss of the unknowable.

To ground the "good" or "value" in being is to bridge the alleged chasm between "is" and "ought". For the good or valuable, when it is this of itself and not just by grace of someone's desiring, needing or choosing, is by its very concept a thing whose being possible entails the demand for its being or becoming actual. Thus, it becomes an "ought" when a will is present that can hear the demand and translate it into action. Therefore, we say that a "command" can issue not only from a commanding will, for instance, of a personal God, but also from the immanent claim of a good-in-itself to be realized. If, however, "the good" or "value" is indeed something by itself, then it belongs to the stock of being in general and in that case axiology becomes a part of ontology. Let us see in what sense being harbors value and where in its self-display that value is visibly situated.

Nature entertains ends or gives play to aims: this we know from their patent and passionate presence throughout animal subjectivity antecedent to and below the level of man. But in having or allowing ends, nature also posits values. For with any *de facto* pursued end (whatever its origin), its attainment becomes a good, and its frustration an evil; with this distinction the predicability of value begins. But from *within* the already decided goal commitment, where henceforth only success or failure counts (whether or not the cat catches the mouse), no judgment about the goodness of the goal itself is possible, and thus, beyond factual interest, no obligation can be derived from it. Therefore, insofar as ends, including our own, are actually at play within nature, they seem to enjoy no other dignity than that of mere facts and would then have to be measured not by their worth but only by their motivating strength and perhaps by the pleasure attending their achievement (or the pain attending their denial). We could then only say that under their spell there is a better and a worse, but not that through them a good-in-itself demands our affirmation. Is there, then, any sense in saying that anything *ought* to be, whether or not it promotes its coming-to-be on its own by influencing desire, instinct, or will? We have said that a "good-in-itself" would be such a thing. But so far good or evil has only shown itself as the concomitant of an already *existing* goal orientation that is left to exercise such power over the will as is *ex post facto* attested by the will's "decisions"—the result of just that power. The implanted purpose looks after itself and requires no "ought" nor could it provide a ground for it in itself. At best it might use the fiction of an "ought" as a means of enhancing its power.

But is what is true of the particular purpose—namely, that its factuality comes first, and the validity of "good" and "bad" relative to it comes second, determined by the first (*de facto*) but not legitimized by it (*de jure*)—also true of "purposiveness" itself, as an *ontological* characteristic of an entity? Here, it seems to me, matters are different. We can regard the mere *capacity* to *have* any purposes at all as a good-in-itself, which we grasp with intuitive certainty as infinitely superior to any purposelessness of being. Whatever measure of self-evidence this judgment possesses, there is plainly no going behind it for something more basic to undergird it. One can only oppose it with the doctrine of *nirvana*, which denies the value of having purpose, but then again affirms the value of liberation from it, making this its purpose. Since indifference is clearly not possible here (what is denied becomes a negative value), at least he who does not embrace the paradox of a purpose-denying purpose must concur in the proposition that purpose as such is its own accreditation within being and must postulate this as an *ontological axiom*. Now it already follows analytically from the *formal* concept of good-in-itself that, whenever this first, self-validating good happens, in any of its individuations, to come under the custody of a will, it addresses an "ought" to this will. And the *content* of this first good is nothing else than what is affirmed in that first, axiomatic intuition: the superiority of purpose as such over purposelessness. Let us try to articulate this intuition somewhat further.

In purposiveness as such, whose reality and efficacy in the world speak through the witness of things alive, we can see a fundamental self-affirmation of being, positing itself absolutely as the better over against nonbeing. In every purpose, being declares itself for itself and against nothingness. Against this verdict of being there is no counterverdict, for even saying "no" to being betrays an interest and a purpose. Hence, the mere fact that being is not indifferent toward itself makes its difference from nonbeing the basic value of all values, the first "yes" in general. This difference rests not so much in the distinction of a "*some*thing" from nothingness (which, when the something is value-indifferent, would merely be the again indifferent distinction between two matters of indifference), but rather in the distinction of goal-interest as such from indifference as such, of which we could regard nothingness to be the absolute form. An indifferent *being* would be only a less perfect form of nothingness (because afflicted with the blemish of senselessness) and not really thinkable. That being is concerned with something, at least with itself, is the first thing we can learn about it from the presence of purpose within it. The subsequent value, deriving from the basic value of being as such and enhancing its difference from nonbeing, would be the maximization of purposiveness, that is, the growing wealth of goals striven for and thus of possible good or evil. The more manifold the purpose, the greater the difference; the more intense it is, the more emphatic the affirmation and, at the same time, its justification. In it, being makes itself worth its own effort.

In organic life, nature has made its interest manifest and progressively satisfies it, at the rising cost of concomitant anxiety, frustration, and extinction, in the staggering variety of life's forms, each of which is a mode of being and striving. The price is necessary, since each purpose can only be realized at the cost of other purposes. The existing generic multiplicity represents such a selection, of which it is impossible to say whether it was always the "best," but whose preservation is certainly a good compared to the alternative of annihilation or impoverishment. But more still than in the extensiveness of the generic spectrum, nature's interest manifests itself in the intensity of the goal-striving of the living creatures themselves, in which the natural purpose becomes increasingly *subjective*, that is, increasingly the individual executants' very own. In this sense, every feeling and striving being is not only an end of nature, but also an end in itself, namely, its own end. And precisely here, the self-affirmation of being becomes emphatic in the opposition of life to death. Life is the explicit confrontation of being with not-being. For in its constitutional neediness, given with the necessity of metabolism, which can be denied fulfillment, it contains within itself the possibility of not-being as its ever-present antithesis—as threat. Its mode of being is preservation through doing. The "yes" of all striving is here sharpened by the active "no" to not-being. Through the negated not-being (which the warding off of extinction through self-preservation is), being becomes a positive concern, that is, a constant choosing of itself. Life as such, in the inherently co-present danger of not-being, is an expression of this choice. Thus, it is only an apparent paradox that it should be *death*, that is, the being-liable-to-die (being "mortal"), and being so at every moment and its equally ceaseless deferment every moment by the *act* of self-preservation that sets the seal upon the self-affirmation of being: in this contrapuntal pairing, the self-affirmation of being turns into single efforts of individual beings.

This blindly self-enacting "yes" gains obligating force in the sighted freedom of man, which as the supreme outcome of nature's purposive labor is no longer its automatic executor but, with the power obtained from knowledge, can become its destroyer as well. He must adopt the "yes" into his will and impose the "no" to not-being on his power. But precisely this transition from willing to obligation is the critical point of moral theory where attempts at laying a foundation for it come so easily to grief. Why does what "being" itself hitherto attended to through all individual willings now, in man, become a duty? Why this standing out of man from nature, such that he is supposed to come to the aid of her governance with norms and therefore to impose limits on his own unique, natural inheritance, arbitrary will? Would not the fullest exercise of just this arbitrariness be the fulfillment of the natural purpose which brought it forth— wherever it might lead, and be it spectacular self-extinction? A heroic tragedy, thus, willed by nature? Just this completion of the species' destiny by its own deeds would then be the value-in-itself toward which the movement of being had striven, and this its vote, forecast in the crazy venture that nature permitted herself with men—the fitting tragic conclusion thereof. Something like this would not be ruled out for individual lives: did not Homer excel the grand perishing of heroes like Hector and Achilles and prefer it to the survival of a Thersites?

But is *mankind* free to commit suicide, as the individual and even the virtuous well may? We are back at the dichotomy of "will and duty." To be sure, no *will* to perish can be imputed to "mankind" nor even the willingness to risk it. But who is "mankind" and where in its case lies the willing? Ultimately nowhere than in the individuals, through whom also the urge to self-preservation operates. And there it is the very ways of short-term self-preservation and self-satisfaction that may lead in the long term to perishing—and most perhaps through their mightiest triumphs with the help of technology, which by inherent purpose is the servant of life. Each of its single and immediate ends, necessary as well as gratuitous, is indeed life in one of its wants or desires—wealth, health, ease, pleasure, power, security, and so on. But the sum of all these currently satisfied ends of the moment (and even Five-Year-Plans are "of the Moment") can by its sheer magnitude issue into their opposite: the great nothing of the exhaustion of their sources in the bounded order of terrestrial life.

Therefore, the capacity of having and pursuing ends—that primary value that being ushered in with life—must in man be complemented by an "ought" that confronts the will with an independent force. Animals have neither the need nor the capacity for it. The "ought," however, can emanate only from the concept of an objective good. And whence do we obtain that? From the contemplation of being, of which again only man is capable. The good-in-itself discerned there, independent of desire, demands to *become* an end. It seems, then, that we must distinguish between "value" and "the good": value draws, the good obligates. We must examine once again the meaning of "value" and of "good."

Linguistically, "the good" as compared with "value" has the objectively greater dignity. We are inclined to understand it as something independent of our wishing and thinking. "Value," on the other hand, is easily tied to the questions "For whom?" and "How much?" The word stems from the sphere of appraisal and exchange. It thus designates at first only a measure of willing, namely, of the will to spend, and not of an honor due. I set myself something as an end because it is worth something to me, or it is worth something to me because it is already, prior to all choosing, set as an end to my indigent nature by one of its congenital needs: in acting on it, perhaps by selection from among competing ends, I make the specific natural end my actual own for the moment. Thus, *every* purpose I set myself is by this alone identified as a "value" that is now worth the effort of pursuing (plus the forsaking of those ends I consequently cannot pursue). The exchange value of the effort—its "recompense"—is here pleasure, including its most refined varieties. If the attained end disappoints me in this and leads me to the conclusion that it was not worth the effort after all, then in the future, too, my better informed desire will only consult itself regarding a more rewarding choice of ends, but not these ends themselves regarding their claim upon my choice. Even the revised judgment, although better informed and thus perhaps more successful, need be no less subjective and hence no more binding than the original one.

Nevertheless, we do not let ourselves be dissuaded from distinguishing between worthy and unworthy ends, and this independently of whether or not desire will get a good bargain out of them. We postulate with this distinction that what *is* worth my effort does not of itself coincide with what just *appeals to me* as worth my effort. However, what is truly worth my effort *should* also become *to me* a matter worth it and therefore *made* by me into a purpose. Now "truly worth the effort" must mean that the object of the effort is *good*, independently of the verdict of my inclinations. Precisely this makes it the source of an "ought," with which it addresses the subject in the situation where the realization or preservation of *this* good by *this* subject is a concrete issue. No voluntaristic or appetitive theory that defines the good as what is desired, does justice to this primordial phenomenon of *demanding*. If the good is a mere creature of the will, it lacks the authority to bind the will. Instead of determining its choice, it is subject to it and is one time this, another time that. Only its foundation in being places it over against the will. The independent good demands that it become purpose. It cannot compel the free will to make it its purpose, but it can extort from it the recognition that this would be its duty. If not in obeying, this recognition manifests itself in the feeling of guilt: we failed to give the good its due.

However, just as we are not willing to part with the distinction between desire and obligation, we will always feel certain that doing the good for its own sake also in some sense benefits the agent, and this regardless of the success of his action. Whether he is allowed to enjoy the achieved good himself or not, whether he lives to see it achieved or not, even should he see his action fail, his moral being has gained with the obedient acceptance of the call of duty. Yet *this* benefit must not have been the good he willed. The secret or paradox of morality is that the self forgets itself in the pursuit of the object, so that a higher self (which indeed is also a good in itself) might come into being as a concomitant effect. To be sure, I am allowed to say, "I wish to look myself in the eye (or pass God's scrutiny)," but just this will be possible only if my concern was with the object and not with myself: the self must not itself become the object, and the deed's object only the occasion for it. The good man is not he who made himself good but rather he who did the good for its own sake. But this good is a "cause" at issue out there in the world; indeed, in its generic principle, it is *the* worldly cause as such. Morality can never have itself for its goal. That is, it is not the moral law that motivates moral action by the reverence it evokes for itself (as Kant said); the prime mover is rather the appeal of this or that possible good-in-itself in the world, an appeal that confronts my will and demands to be heard—*in accordance with* the moral law. To grant that appeal a hearing *is* precisely what the moral law commands; this law is nothing but the general enjoinder of the call of all action-dependent "goods" and of their situation-determined *right* to just *my* action. It makes my duty what insight has shown to be, of itself, *worthy* of being and in *need* of my acting. For that enjoinder to reach and affect me, so that it can move the will, I must be receptive to appeals of this kind. Our emotional side must come into play. And it is indeed of the essence of our moral nature that the appeal, as insight transmits it, find an answer in our feeling—the feeling of responsibility.

Our position, then, can be stated quite simply: things, not states of my will, matter. By engaging the will, the things become ends. *Being* (or instances of it), disclosed to a sight not blocked by selfishness or dimmed by dullness, may indeed instill reverence—and can with this affection of our feeling come to the aid of the otherwise powerless moral law, which bids us to honor the intrinsic claim of being. Yet not even "reverence" is enough, for this emotional affirmation of the perceived dignity of the object, however vivid, can remain entirely passive. Only the added *feeling of responsibility*, which binds this subject to this object, will make us act on its behalf. We contend that it is this feeling, more than any other, that may generate a willingness to sustain the object's claim to existence by our action. Finally, let us remember that the care of progeny, so spontaneous that it need not invoke the moral law, is the primordial human case of the coincidence of objective responsibility and the subjective feeling of the same. Through it, nature has educated us in advance and prepared our feeling for all the other kinds of responsibility not so buttressed by instinct.

The responsibility for later posterity and the future of mankind in general, let alone the future of life on earth, is not so buttressed by instinct. How do our very broad musings on the intrinsic claims of things apply to these distant and seemingly abstract objects? Well, they are not so abstract anymore since they have moved into the lengthened reach of our present, everyday actions. Responsibility is a correlate of power, and our power today encompasses these things. They are also in the class of things corruptible and thereby fulfill the other condition for objects of responsibility. What time cannot affect and to which nothing can happen—the eternal—is an object not of responsibility but of emulation, as was the object of the Platonic *eros*. Only for the changeable and the perishable can one be responsible, for what is threatened by corruption, for the mortal in its mortality. Life is such in its very essence, and not merely the lives of individuals but the life of the species as well—and the whole flimsy film of organismic life on the surface of the globe. With all of this, nature put herself in jeopardy when she let man emerge. By endowing him with the terrifying gifts of free-roaming intellect and will, enabling him through them to imperil her other creations and most of all himself, she has also burdened him with responsibility in the use of those powers. Teeming nature, we may rest assured, however despoiled, will survive the worst follies of man. We may not be so sure whether man will survive man. We declare precisely this to be his preeminent duty. But is he really worth it? May he not justly perish from the earth if he foolishly or knavishly abuses the powers bequeathed him? Why is mankind forbidden the exit of suicide that every individual is allowed? We must answer this question.

Lest we indulge ourselves in unbecoming pride, I hasten to say this first about man's prerogative among the claimants on human responsibility: it has nothing to do with a balance sheet of mankind's performance on earth, that is, with whether mankind has so far been deserving of the preference. The Socratic life or the Beethoven symphony, which one might adduce for the justification of the whole, can always be countered with such a catalogue of incessant atrocities that, depending on the appraiser's disposition, the balance can turn out to be very negative indeed. The pity and outrage of the pessimist are not really refutable here. The price of the human enterprise is, in any case, enormous; man's wretchedness is at least equal to his greatness. On the whole, I believe the defender of mankind, despite the great atoners like Saint Francis on his side, has the more difficult case. But such value assessments have as little bearing on the ontological issue as the hedonistic balance of happiness and unhappiness (which also tends to have a negative outcome when—and because—attempted). The dignity of man *per se* can only be spoken of as potential, otherwise it is the speech of unpardonable vanity. Against all this, the *existence* of mankind comes first, whether deserved on its past record *and* its likely continuation or not. It is the ever-transcendent *possibility*, obligatory in itself, that must be kept open by continued existence. To preserve this possibility is a cosmic responsibility—hence mankind's duty to exist. Put epigrammatically: The possibility of there being responsibility in the world, which is bound to the existence of men, is of all objects of responsibility the first.

It is so because with the capacity for responsibility something transcendent has come forth from the labors of evolution. It is bound up with the two other transcendent capacities that it presupposes and complements: reason and free choice. Now this threefold innate endowment of our nature, which is nothing other than the capability (albeit fallible) for truth, valuation, and freedom, is a thing unique and stupendous to behold in the stream of becoming, from which it emerged, and which in essence it transcends, but by which it can also be swallowed again. Therefore, its possession, as much as we are granted it, purports that there is something *infinite* for us to preserve in the flux, but also something infinite for us to lose. Most evidently, the authority which it imparts can never include the disfiguring, endangering, or refashioning of itself. No gain is worth this price, no hope of gain justifies this risk. And yet, today, this very share of transcendence is also in danger of being thrown into the crucible of biotechnological alchemy—as if the enabling condition of all our freedom to revise the given were itself among the revisable. What in all our technological gamblings we must never forget is this: among the stakes risked in the game, there is one of metaphysical rank (physical as its origins may be), an "absolute" that, as a supreme and vulnerable trust, lays upon us the supreme duty to preserve it intact. This duty is incomparably superior to all the injunctions and wishes of a meliorism in the peripheral zones, and where it is concerned, the question is no longer one of weighing chances of finite profit and loss, but one of contraposing the risk of infinite loss against chances of finite gains. No weighing (for example, of probability differentials) has a place between these incommensurables. When it comes to this core phenomenon of our humanity, which is to be preserved in its integrity at all costs and which has not to await its perfection in the future because it is already whole in its essence as we possess it, then indeed the well-founded prognosis of doom has greater force than any concurrent prognosis of bliss. For be it equally well or even better founded, it necessarily pertains to matters on a lower plane. The reproach of "pessimism" leveled at such partisanship for the "prophecy of doom" can be countered with the remark that the greater pessimism is on the side of those who consider the given to be so bad or worthless that every gamble for its possible improvement is defensible.

With what we have learned on our tortuous journey through the landscape of "is" and "ought," we have also gained an answer to the question we earlier called "the critical point of moral theory," namely *what passage leads from willing to obligation*: from willing, which in every case, just by pursuing any end, actualizes nature's purpose of purposiveness in general and thus is a "good" in itself, to the "ought" which commands or forbids it particular purposes? The transition is mediated by the phenomenon of *power* in its uniquely human sense, in which causal force joins with knowledge and freedom. "Power" as purposive causal strength is in evidence through much of animal life. Great is the power of tigers and elephants, greater that of termites and locusts, greater still that of bacteria and viruses. But it is blind and unfree, although driven by purpose, and it finds its natural boundary in the counterplay of all the other forces that carry on the natural purpose just as blindly and choicelessly and, in the process, hold the manifold whole in symbiotic equilibrium. Here, we may say, natural purpose is administered severely but well, that is, the instrinsic self-set task of being discharges itself automatically. Only in man is power emancipated from the whole through knowledge and arbitrary will such that it can become fatal to him and to itself. His capacity is his fate and increasingly becomes the general fate. In him therefore, and in him alone, there arises out of the willing itself the "ought" as the self-control of his consciously exercised power—and first of all with reference to his own being. Since in him the principle of purposiveness has reached its highest and self-jeopardizing peak through the freedom to set himself ends and the power to carry them out, he himself becomes, in the name of that principle, the first object of his obligation, which we expressed in our "first imperative": not to ruin (as he well *can do*) what nature has achieved in him by his way of using it. Beyond this commitment to himself, he becomes the custodian of every other end-in-itself that ever falls under the rule of his power. We omit here what lies beyond these duties of guarding and preserving: obligations to ends that he first *creates* as it were out of nothing. For creativity lies outside the bounds of duty, which extends no further than to making it possible, that is, to keeping intact its ontological premise, the being of man as such. This is its more modest, but more stringent duty. In sum, that which binds will and obligation together in the first place, *power*, is precisely that which today moves responsibility into the center of morality. That this must issue in a *political* ethics follows from the fact that the power, as a collective-social one, must be collectively controlled. That its ultimate norm needs a valid grounding was the philosophical premise of this paper. To find it in the breadth and depth of being was the object of its, sometimes heretical, groping.

Author's Note: This paper embodies extensive parts from various chapters (mainly 2 and 4) of my book *The Imperative of Responsibility: In Search of an Ethics for the Technological Age*, The University of Chicago Press: Chicago and London, 1984, which was still in the manuscript stage when the paper was delivered. The passages in question are not marked as quotations and are here reprinted with the summary permission of The University of Chicago Press.

Jean-François Lyotard

9. *Notes on Legitimation**

I would like to explore here the question of totalitarianism from an apparently narrow point of view: that of the language of legitimation. I believe this approach to be more radical than any other—be it politico-logical, sociological, or historical—to the extent that it operates without recourse to certain received entities that often go unquestioned, such as power, society, the people, tradition, and so on. It seems to me, moreover, that this approach allows us to distinguish between states of totalitarianism whose differences are hidden or confused by the somewhat totalizing nature of the term itself.

I.

Without attempting to explain here my recourse to this choice, I will begin by recalling a certain distinction made by Kant, one that belongs to the political philosophy of the critical Aufklärung. In *Perpetual Peace* (second section, first article), Kant distinguishes the *forma imperii*, the form in which denomination is exercised, from the *forma regiminis*, the principle according to which the state makes use of its power. The first form, that of domination (*Beherrschung*), consists of the delegation of the supreme power, either to a single person (autocracy), to a few (aristocracy), or to all (democracy). The form of the regime (*Regierung*) is either despotic or republican, depending on whether the executive and legislative powers are merged. Kant immediately adds that the democratic form, which is the mode of domination that accords the exercise of public power directly to all citizens without the mediation of representative instances, calls for a regime that is necessarily despotic, since the people is then, as sovereign, at once the legislator and the executor of its own decisions. Inversely, according to Kant, an autocrat like Frederick II of Prussia can exercise his domination in a mode that is analogically republican in respect to its regime.

Clearly the question of legitimation is not directly treated in this passage from *Perpetual Peace*. However, I would now like to graft that question onto the distinction between despotic and republican regimes.

---

*Translated by Cecile Lindsay.

The subject of a normative phrase can be termed the *instance* of legitimation. A phrase is called normative when, having as its object a prescriptive phrase, it gives that prescriptive phrase the force of a law. Take the prescriptive, *It is obligatory for x to accomplish action a*. The normative phrase would be enunciated as, *It is a norm decreed by y that it is obligatory for x to accomplish action a*. Formulated in this way, the normative phrase designates, here under the name of y, the instance that legitimates the prescription addressed to x. The legislative power is held by y. Kant's formulation of despotism and republicanism can easily be situated within this small complex of phrases.

If one now asks who could be y in order to hold this legislative authority, then one immediately falls back into the customary forms of aporia: either that of the vicious circle (y has authority over x because x authorizes y to have it); or that of *petitio principii* (authorization authorizes authority; that is, it is the normative phrase that authorizes y to make norms); or the aporia of infinite regress (x is authorized by y who is authorized by z, and so on); or, finally, the paradox of the idiolect, in Wittgenstein's sense (God, or life, or some capital "A" designates y to exercise authority, but y is the only witness to this revelation).

I would claim that, at least within the framework of a reflection on totalitarianism, two major language procedures come to mask the logical aporiae of authorization (or to fill in the ontological abyss) witnessed by that reflection. Both procedures have recourse to narration; that is, on the surface at least, both dissipate this lack by spreading out the initial difficulty along the diachronic axis. But that is their only point in common. For while one effects this expansion backwards, towards an origin, the other one extends forward, toward an end. To simplify greatly, for which I hope I will be excused, let me say that one of these narrations shapes the mythic narratives that are indispensable to traditional communities, while the other shapes the narratives of emancipation (which I call metanarratives in *The Postmodern Condition*).

Without losing sight of the question of totalitarianism, it is appropriate at this point to specify the respective functionings of these two procedures.

II.

In order to be entirely clear, I ought to begin by exposing what underlies the argument of this presentation, which has to do with language. But I cannot do that here; I will have to settle for an abridgment. Language is the object of an Idea. It does not exist as a stock of tools from which "speakers" (generally humans) draw in order to express themselves or to communicate. Freed from this functionalist approach, we will see that the only *givens* are phrases: myriads of phrases. We will see that these phrases, no matter how modest and ephemeral (or silent) they may be, not only express meanings but also situate within the universes that they present an addressor, an addressee, and a referent. We will see that families or regimes of phrases can be distinguished by the fact that it is impossible to convert one phrase into another without modifying what can be called, for the sake of simplicity, the pragmatic situation of the instances I have just designated (referent, addressor, addressee). The phrase *The door is closed* is a descriptive; it presents a universe where the question posed is whether or not the door is closed, a universe that is thus governed by the criterion of truth or falsehood. The phrase *Close the door* is a prescriptive; the question it calls for bears on the justice of the obligation it directs to the addressee and on the execution of the act it prescribes. We have just seen that a normative phrase obeys a regime completely different from that of a prescriptive. The same holds true for an interrogative, a performative (in the strict sense), or an exclamative.

The other underlying aspect of my argument, one which I think has a great deal more importance for an understanding of totalitarianism, is that each phrase, no matter how ordinary, happens as an event. I do not mean that the phrase is exceptional or sensational or that it marks an epoch, but that it is never necessary as far as its particular content is concerned. It is necessary *that* something happen, an occurrence, but *what* happens (the phrase, its meaning, its object, its interlocutors) is never necessary. It is the necessity of contingency, or if you will, the being of nonbeing. The link that exists between one phrase and another is not, in principle, predetermined. Certainly various genres of discourse exist: the exposition (of which this is an example), the dialectic (which we call discussion), the tragic genre, the comic genre, satire (the genre of genres), the essay, the diary, and so on. These genres of discourse impose upon the linkage of phrases a set of rules that assure that a given discourse proceeds properly towards the end assigned it by a particular genre: to convince, to persuade, to provoke tears or laughter, and so forth. Respect for these rules thus permits the linkage of phrases toward a generic end. But as we know, these rules for linkage only pass as respectable (if they do at all) in classical poetics and rhetoric. Modern writers and artists multiply their infractions of these rules, precisely because they accord a greater value to the pursuit of the event than to any concern for imitation or conformity. Like Auerbach, I would classify Augustine among the moderns, alongside Rabelais, Montaigne, Shakespeare, Sterne, Joyce, or Gertrude Stein. Modern infraction is of interest not because it constitutes a transgression, as Bataille thought, but because it reopens the question of nothingness, of the event, which is something that Benjamin demonstrates in respect to Baudelaire, or Barthes in his theory of the text and of writing.

III.

I now return to a consideration of the legitimating narrative and totalitarianism. Let us first look at mythic narration.

It's an old question, one already elaborated by Schelling: Is the myth originary, or is the origin mythic? Freud came up against the same question. A corpus of narratives from a traditional culture, that of the Cashinahua Indians, is documented, along with its ritual of transmission, by André Marcel d'Ans. This corpus includes narratives of origin and what may properly be called myths, but it also includes little stories, tales, and legends. What is important for our question, it seems to me, lies in the pragmatics of the narration rather than in an analysis of the narrative content. In order to *hear* the Cashinahua narratives, one must bear a Cashinahua name (as in the case of the anthropologist) and be a male or a young girl before puberty. In order to *recount* these narratives, one must have a Cashinahua name and be a man. Finally, any Cashinahua, without exception, can *be the object* of one of these narratives. Narrative transmission thus operates under certain constraints. These constraints bring into play the division of the community into kinship groups that regulate exogamic unions. The Cashinahua distinguish two masculine "halves," two feminine ones, and two age groups within each half, resulting in eight kinship groups. As the ethnologist notes, "The explicit function of the exogamic unions is the transmission of *names*." The constraints on the narrative pragmatic must be understood as rules for the authentification and conservation of narratives, and thereby of the community itself, through the repetition of names.

The ethnologist confirms this when he notes that every narrative opens with a fixed formula: "This is the history of. . . , such as I have always heard it told. I will tell it to you in my turn; listen to it!" And this recitation, he adds, invariably closes with another formula that says: "Here ends the story of. . . .He who has recounted it to you is. . . (Cashinahua name), known by the Whites as. . . (Spanish or Portuguese name)." By attaching the story told to the names of its three instances—the narrator, his listener, and the hero—the narrative ritual legitimates the story by inscribing it within the world of Cashinahua names.

The result is a characteristic treatment of historical time. Each narrator affirms that he has "always heard" the story he recounts. He has been the story's listener, and his narrator was formerly, in his own turn, a listener. The same thing can be said of the whole chain of transmission. Thus, the heroes themselves must have been their own first narrators. The time of the diegesis, where the recounted action takes place, communicates without interruption with the time of the present narration, which recounts that action. Two operations assure this panchronicity: first, the stability of the names, which are finite in number and are distributed to individuals according to a system that is independent of time; second, the permutability of the individuals named in respect to the three narrative instances (narrator, listener, hero)—a permutability regulated by the ritual at each occurrence.

I believe this language apparatus to be exemplary for our first *forma regiminis*, our first regime, the one Kant calls despotic, as well as for the legitimation of the normative instance that corresponds to it. Names—those "rigid designators," as Kripke says—determine a world: a world of names that is the cultural world. This world is finite because the number of names available here is finite. This world has always been the same. Each human comes into it in his place, that is, under a name that will determine his relations to other names. This place governs all the sexual, economic, social, or language exchanges that he has the right or the duty to have or not have with other bearers of names. An event (here we are) is introduced into the tradition only if it is clothed in a story that is itself subject to the rule of names, as much by what it recounts (its referents: its heroes, its setting, its time) as by its way of being recounted (its narrator, its listeners). Thus, the void that in principle separates two phrases and that makes a phrase an event is filled in by the narrative, which is itself subordinated to the repetition of the world of names and to their permutations on the different instances. The Cashinahua identity, the "we" that gathers together the three narrative instances, escapes in this way the vertigo of contingency and nothingness. And because it is in the nature of narrative to be able to gather, put in order, and transmit not only descriptions but also prescriptions, evaluations, feelings (for example, exclamatory or interrogative phrases), then tradition transmits the obligations attached to names along with prescriptions bearing on a given situation. And tradition legitimates them simply by placing them under the authority of the Cashinahua name.

The Cashinahua call themselves "the true men." Any natural or human event that lies outside their tradition, any event having no name, *is not*, because it is not authorized (not "true"). Authority is not *represented* in the modern sense; the Cashinahua people legislate through the transmission of their narratives, and in executing them (for the names create obligations of all kinds), the people exert the executive power. A politics is thus very much at stake in this narrative practice; but it is immersed in the whole of the life instituted by the narratives, and in this sense it can be called "totalitarian."

I am aware that my description is in certain ways simplistic. An ethnologist would have no trouble refuting the conclusions I draw from it. He would show the extent to which my analysis derives from the West's perennial desire to discover in exoticism the figure of what it has itself lost, as Plato previously did in Egypt or Atlantis. I fully share in this critique. Our vision of myth is itself probably mythical, and we are surely much less humorous with the Cashinahua stories than are the Cashinahua themselves. But our tendency to overload the narrative by considering it as a form of antique legitimation is in itself interesting in the context of the problematic that is our own, that of modern totalitarianism. It is even of the essence.

It is this overevaluation, always widely present in people's minds, always potentially active, that explains how Nazism was so successful in its recourse to myth as a means of opposing its own despotic authority against the republican authority that structured the political life of the modern West and of the Weimar Republic. Nazism put the name Aryan in the place of the Idea of the citizen; abandoning the modern horizon of cosmopolitanism, it grounded its legitimacy in the saga of the peoples of the North. It succeeded because it flattered in a sovereign people—"democratically," in Kant's sense of the word—the desire to "return to sources" that mythology alone can satisfy. Nazism gave to this people the names and narratives that allowed it to identify exclusively with the Germanic heroes and to heal the wounds left by events of defeat and crisis. Xenophobia and chronophobia are necessarily implicated in this legitimating language apparatus. I will return to this question later.

IV.

Republicanism is more than the separation of powers; it calls for the fission or perhaps even the explosion of the popular identity. Republicanism is more than a matter of representation; from the point of view of language, it is an organization of the regimes of phrases and the genres of discourse that is based on their dissociation and that therefore allows for a measure of "play" among them. Or if you will, an organization of regimes and genres that preserves the possibility that the event in its contingency can be taken into account. I call this organization a *deliberative* one.

It has been noted that in traditional narration, the conflation of the various stakes—persuading, informing, convincing, converting—is hidden behind the homogeneity of the affair unfolding before us. The narrative's organic or, better, *totalizing* nature does not favor analysis. In a deliberative politics, the arrangement of the genres of discourse and regimes of phrases is allowed to break up, to disintegrate. A simple and even naïve description of the steps of the deliberative process makes this clear.

The first step: the ultimate end is formulated by a canonical phrase, which we can call the *stakes* and which is an interrogative prescriptive—*What must we be?* The question is weighted with a variety of possibilities: *happy, wise, free, equal, rich, powerful, artistic, American?* Answers are formulated in philosophies of history; while they are the subject of little debate in the political arena, they are nevertheless present under the name of "spiritual families."

The second step: To the question *What must we be?* is now linked the question *What must we do in order to be thus?* In this way, we pass from pure, almost ethical, prescription to a hypothetical imperative on the order of: if you want to be this, then do that.

The third step: The last question enunciated calls for an inventory of the means of achieving the desired end. These means include the analysis of the situation, the description of all available potentialities both of partners and of adversaries, and the definition of the respective interests involved. This constitutes an entirely different genre of discourse: the properly cognitive discourse of specialists, experts, counselors, and consultants, introduced in the form of surveys, reports, polls, indexes, statistics, and so forth.

The fourth step: Once this information is obtained in as complete a form as the nature of the game allows, a new genre of discourse is required, one whose stakes are the question *What will we be able to do?* Kant would see in this an Idea of the imagination (intuition without concept), while Freud would see free associations. I will call it montages of scenarios or simulations, narrations of the unreal.

The fifth step: Deliberation in the proper sense of the word takes place on the subject of these scenarios. This deliberation falls within the regime of argumentation. Each of the deliberators aspires to prove that the other is wrong, and why. This is the genre that Aristotle called dialectical. But rhetoric also enters in. The *logoi*, or arguments, combine with the *topoi*, the classic places of persuasion. One does not simply aspire to refute the opponent, but to persuade the third party (the judge, the presiding official, or the democratic electoral body).

The sixth step is the moment of decision, that is, of judgment, the most enigmatic of the phrases, according to Kant: the phrase *par excellence* of the event. Here are the resolutions, platforms, ballots, and arbitrations.

The seventh step: The judgment must be legitimated, which is the task of normative discourse ("has one the right to decide in this manner?"). Then it must be made enforceable (by decrees, writs, laws, edicts), and any infractions must be punished.

This arrangement is paradoxical in its linkages, despite appearances, because of the heterogeneity of its components; how can a prescriptive (*We must*) be deduced from a descriptive (*Here is what we can do*)? How can a prescriptive be linked to a normative phrase that will legitimate it? In this light, there is a certain fragility to the deliberative apparatus. This fragility is aggravated by the importance given to the role of knowledge (or technoscience in the service of the political), which is itself subject to the constant deliberations of scientists. The unity of the heterogeneous genres put into play in this organization resides only in the answer given to the first question: *What must we be?* The deliberative organization resists the division of its elements only because it is the organigram of free will, of pure practical reason.

In a republic, there reigns by principle an uncertainty as to ends, which is an uncertainty as to the identity of the "we", the "us". As we have seen, the question of ultimate identity simply isn't posed in a narrative tradition: the Cashinahua narrative always answers that we must be what we are, the Cashinahua. (And the Aryan narrative answers in the same way). In a republic there are several narratives because there are several possible ultimate identities. Despotism has a single narrative because it has a single origin. A republic does not offer matter for belief, but for reflection and judgment; it wills itself.

The grand narratives required by the republic are narratives of emancipation; they are not myths. Like myths, these narratives fulfill a function of legitimation: they legitimate social and political practices and institutions, legislations, ethics, ways of thinking, and symbolic systems. In contrast to myths, however, they do not base this legitimacy in any originary "founding" acts, but in a future to be brought about, in an Idea to be realized. This Idea (of freedom, of "enlightenment," of socialism, of general enrichment) possesses legitimating value because it is universal. It gives modernity its characteristic mode: the *project*; that is, a will oriented toward a goal.

To pursue this question, it would be necessary to return to Kant's short works on the historico-political, not only *What is Enlightenment* but also *Perpetual Peace*, *Idea for a Universal History from a Cosmopolitan Point of View*, and especially the second *Conflict of the Faculties*, the one dealing with the conflict between philosophy and the faculty of right. But I cannot pursue this here. The general sense that could be drawn from these works is that the narrative of the universal history of humanity cannot be asserted in the mode of myth; it must remain suspended from an Ideal of practical reason (freedom, emancipation). It cannot be verified by empirical proof, but only by indirect signs and analogues that signal, in experience, that this ideal is present in people's minds and that the discussion of this history is "dialectical" in Kant's sense—that is, without conclusion. The ideal cannot be presented to our perception; a free society can no more be shown than a free act, and in a sense the tension between what one must be and what one is will always remain equally strong.

The only thing that is certain is that right cannot be a question of fact, and that a real society does not draw its legitimacy from itself, but from a community that is not nameable, but only necessary. Thus, one cannot proceed from what a people is today to what it must be, nor can one proceed from one's identity as a Frenchman or an American to the concept of the universal citizen, but rather the reverse. This is why, as I have said, there exists a certain ferment of disintegration in the real community inscribed in the republican principle and in the history it develops. Sovereignty does not go to the people but to the Idea of a free community. And history only serves to mark the tension of this lack. The republic invokes liberty against security.

V.

Taking these summary reflections as a point of departure, it is possible, I think, to know more fully what we are aiming at with the word *totalitarianism*. Obviously a distinction must be made between the totalitarianism that turns its back on modern legitimation by the Idea of freedom and the one that, on the contrary, springs from that Idea. When a power authorizes itself by a national or ethnic name that is itself inscribed in a corpus of more or less fabulous stories, such as the Germanic (or Celtic or Italic) saga, then this can only take place as a complete rupture with the heritage of the Declaration of the Rights of Man of 1789. Here it is not a question of the "abandonment" of the modern project, as Habermas claims with respect to postmodernity, but of its "liquidation". What is then irreparably inscribed, with this annihilation, in the Western or at least the European consciousness is the suspicion that universal history does not inevitably move "toward the better," as Kant said, or rather that history does not necessarily possess a universal purposiveness. The proper name takes its authorization from the narrative pragmatic that I have described: I, an Aryan, recount to you, Aryans, the history of our Aryan ancestors as they have transmitted it to us; listen to it, repeat it, and execute it. This organization implies what I will call the exception. Aryans are the true men, the only ones. Whatever is not Aryan lives only through some lapse in the vital principle. It is already dead; it need only be finished off. The Nazi wars were sanitation procedures, purifications. Nothing could seem more foreign to republican legitimacy, to the deliberative organization of discourses for which republicanism calls, nor, finally, to the idea of history which it develops.

But things are not so simple. With the republic, the question of what the community must be and the ideal of freedom that responds to that question actually presuppose rather than preclude the fact that this community is already real; that is, it can name itself and honor its name with heroism and "noble deaths". If we are not yet citizens of the world, it is because we are still only French people. The fact remains that we are still French. This imbrication of authority by tradition and authority by the Idea is apparent when we analyze, for example, the Preamble to the Declaration of the Rights of Man from 1789. Who—what *y*—should have the authority to declare the rights of man? We have here an aporia of authorization. It is nevertheless surprising to find in the position of legitimizing instance the name of an Assembly representing a singular people, the French people, even if it places its declarations under the auspices of the supreme Being. Why should the assertions of the universal normative instance have universal value if it is a singular instance that declares them? How can we ever know if wars conducted by the singular instance in the name of the universal instance are wars of liberation or of conquest?

Nor with totalitarianism is the opposition to republicanism absolutely distinct. Nazism maintains the trappings of the deliberative organization: the Parliament, the parties. It may even make use of the republican epics of revolutionary war in order to disguise the ethnocentrism of its conquest (that is, Hitler replacing, with great ceremony, the ashes of Napoleon's son in the Hôtel des Invalides). It is without doubt a question of parody. What is the motive? To mask the reversal of legitimation. In this way, despotism recognizes an audience within republicanism. Indeed, it needs one: some remnant of universalism persists in the logic of the exception when the latter is extended to all of humanity.

The root of this equivocacy resides in the idea of the people. We know to what extent Nazism valorized this idea. The name *people* covers at once the singularity of a contingent community and the incarnation of a universal sovereignty. When we say *people*, we don't know exactly what identity we are talking about. When the people, *das Volk*, is put in the position of the normative instance, it isn't clear whether the authority invoked is despotic and requires the tradition of a narrative of origins, or whether it is republican and calls for the systematic institution of the deliberative procedure directed toward an Idea of liberty.

The unusual importance accorded to staging in Nazi politics has often been noted. The aesthetics—notably that of the "total work of art"—elaborated by Postromanticism and by Wagner, which privileges opera and cinema as "complete" arts, is put in the service of despotism, toppling the whole economy of the Schillerian project. Far from educating humanity and making it more fitted for Ideas, the tangible representation of the people to itself favors its identification as an exceptional singularity. Nazi "celebrations", whether monumental or familiar, exalt the Germanic identity by making tangible to the eyes and ears the symbolic figures of Aryan mythology. It is a question here of an art of persuasion that has been able to make a place for itself only by eliminating avant-garde currents turned toward reflection.

This attempt at orthopedic figuration, elaborated and put into action from the earliest beginnings of Nazism, proved fruitful only because the German community was experiencing a serious crisis of identity. This crisis, condensing within itself the defeat of 1918, the partitions made at Versailles, and the great socio-economic depression of the thirties, is generally considered to be the cause of Nazism. But the idea of a cause in these matters is inappropriate. It is more interesting for our purposes to remember that the crisis of identity that Nazism tried to remedy, but only succeeded in spreading to all of humanity, is potentially contained within the republican principle of legitimation.

In *The Phenomenology of Spirit*, Hegel describes the negativism of the modern ideal of freedom as a power capable of disintegrating any singular, concrete objectivity, and notably that of traditional institutions and, I would add, that of any community that is despotic in the Kantian sense, which draws the legitimation of its ways of life from its own name and past. The dialectic of the singular and the universal that Hegel deploys under the name of absolute freedom can only lead, he says, to the Terror. For the ideal of absolute freedom (which is empty), any given reality is suspected of being an obstacle to freedom; its existence has not been willed. I would say that in this case, the only normative instance, the only source of law, the only y is pure will—which is never this thing or that thing, never determined, but only the power to be anything at all. This pure will thus judges that any singular act, even one prescribed by law and executed accordingly, falls short of the ideal. The Terror confirms the suspicion that no one is emancipated enough; the Terror turns this suspicion into a politics. Any singular reality plots against pure universal will. Even the individual occupying the position of the normative instance is contingent in comparison with this ideal and is therefore suspect. Robespierre had nothing to object to in his own execution, except that his judges were no less suspect than he. "In whose name" is appeal made to the army against the Assembly, he asked Couthon the day before his death. The suppression of reality through the death of suspect individuals fulfills this logic that sees in reality a plot against the Idea, and the Terror thereby throws the real community into a state of distress over its identity. The French stop deserving the name of citizens when they retreat in fear before the grandeur of the crime by which they have tried to institute a republican legitimation. But in wanting only to be French, the French give up deliberation, universal history, and the ideal of freedom. The *Front populaire* frightens the country (including the Left), while the Anti-Dreyfus and Pétain States make the republicans (including the moderates) ashamed.

VI.

It seems certain that a politics of terror must not be confused in principle with the politics that can result from a despotic regime, even if, as is frequently the case, the distinction is not easy to make in historical reality. But let us imagine this: the normative instance must remain empty; any singularity (individual, family, party) that intends to occupy this place is suspected of doing so only by usurpation or imposture. The y who authorizes the order and makes a law of it has no name; it is pure will, assigned no determination, linked to no singularity. At whatever scale this arrangement occurs, be it the small, Puritan community of Salem or the French nation, it very probably induces a politics of terror. But far from eliminating deliberation and its institutional organization, this politics requires it. For it is this organization alone that brings into play each person's responsibility—both that of the representative and the represented—in respect to every genre of discourse necessary to a political decision. It is not only, or perhaps not essentially, one's life that one puts into play in these deliberations but one's judgment—that is, one's responsibility before the event. I will recall here that, in principle, the complex deliberative organization leaves open the way in which one phrase is linked with another, or one genre of discourse with another, and that this occurs at every step in the process of the will.

The republic is constitutionally attentive to the event. What is called freedom is precisely this attention to whatever might happen, which will have to be judged beyond all rules. The Terror is one way of taking into account the indetermination of what happens. Philosophy is another way. The difference between the two stems from the amount of time available for assimilating and judging. Philosophy takes its time, so to speak, while a certain urgency speeds up the republican decision, which is usually political in nature.

Totalitarianism would consist of the subordination of institutions legitimated by the Idea of freedom to a legitimation by myth. This is clearly a despotism in the Kantian sense, but one that borrows from republicanism its powers of universalization. It is thus not only *Let us become what we are, Aryans* but also *Let all humanity be Aryan*. The singular "we", once named, aspires to give its own name to the ends pursued by human history. It is in this way that totalitarianism is modern. Totalitarianism doesn't just need a people; it needs the people's disintegration into "masses" in search of their identity by means of the multiple parties authorized by the republic. Totalitarianism needs the equivocacy of democracy in order to overthrow the republic.

I will make a further distinction between Nazi totalitarianism and Stalinist totalitarianism. The mode of legitimation of the latter remains republican in its principle. Socialism is one of the versions of the narrative of universal emancipation born of the Declaration of the Rights of Man. The first International took as its authority a declaration of the rights of the universal worker. Communism is a philosophy of the history of humanity. Its internationalism clearly signified that no legitimacy could be recognized in local powers, which, being singular, are necessarily despotic. An immense effort was made to give the universal proletariat a reality beyond those working classes still attached to their national traditions and their partisan claims. The fact that this effort failed and that, with Stalinism, bolshevism became an incarnation of chauvinism does not imply that the mode of legitimation of the Soviet power has ever been, in principle, slogans on the order of: *Let us be Russian* and *Let all humanity be Russian*. In principle, the very idea of the people underwent a radical critique in Marxism, thanks to the concept of class struggle. Marxism greatly advanced the disintegration of the singular nominal community, and did so in the spirit of working class republicanism.

The question I ask myself now is if Stalinism isn't more a politics of terror than of despotism. All the analyses sketched here lead me to this conclusion. The very disintegration of Russian civil society by the Stalinist and post-Stalinist machine argues for this hypothesis. This disintegration has no equivalent in Nazism, which, on the contrary, solidly and durably structured the German ways of life and social-economic reality in conformity with the despotic principle, thus engendering in Germany a sense of guilt unknown in communist nations. The Stalinist terror was able to deceive people for a long time because it seemed to move towards the realization of the socialist republic. It took as its authority bolshevism, the Marxist cousin of Enlightenment Jacobinism. It took nearly half a century for the imposture to be revealed. And it still has not completely lost its allure for those nations which, because of imperialism, have undergone a crisis of identity analogous to the one experienced by Germany in the 1930s. The fact remains that in all the countries we call communist, the normative instance only authorizes the law in opposition to those to whom the law applies. The normative instance cannot invoke the life of the people or the preservation of its origins and identity; it cannot reign as a true despotism, one of singularity. On the other hand, however, it has been a long time indeed since the normative instance of communism has constituted a republican reign of terror, since it is also unable to cite a process of infinite emancipation as its authority without making those it oppresses either laugh or weep. The peoples of those countries we call communist know what bureaucratic power is: the delegitimation of the legislator.

I have said nothing of capitalism. I would simply like to indicate this: The principle that *every* object and *every* action is acceptable (or permitted) if it can enter into economic exchange is not totalitarian in a political sense, but it is totalitarian in terms of language since it calls for the complete hegemony of this type of economic discourse. The following is the simple canonical formula of this economic discourse: *I will surrender this to you if you will surrender that to me in return*. One property of this discourse is to always call for some new *this* to enter into the exchange (for example, today, technoscientific knowledge) and to neutralize its force as an event by means of payment. Clearly this extension of the marketplace has nothing to do with republican universality. Capital has no need for deliberation either politically or economically. It only needs deliberation socially, because it needs civil society in order to repeat its cycle. Deliberation is for capital the indispensable moment of the destruction (consummation) of the singular *thises* and *thats*.

It would be of great importance to examine the present status of capitalism from the point of view of totalitarianism. Capitalism adapts itself to the republican institution, but it has little tolerance for terror (which destroys its market). It can make a good bedfellow for despotism (as we saw with Nazism). It is scarcely troubled by the decline of the great universalist narratives, even that of the enrichment of humanity. It would seem that capital has no need for legitimation, that it prescribes nothing in the strict sense of an obligation, and that consequently it does not manifest an instance that makes norms of prescriptives.

It is present everywhere, but as a necessity rather than a purposiveness. I believe that one can understand why it appears as a necessity by analyzing the canonical formula of the genre of discourse that is its own. One would see that a purposiveness nevertheless hides beneath this appearance: to gain time. Is this a universally valid end?

III

A Descriptive Philosophy of Politics

Bernhard Waldenfels

10. *The Ruled and the Unruly: Functions and Limits of Institutional Regulations**

Certainly I am expected to make a contribution to political philosophy. But it's not so easy to say what political philosophy (or practical philosophy, which I teach at my home university) really means. Nevertheless, I don't suppose that politics is a mere application of principles or a realization of ideas to be found elsewhere, in a philosophical heaven. But I am just as little inclined to turn the tables, reducing philosophy to another kind of politics. Rather, I would suggest that there is a political dimension to every sort of thought or research, and vice versa: that philosophy always has a bearing on the pragmatics and tactics of everyday politics. In brief, I wish to speak of a mutual implication of philosophy and politics. This thesis has, surely, to be rendered concrete, but my short remark may be sufficient to dissipate some initial misunderstanding. Philosophers and politicians don't live on different islands, and the connection between philosophy and politics is not entirely a question of personal involvement or noninvolvement. It is useless to wail for a *philosophie* or a *science engagée*. We *are* involved whether we want to be or not.

My contribution consists of three parts. First, I will briefly raise the problem of rules and institutions. This leads us to the general question of order and its history. After this far-reaching overture, I shall narrow the thematic field. So in a second move, which is much more analytical, I shall pick up Peter Winch's theory of action, which centers on a certain concept of rule. This theory, following Wittgenstein and Max Weber, arrives at the field of institutions indirectly, through the realm of language. This part of my paper will not be much more than a reminder because I assume you are sufficiently acquainted with the essential aspects of this theory. In the third and last part, I shall come back to the problems with which I began. Critical reflection on Winch's theory will help us

---

*From *Graduate Faculty Philosophy Journal*, Vol. 9, No. 1 (Winter 1982).

to take up the question of order once again, but more pointedly. The power of rules and institutions will reveal its limits.

The Problem of Order

First, I propose to distinguish between two types of order: the classical and the modern. This distinction should be taken in a heuristic sense; we should not expect any form of thinking or living to fit into it completely. Its purpose is not to resolve any questions but to raise some. In this sense, the question of how order and rationality are conceived precedes the question of how they are to be detected or justified.

In the case of the classical type, we are confronted with an order that is firmly embodied in the nature of things, whether a cosmic world in the Greek sense or a created world in the medieval Christian sense. This kind of order is all-encompassing. It comprises even the spectator, whose highest activity consists in reproducing and repeating the given order in his own soul. In such a process of "mimesis," macrocosmos and microcosmos mirror each other; the modern concepts of reflection or speculation are still connected with this tradition. Within such a well-formed whole there are fixed boundaries that separate what is essential from what is inessential and finally from what may be called antiessential in the sense of an antinature. The essence is the heart of reality; it is reality in its highest form. This central zone is surrounded by a gray zone of the incidental or contingent, and it contrasts with the totally dark zone of the chaotic and orderless. The highest paradigm for human life and action is to be found in the revolutions of celestial bodies; another paradigm is given by the evolution of the organism. Human beings are not privileged because they create order, but because they know about order. There is no place for real innovations or inventions. The overwhelming order of reason does not allow for new kinds of things. There is nothing new under the sun unless it is the indefinite number of shadow forms, which flee the daylight. Innovations are suspect as signs of disorder. (Take for example Plato's warning against new forms of music.) There remains only the great divorce between Reason and Chaos. Every deviation turns out to be a deviation from the one path of Truth and Virtue, as in the case of Heracles at the crossroads.

Now take the second type of order, which I call the modern one. Certainly, I don't want to claim that this new order sprang up in history as a ready-made form. Rather, we should speak of a long process of modernization, which has been going on since the fifteenth century, unevenly, to be sure, and which has affected the different fields of ethics, politics, religion, science, technique, art, education, and so on. Order in the new sense is not pre-established once and for all, but has grown up under certain circumstances and is capable of further change. There are not only histories within a unique order, like the rise and decline of empires; order itself has its history. We must not go so far as to claim that every order is arbitrary. To deny the inner necessity of the one order, it is sufficient to say that every order is contingent or conventional, that is, it *can* be other than it is. To be sure, this is the very definition Aristotle applies to the realm of human practice. But to be precise, we must add: it is the concrete forms and means of human life and not their goal that can be changed. Now if cognitive and practical order is subject to change, the great and solid order splits into different orders that are no longer all-encompassing but restricted in each case. The boundaries between that which is governed by rules, that which remains open, and that which is against rules are more or less indeterminate. Deviation does not necessarily militate against reason, conjuring up chaos: it may be the formation of a new kind of order. When such alternatives and selections are possible, Reason becomes plural—*rationalities*.

If it is true that such a shift from one type of order to the other has taken place, many problems will arise. For instance, in the classical view there is no real problem of freedom. Every individual demand or request that is legitimate and acceptable is fulfilled by the order of the whole. The contrast between order and freedom, between regularity and spontaneity, only appears when order proves to be restrictive and exclusive. *"Vernunft wird Unsinn, Wohltat Plage . . ."*—that's Mephisto's voice; nevertheless, it is an earthly voice. The problem that arises has provoked many attempts at solution, which are no more than half-hearted compromises and compensations. For example, one tries to transfer metaphysical order into history instead of transforming this kind of order. In what follows, I don't want to tackle these problems head on; I prefer to make a detour. A social philosopher like Winch does not argue against classical order; he simply bypasses it. This theory of action is no longer oriented to the revolutions of stars but to linguistic rules, and that means a conventional order, infected by contingency.

Action as Rule-Governed Behavior

In his well-known book on the *Idea of Social Science,* Peter Winch develops a theory of action in which Max Weber's conception of social action is combined with Wittgenstein's linguistic approach. Winch takes up Weber's famous definition: "Action is human behavior if and insofar as the agent or agents associate a subjective sense with it." But this sense is not defined by the intentions or experiences of agents, but by public rules. In this way language becomes not only the medium for analyzing action but the model for defining it. It is not necessary to repeat the way in which Wittgenstein explains the meaning of words by their use in language, passing from speech acts to language games and ending with certain forms of life. Here, speaking is embedded in acting and living in such a way that the theory of language includes a theory of institutions, at least in a rudimentary form. In Saussure's semiology, too, we find social implications. To speak thoroughly about language is to speak about more than pure language.

Picking up Winch's theory of action, where sense, rule, and social control are closely connected, I shall single out four aspects that are decisive in understanding how a rule functions.

The Prescriptive Character of Rules

First, a rule governing human behavior is prescriptive and not descriptive. It doesn't refer to what is done or said under certain circumstances but to what has to be done or said. It doesn't explain what happens but enables us to judge and justify what is done or said, insofar as there is a clear-cut distinction between natural laws and conventional rule. Natural laws are applied to regular or uniform processes from without, whether physical events or psychological habits, whereas conventional rules are only to be grasped from within by learning the rules and participating in the respective form of life. Winch gives a criterion for deciding whether there is rule-governed behavior. We have to ask whether it makes sense to distinguish between right and wrong procedure (Winch, p. 58). It may look like a bad habit to drink ten whiskies every night, but it is not wrong unless you are on a strict diet or you are a member of a nonalcoholic group.

The Constitutive Character of Rules

Rules are not only the framework of action at a preinstitutional level and only regulated afterwards. There are at least some rules that constitute actions. In this connection, Searle distinguishes between brute and institutional facts, defining institution as a "system of constitutive rules" (*Searle,* p. 51). We all are ready to make a distinction between marking a paper and voting, between a red cloth and a flag, between red lamps and traffic lights, between moving little horses and towers on a wooden board and making a move in a game of chess, between hearing a noise and deciphering phonemes, and so on. But we cannot maintain these distinctions if we refer only to physical features or psychological events. Rather we have to invoke the rules of a parliamentary system, of a certain political symbolism, of a traffic system, of the game of chess, or of a phonematic system of language. Otherwise the so-called "institutional facts" would simply not exist. This insight corresponds to what is encountered in the tradition of Durkheim and Saussure. For Lévi-Strauss, systems of kinship or rituals of the table are constitutive for the cultural order that from the beginning transcends the pure fulfilling of biological needs. There is no place for such things as pure reality, whether the reality of real things or of real needs.

The Social Character of Rules

There are no rules without conventions that introduce rules and without sanctions that control their observance. This is not a new assertion. Aristotle already explains sign (σημεῖον) by referring to convention (συνθήκη), and he gives social reactions like praise and blame an important if not the major role in his ethics. Without internalization of social rules there would be nothing but a process of conditioning, which could not produce any obligation. The distinction between right or wrong would be void. To reproach someone about his bad behavior would be like reproaching the weather because it is bad. Consequently, sociality inheres in rules and is not merely added to them. Without such a court of appeal, the individual would be in the position Wittgenstein describes with black humor: trying to verify the content of a morning paper by buying another copy of it.

The Practical Character of Rules

Finally, we must not suppose that rules are only rules when explicitly formulated and promulgated and when reflected upon by the persons who are subject to them. If we made this claim there would be a *regressus ad infinitum* because the setting of rules would require rules for the setting of rules and so on. Achilles would never reach the tortoise by arguing about arguing. As Lewis Carroll demonstrates, we have to learn to do something even in thinking (see Winch, p. 57). Learning to do something does not mean that we learn rules that are to be applied to situations, but we learn rules by acting according to them. To mention Aristotle once more: playing the zither is learned by playing the zither and not by studying books about zither playing, and he adds, the same holds good for becoming a righteous man. From the beginning, knowledge of rules belongs to knowing *how,* not to knowing *that.* It is sufficient to suppose that we can reflect on rules under certain conditions. This incidental form of reflection has not much to do with the great mirror of consciousness and self-consciousness that reflects everything, including itself. Rather, it may be compared with a commentary that neither replaces the original text nor absolves us from reading it again and again.

Critical Reflections on the Limits of Rules

Perhaps you will agree with me that most of what has been said sounds rather plausible. But many questions will arise when we explore the surroundings, presuppositions, and effects of rules. Theory may get on well with some of these questions but not with others. There are lacunae not only in the theory of rules but in rule systems themselves. For me it is not a question of *whether* human behavior is rule-governed but to what extent. In my opinion rules are systematically overemphasized in a theory like this. The following reflections will lead us back step by step to the problem of order we began with.

The Range of Rules

Asked how far rules are constitutive for actions I would make two restrictions.

Any action whatsoever is more than a mere following or not following of rules. It is not difficult to give you some examples. A man who speaks or writes correctly does not necessarily speak well, with elegance, vigor, or imagination. Winch mentions the looser form of stylistic canons (p. 53). A musician who avoids missing the right key is not yet an excellent interpreter or a virtuoso. And somebody who masters the rules of chess may be a bungler without any tactical skill.

According to Wittgenstein, we should speak of an openness of rules. The field of application is always more or less outlined. As Wittgenstein remarks, when serving in tennis there are no rules regulating how high one throws the ball or how hard one hits it *(Phil. Invest., #68)*. Moreover, the field of application is more or less open. Because the rules that govern our acting and perceiving are not universal rules or essential structures, it is impossible to anticipate new kinds of things. We must always reckon with surprises in the good or the bad sense (see Winch, pp., 154 f.). Our acting and speaking always moves within a certain realm of play *(Spielraum)*. The application of rules cannot be timed by further sets of rules. If the gap between rules and situations could be completely filled, we would live in a closed world. There would be no room for new rules but only for new combinations within the given repertoire. Of course, we can approach the nightmare of what Horkheimer called the "administered world" or Huxley's negative utopia in *Brave New World*. But these are degenerate forms we will have to speak about later. Now, another question lurks behind this one. What is really left open by rules? What comes to stand in the breach? Where is the frontier between production *by* rules, production *according to* rules, and production *of* rules? But let us pass to a second form of restriction.

All actions are not rule-governed to the same extent. The useful model of language may seduce us into simplifying the phenomena. Take actions like walking, eating, cooking or fishing. In which sense could they be qualified as right or wrong, using Winch's own criterion? McIntyre made this objection long ago. In my opinion we have to weigh them on a scale of increasing and decreasing regulation. Actions are more or less embedded in public institutions, and they are more or less formed by conventions and rituals. On one end of the scale, we would find actions that are prefabricated and utterances that are preformulated to a high degree—we would speak of "ceremonials." On the other end of the scale, we would find a high degree of spontaneity, which is not the same as arbitrariness. There may be deeper structures and something like a language of desire, but the rules of this language would differ from the common rules just as much as dreaming, sleeping, or loving differ from common acts.

In legal or moral terms, we may speak of a middle zone, which is neither commanded nor forbidden but allowed. This margin is greater or smaller according to cultural and historical differences. It is not for nothing that Lévi-Strauss, while looking for a universal code of human culture, turns to so-called primitive societies whose individual behavior is much more uniform than ours has been in a long time.

In general, I find in analytical philosophy a certain tendency to minimize that which is not guided by rules. The unruled turns out to be a remainder. But if conventions are so overrated, acting and speaking are cut off from the impulses, forces, and motives which animate them. They are partly disembodied. This failure cannot be repaired by taking refuge in a physiology that is completely dominated by natural laws. By such a double strategy the old "animal rationale" becomes all too domesticated by the two sets of rules, the conventional and the natural. Conventionalism and behaviorism complement each other; they simply work two sides of the Cartesian street. If we take the realism of rules as coextensive with the realm of sense, we would have to refine the concept of rule much more than analytic philosophers are used to doing. With this less simplistic concept of rule, institutions would take the form of what Merleau-Ponty calls embodiment, which is more than a pure system of rules.

Mutability of Rules

In social science Winch proposes to comprehend the "inner logic" of different forms of life. He claims to practice a participatory kind of observation, but confronted with competing ways of life and views of the world, he refuses to permit any intervention. The inquiry has to remain uncommitted (pp. 102 f.). Wittgenstein is invoked as an authority: "Philosophy leaves everything as it is" *(Phil. Invest.* #124), or "What has to be accepted, the given, is—someone could say—*forms of life*" (p. 226ᵉ).

You could easily argue against this modesty, taking it as a new version of a Diltheyian historicism. But Winch would defend himself with Wittgenstein's arguments. A form of life cannot be founded or justified as a whole; it is the soil that makes justification and reasons possible. "If I have exhausted the justifications, I have reached bedrock, and my spade is turned. Then I am inclined to say: 'This is simply what I do' " *(Phil. Invest., #217).* A form of life is neither good nor bad, neither true nor false, just as language, which functions as the matrix for true or false sentences and legitimate or illegitimate demands, cannot be justified as such. There are conditions of truth and goodness that are not themselves true or good. "What people accept as a justification—is shown by how they think and live" *(Phil. Invest., #325)*. You may change the soil, but not without uprooting certain forms of arguing and justifying. All this means that the mutability of rules is not excluded by Winch, but it is only stated incidentally as something that happens, and just at this point new difficulties arise.

Competing forms of living, thinking, and acting do not simply exclude each other; they are more or less overlapping, as Winch himself concedes (p. 101). An action may be evaluated as irregular when seen from the standpoint of the established rule system, and the "same" action may be taken as an inauguration of new rules when seen from the standpoint of a not yet existing system. This ambiguity, this oscillation from irregularity to deregulation, disappears when we place one form of life beside the other.

The transition from one form or system to the other cannot be explained or even described when we neglect the tensions, gaps, and breaches that are to be found in the given structures. But if we accept such blind spots and such deficiencies, we must also accept our saying, acting, and living as never completely included within a certain system or institution but always transgressing its borderlines. There must be something of the unruled or unruly within the ruled that is responsible for change. This reminds us of the openness of rule we discussed before.

The Critique of Rules

We come back to the original problem, which was characterized in the beginning as a problem of order. What about the critique of rules, rule-systems, institutions, and forms of life? In the first place, we have to mention the classical answer once more. It has not lost its attraction, as can be seen, for example, in the work of Leo Strauss. Here the given forms of life are criticized in light of a true form of life whose norms and goals are reasonable in the strong sense. It may be that we claim to realize this highest form of life or that we content ourselves with trying it. Nevertheless, there is a final end that guides our attempts. Now this conception has to be contested if it is true that every institution has its "positivity" (in the sense of "positive law"), which cannot be integrated or elevated into an all-encompassing whole. And I want to claim that this *is* true. Take once more the paradigm of language: there is no true language, and it is hopeless to expect that the different languages will someday be arranged in a complete and final hierarchy.

There are other perspectives that accept the fact that cultural orders arise and change in history and are not given once and for all by nature. Here the limits and constraints of the given factual orders are the targets of an attack that runs through several different strategies. I shall mention three typical forms they take.

First, you may look for a universalization of rules. The limits of concrete forms of life are moved, and they are moved in such a way that in the end every reasonable being will have access to this form of super-institution. You could call this strategy the taming of the unruly. This is the classical answer modified under modern circumstances. We have to establish order, not seek it in the nature of things. *We*—who's that? Reason, a transcendental ego, a universe of monads or mankind? There is one deficiency in this project. The more general the rules and institutions are, the more the particularities of life remain outside their reach. Concrete interests, needs, and fantasies are shunted into hiding places where they rumble about, shying from the public light. Not only Goya's sleep of reason but an over-wakeful reason, too, generates monsters. Besides, universal rules are impotent in the full sense of the word. They are able neither to guide nor to generate concrete enterprises. At best they are to be used as correctives: they represent the forum of reason.

A restrictive form of reason finds its complement in a certain kind of anarchism. Here life is to be dispensed from the constraints that lurk in rules and order. Let's overcome institutional oppression; let's remove the chains, and the spontaneity of life will bloom. Common to anarchism's soft and hard forms is its flirtation with an innocence in nature, which only has to be emancipated. But is there any speaking and understanding without rules? Is there any creation that can free itself totally from the burden and heritage of tradition? Is there any formation without deformation and transformation?

There is a third way of reconciliation. Here one looks for a universal order, which doesn't issue in universal norms but tends to a concrete universality wherein every particular need and aspiration is fulfilled. Perhaps we could call it the great illusion of modern times. The reign of freedom is waiting for us. Where? In history. Nobody prevents us from revising the date and place of the great solution again and again. We have the cake now and eat it tomorrow.

My survey will stop here. Some concluding remarks will do. To begin with, I want to ask if we are not inclined to overrate the function of rules. There is a trend toward a sort of over-regulation that may be the result of the decay of the old cosmos. Without the regulations invented by man, there seems to be a human chaos, which though it goes together well with a physical order is not remedied by it. In Hobbes, for example, formal institutions are systematically over-charged. Man, the support of reason, is groaning under the burden of the world like a modern Atlas. The announcement of the death of man, would it mean a *coup de grâce?*

It would be better to accept the openness and limits of institutional rules as two sides of the same coin. To be sure, every institution has its limits. Nevertheless, there is no pre- or suprainstitutional realm which could be a refuge against institutional constraints. No, the limits are inherent in the rule system itself.

Something unruled is to be found within what is ruled, just as the invisible or the unsayable is not beyond what is seen or said, but within. This unruly may be called *sens sauvage,* a sense that cannot be completely domesticated. Searle's distinction between "brute facts" and "institutional facts" has to be modified. In every work of culture, there remains some brutishness, which is not to be devalued as simply awaiting rationalization or fleeing from it. Rather we should take it in the sense Dubuffet intends when he speaks of *art brut.* If we should one day succeed in taming all that resists, in ruling out the unruly and in filling in all the blanks, the game would be up.

References

Searle, John R., *Speech Acts: An Essay in the Philosophy of Language.* London: Cambridge University Press, 1969.

Winch, Peter, *The Idea of a Social Science and its Relation to Philosophy.* New York: Humanities Press, 1958.

Wittgenstein, Ludwig, *Philosophical Investigations.* Trans. G. E. M. Anscombe, New York: Macmillan, 1968.

Michel Henry

11. *The Question of Life and Culture from the Perspective of a Radical Phenomenology*

To speak of the active life and of the contemplative life implies the prior knowledge of what life is. This knowledge of life implies in its turn, it seems, that we have available to us a method, or even a philosophy, that would allow us to acquire it. And indeed we do. This philosophy is a radical phenomenology. By this I do not mean the historical phenomenology that developed starting with Husserl, but instead an ideal phenomenology that would get to the bottom of the questions that define its object. The object of phenomenology is not the totality of phenomena studied by the sciences, but what in each case permits a phenomenon to be what it is, that is, its phenomenality, the mode of givenness according to which it presents itself to us and in this way is a phenomenon for us.

Since Descartes, this mode of givenness has been interpreted as consciousness. However, what this consciousness is remains difficult to grasp. In Husserlian phenomenology, this consciousness is brought to light by means of a remarkable method: the phenomenological reduction. In the *Krisis*, where it is presented for the last time, it is developed in two stages. There is first of all the epoché of the world of Galilean science, the science that overturned the European manner of thinking and its conceptions, making us what we are today. The world is given to us in its sensible, subjective, and variable appearances; however, according to this science, it is possible to display, beyond the relativity of its subjective appearances, a true being of the world, a world in itself. And this is so to the extent that, in our knowledge of this world, we abstract precisely from sensible qualities and in a general manner from all that is relative to subjectivity. This allows us to retain as genuine being only those abstract forms of the spatial-temporal universe in which geometrical determinations constitute, henceforth, a univocal knowledge. With respect to the world of the spirit and to human spirituality, these now rest on this scientific nature and are to be explained by it.

The Husserlian reversal of the theses supporting the scientific and positivist ideology of our times is one of the major analyses of philosophical thought. The world of mathematical idealities characteristic of Galilean science cannot account for the sensible and subjective world in which our daily lives unfold because it is grounded in the latter. On the one hand, scientific idealizations have meaning only in relation to this world. On the other, as idealizations they presuppose the transcendental, subjective operation that produces them and in which the idealization actually consists. Instead of reducing subjectivity to mere appearance, the world of science finds in it the principle of its continual generation. Finally, the nature on which all human or animal spirituality is constructed is not the world of science and its abstract idealities, but the world of life, a world constantly open to intuition and to experience in the sensible modes of its subjective givenness.

Subjectivity, therefore, not only produces the idealizations of the mathematical world of science, it first produces the life-world itself, being nothing other than the set of procedures and of modalities in accordance with which the world offers itself to us. In other words, subjectivity produces the fundamental methodology by virtue of which it exists. All the beings *(onta)* that inhabit the life-world are never given immediately and as if by themselves, as the substrata of their qualities; nor is this life-world itself so given. They are as they are as a result of the ensemble of subjective operations that make them visible and thus carry them in their very condition of phenomena, or as Husserl says, "constitute" them. These transcendental offerings, which give meaning and being to all that is and can be for us, are highly complex. Our perception of the side of a cube, for example, or of a house is connected to the potential perceptions of the other sides, following an endless series of referrals. Now in the natural attitude, we only pay attention to beings and to the ends they propose for our practical action. The transcendental operations that constitute the phenomena are not perceived, but remain "in anonymity" as phenomenologists say. I perceive the house, not the perception of the house. I am always conscious of the world and never conscious of my consciousness of the world. This is why, after the first epoché, which takes us from the world of science to the life-world that serves as its ground, there is need for a second epoché that performs the questioning back from the life-world to the consciousness of this world.

This is where we have to split off from historical phenomenology however remarkable its developments may have been, particularly in Husserl. If we want to be able to speak about the subject of our discussions—namely, life—then a more radical phenomenology is needed. For Husserl, consciousness is consciousness of the world. It is consciousness of something, in other words, intentionality. To say that consciousness is in its essence intentionality means that intentionality is posited as the condition for phenomenality, that it is phenomenality itself, that it is what makes something visible. How does intentionality make things visible? Inasmuch as it refers to something that stands before it as transcendent, intentionality is this power of placing something before itself and therefore of breaking a path to what is standing before it. It is in this profound sense that consciousness is consciousness of the world: being a consciousness means making visible, and making visible is placing before, putting in a world.

Now in the consciousness that we have of the life-world within the natural attitude, we are conscious of beings *(onta)* and not of our consciousness of the world. How, then, are we able to acquire consciousness, not of the world this time but of our very consciousness of the world? Husserl's solution is still intentionality. The phenomenological reduction that is supposed to make us conscious of our consciousness of the world remains a reflection on spontaneous consciousness. It remains an intentional gaze directed to transcendental experience. To be sure, this reflection presupposes retention, but retention is itself an intentionality. So if we ask the ultimate question concerning how consciousness is consciousness of itself and not of the world—the question of the self-revelation of absolute subjectivity—the answer is that absolute subjectivity is revealed to itself inasmuch as it relates intentionally to itself. According to Husserl this occurs in the self-constitution of the flux of absolute subjectivity, a self-constitution that is its self-temporalization. Temporalization is the flowing, the rising up of a split, the first putting at a distance, an ecstasy, and the intentional gaze of retention, and then of reflection, moves within the space opened up by this ecstasy, which is the first opening up of a world.

This is the moment to point out Husserl's failure with respect to our problem—the self-revelation of absolute subjectivity—since this self-revelation is life itself. Husserl argues that the flux of absolute subjectivity appears to itself to the extent that it constitutes itself, that it is intentionally related to itself. Since it is always so related in its phenomenally constituted phases, these constitutive phases themselves never are given except in this way, in and through intentionality. This means that they never give themselves as constitutive, that intentionality never reveals itself as such, that is, as operative and in its functioning. What this means, in other words, is that what makes things visible is, itself, never seen. Thus, in Husserlian phenomenology, there is an ultimate constituent, an "absolutely unique, ultimately functioning ego" (*Krisis,* § 55), concerning which a 1933 manuscript states "I am not only something for myself, but I am myself" (Ich bin nicht nur etwas für mich sondern ich bin ich). Yet nothing more is said about this supreme authority, which is nothing other than the absolute life of transcendental subjectivity (that is, real life) and which remains in Husserl—but also in philosophy in general—in an inviolable anonymity.

In order to glean something more about this life, to learn whether or not we can know something about it, let us turn towards Descartes and the *cogito.* In his lecture, *The End of Philosophy and the Task of Thinking,* Heidegger says that the *Cartesian Meditations* were not for Husserl simply the lectures he gave in Paris in 1929. Instead, their spirit guided his entire work. Nevertheless, I think that this Cartesian meditation, regardless of the fact that it proved fruitful in so many respects (as did Heidegger's own critique of the *cogito*, which he reduced to an "I represent myself to myself") misses Descartes' fundamental intuition. It is true that even today, this fundamental insight still remains to be discovered. In § 50 of the *Krisis,* speaking of the Cartesian headings *ego, cogito, cogitata,* Husserl declares that, for his own part, he intends to pursue them in the opposite order, that is, by beginning with the *cogitatum* rather than by moving from the *ego cogito* to the *cogitatum.* As a general rule, phenomenological analysis always takes the intentional object as its starting point, as a "transcendental guide," moving from it to the constitutive syntheses that account for it, and this is the case even in noetic analysis.

However, according to the first two *Meditations* of Descartes, it is impossible to start from the *cogitatum,* be it reduced to itself, to its simple appearance. The *cogitatum qua cogitatum* cannot provide the starting point since it is excluded by the Cartesian doubt. Self-evidence, the apodictic seeing of something certain, cannot provide a foundation. Indeed, something that cannot be otherwise—for example, "if I think, then I have necessarily to exist"—can nevertheless be false in its self-evidence (if this is the will of the Evil One), because the apodictic seeing is perhaps fallacious. What if every possible world, whether real or ideal, sensible or intelligible, is rejected? What if the ecstatic milieu of visibility in which these worlds appear to me is not actually such, is not a "making visible" or a "giving to be seen," but instead an "inducing into error," "misleading me"? Then what remains?

At certe videre videor, states the *Second Meditation* (Adam and Tannery, VII, 29). "At the very least, it seems to me that I see." What subsists at the end of doubting is the subjective experience of vision, that is, the self-revelation of this vision itself, *inasmuch as this revelation of seeing (which reveals seeing) does not consist itself, as revelation, in a seeing such as this*—for otherwise it too would be doubtful. The seeming in which it seems to me that I see, in which seeing feels itself—*"sentimus nos videre"* (AT, I, 40)—experiences itself. But how? It reveals itself to itself, not as that seeing which reaches its object. It is not the illumination of an ecstasy. Therefore, seeing itself needs to be grounded. It is a matter of providing a guarantee for any self-evidence (and of doing this without taking as a foundation either seeing or self-evidence). This can only be done by showing how this seeing is properly established in itself in such a way that in life's primordial immersion in itself, an immersion in which it touches all the points of its being, there exists neither seeing nor ecstasy, and so neither doubt nor any possible error.

This originary establishing of subjectivity in itself, which makes it life, can be expressed by means of a Cartesian terminology. We would say that it is the idea in its original acceptation; it is the idea of the mind as it differs from all other ideas (AT, VII, 443), inasmuch as it has no *cogitatum.* Once it is stripped of objective reality and reduced to its material or formal reality alone, to pure *cogitatio,* it is the power by which the latter reveals itself to itself as *cogitatio* and as it is in itself. In this way, subjectivity is self-revelation, the revelation of thought itself and not of anything else, whether otherness, some sort of objectivity, or any *cogitatum.* This is why the formal reality of the idea does not designate something formal (like the Kantian subject), the mere form of a content located outside it, or a representation. It designates instead, in the absence of any externality, the reality proper to thought. The idea is its material reality, namely, the phenomenological materiality of pure phenomenality to the extent that the latter consists not in an ecstasis but in its radical self-immanence. The idea of mind is not a particular idea opposed to all others; it is their common essence. "By the name 'idea' I mean that form of each of our thoughts, by means of whose immediate perception we have knowledge of these same thoughts" (AT, VII, 160). In Descartes, ideas are thus first of all the radically immanent modalities of subjectivity, not the data of internal time-consciousness but that which, before any constitution or self-constitution, is to be thought of "as the ideas which are simply in our soul" (AT, IX, II, 56).

The Cartesian reduction, if we want to name doubt in this way, therefore has nothing to do with the Husserlian reduction. The latter excludes the world only in order to take into account its givenness, that is, the consciousness of the world, intentionality, so that the *cogitatio* signifies the phenomenality of the *cogitatum,* the light of ecstasy. What is not mentioned—and this explains the aporia that Husserlian phenomenology will run up against, its incapacity of giving a phenomenological status to the ultimate constituent—is nothing less than what Descartes called the "knowledge of the soul." According to the *Second Meditation,* this knowledge precedes the "knowledge of the body." This is not to say that there is one knowledge and two objects for this knowledge, the soul and the body. Rather there are two fundamental modes in which the phenomenalization of pure phenomenality takes place. The first of these modes is intentionality and that which grounds it, the ecstasy in which it unfolds; the second is life. *"Cogito"* and *"consciousness"* do not mean the same thing but rather two things, which are basically different and heterogeneous.

In this way we have distinguished between the world of science and scientific knowledge, the life-world and the consciousness of this life-world and, finally, life. Scientific knowledge rests on the consciousness of the world, on intentionality; it is a developed form of this intentionality. The knowledge of life has no relationship to scientific knowledge, nor to consciousness of the world in general. And because it does not carry within it the ecstasy of intentionality, it owes nothing to them.

Consider a biology student reading a work on the genetic code. His or her reading is the repetition in a conscious act of the complex processes of conceptualizing and of theorizing contained in the book, signified by the printed characters. But while the student reads, and in order for this reading to be possible, the student turns the pages of the book; the eyes move across the page, following one after the other the lines of the text. And when our student is tired by the intellectual effort, he or she will rise from the chair, leave the library, take the stairs to the cafeteria, rest, eat, and drink. The knowledge contained in the work of biology, which the student has assimilated in the course of reading, is scientific knowledge. Reading the work as such involves a knowledge on the level of consciousness: the intuition of words, the grasp of the meaning they carry. The knowledge that made possible the movement of the hands, the eyes, the act of rising from the chair, the climbing of the stairs, the drinking and eating, the resting itself, is the knowledge of life.

If we ask which of these three types of knowledge is the basic knowledge, we must cast aside in one fell swoop all the prejudices of our time, its scientific and positivist ideology. This ideology amounts to the belief not only that scientific knowledge is the most important but that in reality it is the only true knowledge, that knowledge means science. Knowledge has become identified with the type of mathematical knowledge of nature introduced in the age of Galileo. According to this common view everything that came before the advent of science in the Western world was no more than prejudice, confusion, illusion. But beginnings are always the most difficult. And how was it that prescientific humanity, possessing in fact none of the means that science would later make available to it, was able not only to survive and develop but also to produce in so many areas— in the areas of art and religion for example—extraordinary results that today's humanity would be incapable of attaining if it did not have a basic knowledge available to it? (This is a point we shall return to later.)

The knowledge belonging to life has no object because its essence is not the relation to an object. If the knowledge involved in moving our hands, and which makes it possible to do so, had an object—in this case our hands and their potential motion—this movement would never occur. Knowledge would stand before it as before something objective, from which the distance of objectivity would forever separate it, something it would be incapable of ever reaching. On the contrary, only a knowledge that possesses the capacity of uniting with the power of the hands and of identifying itself with it, of being what it is and of doing what it does, can merge with this power because it is nothing other than the experience that this power has constantly of itself. Such knowledge is nothing other than its radical subjectivity. Only in and through the absolute immanence of its radical subjectivity is the power of the hands—that is, any such power in general—possible. In other words, only in this way is it in possession of itself and thus *able* at every instant to be unfolded. A knowledge like this, which excludes all *ecstasis* from itself, a knowledge that sees nothing and consists in the radical subjectivity of its pure experience of itself and in the pathos of this experience, is precisely the knowledge of life.

Life, then, is not merely the external condition for scientific knowledge, in the sense that the scientist must first know how to turn the pages of books; it is also the internal condition for it. Scientific knowledge is just one mode of the knowledge of consciousness, that is, of the relation to an object. But this relation itself is possible only against the backdrop of life within it. Relating to an object is seeing an object, whether this is the sensible seeing of a sensible object or the intellectual seeing of an intelligible object, an abstract relation or an ideal object. However, as we have shown, the knowledge implied in seeing an object is by no means exhausted in knowledge of the object. It implies the knowledge of seeing itself, which is no longer consciousness, the relation to the object, but life.

One cannot escape such an originary notion of life if it is granted that seeing the object presupposes seeing itself, or the pathos of its own self-experience. To put it more explicitly, the auto-affection of absolute subjectivity, which makes it subjectivity, finds its phenomenological realization in the pathos of its experiencing itself by itself, that is, in a transcendental affectivity. If this is granted, then the vision of the object is never a simple seeing but, inasmuch as it constantly affects itself by itself, it is a sensibility. And this is also why the world of science, which excludes sensibility, is necessarily an abstraction in relation to this primordial world.

Our thesis is the following: culture is the culture of life, in the twofold sense in which life constitutes both the subject of this culture and its object. It is an action that life performs on itself and by which it transforms itself, inasmuch as it is itself what transforms and what is transformed. "Culture" designates nothing other than this. "Culture" designates the self-transformation of life, the movement by which it never ceases to modify itself in order to attain forms of realization and of accomplishment that are increasingly more elevated—in order, that is, to grow. But if life is this movement of self-transformation and of self-accomplishment, then it is culture itself, and it carries the latter within itself, intended by it as the very thing it is.

Why does life want to grow? But let us stress first the fact that this self-transformation of life rests on a knowledge. This knowledge is precisely the knowledge of life, in a twofold sense. First, it is a knowledge *of life*. It has life as its content. It is never the knowledge of an object. It is a knowledge that is totally lacking in consciousness, in the knowledge of the world just as in the knowledge of science, which is always a knowledge of something other than life. In this way, for example, biology is the knowledge of a certain type of natural processes external to this knowledge and never the knowledge of the life of which we are speaking, which is the phenomenological life of absolute subjectivity. Second, the knowledge on which culture rests is constituted, as knowledge, by life itself: it is *life that knows* what is in question here and, moreover, that what is in question is itself. How best describe this knowledge? To the extent that it has to do with life, that it stems from life on the one hand and that it has life as its content on the other—to the extent, then, that in it life knows and at the same time is known—I shall call that knowledge *praxis*. Whether the issues are great or small, we always speak about a theoretical point of view and about a practical point of view, as well as of the difference between them, as if it were obvious. This difference, however, is obscure when we seek its principle, because it is rooted in the ultimate structures of Being and finally in its invisible Ground—and it is only here that it can be clarified.

Inasmuch as culture is the culture of life and rests on the knowledge proper to it, it is essentially practical. It consists, we shall say, in the self-development of the subjective potentialities that define this life. As concerns the eye, for example the subjective potentiality of seeing—it is easy to distinguish between the crude eye and the cultivated. The crude eye, as Marx mentions in the *1844 Manuscripts,* is an eye incapable of a fine perception of what it contemplates, incapable of any aesthetic appreciation. It cannot discern the beauty of the material, the beauty of form, and so on. Of the cultivated eye, on the other hand, the refined functioning is, in its pathos, aesthetic pleasure as such. If it is a matter of motor subjective potentialities, we can all distinguish in the same way between the body of a dancer, which can master its own strength, hold it in or free it, and the body of an individual who is inexperienced and awkward. As the self-development of the potentialities of life, culture can be considered their being put to work, their exercise, which presupposes that life does possess these powers and is capable of exercising them. Culture presupposes that to life belongs the fundamental ontological condition that is its very essence as auto-affection and transcendental affectivity. For it is in the auto-affection of this transcendental affectivity that each of its powers is attained in itself and thus grows of itself.

We were asking, Why does life want to grow? We can reply, Because this is its nature, because it is the original attaining in itself that, as such, is self-growth—what Nietzsche called the Will to power. In this way, the self-development of the powers of life never signifies that they are simply put to work, but instead that they are unfolded in such a way as to verify what they are, namely, the movement by which they take possession of their own being, never ceasing to grow in and of themselves at every instant. Insofar as it is subjectivity, life does not exist; it is a perpetual becoming as a coming to be itself, within an attaining in itself. This growth of life in the sense of its eternal coming into itself is indeed a pathos, an experiencing of itself, so that in this experiencing of itself life lives itself out as something it has not posited but as something that comes to it, happens to it, and never ceases to do so—as something it constantly undergoes in a submission that is stronger than its freedom. This submission, in which life is constantly assailed by its own being and submerged by it, projects it ahead, spurs it to action. This does not occur first in the exteriority of a world but precisely in the form of this submission, as an increase of power and as its unfolding. Every eye can see something more and every force can increase. It is not what it sees (unless it is spread out before the eye for this very purpose) that makes the eye open wider, it is its seeing. What stimulates its power and drives it towards even greater power is not its possible effect or some predetermined aim, but its own intoxication.

Culture, as the self-development of life, involves several different forms: an immediate form, namely, the social organization, the system of needs and of labor aimed at satisfying these needs. Needs and labor are two basic modes of praxis, each a sort of extension of the other—labor, or rather original activity, being nothing other than the growth of need. On the other hand, there are also superior forms: art, ethics, and religion. Particularly remarkable moments in the development of culture occur when the superior forms explicitly seek to relate inferior forms to themselves. In the modern world we can cite the current of thought that begins with Ruskin and William Morris and leads to the extraordinary attempt of the Bauhaus movement in Germany to give to industrial production the characteristics of aesthetic production.

At times the opposite movement is produced. Not only does the mastery of the superior forms over the inferior forms decline, but instead of pursuing its own development, each of these forms of the realization of life is impoverished and the whole of life seems to be in decline. Humanity then enters a period of barbarism. Barbarism is always second to a state of culture prior to it, necessarily, and it is only in relation to this former state that it appears as a degeneration. As Joseph de Maistre says, barbarism is a ruin, not a rudiment. Culture is therefore prior. Even the rudest forms of activity and human organization are already forms of culture, for they do offer an organization, implicit laws, and modes of behavior that are all intended to make the existence of the group and its survival possible. As the mere maintenance and the conservation of the forces concerned, these appear as the condition for subsequent progress.

The self-development of life as its self-growth is intended and prescribed by it, in the sense that this is identical to its essence. If this is so, the arrest of that development, even to the point of regression, and the slipping of culture as it falls into barbarism are incomprehensible. It is Nietzsche's stroke of genius to have seen this aporia and to have been forced, in order to solve it, to undertake some extraordinary analyses. These show, in the first place, that the domain of life is not that of the vague and the indeterminate, which would then lend itself to fanciful assertions alien to rigorous science, but that, in it, one can find eidetic and *a priori* correlations, the object of an apodictic knowledge. With respect to our problem, Nietzsche would have it as follows: if the decline of civilizations is possible, this is not because the life-force is capable of diminishing and of gradually changing itself into weakness. Instead, this is because the life-force is infinite and, in its Ground, never weakens. Only it happens that, in the case of what we call weakness, the infinite life-force is turned against itself—in bad conscience, hatred, resentment. If the weak can conquer the strong and even if, according to Nietzsche, they unfailingly do so, it is because they draw support from this force in themselves which, at the very heart of their degenerateness and their decrepitude, remains intact.

Why and how can life turn against itself? Because it is life; it is the "submitting to itself" and the "bearing with itself" of absolute subjectivity, finding its full phenomenological actualization in Suffering and in the extremes of this suffering, which, when this is insufferable (that is, when it can no longer bear with itself) undertakes to undo itself (that is, to break the irremissible tie attaching life to itself). It is only in this mad project of undoing itself that life becomes weakness, precisely because the tie that ties it to itself cannot be untied. It is then that life turns its powerlessness against others or against itself in resentment, abandoning itself to destructive efforts. Great civilizations do not die submerged by external forces; their death arises from within them.

Today humanity is again entering into barbarism. This barbarism, however, presents particular characteristics that should be underscored. These are mainly the result of the fact that our civilization is one based on science and its applications. Since science is the science of nature, it neglects life. It neglects life, in particular, because in the world that it studies, science has abstracted from that by reason of which this world is a life-world, namely, sensibility. Naturally the mathematical science of nature has its own right to exist; its prodigious development in modern times has led to extraordinary results, many of which, if placed in the service of life, would offer it new possibilities. But when we say "placed in the service of life," we are assuming that it is life that judges and decides, in terms of a knowledge that is its own and that concerns it. Except that along with the theoretical development of Galilean science, there is also a belief, to which we alluded earlier, that this science constitutes the only type of real or possible knowledge. Given the reign of this belief, the development of science signifies that any other form of knowledge is excluded and, in particular, the knowledge of life in its fundamental, practical developments—art, ethics, and religion. Eliminating the fundamental knowledge of life at the very heart of the extraordinary development of the mathematical science of nature and for the benefit of this science itself: this is what produces the barbarism proper to our world, and this is what defines it.

The collapse of the fundamental practical knowledge of life is manifest practically, on the level of the life of human groups: churches are empty; there is no ethics. It is true, one can see in this (and some actually do see), a positive factor: the liberation of humanity with respect to taboos and unfounded beliefs. But there is no belief without a foundation. Every belief, however strange or absurd it may seem, is a belief that life has in itself and, ultimately, is identical with life itself. The disappearance of beliefs in the modern world is in strict correlation with the exclusion of the fundamental knowledge of life and the consequence of this. Moreover, the fact that this elimination of the knowledge of life is interpreted as a "liberation" is significant. Thus, the liberation of sexuality means that sexuality is to be considered as a natural process calling for a scientific description and explanation in the sense of natural science. The behavior one is to have in relation to sexuality has its principle in this knowledge of nature or in a knowledge patterned after it, rather than in eroticism or in love understood as radically subjective experiences. Life has ceased to dictate its own laws to itself; it receives them from a scientific backdrop. In this regard, there is endless food for reflection in the popular success encountered in our age by a doctrine such as psychoanalysis.

Here, however, we touch upon an absolutely general point, which could be termed the naturalization of man. Since it is given that the sole type of knowledge is the mathematical knowledge of nature, we can know something about human beings only to the extent that we treat them, in one way or another, as fragments of that nature, that we dismiss their ontological claim, as astronomy has done before us, in short, that we convert the transcendental life of absolute subjectivity into so many objective, empirical data offered to the various positive types of knowledge, which, employing the most rigorous logical and mathematical apparatus possible, will finally tell us what human beings are. The practical elimination of the practical knowledge of life leads to this consequence on the theoretical plane and becomes apparent there.

In this regard, the study of the modes of communication of knowledge, a communication that assumes to begin with the choice of types of knowledge considered as fundamental and primary, would be especially enlightening. From this point of view, the university is a veritable microcosm, and the series of reforms that follow one another at a frantic pace always have as their aim, on the level of teaching as well as on the level of research, the exclusion of the traditional disciplines of culture, which deal with life in an "obscure" way as a specific reality, to the benefit of the scientific disciplines that are defined by their inability to recognize this specific character. The very choice of mathematics as a criterion for separating and classifying high-school and college students is revealing in this regard. What is more, in the disciplines of culture, the invasion of scientific methods robs these disciplines of their proper object, giving rise instead to the appearance of new objects defined by the potential application of these methods. In this way, philosophy has given way to social sciences characterized by the highly technical nature of their distinctive methodologies, a technical nature that goes hand-in-hand with a growing ignorance concerning the final object of investigation. Within philosophy itself, it has been replaced by epistemology, that is, by a reflection on scientific knowledge—which alone is of importance, which alone exists—by mathematical logic, and so on. In

France, in the discipline called "French literature," literature is cast aside in favor of linguistics, of various sociological, psychological, or Freudian approaches to texts whose literary—that is, aesthetic—characters are not even perceived. The texts of great authors are replaced today by texts taken from newspapers, for which an aesthetic analysis would have no point. Last year, for the Aggregation program in English, English literature became optional. In this way the university, which has traditionally played the role of a cultural center, has become in the modern world one of the extensions and one of the centers of the spread of barbarism.

The assertion that science, considered as the only possible mode of knowledge, generates barbarism will not fail to seem overly general as well as excessive. Allow us, therefore, to demonstrate this using precise examples. In Greece, at Eleuthera, are the ruins of one of the fortresses that guarded Attica in the fourth century. It is an admirable wall of huge blocks of stone, resplendent in the sun—above which, unfortunately, a high-tension electrical wire passes. If it is a matter of carrying electrical current from one place to another and of calculating the best way to do this, then the solution adopted by the Greek engineers was certainly the right one. If it suggests itself to us as one of the innumerable examples of the barbarism ravaging our world, this is because in these calculations—and making them possible—it was necessary to abstract from sensibility, that is, from the Whole of absolute subjectivity as the ultimate criterion and as the ultimate reason for all things. If, generally speaking, the "decision makers" of today are barbarians, this is because life, transcendental phenomenological life, is no longer part of their knowledge.

Another example: In the midtwentieth century, from an aesthetic point of view (that is, on the level of praxis, even if this were a past praxis), three main cultivated countries could have been said to exist in the world: Italy, Germany, and, to some extent, France. In these countries much destruction had however been wrought. In these three countries one could still contemplate cities that in themselves, as places where people lived and worked, were works of art. The destruction of German cities during the second World War—specifically, the destruction of their architectural core done without any real military or economic reason—is a striking example of the barbarism of political and military decision makers. Likewise, the absence of any subsequent reaction in the face of this irreparable damage done to an extremely important part of the cultural heritage of humanity shows to what degree the very idea of an aesthetic dimension of existence—that is, an aesthetic praxis—has been excluded from the sphere of human experience. One could say, in this regard, that there is a circle of barbarism: only people devoid of any aesthetic sense could live in the monstrous suburban developments built in the twentieth century—and yet, because life is never completely eliminated, they cannot really.

A final example concerns the intervention of science in aesthetics itself. For if aesthetics still enjoys some rights among us, this is only inasmuch as it is scientific and sets for itself rational aims and methods. But if science excludes sensibility, what can be the meaning of a scientific aesthetics? Not far from Eleuthera, at Daphni, there is a monastery dating from the fifth century, with a church covered with magnificent mosaics. Thanks to numerous and patient restorations, these mosaics had survived. But in 1976 a new restoration process was applied—a scientific one, this time—which resulted in the destruction of a large number of mosaics, the remaining ones being covered with splotches of cement rendering them unrecognizable and disfiguring them forever. What happened? Today various processes, in particular the use of carbon 14, allow the precise dating of materials and, consequently, permit experts to distinguish in a restored work what is original from what is not. What matters to science in the Byzantine monastery at Daphni is what can be established scientifically, that is, being able to separate out additions, touch ups, repaintings of the original work. The irreversible destruction wrought by hammer blows on the mosaic tiles is the consequence of the theory and its own intention. It may be objected that it is not carbon 14 that tells us to reduce to dust everything that does not date from 1160. But who or what will tell us? On what knowledge can we base our decision if there is no knowledge other than scientific knowledge?

The interpretation of culture on the basis of absolute phenomenological life, which is essentially practical, does, to be sure, raise a number of questions. We may ask whether there is not a theoretical culture, whether humanity does not necessarily seek *to know* the life it cannot be content simply to live in the spontaneity of the immediate—in other words, to live blindly, because it is thought that knowing means seeing, that knowledge is precisely theory. And what we ourselves have said about life in this brief presentation, is this not a theoretical knowledge of life? And how is this knowledge possible if life is never an object, if it is by nature invisible?

A theoretical culture, that is, a theorizing of praxis, presupposes the operation—whether implicit or explicit—by which for life is substituted something else, something that takes its place, an objective equivalent, a mere representation of it, in such a way that this representation never gives us life in its reality but only an unreal copy. Political economy, for instance, consists entirely in a substitution like this whereby the real practical life of individuals is replaced by a set of determinations that are supposed to represent it and that are general economic determinations: abstract labor (obtained by excluding all the subjective features of labor, that is, its reality, what Marx called "real labor," "living labor"); exchange value; money; capital; variable capital; and so on. As a result, on the theoretical plane these determinations cannot be explained by themselves. Quite the opposite, they are the source of insurmountable dilemmas on their own level, and on the practical level, they give rise to a deep-seated uneasiness.

In the same way, if we ask how a radical phenomenology of absolute subjectivity is possible—that is, if a theory of life is possible in general—it indeed will have to be constructed as the theory of the possible adequate representations of that life. We shall then observe that in Husserl, for example, there is an unintended shift from the alleged grasp of the reality of transcendental experience in intuitive self-evidence to the intuition of essences that govern this experience but are themselves no more than unreal idealities opening up to the phenomenologist a universe of pure possibilities.

The opposite turn, the passage from the reign of pure, ideal possibilities to that of reality, is accomplished by ethics. Ethical utterance or religious commandment is theoretical only in its mode of presenting itself to consciousness. In its very meaning it refers to theory's other, to praxis as the place of all reality: "it is necessary to act"; "philosophers have only interpreted the world in various ways; the point, however, is to change it." With real action, we are carried back to real culture, to which ethics indeed belongs. The same thing is true of art, whose productions are only apparently objective, and of religion.

Life, then, is praxis. It is, of its very essence, active life. When we speak of someone who leads an active life, who has a lot of telephone calls and important meetings during the day, we are talking about something else, not about the essence of life but about an existential modality of life, in which life tries to flee from itself. Life's attempt to flee from itself is still simply a mode of this life, a singular one even if it is universally widespread. It is weakness and despair.

The contemplative life is, in itself, no less praxis than the active life; it is therefore the same. The contemplative life is not contemplation in the sense of theory. The person who contemplates sees nothing; Rembrandt's portraits have no gaze. In its active modes, life liberates its own force; in its contemplative modes, it is attentive to the original force that dwells in every force, projecting it in itself before it unfolds. It is a life that entrusts itself to its own essence and that, losing itself in the untiring movement of its own coming into itself, experiences it even more intensely.

William J. Richardson

12. *Contemplation in Action*

> Thinking had come to life again; the cultural treasures of the past, believed to be dead, [were] being made to speak . . . . What was experienced was that thinking as pure activity—and this means impelled neither by the thirst for knowledge, nor by the drive for cognition—can become a passion which not so much rules and oppresses all other capacities and gifts, as it orders them and prevails through them. We are so accustomed to the old opposition of reason versus passion, spirit versus life, that the idea of a passionate thinking, in which thinking and aliveness become one, takes us somewhat aback. (Arendt 1971, pp. 51f).

These are the words of the mature Hannah Arendt reflecting on the great moment of her youth when she fell in love for the first time. It came to pass at the age of eighteen in "the extraordinary, the magical" (Young-Bruehl 1982, p. 51), heart-rending year at Marburg (1924) when she began her university studies there. For it was then that she first met Martin Heidegger.

That the two allegedly became lovers, as her biographer reports, is perhaps none of our business. What is our business, at least in these pages, is that he awoke in her through his own passionate thinking a passion for thought that marked her entire career. This passion took her down a different path than the one Heidegger himself followed, but when it came to its end, with the undelivered lectures on the nature of willing that would culminate with a philosophical distance from Heidegger on an analysis of his notion of "willing non-willing," one can wonder about the ultimate distance between them and the strange history of their common passion. *Eine starre Hingegebenbeit an ein Einziges* ("an unbending devotion to a single one") (Young-Bruehl 1982, p. 53), she had called it in the full flame of her teenage ardor, and her biographer takes it as testimony of her adolescent love. But was it only that? What may have remained of this initial devotion in the recollection of maturity as her own path came to an end?

The question is legitimate, for after their brief but intense romance their paths were clearly divergent. If Heidegger was the prototypical thinker, concerned only with the meaning of Being, Hannah Arendt's concern was for doing, the *vita activa,* as she liked to call it—indeed, she never considered herself a "philosopher" in the Kantian sense of a "professional thinker" (1978a, p. 3). It is significant that the term *vita activa* should have so captured her fancy, even to the point of becoming the original title for *The Human Condition.* For it comports with it, and hence makes ingredient to the thinking of it, its correlate in the Graeco-Roman tradition, the *vita contemplativa.* For Hannah Arendt, then, the problematic of contemplative life by way of counterpoise becomes ingredient to her reflection on the active life, and she seems to nurture a fondness for it, even a yearning for it, born perhaps of her empathy with the Greek mind that valued it so highly.

How she conceived these two notions emerges clearly in *The Human Condition.* There she proposes to make a rigorous effort to "think what we are doing" (1958, p. 5). The emphasis is on the doing, of course, and leaves out of consideration the "highest and perhaps purest activity of which mean are capable, the activity of thinking" (1958, p. 5). For it is doing, far more than "labor" or "work," that characterizes what for her is the specific prerogative of a human being, that is, "natality"—that "new beginning inherent in birth that can make itself felt in the world only because the newcomer possesses the capacity of beginning something anew, i.e. of acting" (1958, p. 9). And since action is the "political activity" par excellence, natality rather than mortality "may be the central category of political, as distinguished from metaphysical, thought" (1958, p. 9). Nevertheless, it is what profoundly specifies the human condition. And when the medieval Latins translated the Greek term for "political life" *(bios politikos),* they did so by the formula of *vita activa.*

Whether the *vita activa* is identified with political life as such, (that is, with the active engagement of the free citizen in the *polis*) or whether the notion is broadened to include other activities as well, it remains essentially an "unquiet" life, concerned with what man makes, or brings about, himself. As such it differs profoundly from the *bios theoretikos,* life given over to *theorein,* essentially a "beholding." Arendt traces the origin of the term *theorein,* as others have done, back to the word *theasthai* in Homer, where it signifies a kind of "wonder-struck beholding" on the part of those humans to whom a god (usually in some human disguise) appears. She emphasizes here the fact that both the appearing of the god in disguise and the response of humans to this appearance are utterly gratuituous on the part of the god, hence, something to be suffered *(pathos)* (Socrates' term in *Theaetetus,* 155d) or received by men as gift, rather than achieved by human effort. Moreover, she finds this "wonder-struck beholding" cognate with the *thaumadzein* of Plato, that "admiring wonder" that is the true "passion" *(pathos)* with which philosophy itself begins. Wonder at what? For the prephilosophical Greeks, it was the wonder at the invisible harmonious order of the *kosmos,* beyond all the rhythms of change (Arendt 1978a, pp. 142-143).

We can see, then, how this *bios theoretikos,* the life of contemplation, came to enjoy a place of privilege for the Greek mind among all forms of human activity. "The primacy of contemplation over activity rests on the conviction that no work of human hands can equal in beauty and truth the physical *kosmos,* which swings in itself in changeless eternity without interference or assistance from outside, from man or god" (Arendt 1958, p. 15). But as the notion of contemplation is developed by the philosophers, it becomes clear that on the part of one who contemplates such truth, the *pathos* (passivity) must be complete. "Every movement, the movements of body and soul as well as of speech and reasoning, must cease before truth. Truth . . . can reveal itself only in complete human stillness" (Arendt 1958, p. 15), stillness that, whatever its attraction, blurs for Arendt all distinctions and differentiations in the life of activity. Moreover, it implies a stepping out of time, however briefly (as in Plato's cave metaphor), in a kind of *nunc stans* ("the standing now"), to feel the touch of eternity as if in a transitory brush with death (Arendt 1958, p. 20).

When these Greek categories passed into the Christian tradition, the same hierarchy remained. Instead of the harmony of the *kosmos* or the Platonic Ideas, the eternally true is God himself. Contemplation of this truth is the highest form of human existence, to which everything else, that is, all the complexities of the active life, must be subordinated (see Arendt 1958, p. 303). And even if the contemplative experience is filtered through the categories of love that plunge it back into the world in the service of others, it remains for Arendt a kind of fleeing from the world and hiding from its inhabitants that "negates the space the world offers to men, and most of all that public part of it where everything and everybody are seen and heard by others" (Arendt 1958, p. 77).

For our purposes, let us accept in broad outline Arendt's reading of the polarity between contemplation and action, especially in the monastic tradition of the West—though a more thoroughgoing treatment would require further nuance. But in the sixteenth century, while Martin Luther was preaching salvation through faith alone in Germany and Theresa of Avila was founding convents in Spain, there emerged another kind of religious personality in Europe who introduced into the tradition another kind of contemplation; his name was Ignatius of Loyola.

There is no need here to recount his history. It is common knowledge that after his conversion at the age of thirty, following a battle wound at Pamplona, Ignatius spent eleven austere months of withdrawal at Manresa seeking to know God's will for him. The anguish of this time: the neglect of his bodily needs, the fasting, the seven hours on his knees in daily prayer, the mood swings from consolation to desolation, the torture of scruples, the temptation to suicide, all such signs of the "dark night of the soul" yielded at last to several mystical experiences, one of which was classically contemplative. As reported later: "He saw in a marvelous manner into the divine mysteries. This light was extended also to the power of discernment between good and evil spirits, and was so overwhelming that he beheld, so it seemed to him, all human and divine things with wholly new eyes of the spirit" (cited Rahner 1953, p. 53). Such was the ascetical way of the entire monastic tradition that led Ignatius by the Cardoner River to the passive gaze of the classic contemplative.

But if we look at the same man forty years later in Rome, fully engaged in the active life of governing the religious order he helped found, he is still very much a mystic, but of a different sort. Now the contemplation of the Holy Trinity did not withdraw him from the world but immersed him in it. Thus, Jerome Nadal, his longtime secretary, would write:

> We know that Father Ignatius had received from God the exceptional grace of being able without effort to pray and rest in the contemplation of the Most Holy Trinity. . . . To this was added that in all things, actions, conversations, he felt and contemplated the presence of God and the attraction of spiritual things: he was contemplative in action, something he habitually expressed by the words: we must find God in all things. (Stierli 1977, p. 140)

The claim here is that this is an acceptable use of the word *contemplation*. It should be noted that what is at stake for Ignatius is not a vision of God as some neo-Platonic object of knowledge in which one could repose in a passive beholding, but awareness of God as *acting* in the world. God's will for Ignatius was not the divine nature or divine truth but divine action that invited the collaboration of his "servant" and "instrument" in the accomplishing of it. This conception of God as being *at work* in the world may indeed derive from the vision by the banks of the Cardoner. Nevertheless, it is found in the book of the *Spiritual Exercises,* the notebook record of the Manresa experience for use in the guidance of others. There we find an exercise under the title of "Contemplation for Obtaining Love."

This meditation summarizes and concludes the entire set of spiritual exercises and begins with two preambles: (1) love is proved by deeds rather than words; and (2) love consists in a mutual exchange of gifts. He proposes to consider how God's love has shown itself by deeds rather than words and invites the exercitant to respond by a corresponding gift of himself or herself. Ignatius then suggests that one reflect on the countless gifts that God has bestowed on human beings, beginning with creation itself, and then on how God himself actually dwells in his gifts by his presence, works in them through his power, is the source of everything that comes to human beings, like rays emanating from the sun. The appropriate response from humans, then, would be a loving surrender to the divine bounty by engaging itself in active collaboration with the divine will at work in the world. It is a gesture of loving gratitude, of meditation as thanksgiving, if you will. In short, this constant effort to discern and realize, that is, coactivate, the divine will in the world and collaborate with it is precisely what Ignatius meant by "finding God in all things" (1960, pp. 127-30).

How this conception functions in the spirituality Ignatius offers those who follow his inspiration may be seen in the advice he offers young men in training, whose preoccupation with studies does not permit them long periods of prayer. Let them "exercise themselves in seeking the presence of our Lord in all things—for example, in conversing with someone, in walking, looking, tasting, hearing, thinking, and in everything they do, since it is true that his Divine Majesty is in all things by his presence, power and essence" (Stierli 1977, p. 145). When the conception worked well in history (obviously not always the case), the results were good: from the foundation of colleges to the reductions in Paraguay, from Matteo Ricci to Teilhard de Chardin.

What, then, do we infer from all this? Ignatius appeared on the scene precisely at the time when the hierarchy between contemplation and action was, according to Arendt, on the point of reversal. For after the calculations of Copernicus that made it possible to conceive of "virile man standing in the sun . . . overlooking the planets" (1958, p. 264), and after the discovery of the telescope by Galileo that made it possible for man to measure truth by an instrument of his own fashioning, and after the meditations of Descartes on a guaranteed way to certify knowledge, truth was no longer something to be beheld (in contemplation) but rather something to be achieved by human action. Archimedes' dream had finally been realized—a point had been discovered outside the earth from which man, while still on earth, could dislodge the world. This shift for Arendt is the most decisive characteristic of the modern era (1958, p. 320): the *vita activa* had lost all point of reference to the *vita contemplativa*. And yet, at least in the religious tradition, Ignatius was there to say that the two were still reconcilable—not that his personal experience could be shared, of course, but that the structure of it was somehow viable and sharable with others.

But that is in the religious sphere. In the secular sphere, the distinction between knowledge and though became paramount.

> Certainty of knowledge could be reached only under a twofold condition: first, that knowledge concerned only what one had done himself—so that its ideal became mathematical knowledge, where we deal only with self-made entities of the mind—and second, that knowledge was of such a nature that it could be tested only through more doing. (Arendt 1958, p. 290)

Henceforth the role of thought itself would be radically changed. Although it never had been identified with contemplation as the beholding of truth, it had always been conceived as the dialogical discourse within one's self that would lead to it. Now that truth was not to be beheld but to be fashioned, thought was no longer the handmaid of inchoative contemplation ("theology") but of the human doing that would produce certifiable knowledge (1958, p. 291-292).

But not for Hannah Arendt! She had come to know thought at Marburg—real, passionate thought: thought that was "pure activity" in which the cultural treasures of the past could be "made to speak," in which "thinking and aliveness become one." And when after thinking about what we do she came at last to think about how we think. It is not surprising, then, that she took this model as her standard of excellence. We know that she came to the task in the Gifford lectures after the Eichmann study, where, impressed by the "banality of evil," she found that the problem lay not in his stupidity but in his thoughtlessness (1978a, p. 4). What, then, does she mean by thought?

First, it is not the privilege of the few, but the "natural need" (Arendt 1978a, p. 191) of all human life that must not be left to the specialist, "as though thinking, like higher mathematics, were the monopoly of a specialized discipline" (Arendt 1978a, p. 13). On the contrary, it "accompanies life and is itself the dematerialized quintessence of being alive . . . Unthinking men are like sleepwalkers" (Arendt 1978a, p. 191). To be alive in thought, then, is the only remedy for the "thoughtlessness" of an Eichmann or the sleeplike existence of "unthinking men." Deep as life and broad as life, thinking is not just a cerebral discipline but encompasses the whole of life and, hence, is the source and inspiration of all art (Arendt 1958, p. 170). Thinking is "sheer activity" (pure *praxis*), that is, it does not serve any aim outside itself but rather is its own end (Arendt 1958, p. 170).

In all this, the great model, of course, is Socrates—not simply because of his own passion for the dialogue of thought but because this found its place within the *polis*. Socrates was equally at home in both spheres (Arendt 1978a, p. 167-68). But he also manifests the limitations of thought, inasmuch as thought interrupts all activities and is interrupted by them. Identified with life, the activity of thinking demands a certain withdrawal from life, as indicated by Xenophon's stories of Socrates' distractedness in the military camp.

More precisely, what is thinking? Hard to define, it is at least different from knowing. Hannah Arendt makes her own Kant's distinction between reason *(Vernunft)* and intellect *(Verstand)*, taking the latter to signify the faculty of cognition (primarily scientific) and the former to signify the faculty that reaches beyond what can be known as objects to ultimate unities, or unifying principles, of meaning (like Ideas of God, freedom and immortality) that thought cannot know as objects, but cannot dispense with either. Thinking, for Hannah Arendt, is the functioning of just such a faculty of reason.

Who is it that thinks? Kant, as we know, makes a distinction between the "self" of everyday experience that appears in consciousness (the "phenomenal" self) and the subject that is thinkable but not knowable (the "noumenal" subject). Arendt makes her own Kant's formula from the *Critique of Pure Reason:* "In the consciousness of myself in the sheer thinking activity [*beim blossen Denken*], I am the thing itself [*das Wesen Selbst,* that is *das Ding an sich*] although nothing of myself is thereby given to thought" (B 429). This is what encourages her to speak of this subject as "sheer activity," and she adds, "The thinking [subject] is . . . therefore ageless, sexless, without qualities, and without a life story" (Arendt 1978, p. 43).

But if the thinking subject is "sheer activity" and "ageless," is it therefore timeless? It is in addressing this question that Arendt makes her own most personal contribution to the notion of thinking. To explain her position she makes use of a parable of Kafka, entitled "He":

> He has two antagonists; the first presses him from behind, from the origin. The second blocks the road in front of him. He gives battle to both. Actually the first supports him in his fight with the second, for he wants to push him forward, and in the same way the second supports him in his fight with the first, since he drives him back. But it is only theoretically so. For it is not only the two antagonists who are there, but he himself as well, and who really knows his intentions. His dream, though, is that some time in an unguarded moment—and this, it must be admitted, would require a night darker than any night has ever been yet—he will jump out of the fighting line and be promoted, on account of his experience in fighting, to the position of umpire over his antagonists in their fight with each other. (Arendt 1946, pp. 276-277)

For Hannah Arendt, this Kafka parable describes the "time sensation" of the thinking subject when it directs attention to its own activity and is withdrawn from the business of everyday life (1978a, p. 206), where two tenses of time, past and future, are experienced as antagonistic forces that crash into the present Now (1978a, p. 203). For Kafka, it is a metaphor for the whole of life.

Arendt insists that the thinking subject here is not the self of phenomenal (or phenomenological) awareness. "It is because the thinking [that is, the noumenal] subject is ageless and nowhere that past and future can become manifest to it as such, emptied, as it were, of their concrete content and liberated from all spatial, categories" (1978a, p. 206). For the thinking subject, time is an enemy, since it interrupts the "immobile quiet in which the mind is active without doing anything" (1978a, p. 206). The subject rests, then, in a kind of *nunc stans,* that is, a quasi-"eternal presence in complete quiet" (1978a, p. 207), and hence is apparently timeless.

Arendt is sensitive to the fact that Kafka's "He" seems to jump out of the world altogether, and she admits that without man in the world there would be no difference between past and future but only everlasting change. Instead, she suggests the metaphor of a parallelogram of forces: past and future are conceived as two vectors, each proceeding out of an "infinite" distance, that intersect in man as if at the apex of a ninety degree angle that represents the present:

> Ideally, the action of the two forces that form our parallelogram should result in a third force, the resultant diagonal whose origin would be the point at which the

forces meet and upon which they act . . . . This diagonal force, whose origin is known, whose direction is determined by past and future, but which exerts its force toward an undetermined end as though it could reach out into infinity, seems to me a perfect metaphor for the activity of thought. (1978a, p. 209).

The thinking subject reposes in such a present, like "the quiet center of a storm that, though totally unlike the storm, still belongs to it" (1978a, p. 209).

Arendt is aware of the tenuous nature of her proposal, insisting that it applies only in the realm of "mental phenomena," hence not to "historical or biographical" time where "gaps do not occur" (1978a, p. 210). Springing from the clash of past and future, such a present is outside of historical time, "coeval with the existence of man on earth"—"the small, inconspicuous track of non-time beaten by the activity of thought within the time-space given to natal, mortal men" (1978a, p. 210).

But what is to be said about such a conception of thinking? Of course, we do not have Arendt's own final redaction of these texts, but given what we have, it seems that we can at least say this much: In *The Human Condition,* "thinking" was spoken of, usually in the Greek sense, as different from contemplation, to be sure, but as discursive activity that was a propaedeutic to contemplation. In *The Life of the Mind,* she speaks in her own name, synthesizing Plato with Kant, so that thinking becomes the activity of the noumenal subject that takes place in a gap between future and past, a *nunc stans* that, if not eternal in the sense that divine truth is eternal, is nonetheless outside of time. This I find highly problematic, for it seems to make thinking in its purity essentially ahistorical. But this does not follow her own style of thinking which is profoundly historical and historicizing. It also does not follow, I believe, the essential dynamism and historicity of natality and the whole problematic of storytelling.

There appears to be, then, in her own experience of "passionate thinking," a kind of nostalgia for the contemplative ideal of the Greeks that is inimical to the life of action, at least to the extent that thought (witness Socrates) demands some kind of withdrawal from action. But in her own work, she seems to have achieved a kind of operational synthesis of the two, though on the conceptual level she found no philosophical paradigm to parallel the one that Ignatius discovered in the religious sphere. This is said with reserve, of course, for we do not know how she might have explored the role of contemplation in the functioning of judgment, since this relates to political action. An explicit treatment of judgment was to have brought *The Life of the Mind* to a close, and presumably it would have followed a Kantian paradigm (1978b, pp. 242–243, 255–273). How it might have been developed, however, is a matter of speculation. The present reflection makes no pretense at writing the book that Hannah Arendt left unwritten, but proceeds with the data as we have them. In such a context, we ask simply if there is some analogue of the Ignatian paradigm possible for thought.

We are suggesting here that there is, if only to explore the relationship with Heidegger that began when she fell in love with him in 1924.

Let us begin with her own explicit interpretation of Heidegger's philosophical enterprise as it appears in the Gifford Lecture that she never delivered. It appears in Part II of *The Life of the Mind* where she traces the history of the notion of will, culminating in a discussion of Nietzsche's "repudiation" of the will and Heidegger's apparent endorsement of that "repudiation" with his "passionate insistence" (Arendt's phrase) on willing "not to will" (Heidegger's phrase). Allegedly this insistence was a new development on Heidegger's part and derived from a shift in his thinking that took place in the midst of the ten-year span (1936–46) in which he devoted his university courses chiefly to the study of Nietzsche. This shift constitutes what Heidegger himself later called the "turning" *(Kehre)* in his thought. If Heidegger claims that this turnabout is a sign of deep continuity with his earlier endeavor, Arendt dismisses the claim as a *post factum* "reinterpretation" of the "original" shift that consists of a "concrete autobiographical event precisely between volume I and volume II [of his Nietzsche book, *ca*. 1940]": "What the reversal originally turns against is primarily the will-to-power. In Heidegger's understanding, the will to rule and to dominate is a kind of original sin [of destructiveness (Arendt 1978b, p. 178), of which he found himself guilty when he tried to come to terms with his brief past in the Nazi movement" (Arendt 1978b, p. 173).

That's the heart of her interpretation. She expands her analysis of the relation between the earlier and later period in Heidegger's development by showing how certain themes of *Being and Time* (such as care, death, and self) emerge after the turn (1978b, pp. 176, 236 [n. 52])—all in light of that interpretation of the turn.

It would not serve any purpose to quarrel with her in her absence about this interpretation of Heidegger's development, except to say that it is doubtful that many Heideggereans today would agree with her. Elsewhere (Richardson, 1973), the present writer argued that the turn was apparent in Heidegger's work at least ten years earlier than she claims (by 1930), and on the basis of recently published materials one could argue for its being in play much earlier. That is why it seems gratuitous to dismiss Heidegger's own explanations as "reinterpretations" of some more "original," unacknowledged fact. When Heidegger was once asked explicitly, "given the turning, how did it come about?", he replied:

> The thinking of the turning *is* a change in my thought. But this change is not a consequence of altering the standpoint, much less of abandoning the fundamental issue, of *Being and Time*. The thinking of the turning results from the fact that I stayed with the matter-for-thought [of] "Being and Time," i.e., by inquiring into that perspective which already in *Being and Time* (p. 39) was designated "Time and Being.". . . . The distinction you make between [the early and later Heideg-

ger] is justified only on the condition that this is kept constantly in mind: only by way of what [the early Heidegger] has thought does one gain access to what is to-be-thought by [the later Heidegger]. But the thought of [the early Heidegger] becomes possible only if it is contained [in the later Heidegger]. (1963, pp. xvi-xxii, Heidegger's italics).

It seems clear, then, that the turning had nothing to do with the influence of Nietzsche and still less to do with the tragic events of 1933. Rather, it had everything to do with his most primordial philosophical experiences of the early 1920s:

I was trying to follow a way which was leading I knew not where. Only the immediate prospect was known to me, for this was continually opening up, even if the field of vision often shifted and grew dark (Heidegger, 1959b, p. 6)
. . . .The course was a scarcely perceptible promise of a liberation unto freedom, now dark and confusing, now a lightning-flash of sudden insight which then again for a long period of time withdrew from every attempt to utter it. (Heidegger 1959b, p. 41, translation modified; cited by Richardson 1973 p. 632).

The point is that the dynamics of the turn were always already operative in Heidegger's thought, and this was part of the *pathos* of the "passionate thinking" that set Hannah Arendt aflame in 1924.

That said, no pretense is made here at a formal critique of Arendt's analysis of Heidegger. It will be more useful if we simply extract certain themes for comment that may throw light on her or him or them both. To begin with, she is very aware of the import of Heidegger's endeavor to engage in the "thinking of Being" where the "of" is both subjective and objective genitive, that is, suggesting that Being is the origin and the term of Dasein's thought. But she then proceeds to "ontify" being almost to the point of ridicule, speaking of it as analogous to Hegel's Absolute Spirit, hence a "ghostlike existence," a "Somebody," or a "Nobody"—Nevertheless an apparently Ontic Something that "behind the backs of acting men" secretly guides the course of history (Arendt 1978b, pp. 186–87). Understandably she objects to the determinism involved. She speaks disparagingly, too, of the role assigned to the thinker in this process. He is one who responds to Being and by "sheer thinking" enacts "the countercurrent of Being underlying the "foam" of beings—the mere appearances whose current is steered by the will-to-power" (Arendt 1978b, p. 187). And all this takes place while the thinker remains a solitary "in 'existential solipsism,' except that now the fate of the world, the History of Being, has come to depend on him" (Arendt 1978b, p. 187). She remains skeptical, too, about an identification of thinking and acting. She quotes Heidegger, who puts it this way: "If to act means to give a hand to the essence of Being, then thinking is actually acting. That is, preparing [building an abode] for the essence of Being by which Being transposes itself and its essence into speech" (Heidegger 1962, p. 40; cited by Arendt 1978b, pp. 180–81).

If these are her reserves, there are at least three ways in which she finds the thought of the later Heidegger congenial. In the first place, she seems to be comfortable with Heidegger's conception of thinking as letting-be:

> And letting-be as an activity is thinking that obeys the call of Being. The mood pervading the letting-be of thought is the opposite of the mood of purposiveness in willing; later. . . . Heidegger calls it *"Gelassenheit,"* a calmness that corresponds to letting-be and that "prepares us" for "a thinking that is not willing" (Heidegger 1959a, p. 33/60).
> This thinking is "beyond the distinction between activity and passivity" because it is beyond the "domain of the will," i.e., beyond the category of causality. (Arendt 1978, pp. 178–79).

Implicitly she recognizes here that the process of thinking lies deeper than willing and, indeed, makes it possible.

A second aspect of Heidegger's thought that she finds congenial is the conception of thinking as thanking. Conceding an etymological warrant for the correlation Heidegger finds between *Denken* and *Danken*, and even finding it acceptable insofar as it resonates for her with the tones of Plato's "admiring wonder" (*thaumadzein*) with which philosophy begins, nonetheless thinking as thanking makes impossible the discernment "of disharmony, of ugliness and finally of evil" (Arendt 1978a, p. 150), whether that evil be "radical" or "banal." Perhaps that explains why she finds so congenial what she takes to be a "new outlook, so isolated from the rest of his thought [that it] must have emerged from another change of 'mood' no less important [than the original turning]" (Arendt 1978b, p. 188), namely, a theme that emerges in Heidegger's analysis of Anaximander. There, in meditating on the "coming-to-be and passing-away" (*genesis-phthora*) of beings, Heidegger emphasizes the concealment inherent to the process of revealment, that is, the untruth ("errancy") intrinsic to the process of truth (*aletheia*) as it emerges in history (Arendt 1978b, pp. 188–92). The issue here is important, for it is not something new in Heidegger's thought, and it is interesting that she finds it so fascinating. Curiously enough, the theme emerged the first time he thematized the notion of letting beings be.

In his essay *On the Essence of Truth* (1930), Heidegger begins with an analysis of the traditional notion of truth as correspondence and argues that the essence of such truth is freedom: "To free oneself for a binding directedness is possible only by *being free* for what is opened up in an open region. Such being free points to the heretofore uncomprehended essence of freedom. . . . *The essence of truth is freedom"* (1930, p. 125, Heidegger's italics). This freedom, already analyzed in *Being and Time* in terms of Dasein's "disclosedness" (1927, pp. 256-73, 212-30) had been addressed again in *On the Essence of Ground* (1929b) as the "transcendence of Dasein, i.e., its passage beyond beings to Being (discerned there as World).

Call it "disclosure," "transcendence," "ek-sistence," Dasein is free insofar as it is open to the Open of Being. What, then, is the essence of freedom? Letting beings be! "To let be—that is, to let beings be as the beings that they are—means to engage oneself with the open region and its openness into which every being comes to stand, bringing that openness, as it were, along with itself. Western thinking in its beginning conceived this open region as *ta alethea*, the unconcealed" (Heidegger 1930, p. 127), that is, as truth.

Heidegger continues to meditate this notion of *a-letheia* in the essay and for the first time orchestrates it as revealing itself to—but also concealing itself from—human beings:

> Considered with respect to truth as disclosedness, concealment is then undisclosedness and accordingly the untruth that is most proper to the essence of truth. . . . The concealment of beings as a whole, untruth proper is older than every openness of this or that being. It is older than letting-be itself which in disclosing already holds concealed and comports itself towards concealing. (1930, p. 132).

He then proceeds to meditate the untruth that is ingredient to truth as a process of concealment-revealment. It takes two forms: (1) the concealment itself is concealed, and Heidegger calls this "mystery"; (2) the concealment not only conceals itself but beguiles man into obliviousness of it, thereby leading him astray—and this he calls "errancy" (*Irre*):

> Errancy opens itself up as the open region for every opposite to essential truth. Errancy is the open site for and ground of error. . . . Error extends from the most ordinary wasting of time, making a mistake and miscalculating, to going astray and venturing too far in one's essential attitudes and decisions. However, what is ordinarily and even according to the teachings of philosophy recognized as error, incorrectness of judgments and falsity of knowledge, is only one mode of erring and, moreover, the most superficial one. The errancy in which any given segment of historical humanity must proceed for its course to be errant is essentially connected with the openness of Dasein. By leading him astray, errancy dominates man through and through. (1930, p. 136).

The problematic of errancy, then, that Arendt finds so fascinating in the analysis of Anaximander's use of *genesis-phthora* is indeed not a "new outlook . . . isolated from the rest of his thought" (Arendt 1978b, p. 188) but ingredient to it and there from the beginning of his meditation on truth. In any case, it is in this context that the problem of evil must be confronted in Heidegger: "With healing (*Heilen*), evil (*das Böse*) appears all the more in the lighting of Being. The essence of evil does not consist in the mere baseness of human action but rather in the malice of rage (*Bösartigen des Grimmes*). Both of these, however, healing and raging, can essentially occur only in Being, insofar as Being itself is what is contested (*das Strittige*)" (Heidegger 1947, p. 237).

But how does Dasein respond to this if thinking is thanking? The argument has been made elsewhere and can only be summarized here. In *Being and Time*, thinking consisted in the phenomenological analysis of Dasein, whose structure was discerned in its unity as care and whose authenticity was achieved in a dynamic way by a gesture of acceptance—acceptance of its transcendence, acceptance of its finitude—in "advancing resolve." In the later period, the problem of thinking is everywhere, but it is thematized most explicitly in *What is Called Thinking?* There, among other things, Heidegger meditates on the etymology of *Denken* as related to *Gedächtnis* on the one hand, and *Gedanc* on the other. *Gedächtnis* is not just "memory" but "re-collection" in the sense of that "heart" of man where he is exposed most profoundly to Being: Meister Echkart's *Seelenfuenklein*.

Gedanc, on the other hand, suggests thanksgiving, that gesture by which the thinker acquiesces to the to-be-thought in the most profound gesture of acceptance. One finds here a complete analogue to what was found in *Being and Time*: thinking as the re-collected "heart" of Dasein, corresponds to what was the unified structure of care; thinking as thanksgiving corresponds to what was the gesture of resolve. Nonetheless, it is in this context that we are to understand Heidegger's admonition about "willing non-willing," upon which Arendt has laid such stress. "The occasion for releasing oneself to belonging [Being] requires a trace of willing. This trace, however, vanishes while releasing oneself and is completely extinguished in releasement (*Gelassenheit*)" (Heidegger 1959a, p. 80). But this is the gesture of resolve: "The essence of thought, i.e., release unto [Being], is resolve into truth as it comes-to-presence" (Heidegger 1959a, p. 81, translation modified).

It is just such a gesture of resolute acquiescence in spite of *das Strittige* (the Contentious) that is at stake, it seems to me, when in *Introduction to Metaphysics* (1953) Heidegger analyzes Heraclitus' term *polemos* (struggle). "The *polemos* named here is a conflict that prevailed prior to everything divine and human" (Heidegger 1953, p. 62). It is the primal struggle between revealment and concealment that constitutes the very essencing of truth (Heidegger 1950, p. 177). He continues:

> The struggle meant here is the original struggle, for it gives rise to the contenders as such; it is not a mere assault on something already there. It is this conflict that

first projects and develops what had hitherto been unheard of, unsaid and unthought. The battle is then sustained by the creators, poets, thinkers, statesmen. Against the overwhelming chaos they set the barrier of their work, and in their work they capture the world thus opened up. It is with these works that the elemental power, the *physis* first comes to stand. Only now do beings become beings as such. This world-building is history in the authentic sense. (1953, p. 62, translation modified).

We see here, then, at least in general terms, how Heidegger conceives the function of the statesman in the *polis*. This surely is more than a solitary gesture of thought consummated in "existential solipsism." May one consider it a legitimate expression of the *bios politikos*, hence a recognizable form of the active life? This opens up larger questions, of course: What is the relation between action and thought in Heidegger? Does thinking as resolute thanksgiving permit action of any efficacious kind, let alone political action? At this point we are on the threshold of the entire discussion that has been launched by Reiner Schürmann concerning the possibility of an eventual practical philosophy emerging out of Heidegger's thought. Schürmann's position on the matter is challenging and provocative, but a discussion of it lies outside the scope of the present reflection. Rather, the question here is whether it may be called a contemplation at all, and if so, whether this kind of thinking may be called a "contemplation in action," following the structure of the Ignatian paradigm.

In the first place, it seems legitimate to find in Heidegger's thought an analogue to the Greek ideal of contemplation by Arendt's own testimony: "Philosophy [for Heidegger] is the exceptional existential possibility of human reality—which is, in the end, only a reformulation of Aristotle's *bios theoretikos*, of the contemplative life as the highest possibility for man" (Arendt 1946, p. 48). As such, it emulates the "admiring wonder" with which, for Plato, all philosophy, that is, all true thinking, begins (Arendt 1978a, p. 142). For Heidegger, this "wonder of all wonders: that beings are" becomes the ground-question of all metaphysics: "why are there beings at all and not much rather no-thing?" (Heidegger 1929a, p. 112).

Such, then is the *pathos* (the passion) of Socrates. And if he is taken by Arendt to be the model thinker because he is equally at home in both activity and thought, the reason, as Heidegger sees it, is the following:

> Throughout his life and up to his death Socrates did nothing other than place himself in this draft, this current [of thinking], and maintain himself in it. This is why he is the purest thinker of the West. This is why he wrote nothing. For anyone who begins, out of thinking, to write must inevitably be like those people who run for shelter from a wind too strong for them. . . . All thinkers after Socrates, their greatness notwithstanding, had to be such refugees. (Heidegger 1954, p. 17, translation modified).

Socrates alone, then, among the great philosophers was no refugee. It should be noted that this draft into which Socrates was drawn was the draft of Being's withdrawal. For the withdrawal (*Entzug*) of Being draws the thinker with it and constitutes him or her in that privileged relationship (*Bezug*). It is the hailing and being hailed, the call and responding to the call in acquiescence that Socrates was caught up in a gesture of thanksgiving.

I suggest that this be regarded as contemplation, not as the Greeks, or even Socrates, understood it but as an Ignatius would find understandable—as total accepting exposure to Being advancing toward human beings as their history and inviting their collaboration to bring it to expression.

It is to be regarded as contemplation, then, but also as action, at the very least through the action of speech. First, Heidegger:

> If to act means to give a hand to the essence of Being, then thinking is actually acting. That is, preparing [building an abode] for the essencing of Being, in the midst of entities by which Being transposes itself and its essencing into speech. Without speech, mere doing lacks the dimension in which it can become effective and follow directions. Speech, however, is never a simple expression of thinking, feeling, or willing. Speech is the original dimension in which the human being is able to respond to Being's claim and, responding, belong to it. Thinking is the actualization of that original correspondence. (Heidegger 1962, p. 40; cited in Arendt 1978b, pp. 180-81).

But for Hannah Arendt, action and speech belonged close together in the life of the *polis*. Just as for the prepolitical Greeks of Homer, great actions and great words were "coeval and coequal," so "to be political, to live in the *polis*, meant that everything was decided through words and persuasion, and not through force or violence" (Arendt 1958, p. 26). The result was that Aristotle's famous formula for man (*zoon logon echon*) was not so much a metaphysical definition as a sociological description of a way of life in which speech and only speech made sense, and where the central concern of all citizens was to talk with each other. Thinking that founds speech is, then, a form of action.

In conclusion, what is the essential in all this?

1. In taking Socrates as model of the thinker in the *polis*, Hannah Arendt invites us to think of the *pathos* that impassioned him as the draw of Being's withdrawal that drew him with it in its wake. The argument has been that, given the Ignatian paradigm, this is a form of contemplation in a unique but legitimate sense; that insofar as that draw—withdrawal—drawing-with is the origin of speech, then given the identification of speech and action in the *polis* (speech, then, as a species of action), it is a contemplation mediated through action in a

unique but legitimate sense. That is why, given the divergence of their ways, it is possible now to think of Hannah Arendt and Heidegger as dwelling together on mountains a chasm apart.

2. If we think of them this way, we might find a better way than she has offered to understand the true natality of thought, even when—perhaps especially when—it tells again an old story, for example, of the founding of the city. It would be grounded in the temporo-historical structure of a recollective thought (*andenkendes Denken*) such as the following:

> If the thinking-upon-what-is-past allows the past [to follow the law of] its own essence . . . , then we experience that what-is-past, in its return through [our] thinking upon it, swings out over our present and comes to us as a future. All at once our thinking-upon-what-is-as-having-been must consider this past as something-not-yet-unfolded. (1951, p. 95, writer's translation).

Moreover, we would conceive of thought as a quest for meaning that, on the one hand, finds a way to account for errance and evil in the historization of truth and, on the other hand, accounts for the thinking of it as corresponding in the event of truth, without resorting to the hypothesis of a timeless, worldless, speechless subject.

3. Finally, that we may end where we began, we are left to wonder about the *pathos* of that common passion that took flame in 1924. What is the nature of such visitation that is a constant of human experience from Homer down to Michel Henry?

> What I called the "quest" for meaning appears in Socrates' language as love, i.e., love in its Greek significance of *Eros*, not the Christian *agape*. Love as *Eros* is primarily a need; it desires what it has not. . . . By desiring what it has not, love establishes a relationship with what is not present. (Arendt 1978a, p. 178)

If quest for meaning, that is, thought, is for Socrates essentially *Eros* we cannot reflect upon the *pathos* that awoke in 1924 without wondering about the *Eros* that was interior to it. For when all is said and done, Arendt's commitment to the political enterprise was a form of *Eros*, according to which she could say to the world, *amo et volo ut sis* ("I love you and want you to be"). But this poses the question of the relationship between love and desire (that is, as want-to-be) as it came to pass in her at the time she first fell in love. What, then, is the relationship between desire and thought? And how can it be shared by two human beings beyond their awareness (in the unconscious), so that after sixty years of divergence it leaves them together on mountains a chasm apart?

On Heidegger's tombstone is engraved a star—as if to suggest the line from one of his epigrams: *Auf einen Stern zu gehen, nur dieses* ("to follow a star—

only this"). If one were to imagine a comparable epigram for Hannah Arendt's tombstone, it might well be: *eine starre Hingegebenheit an ein Einziges* ("an unbending devotion to a single thing"). For such is the spirit that motivates a symposium like the present one. Presumably dedicated to political philosophy, it evoked very little about this theme. The reason may be that this remarkable woman was more than a political philosopher. She was a contemplative in action—and, in the very best of senses, remains for us now the prototype of a political . . . refugee.

References

Arendt, Hannah (1946), "What is Existenz Philosophy?" *Partisan Review* 8/1 (Winter 1946): 34–56.

─────── (1958), *The Human Condition*. Chicago: University of Chicago Press, 1958.

─────── (1971), "Martin Heidegger at 80." *New York Review of Books* 17/6 (October 21, 1971): 50–54.

─────── (1978a), *The Life of the Mind*. Ed. M. McCarthy. New York: Harcourt Brace Jovanovich, 1978a. I. Thinking.

─────── (1978b), *The Life of the Mind*, ed. by M. MacCarthy. New York: Harcourt Brace Jovanovich, 1978b. II. Willing.

Heidegger, M. (1927), *Being and Time*. Trans. J. Macquarrie and E. Robinson. New York: Harper & Row, 1962.

─────── (1929a), "What is Metaphysics?" Trans. D. F. Krell. In *Basic Writings*. Ed. by D. F. Krell. New York: Harper & Row, 1977.

─────── (1929b), "Vom Wesen des Grundes." *Wegmarken*. Frankfurt: Klostermann, 1967. (*Gesamtausgabe*, Abt. I: Veroeffentlichte Schriften 1914–1970, Bd. IX. Frankfurt: Klostermann, 1976).

─────── (1930), "On the Essence of Truth." Trans. J. Sallis. In *Basic Writings*. Ed. D. F. Krell. New York: Harper & Row, 1977.

─────── (1947), "Letter on Humanism." Trans. F. A. Capuzzi, J. G. Gray, and D. F. Krell. In *Basic Writings*. Ed. D. F. Krell. New York: Harper & Row, 1977.

─────── (1950), "The Origin of a Work of Art." A. Hofstaedter. In *Basic Writings*. Ed. D. F. Krell. New York: Harper & Row, 1977.

─────── (1951), *Erläuterungen zu Hölderlins Dichtungen*. Frankfurt: Klostermann, 1951.

─────── (1953), *Introduction to Metaphysics*. Trans. R. Manheim. New Haven, Conn: Yale University Press, 1974.

─────── (1954), *What is Called Thinking?* Trans. F. Wieck and J. G. Gray. New York: Harper & Row, 1972.

―――― (1959a), *Discourse on Thinking*. Trans. J. M. Anderson and E. H. Freund. New York: Harper & Row, 1966.

―――― (1959b), *On the Way to Language*. Trans. P. D. Hertz. New York: Harper & Row, 1971.

―――― (1962), *Die Technik und die Kehre*. Pfullingen: Neske, 1962.

―――― (1963), Preface to Richardson, W. J., *Heidegger: Through Phenomenology to Thought*. The Hague: Nijhoff, 1963.

Ignace de Loyola. *Exercises Spirituels*. Trans. F. Courel. Paris: Desclée de Brouwer, 1960.

Kafka, F. (1946), *The Great Wall of China*. Trans. W. and E. Muir. New York: Schocken, 1946.

Kant, I. (1787). *Kritik der reinen Vernunft*. Hamburg: Meiner, 1952.

Plato. *Theaetetus*. Trans. F. M. Cornford. In *The Collected Works of Plato*. Ed. E. Hamilton and H. Cairns. New York: Panetheon, 1961.

Rahner, H. (1953), *The Spirituality of St. Ignatius Loyola*. Trans. F. J. Smith. Chicago: Loyola University, 1953.

Richardson, W. J. (1973), *Heidegger: Through Phenomenology to Thought*, 3d ed. Preface by M. Heidegger. The Hague: Nijhoff, 1973.

Schürmann, R. (1982), *Le principe d'anarchie. Heidegger et la question de l'agir*. Paris: Seuil, 1982.

Stierli, J. (1977), "Ignatian Prayer: Seeking God in All Things." *Ignatius of Loyola. His Personality and Spiritual Heritage. 1556–1956*. Ed. F. Wulf. St. Louis: Institute of Jesuit Sources.

Young-Bruehl, E. (1982), *Hannah Arendt. For Love of the World*. New Haven, Conn.: Yale University Press, 1982.

Jürgen Link

13. Collective Symbolism in Political Discourse and its Share in Underlying Totalitarian Trends

If linguistics and literature, or to be more precise, if discourse theory is to have a voice in the discussion of totalitarian threat,[1] it should, of course, point out right from the beginning that its contribution is far from comprehensive. In the establishment and maintenance of totalitarian regimes, economic, political (in the narrower sense), and, above all, military factors are invariably as important as discursive, symbolic-cultural factors; indeed, their significance often outweighs the latter's. On the other hand, however, we need not overdo our modesty, as hardly any theory or historical description of totalitarianism fails to emphasize the significance of cultural factors, which are usually somewhat helplessly defined as "psychological" or "socio-psychological." We might even go further and assume that literary concepts play a constitutive role in quite a few theories of totalitarianism; recall the connotative dependency of various theories on Kafka's, Orwell's, Camus', and Sartre's imaginary models.

Though I will address only a particular, yet hardly marginal aspect of those phenomena called "totalitarian," you will rightly ask for my definition of the term. I must admit that I regard this concept as indispensable to understanding and analyzing modern industrial societies, but I am not inclined to accept any of the theories I know without reservations. In the course of my empirical studies on structures of political discourse in modern mass media, I have tried, rather, to "assemble" various elements into a more heuristic and flexible concept that I have used as an instrument in my discourse analyses in particular. I proceeded, above all, from materialist approaches (Gramsci, Jean-Pierre Faye, Macciocchi, Poulantzas, Laclau),[2] yet tried to integrate especially those findings that were undisputed even by strongly oppositional stances.

In this connection the concept of a "civil society" (following Gramsci) plays a vital role:[3] when Carl Schmitt, for instance, regards the state as pressured into totalitarianism by growing chaos in and rebellion of "society" (he uses this German word precisely in the sense of civil society) against the government, he seems to pinpoint fundamental dialectics, which—though in a different terminology—reappear in most theories of totalitarianism in one way or another. Take Hannah Arendt, for example: what she describes as the atomization of the modern individual in industrial societies, as the collapse of structured class societies into unsteady "masses" devoid of any structure, is for her coextensive with the politicization of the private sphere, with the breakdown of fundamental social ties like the family or friends.[4] In other words, fundamental institutions of a civil society break down and expose individuals who are unprotected, even deprived of any shelter of privacy, to totalitarian control. Therefore, I believe that despite discrepancies in terminology and political options one may define a first basic characteristic of totalitarianism: it is manifested in the politicization of private life in a civil society, with private life rendered uniform and *gleichgeschaltet,* (the Nazi metaphor meaning "forced into the pattern" or "synchronized" in the sense of electric control) thus, ultimately suffering total encroachment by the total state. I am aware that in two respects I have deviated from Hannah Arendt's emphasis: I do not think that the fundamental institutions of a civil society, such as the family or a neighborhood, break down and disappear altogether; in my opinion, they are simply *gleichgeschaltet* (here the German word hits the nail on the head) and partially overdetermined as totalitarianism makes headway. Hannah Arendt would question my statement, "Suffering total encroachment by the state," and would point out that fascist movements have been totalitarian in the full sense of the word already before they seized power. Though I agree, I think that the Fascists' "recipe" (and here, in fact, one finds a disturbing parallel not only to the post-Leninist but even to the Leninist recipe—despite all other important differences) actually aimed at developing and imposing state-apparatuslike and, above all, military forms of organization on all institutions in a civil society.[5]

A second major point of agreement regarding totalitarian structures is that totalitarianism means denial and abolition of "pluralism" or "plurality." A key to understanding this thesis can likewise be found in the civil society itself: how does one pave the way for rendering individuals of a civil society uniform, indoctrinated, *gleichgeschaltet*, and militarized? I would offer the following hypothetical answer: a civil society's paradoxical disposition to uniforming and militarizing its "everyday life," including family relations, friendships, neighborhoods, or circles of colleagues, can emerge at a time of cultural revolution. According to my understanding, this would be a situation in which the existing cultural "hegemony" (Gramsci), that is, the cultural hegemony in an accumulative industrial society threatened by totalitarianism, is in a severe crisis resulting in a decline in the civil society's capacity to integrate its diverse elements spontaneously. I assume that Hannah Arendt was thinking of similar phenomena when she developed her peculiar thesis of the "breakdown of class society":[6] this thesis also highlights the diminishing capacity of industrial societies to allow different social classes and groups a satisfactory "everyday life" in a civil society and to integrate the whole range of elementary cultural lifestyles spontaneously under the dominant cultural hegemony. One may assume that such a severe crisis invariably arises when elements of an alternative culture negating the cultural hegemony of accumulative industrial societies have emerged in a civil society itself. In the past, these alternative cultures have often been proletarian-plebian or nostalgic-aristocratic; at present, alternative cultures of the Third World and ecologism, for instance, are gaining importance.

The process, therefore, could be outlined hypothetically as follows: people in the institutionalized plurality of a civil society suddenly become aware of an antagonism within certain everyday cultural phenomena. These may be a growing number of workers' demonstrations, strikes and squattings, for instance, which hegemonial sections of civil societies semiotically code as "chaos," or "waves of waste"[7] (the situation in Italy shortly before the fascist movement came to power would be a good example); or it may be a question of immigrant groups whose women wear headscarves, for instance, being coded as "unwilling and incapable to integrate" and as "too alien." (At present, we may find examples to illustrate this in several West European countries, among them the Federal Republic of Germany.) Once such a fundamental antagonism within a civil society has emerged, a totalitarian cultural escalation may start, whose mechanism I now will describe in more detail.

But first I would like to outline briefly a theoretical model that illuminates the connection between social conflicts, the structure of a civil society, and the possible integration of cultures. Again and again, it has been rightly pointed out that class conflicts are not directly reflected on a cultural and political level. Diverse "mediation models" have been constructed. I would suggest tackling the problems as follows: I assume that the most striking distinctions in "everyday life," that is, in the elementary social culture of a civil society, are to be found on the discursive level. In assuming this, I'm using the term *discourse* in the sense of Michel Foucault, that is, I understand discourse as an institutionalized special knowledge including the corresponding ritualized modes of speech, modes of behavior, and effects of power.[8] This means, for instance, that the class differences between a skilled worker and a civil servant are as such hardly conceivable in everyday life, whereas the discourse difference between a skilled worker and a teacher or doctor is much more obvious. The more the division of labor in industrial societies and, in accordance with this, the specialization of knowledge and diversity of discourse develop, the more urgent the reintegration of a civil society in everyday life becomes. According to my thesis, this reintegration proceeds spontaneously by what I would like to call "interdiscourse."[9] This term covers all those discourse elements that are not specialized, but that are common to several individual discourses. As the term *fairness* shows, for example, certain discourse elements are no longer restricted to a particular initial discourse, in this case the discourse of sports, but come to be used as "metaphors" in a multitude of discourses (in this case, for instance, in the political, legal, or other discourses), thus immediately becoming fundamental ideological concepts of a civil society. It is essential to see that even the interdiscourse in a civil society is a discourse in the sense of Foucault; that is, even here (in his view), ritualized modes of speech, modes of behavior, and power effects are connected. In practical terms, this means that an interdiscursive element like "fairness" is not merely a simple metaphor but at the same time a "representative" and "pragmatic symbol":[10] "fairness" plays a constituting part in all everyday rituals, from traffic to economic competition. If a whole group of the population is charged with "unfair" business practices (as was the case with the Jews in the past), the charge has an obvious significance, since "fairness" is an absolute value in a civil society, a value that is not questioned by any social group.

Since "fairness" is part of the sports or football symbol, it belongs to the most important aspect of interdiscourse, which I now intend to scrutinize. I am thinking of the whole range of symbolism, "imagery," metaphors, clear stereotypes, "models" and clichés. In various studies I have attempted to describe this ensemble in both a "structuralist" and a "poststructuralist" way as a synchronic system in permanent fluctuation, which I call a "synchronic system of collective symbols."[11] Here I have to be brief: I speak of a synchronic system because collective symbols of a culture (for example, football, car, aircraft, missile/rocket, cancer, and so on) do not generate interdiscursive constituents on their own, but only when connected with each other. Symptomatic for this is the basic figure of the journalistic interdiscourse, which I would like to call "Catachreses meander" according to the following model:[12] "The wave of expenditure cuts in the social safety network (a German metaphor for the social welfare system) has to be dyked by boosting the economy." (If one were to translate the German word literally, one would not speak of "boosting," but of "cranking"). I have generated this example for demonstration purposes, but journalistic and political interdiscourse is, in fact, full of such phrases (at least in West Germany). You will see that the different symbols stand in a series of equivalences and oppositions within the system: cranking (car symbol) symbolically equals upswing (balloon or sport symbol) and injection in the economy (body and disease symbol), so that the discourse may shift between these images in a process of continual meandering.

I think that even this brief sketch contains a plausible explanation why the interdiscourse and the synchronic system of collective symbols, in particular, integrate the specialized fields of discourse and knowledge up to a certain degree in everyday culture: the individual images originate from various discourses (for example, "fairness" from sports, "injection" from medicine, "cranking" from engineering), thus virtually allowing different specialized dis-

DEAR FATHERLAND . . .
"Wellll---What's a little undermining?"
(from *Frankfurter Allgemeine Zeitung, 19 April 1972*)

courses a connotative role in the common interdiscourse in the everyday life of a civil society. I would now add that social conflicts are immediately reflected (and thus always slightly "shifted") on a linguistic level in the medium of interdiscourse. It is quite obvious that all collective symbols imply fundamental ideological value judgments in themselves: for someone who is flooded, *flood* certainly has a negative connotation, whereas a *dyke* has a positive one. If workers go on strike, employers and most of the media will say: "the wave of strikes has to be dyked." As is apparent, the synchronic system of collective symbols functions like a game of chess. I call a certain, comparatively coherent use of the system "discursive stance." The environmentalist movement and the Green Party in West Germany are topical examples that may illustrate this. Since industrial societies have been established, there is a discursive stance that one may define as "Rousseauist"; for this stance, industrial symbols (such as machine, as city) are negative and stand in opposition to positive nature symbols.

The Greens have incorporated this symbolism already into their name and have begun an effective symbolic campaign against gigantic plants, aircraft, missiles/rockets, cars, concrete, and for the protection of the German forest, and so forth. The opposite discursive stance, which favors concrete, machines, and missiles/rockets, has been pressured into a completely defensive position within only a few years. A process like this certainly depends on real developments (the ecological crisis, dying trees, and so on) that cause "discursive events." (A German example was the conflict over the expansion of the Frankfurt airport, where an abundance of collective symbols, such as the German forests—which were cut down—concrete and aircraft, were applied pragmatically). Such "discursive events" strengthen or weaken one discursive stance or another.

At this stage it may be asked ironically how "pluralistic" and how "fair" a synchronic system of collective symbols is for all the different groups that have to use it. Theoretically, the following model may be constructed: take a society that is formed by a number of social groups Gl . . . Gn; furthermore, by a number of discourses Dl . . . Dn. From these discourses a similar number of collective symbols (Pl . . . Pn: with "P" for "pictura" = symbol) is generated, which, in turn, would be used equally positively or negatively by all groups with regard to all other groups in changing discursive stances. A little intuition is enough to see that reality is quite different from a model like this and that the discrepancy results from the domination of a "hegemonial" interest. Space does not permit me to outline the vast number of sometimes complicated rules of selection and dominance in which cultural hegemony is revealed;[13] I will restrict myself to the most important. First is the symbolizing of the system's borderlines: one of the basic rules of the system is the assumption that groups that are symbolically coded as "outside the system's borderlines" are transformed into "enemies." The West German press provides some typical examples: On April 19, 1972, the well-known liberal right-wing *"Frankfurter Allgemeine Zeitung"* (FAZ) published a cartoon with the caption "Dear Fatherland . . . " depicting a single family home with flowers in the windows and the German eagle on the roof, clearly signalling a symbolic equation of the home with "Germany." Beside the house is a car symbolizing "freedom" and "prosperity"; in front, "German Michael," the proverbial allegory for the sleepy, apolitical, and thoroughly exploitable German, sits in a swing (= "prosperity" + leisure). A horizontal line divides the house from the ground underneath, where in black and white colors we see an army of rats is gnawing the supporting piers of the house to pieces. The caption, "Dear Fatherland . . . " quotes the well-known nationalist song "The guard at the Rhine" ("Dear Fatherland, you may be calm. The guard at the Rhine is standing firm and loyal"). German Michael says, "What's a little undermining?," or literally "That little bit of undermining." The German word *unterwandern* alludes to "wandering" or hiking, which is deemed to be a particularly German occupation and is thus a typically German collective symbol. The term refers to the so-called undermining *(Unterwanderung)* of civil services by Marxists and other representatives of the extreme left, a problem that was solved by banning some thousands of real or alleged Marxists from their professions. The FAZ quotes "Guard at the Rhine" ironically: carefree "Michael" believes that there is "only a little undermining" and that the state's position against this underminding is as firm as was the Prussian position embodied in the Rhine fortresses against France in earlier days. Thus, according to the "FAZ," Michael is suffering from typical delusions; in reality everything is already lost, and West Germany is on the brink of a "collapse." Of seminal importance here is the symbolization of the system's borderline: rats are unconditionally negative symbols; their meaning can hardly be reversed or used in a positive sense.

On August 30, 1973, the following comment was published in the "Bildzeitung," which has by far the widest circulation of all German dailies (and is edited by Axel Springer):

> Turks have paralyzed the Cologne Ford works against the will of the German workers. This a new warning signal. . . . Now the tight paragraphs of Immigrant Law ("Ausländergesetz" literally means "foreigners' law") must be applied. Foreign trouble-makers have no business in German plants. The word migrant worker (or, more literally, "guest worker") originates from the word guest. A guest who cannot behave himself has to be turned out. Others are welcome.

Once again, we find the family house symbol underlying the comments: Here, the system's borderline is constituted through "ill-behavior" (with the help of the meaning of *guest*). This is deliberately connected with the national opposition "Germans" versus "Turks."

On May 28, 1980, it was again the "FAZ" that published an article with the headline "Dams against spring tide of asylum seekers" ("Asylanten": I will comment shortly on this neologism). Among other things one could read:

> There is a growing view among politicians that the inflow of foreigners seeking political asylum in the Federal Republic of Germany . . . has to be dyked. . . . But all those who have followed the desire to enjoy a higher standard of living than they can find at home, and even if only by relaxing in our social welfare system ("safety network"), must be sent back. . . . The SPD and FDP have levelled strong criticism at members of the CDU for using the term "collecting camp" (*"Sammellager"*): However, if the proceedings concerning asylum seekers are conducted in areas surrounding airports, the term "camp" . . . cannot be viewed as a taboo.

This passage is a good example for the above mentioned *catachreses meander*. Several symbols, that of the flood, the social safety network and the collecting camp, are closely connected, uniting to code the so-called "asylum seekers" symbolically as a dangerous "flood" against which "dykes," consisting of deterrent "camps," need to be erected. (This has been recognized by now and has led to a high-level dispute with the U. N. High Commissioner for refugees.)

These examples may suffice for the moment to show that the general symmetrical use of collective symbols is impossible, not only because we have to identify oppositions within the system (for example, machine versus forest) but oppositions between a system and a countersystem, or between a system and chaos. From the start, a term like *extremist* places those groups and individuals it symbolically codes on, or outside, the system's borderline. In cooperation with Willi Benning, I have developed a scheme of topoi that shows the fundamental-ideological functioning of the collective symbols system. The basic scheme is equivalent to that of the FAZ cartoon against "undermining." As in the cartoon, a horizontal line divides the topos into an upper section of "light" and a bottom section of "darkness"; this dimension thus reflects ancient gnostic myths. The system is arranged in a circle around its "center," which is why German election campaigns tend to focus on the question: which party is the closest to the "center." Beyond the borderline, both on the "right" and "left," is chaos.

Another decisive factor now becomes apparent, one that prevents the above-mentioned collective symbols from being freely interchangeable: the system of symbols always has the function of creating subjects—body and house invariably mean "we/us," rats and germs never mean "us." This, however, means that groups of the population who, in purely statistical terms, are almost always placed in the "offside" (to use the football symbol) by the interdiscourse of the media and of leading politicians, for instance, are essentially already excluded, at least partially, from the sphere of tolerance offered by a civil society (or more precisely: by the hegemonial section of a civil society) even if they still enjoy certain equal rights.[14]

One may now define the terms for the "pluralism" potential of systems of collective symbols or a political and journalistic interdiscourse: first, this potential seems to depend both on the relative significance of those symbols that mark the system's borderline and on the relative weight of unconditionally negative symbols; second, it depends on the degree to which symbols are reversible; third, it depends on "how closely woven the network" is (whether a group symbolized as "flood" is automatically also symbolized as "waste," "cancer," and so on, or whether there are less rigid constructions); fourth, and above all, it depends on statistically established referential identities; that is, whether the Jew, the Turk, the Marxist unionist (in Poland, the Catholic unionist) is invariably and stereotypically coded with the symbol of enemy, so that the average citizen of a hegemonial culture automatically thinks of the meaning of "Jew" when confronted with the image of a "rat."

In the concluding section of my paper I will use a topical example from the Federal Republic of Germany to illustrate how such a symbolic escalation of totalitarian trends can begin, even in an atmosphere that is comparatively liberal and free of crises. My example is the symbolic and interdiscursive treatment of foreign, especially Turkish, refugees and immigrants.

Demoscopic surveys provide evidence that the period from 1978 to 1980 saw a dramatic deterioration of the "climate"[15] (that is, the mood of the German people) with regard to immigrants. At the same time, there were noticeable changes in political and media discourses as concerns the topic "foreigner." Above all, the media and politicians invested the neologism "Asylant" (which means, but does not exclusively mean, "asylum seeker") with negative connotations because of the suffix *ant*. The term had earlier been used sporadically in legal discourse and in the specialized discourse of officialese in reference to foreigners; indeed, since 1980 the West German Duden has included an entry on this term (which did not gain currency in the Swiss-German, Austrian and East German interdiscourses). The objective function of this nonword, which calls forth both conscious and unconscious associations with other words ending in *ant*, such as *"Querulant"* (grouser), *"Simulant"* (malingerer), *"Bummelant"* (loafer), *"Mutant"* (mutator), and so on, because of its most pejorative ending, was to replace the German word *Flüchtling* (refugee) for refugees from the South. The "Asylant," however, was just the tip of the iceberg; an entirely new word field with constructions such as "willing to integrate," "able to integrate," and "culturally alien," emerged. But, above all, the mechanism of the collective symbol system began to work in a heinous way: right from the start, the new word appeared (and very often in headlines) couched in symbolic terms such as "floods of asylum seekers," "inflow of asylum seekers," and "dyking and channeling the flood of asylum seekers." According to the tendencies of the symbolic system mentioned above, the danger of symbolic *Gleichschaltung* was also very great; what had been placed outside the system's borderline as "flood," was bound to be burdened with the whole range of negative symbols. I know especially typical examples for "time bomb" (terror complex) and *Belastungsgrenze* (burden limit).[16] Politicians or commentators of all hegemonial parties or media could not repeat often enough that Germany had reached its "burden limit" with regard to foreigners—a metaphor that warrants further comment. The "burden" metaphor belongs to the vertical dimension of the symbolic topos discussed above; it codes a negative influence from outside the system's borderlines, that is, from above, on the system itself, on the house, on the body, on the Submarine (U-boat), and so forth. The connection with "limit" puts particular stress on the system's borderline: one could add the burden borderline to the topos (above the disorder borderline, for instance). The discursive effect of the burden borderline is most tricky in our case here, for it works to a large extent through people's unconscious: until immigration was supposed to be a problem, this metaphor had been used, above all, in ecological contexts (compare phrases such as "the German forest's burden limit with regard to exhaust fumes has been exceeded"). Even pragmatically, poison, waste, deadly disease (dying trees) were the issue. What is going on in the unconscious of "silent majorities"[17] who keep hearing from the Minister of the Interior, Zimmermann, and the media that the two most urgent domestic problems that have to be "tackled immediately," are the dying trees and the problems caused by migrant workers? Already the syntagmatic link suggests a symbolic equivalence to our unconscious precisely because of the mechanisms that govern the system of collective symbols; while the forests are "burdened" by poison, the German people are burdened by immigrants—or is there any denying that the German forest is the original symbol of the German people, as Elias Canetti has pointed out in his book entitled "Mass and Power"?[18] The fact that symbolism plays a part in (almost) all "problems caused by migrant workers" is also reflected in the so-called "square metre regulation," which demands evidence of "sufficient" living space for foreigners and which is likely to be backed by law in the near future, when it will be officially acknowledged as the most important "dyking tool," whereas the ban on reuniting families will be dispensed with. However, the house is a German "original symbol," too, as has been demonstrated with the help of some examples; it is a symbol of a small German family that cannot permit the house to "overflow" with "floods" endangering the "house."

Is all of this speculation? On May 10, 1982, at the height of anti-immigrant propaganda, the "Spiegel," known as liberal and left wing, published an article ambiguously headlined "packing suitcases." The introduction, which appeared in bold print, read as follows:

> Five Turkish families with many children have bought a house in Berlin and are seeking to evict the German tenants by court action.

Though the symbols of flood, burden, and bomb do not appear literally in this article, the text tells a completely symbolic story, a myth, in which every factual figure and every factual situation and action obviously represents something more general: the last Germans being driven out of their country by the Asian flood. Two photos have the strongest impact; in the upper right corner one can see 8 Germans crowded on a balcony; in the lower left corner are 34 Turks, among them 24 children, in front of the "entrance door" (that is, *ante portas*) of the "German house."[19]

You may now accuse me of quite nonchalantly moving away from the refugees to the immigrants (yet another word ending with *ant*). But I have only done what the system of collective symbols has suggested: indeed, it did not take long until the public thinking identified the "floods of asylum seekers" in particular and the "floods of foreigners" in general; both were even merged symbolically with the Third World "population explosion," which people saw "flooding our house." If one now takes Hannah Arendt's view of the refugees' problem after World War I as a prelude to totalitarianism, my choice of this example becomes clear: due to the mechanisms governing the symbolic system and the interdiscourse, there is actually the danger (though it may seem small at the moment) that a connection of discursive events could lead to an underlying totalitarian symbolic coding of certain groups of immigrants, in particular, the Turks. I would like to explain this with the help of a model.

To explain the model: almost 50 percent of all dominant negative symbols are already and invariably used to characterize immigrants (as I have shown); at present, the collective unconscious already sees a close connection between Islamic immigrants as "inner threat" and the Islamic Renaissance movement (above all, the complexes Iran/Khomeiny and Libya/Khaddafi) as "threat from outside." In a different study, I was able to show that the growing resentment against Turkish immigrants, which was visible from 1978 to 1980 as mentioned earlier, coincided with the Islamic Revolution in Iran and with the development of a concept of an enemy "Khomeiny, = the fanatic, Moslem terrorist who wants to go back into the Middle Ages" (the central symbol of this identification is the "headscarf" of Moslem women).[20] At present, we already find symbolic links between the so-called problem caused by migrant workers and the problems of extremism, terrorism, the turning off of "our" oil tap, and ecology, which should be grounds for concern. We use to speak of a "scapegoat" function of minorities[21]: my model attempts to point out the unconscious, symbolic accumulation process that can turn a group into a "scapegoat."

Taking all this into account, my thesis is that we may notice a kind of *Gleichschaltung* at the beginning of an escalation with an underlying totalitarian trend: the interdiscourse of the hegemonial sections within a civil society is "toughening," we may say. The combination of all the system's borderlines is symptomatic for this: while any civil society that functions more or less pluralistically needs a symbolic system with a highly differentiated range of outside borderlines (a "trouble-maker" is not yet a "burden," a "burden" not yet an "extremist," an "extremist" not yet a "terrorist"), the system's borderlines are suddenly likewise *gleichgeschaltet*, the symbolic difference between "burden" and "terror" vanishes. The combination of borderlines leads to the so-called "armour plate" of total "security," everything becomes 'black and white.'

When this point is reached, the civil society involved tends to be split into sections that are completely antagonistic and set against each other; it tends to be incapable of civil-social, that is, interdiscursive and nonviolent reintegration. Symbolic information and *Gleichschaltung* pave the way for political militarization and total encroachment by a state apparatus that is "toughening," militarizing, and "totalizing" at the same moment; it is the point when, according to Carl Schmitt and Ernst Forsthoff, the question arises as to who is governing the state of emergency—since the civil society has maneuvered itself into a permanent (industrial) crisis. It was in this stage that the classic, fascist, mass movements began with their pseudo-revolutionary militarization, with their formation and uniformation of both the hegemonial and terrorized rest of the civil society. There is sufficient evidence that Fasci and the important sections of a government apparatus can be accomplices so that the "seizure of power" and the ensuing formal encroachment of the civil society by the state follow as a logical consequence. There is not much evidence suggesting a repetition of this process, but one must be permitted to ask whether alternative forms of a totalitarian industrial nation would be possible in a longterm state of emergency—through co-operation between "tougher" government institutions, mass media, and "silent majorities," for instance. Indeed, it is precisely these alternative forms that Schmitt and Forsthoff have been discussing since World War II.

One final and brief question: What about totalitarianism in the Eastern hemisphere? I would like to outline my thesis in just a few words: the civil society's split into antagonistic sections leads to the above-mentioned "toughening" of the interdiscourse on the hegemonial side. Revolutionary or cultural revolutionary sections of the civil society have reacted in part with an adverse "toughening" in most cases, thus establishing totalitarian trends in the interdiscourse even on this side, on which many people had pinned their hopes. Due to the discursive rules, one can easily grasp the full symmetry: the simplest rule of polemics in "discourse strategy" is the reversal that follows the pattern "We are the rats? Oh, no, it's you who are the rats!" In addition to this, people in the Leninist and post-Leninist age were of the opinion that a proletarian civil society that was not *gleichgeschaltet*, but left to develop spontaneously, would automatically end in bourgeois restoration. As my friend and colleague Hans Günther says in a dedication he wrote into my copy of his book on "literature as government instrument":[22] "Does total state control require a cultural revolution or does a cultural revolution lead to total state control?" My answer would be that while the former is certainly true, the latter may be. Is there any cure for this? The cultural revolution should resist the symmetrical reversal of the hegemonial system of collective symbols; it has to "dismantle," to "deterritorialize," to "deconstruct" the whole system, including paradoxes, the ironical use of language, the use of favorable discursive events, and so on—multisubject and multiculture instead of monosubject and monoculture.

Translated by Rita Westerholt and Linda Schulte-Sasse

NOTES

1. Here I am referring basically to Michel Foucault's writings.
2. See, for instance, Antonio Gramsci, *Sul fascismo*, Roma 1974; Maria Antonietta Macciocchi, *Eléments pour une analyse du fascisme*, Paris, 1976 (two volumes); Nicos Poulantzas, *Fascisme et dictature*, Paris; Jean-Pierre Faye, *Languages totalitaires*, Paris, 1972; Ernesto Laclau: *Politics and Ideology in Marxist Theory. Capitalism—Fascism—Populism*, London, 1977.
3. "Civil society" is the English translation of the German original term *Zivilgesellschaft*, which I chose to render Gramsci's *società civile* (instead of the totally mistaken *bürgerliche Gesellschaft* that nowadays, in Italian as well as in French and English, would evoke "bourgeois society"!). "Civil society," then, is meant in opposition to "state (apparatus)," with perhaps a slight connotation of "civilian society." See, for further information, Jürgen Link/Ursula Link-Heer, *Literatursoziologisches Propädeutikum*, München, 1980 (which attempts to systematize Gramsci's notes).
4. See her *Origins of Totalitarianism* (New Edition), New York, 1966, pp. 323f., 434, 452, 474ff.
5. Thus, it is evident that I disagree with Hannah Arendt's minimizing the *state* (apparatus) character of totalitarianism (she even speaks of the "so-called" totalitarian state: op. cit., p. 392ff.) She can do so only by *opposing* the "state" to the state's armed units (like the armed forces, the police, the secret police, and so on). She thereby tries to stress the difference (which of course no one can deny) between the totalitarian state and other types of state, overlooking in some way the equally undeniable structural analogies of all states.
6. Op. cit., p. 305ff.
7. See Klaus Theweleit's psychoanalytic hypotheses on the significance and function of such symbols for modern military men's leagues: *Männerphantasien*, Reinbek bei Hamburg, 1980 (two volumes).
8. See, for example, his *Histoire de la folie à l'âge classique,* Paris, 1972, and his *Surveiller et punir. Naissance de la prison*, Paris, 1975.
9. For further information see Jürgen Link, *Elementare Literatur und generative Diskursanalyse*, München, 1983, and my articles in Jürgen Link/Wulf Wülfing, ed., *Bewegung und Stillstand in Metaphern und Mythen. Fallstudien zum Verhältnis von elementarem Wissen und Literatur im 19. Jahrhundert*, Stuttgart, 1978.
10. See, for further information, my book *Die Struktur des Symbols in der Sprache des Journalismus. Zum Verhältnis literarischer und pragmatischer Symbole*, München, 1978.
11. See my article "Über ein Modell synchroner Systeme von Kollektivsymbolen sowie seine Rolle bei der Diskurs-Konstitution," in Link/Wülfing, pp. 63–92.
12. On this notion, see Axel Drews/Ute Gerhard/Jürgen Link: "Moderne Kollektivsymbolik. Eine diskurstheoretisch orientierte Einführung mit Auswahlbibliographie," in *Internationales Archiv für Sozialgeschichte der deutschen Literatur*, Special Vol., 1985, pp. 219–66.

13. For a more detailed study of the mechanisms of cultural hegemony, see *Literatursoziologisches Propädeutikum*.
14. Only in a bourgeois society would the hegemonial section of civil society be "bourgeois"; but bourgeois society in its liberal form is defined by the very feature that a certain amount of liberty is also granted to nonbourgeois subcultures within civil society. It seems that Hannah Arendt focused on this relatively pluralistic structure of civil society in liberal systems when she used the term *class society* in her peculiar sense.
15. Corresponding to an Infratest poll, 60 percent of the West German population of 1978 felt that foreign workers should enjoy the right to stay if they want, whereas the percentage fell to 50 in 1980 and to 42 in 1982.
16. See, for further documents using this notion, Herbert Becher, "Kritische Bemerkungen zur Begrenzungspolitik," in *kultuRRevolution. Zeitschrift für angewandte Diskurstheorie*, no. 5 (1984), p. 33f.
17. The term *silent majority* seems to anticipate a new possible type of *gleichgeschaltete* civil society.
18. See Elias Canetti, *Masse und Macht*, Hamburg, 1960, p. 195f.
19. See my article "Asylanten—Ein Killwort," in *kultuRRevolution*, no. 2 (1983), pp. 36–38, where I quote another article on the same issue (published in Springer's *Welt am Sonntag*), which does not even attempt to mask its racist character.
20. In magazines, the *Bildzeitung* and television, the Iranian revolution was represented symbolically merely by photographs of women wearing headscarves.
21. See Hannah Arendt's criticism of the "scapegoat theory," op. cit., p. 5ff.
22. Hans Günther, *Die Verstaatlichung der Literatur. Entstehung des sozialistisch-realistischen Kanons in der sowjetischen Literatur der 30er Jahre*, Stuttgart, 1984.

Vincent Descombes

14. *The Socialization of Human Action**

I.

Let me begin by explaining what I mean by the phrase *socialization of human action*. We have all heard of something called "the socialization of the means of production," which is meant to convey a change in the juridical status of equipment and tools. That sort of socialization happens when what was first private property becomes public or community property. I would like to use the word *socialization* in a similar way to designate a change that we produce in something by modifying its status within a community. Used this way, *to socialize* is a transitive verb. To socialize in this sense is to socialize something, to transform its status with respect to the law governing a community. What was at one time a private matter or a personal belonging becomes an element in a cooperative undertaking.

My subject in this paper will be human action—more precisely, the way we are inclined to describe human action when we conform to the conceptual schemes of our culture. I shall argue that our current conception of human action is the result of socialization. The socialization I have in mind is not in the first place a change in the way we act; it is not a change in the reality of action. Rather, it is a change in the views we hold about action. The process of socializing human action, as I call it, is primarily an event in the history of our ideas about action. It is first of all an exchange in the descriptions of what human beings characteristically do. After the "event" of the socialization of our practical philosophy, as it were, had taken place, human beings were said to act socially, they were said to act as *social* beings. Whatever they did was supposed to be part of some social transaction. I shall call the general framework for such descriptions of human action the *sociology of human action* (briefly, the sociology of action, since we shall be concerned only with human affairs). I will begin by formulating the principles of a sociology of action. But before doing that, it is worth mentioning that the usual sense of the verb *to socialize* in ordinary English is not connected with the idea of abolishing private ownership of means of production. Rather, socializing means social behavior like going to

---

*From *Graduate Faculty Philosophy Journal,* November, 1986.

parties, returning invitations, indulging in gossip, calling on friends, and the like.

The main example of socialization in the first sense is the founding of a company by several partners. The main example of socialization in the second sense is the process by which "angry young men" finally come to appreciate life in good company, *in der guten Gesellschaft,* to indulge in *mondanités* and "social events."

I now sum up the definition I have been offering: The socialization of human action is a change in the way we describe human action, with the result that human action is made available for sociological analysis and interpretation. My purpose in this paper will be to question the validity of this sociological turn that has affected our *philosophia practica.*

II.

I now return to the subject of the principles of the sociology of action (briefly, of *sociology,* since I shall explain in the next section of this paper that sociology is necessarily sociology of action). I shall distinguish two levels of socialization within the theory of human action. That distinction will help us to capture both of the senses of socializing (the transitive and the intransitive) I have just mentioned. First, we may speak of limited socialization when any collective action, any action performed by somebody with the help of or with any sort of participation by other people is called social action and conceived as the operation of a society formed by the association of the agents. Socialization, in such a view, is restricted to those actions that are explicitly collective or concerted. In saying that they are social, we seek to explain the way in which they are performed by several agents acting together. Our explanation is that each agent acting with other people is acting as a member of the society constituted by him (her) and the people whose actions are coordinated with his (her) action. For such an explanation, we may speak of the *special* sociology of action (the special social theory of action).

Let us now suppose that we hold a stronger thesis: any human action of any kind, even performed without any obvious or conscious coordination with other people, should be conceived as someone's contribution to some society. Sociologists of this persuasion will seek to find the society in which the agent discloses his (her) membership by acting in the way s/he is doing. It would be fair enough to speak in that case of a *general* sociology of action. For example, the sociology of science claims to show that scientists, who have sometimes been viewed as lone heroes confronting the mysteries of Nature, are really social partners engaged in a social enterprise. Scientific discoveries would be described as social events, that is to say, moves in the competitive game called scientific research. What does it mean to say that scientific research is a social game? If we hold the weaker thesis, we shall say that it is always possible, and sometimes useful, to view scientific research as a social game, that is to say, to give an account of it in terms of social motivation, such as seeking success and notoriety, wanting to be the first to achieve something, and so on. Now if we hold the stronger thesis, we shall be prepared to say that scientific research is nothing but a social game and that, by giving a sociological account of that kind of human transaction, we have explained everything about it.

We need to state more precisely the sociological theses corresponding to the two levels of socialization of human action.

1. By *human action* I mean an action that is performed intentionally by a human agent—in other words, an action the subject of which is not just the agent, but the intentional agent (*actus humanus* as opposed to *actus hominis*). Here one could object to my speaking of "intentionality" that it is naïve, not to say "precritical," to attribute "intentionality" to all human actions. The objection would go on to say that it was the irreversible achievement of modern thinkers such as Marx, Nietzsche, or Freud to undermine the idea of a rational agent acting with at least potentially clear awareness of his action and purposes. However, that sort of objection should not worry us since the intentionality we require for an action to be a human action (*actus humanus*) has nothing to do with either mastery over the final result of the action, nor with awareness on the part of the agent of what the agent is doing. For an agent to be acting intentionally, it is not necessary that he know what he is doing or what he wants to do. Whenever it makes sense to say that the agent is trying to do something, we shall be satisfied to say the action is intentional. Actions performed under hypnosis or somnambulistic behavior are nonetheless intentional as long as it would be sensible to ask whether the agent has succeeded (or not) in doing what he was *trying* to do.

2. When several people are acting together, we speak of *collective action*. Collective action is *social action* when the agents are socially connected, that is, when they are subjected to a social bond (what Rousseau and others have called *le lien social*). According to those stipulations, only a group of individuals can act collectively; only an individual can act socially. To act collectively is to act *as* a group, to act socially is to act *in* that sort of group called *society*. The *principle of a special sociology* is as follows: For any joint or collective action in which several agents are engaged there is a true description that presents this action as the operation of a society constituted by the individual agents. The *principle of a general sociology* is as follows: For any action by an individual agent there is a true description that presents this action as the contribution the individual agent is making to some society. In other words, every time somebody does something, it should be possible to relate what that person is doing to what other people are doing somewhere else at the same time and to consider that they are acting together *as if* they were partners in a society, that is, *as if* they had entered into a social agreement.

III.

I now turn to the concept of society. My contention will be: (1) that we currently use the word *society* (as well as other related words) in two different ways; (2) that the difference between the two senses of the word is a logical one. If I am right, it will follow that we ought to distinguish between two concepts of society. If the difference is logical and if our current sociological thinking fails to notice it, it will be small wonder if we run into trouble in our *philosophia practica*.

It is sometimes said, and often assumed, that social philosophy has to do with the plurality of human beings. Social philosophy, so goes the story, begins when the Cartesian solipsism is overcome (without recourse to the proofs of a *Dieu vérace*). We enter into social philosophy by switching from the solitary subject of consciousness to something called "intersubjectivity," that is, plurality of minds. Within such a tradition, the purpose of social philosophy will be to analyze the various forms of *being together*.

The mere notion of *being together*—"togetherness," *Mitsein, coexistence*—however does not give us a subject matter unless we are able to say how we conceive those beings that are said to be together. It is true that in the idealist tradition, philosophers have much too often been satisfied to apply a collective predicate like *being together* to a collection of selves or a set of minds. We may think here of what has been called the problem of Otherness, the *Ich und Du* problem, *"le problème d'autrui."* However, a mere coexistence of minds does not give us a society. For a set of people to constitute a society, it is not even necessary that they be together (in the sense of being there in the same place). But it seems to be necessary that the members of that society *do* something together. Even angels, if they are to be together, have to take part in some common activity like singing together or playing music.

Other philosophers have granted that the account of social life as being together in the same place with an awareness of the disturbing presence of the other people is too abstract. Being somewhere together is not enough if it does not give rise to new relationships between the coexisting beings. Hence, in the phenomenological tradition the appeal of the notion of a public space where the person is supposed to acquire a new quality called "being for the Other" (as opposed to "being for oneself," see Hegel's *Füreinanderessein* and *Ansichsein, Phänomenologie des Geistes*, p. 133). The presence of a public space (like an agora, a forum, a marketplace) makes it possible that something happening to one of us will be part of the private experience of all members of the community. Indeed, in the public space, one's behavior is open to the attention and appraisal of other citizens. In that respect, the phenomenological ideal of a public space would be the small town or the country club.

In order to clarify our concept of society, we would do well to start from its use in Roman Law. It is useful to be reminded that a society (*societas*) was not in the first place a (human) collectively, but a kind of contract between people. A *societas* is primarily what we now call a social contract, that is, the kind of contract that creates between the partners (*socii*) a juridical link (called *vinculum*) from which various mutual obligations arise. A society is a source of obligation.

In Roman Law, the conditions for an agreement to be a *societas* (a social contract) are the following:

1. There must be a common aim of the association and it must be a lawful aim (there can be no *société du crime*).

2. All partners must enter into the society with a personal share, whether a contribution of capital or a contribution of labor services, and so on.

3. There must be a fair distribution of the social outcome. All partners must receive their share of whatever outcome arises from the social activity. No association can be called a society if it does not have a rule of distributive justice. Nobody is any longer subject to a social obligation if he does not get something in return for his contribution to the common undertaking.

4. There must be among the partners an intention of forming a society with such and such person. For an association to be a society, it is not enough that it be aimed at some general interest or that it benefit everyone. No one can *discover* that he is a member of some society. No one can learn that unknown to him, he has been a member of some society for the past ten years. Entering into a society requires a personal commitment. However, according to the Roman Law, there is no unique formal way in which the social contract has to be concluded. It does not have to be written; it does not require any specific *formalitas*. There it may happen that the existence of a society among some people becomes controversial. The question may arise: Was their agreement a *societas*, a social contract? Such a question could lead them into a law court.

The concept of a society with which social theorists analyze human action is not the juridical one. But it is surely an extension of it. Now, it may happen that while extending the use of a concept to new types of situations, the new application we give to it requires such an important reshaping of the concept that the original application becomes irrelevant to its understanding. However, I think that in several cases the connection between the extended application and the original application is not a matter of mere philological inquiry. It is worth remembering that the original concept of society was the idea of a particular source of obligation. Indeed, we do not need to be experts in contemporary social theory to notice that there is a concept that seems to be central to all brands of sociological analysis: it is the concept of *rule*. Moreover, it is not just social sciences as such, in the professional sense, that cannot avoid making an intensive and often unexplained use of the concept of rule. But it seems that we could not even begin to understand what philosophers today say they are doing if we were to write off the word *rule* from our vocabulary.

Therefore, I suggest that we should try the following hypothesis: to analyze human action in the framework provided by sociology is to seek an explanation of why people behave according to rules. The concept of society borrowed from Roman jurists is apt to provide such an explanation since it permits us to elucidate the sociological wonder of the observance of rules through such allegedly unproblematic notions as *personal consent, agreement, mutual interest, reciprocal obligation,* and so on. The concept of society makes it possible to give an answer to the sociological question, namely: Why do people observe rules even when they are not under any natural constraint to do so? Why do human agents put constraints on themselves? The answer is, of course: Because they live in society. Now if that answer is to be of any use, it is clear that living in society will not mean just living together. Living in society must mean living in some sort of arrangement with other people. We may therefore conclude that any significant use of the word *society* keeps some part of the original sense of the word. Our concern will now be to find out how much should be kept in order that the word *society* be both significant in its application and suitable for sociological uses.

Before going into the next subject, let us sum up the characteristics of a *societas:*

1. No society without a specified and non-objectionable aim.
2. No society without some initial share from everybody.
3. No society without mutual advantage.
4. No society without that kind of mutual agreement that creates legal obligation.

IV.

Apart from the juridical, we find in social theory two well characterized senses of the word *society*. Let us call the first one the political sense and the second one the sociological. When social theory was still known as political philosophy, philosophers used to speak of *civil society* (*societas civilis, bürgerliche Gesellschaft*). And they were happy to speak of *societas* precisely because they wanted to consider the *politikè koinōnia,* the *civitas,* as an association of citizens who have decided to live together for some purpose, the major philosophical question now being: For what purpose? What is the aim of civil society? Is it the protection of rights, or the security of the persons, or the greatest happiness of the greatest number? But it is only when the political community is viewed as a social association that it becomes relevant to raise the question of the point of having such an association among ourselves: The idea that the *civitas* is a (civil) society gives us the political sense of society. We will find in more recent social theory a conception of society in the sense of a social system.

How can we obtain the political concept of society from the juridical one? The extension of the use of the word in the political realm is made possible by a reversal of the juridical order of questioning. From a juridical point of view, it is always possible to question the existence of a particular society. One may claim, for example, that the aims of a particular society have already been fulfilled, so that nobody is under any further obligation toward the association. Or one may point out that the aim of the society was such that it has become impossible to fulfill it. (For instance, we could have formed a society devoted to the protection of some natural species, and we could have failed to prevent the extinction of that species.) Another way of questioning the existence of a particular society among ourselves would be to claim there has never been such a society. In that case, the other party would have to establish that there was an agreement among us, even an implicit one. Political philosophers since the beginning of the Modern Age have followed the same line of argument, but in the opposite direction. Instead of arguing that we are under various obligations to the community *because* we agreed earlier to enter into a contract stipulating those obligations, philosophers from Hobbes to Rousseau went the other way. They tried to analyze our political obligations as *social* obligations, that is, obligations exactly similar to the obligations we would have *if* we had entered into a social contract. In other words, the point of speaking of an original social contract is to give an account of the rules people observe in their transactions that presents those rules as arising internally from the will, not externally, like laws and commands. The point of the fiction of a social contract is to equate "what we really want" (*la volonté générale*) and the laws of the community. In order to assert an identity between will and law, we have to distinguish between what we think we want and "what we really want." We even need to distinguish between what we think we really want, while thinking of it without the assistance of the laws, and what we really want. Thus, the philosophy that tries to present political laws as *social rules* is the philosophy of the autonomous agent. The first step in the socialization of human action was the rise of the philosophy of autonomy. But we just saw that a pure philosophy of autonomy will suffer a dialectical reversal. For to give an account of public rules within such a philosophy, it is of course necessary to deny the existence of obligations really arising externally. *Externally* means here, being there whether we like it or not, being there without having first asked our permission to be there. But this is not the end of the story. We cannot dispense entirely with the external localization of the laws. What happens when it is said that our obligations cannot really arise from outside is that the disclosure of what we really want must now come from outside. When philosophy seeks to think of the citizen as an autonomous agent, philosophy is changed into political pedagogy. Of course, if we were rational mature persons, we would know directly—"from inside," so to speak—what we really want, that is, what is good for us. Since we are not (or maybe, not yet) rational mature persons, we need to be taught by some *Magister*. We are in need of a *Bildung*. We must learn, like young children in the classroom, what it is that we really want from the voice of the Law. Unknown to us, at least until philosophers disclose it to us, the voice of the Law is our voice. The public voice we are listening to seems to come from outside. But this is just a childish appearance, since the law is nothing but an expression of our rational will.

The sociological point of view—I do not distinguish here between various competing schools of social theory—pretends to be very different. As early as the eighteenth century, it was correctly argued that philosophers were dealing with an abstract entity of their own invention. The political animal they were placing at the root of civil society was nowhere to be found. The best one could say for this autonomous individual was that it was very like the final product of Western history understood as a process of civilization, that is, a process of socialization. According to sociologists, we must place the society before the individuals. In doing so, we are exchanging the concept of *civil society* for the concept of *social system*.

In order to achieve the political concept of society, we had to modify the last element of the juridical definition concerning the origin of social obligation. Philosophers were happy enough to substitute the fiction of a contract for the actual historical agreement we would ask for if we were on juridical grounds. That was the only way to explain away the apparent externality of the public rules to the agents. Incidentally, giving up the condition of a real contract was also necessary in order to speak of an agreement between us and people we often have never met and whose existence we are unaware of. But we want now to overcome the abstractedness of modern political theory. In order to do so, we need to write off the condition of a social contract entirely. We will agree to have a society whose members have never been asked, even implicity, whether they wanted to join the club. For the *instant* socialization of human agents by a contract, we substitute a *process* of socialization. We admit the fact that individuals do not really enter into society by consenting to be governed by a set of social rules. They are *introduced* to society by various social practices such as being taught a language, being taught to master one's bodily movement, playing games, listening to stories, being praised for some achievements and being mocked or punished by others, and so on. Now we shall say: The reason why people observe the rules of their community is not that, as individual agents, they approve of those rules and have decided to commit themselves to their observance. Rather, they have been trained to think of these rules as their rules in the course of their socialization. A Hegelian would say: they have learned to identify themselves with the rules of their community. Notice here that the sociological quest for a concrete view of human action does not dispense entirely with the contract fiction. At the end of the process of socializing the behavior of newcomers in the community, we get self-governed citizens who behave socially *as if* the social rules were, from the beginning, the expression of their own will.

We may wonder whether social theory—the would-be scientific theory of social systems—is not just an attempt to lend some plausibility to the assumptions of modern political theory. Instead of thinking of the autonomous agent as a precondition for the existence of society, sociologists hold it as a social outcome.

V.

I now come to the thesis of the present paper. The philosophy of social contract corresponds to a restricted socialization of human action, whereas the theory of social systems corresponds to a general socialization. One way of sketching the difference between those two levels is to notice that people who have not been socialized by instant socialization could still have been socialized by means of progressive socialization. Even if they do not associate with each other, they may socialize. Let us take the example of a party traveling in some wild country. We say that travelers united in a caravan are traveling *together*. They travel together in a sense in which people who happen to be in the same plane do not travel together. Joining an expedition is choosing one's companions, whereas in the second case you just discover who your company will be during the trip when you find your seat in the plane. One use of *together* corresponds to the political concept of society, the other to the sociological. Now social theorists claim that they have overcome the fictions of political philosophy, since they are able to explain how people who happen to be together, without any intention of associating, will develop various relationships in dealing with each other. Those people will be engaged in progressive socialization, as opposed to the political step of giving up an alleged state of nature.

Yet in speaking of two levels of socialization, I may seem to imply that there is a continuity between the society of special socialization and the society of general socialization. I now want to argue to the opposite. The political concept of society and the sociological concept of society are logically different concepts. For that matter, it will be enough to show that the first concept—society as civil society—presupposes the logical, if not historical, possibility of a State of Nature whereas the second concept of society—society as a social system—excludes the possibility of a state of affairs in which human agents would not be socialized in one way or another.

The existence of a civil society is an *all-or-nothing matter*. Either you are a member of the club or you are not. There is no intermediate position between the state of nature and the state of civility. The political concept has retained that feature from the juridical notion of founding an association by a mutual agreement. Before we entered into the social contract, there was no society whatsoever between us, even if we had plenty of mutual feelings, intercourse, transactions, and the like. Another way of putting it would be to say: the existence of civil society is such that it must be possible to question it. We would not be in a civil society if it were not at least logically possible that we were not in a civil society.

On the other hand, the existence of a social system is a *matter of more or less*. Whenever you find people dwelling in the same area, there is always some degree of dependence among them and some level of ritualization in their behavior toward each other. Within social theory, independence means degree zero of dependence, wild spontaneity of behavior means degree zero of ritualization. We ourselves are more socialized than anchorites or tramps, but are less socialized than Molière's *petits marquis* or citizens of some utopian *phalanstère*.

If we are socialized in the sense of belonging to a civil society, we are simply social beings. If we are socialized in the sense of having manners, we behave socially to some extent. But in that case, possessing manners is always a matter of degree. We are then social in a sense in which it is possible to be more social or less social than we are. Therefore, the difference between the two concepts of sociality is the difference between a property that one has or does not have without qualification and, on the other hand, a property that admits of all degrees of intensity. Such a difference is a logical one. It is like the distinction made by Aristotle between predicates belonging to the category of substance and predicates belonging, for instance, to the category of quality (*more or less white* makes sense, *more or less man* does not).

VI.

Now let me draw the consequence of the whole argument.

Instant socialization, being an all-or-nothing matter, is *total* socialization. Whatever undergoes instant socialization becomes altogether social, without any restriction. *Progressive* socialization, being a matter of more or less, is *partial* socialization. Whatever undergoes progressive socialization has been less social, in some cases should be more social and in any case could be more social.

The consequence is that socialization is necessarily limited one way or the other. It is not the case that the whole behavior of a human agent can be totally transformed by socialization. Some thinkers, like Jean-Jacques Rousseau, have held that society without dependence is impossible, unless we admit a total socialization of the human being ("*aliénation*"). Others have thought of such a *Vergesellschafteter Mensch* as a true ideal to be sought. But socialization cannot be both *total* and *general*. If it is total, it will be limited to some human activities and operations. For instance, switching from single to shared occupancy of an apartment is a total socialization of one's activity of occupying an apartment, but it is not yet the socialization of one's whole life. On the other hand, if socialization is general, it will be partial. For instance, there is a sense in which people can be said to sleep together, but even if one is sleeping with somebody else, one's sleep will never be totally socialized.

Total socialization means *special* sociology of action. A theory of total socialization cannot be a general theory of action, even if it explains all the features of some of our activities. *General* sociology of action means *partial* socialization. At its best it will explain some features of human action.

To sum up: Sociologists may claim the following:

1. They explain all features of all kinds of human action.
2. They explain all features of some kinds of human action.
3. They explain some features of all kinds of human action.
4. They explain some features of some kinds of human action.

My argument has been that we should reject the first claim. That leaves us with various combinations of *all* and *some* between two undesirable extremes: explaining almost everything about almost nothing and explaining almost nothing about almost everything.

IV

An Institutional Philosophy of Politics

Agnes Heller

15. *An Imaginary Preface to the 1984 Edition of Hannah Arendt's "The Origins of Totalitarianism"*

The twentieth century will go down in history as the age of totalitarianism, and Hannah Arendt will certainly remain the classic source of any forthcoming interpretation of the origins of totalitarianism. True enough, any chronicle by a contemporary, an eyewitness, lacks in certain historical perspectives, even if the witness' story is told in the past tense, for this past is still the "past of the present" and not the historical past of the bygone. This holds true for Hannah Arendt's book as well. Yet it was precisely a certain lack in perspective that made her book powerful. As a deeply involved observer, she gave her testimony in a case that is still far from closed. Her theoretical commitment to understanding totalitarianism, her practical commitment to a stand against totalitarianism, and her emotional reenactment of the path leading to the Golgotha, merged fully in a unique compound.

Arendt's approach to totalitarianism is strictly historicist. She resists the temptation of easy explanations. This is why she insists that totalitarianism, far from being indicative of our having relapsed into some kind of premodern (incidentally Asiatic) barbarism, is rather the offspring of our modern, Western culture, a new form of *modernity*. She sums up her position in the Preface to the first edition in the following manner: "The subterranean stream of Western history has finally come to the surface and usurped the dignity of our tradition." The explanations of totalitarianism are, therefore, to be sought in the dynamics of development and not in underdevelopment, in the Occident and not in the Orient, in certain tendencies specific to our own history and not in any outburst of the instincts of an eternal human nature. This seminal discovery (which of course has never prevented legions of scholars from endlessly pondering the Asiatic mode of production as the possible source of Soviet totalitarianism) has, to my mind, only one flaw. Arendt remained an evolutionist insofar as she attributed to certain kind of necessity to the factual sequence of historical events. Since totalitarianism was, in her view, the novel offspring of Western modernity, it could only emerge after all previous events of modernity had already unfolded. However, the fact that history unfolds in a certain way does not prove that it could not have been otherwise. In my view, the totalitarian option had been present since the dawn of modernity, at least on the European continent, and it was due to certain "accidental" (but, at least, undoubtedly not "necessary") factors (to our everlasting historical fortune) that the nineteenth century took a turn towards parliamentary liberalism, rather than an early form of totalitarianism. However, since alternative histories cannot be written, either for better or for worse, Arendt's reconstruction of the origins of totalitarianism remains valid.

If we read *The Origins of Totalitarianism* together with its companion volumes, *The Human Condition* and *On Revolution*, the message of the first work becomes even more explicit. In Arendt's view, there are two ideal types of modernity: the democratic and the totalitarian. Neither of them is simply a political system. Rather, they constitute *two different cultures* diametrically opposed to one another. Each culture has a singular moral, psychological, sensual texture of its own; each operates with an imaginary contrary to that of the other. Each enhances attitudes and practices counterposed to the other. Fortunately or unfortunately, however, real histories rarely produce ideal-typical, pure cultural types. Although I am convinced that Arendt's typology is, in the last instance, revelatory, the understanding of the development of totalitarianism after Stalin calls for certain refinements and further specification. In her 1966 preface to *The Origins of Totalitarianism*, Arendt refers to the "rich recovery of the arts during the last decade" as "the clearest sign that the Soviet Union can no longer be called totalitarian in the strict sense of the term." Arendt, as so many among us, drew far too hasty conclusions from certain phenomena associated with the Khrushchevian intermezzo. Almost two decades have again elapsed since this preface was committed to paper, and totalitarianism has remained vigorous, indeed, it has even gained more ground. If Arendt lived today, she would surely write a new preface to her book, as she did every time historical junctures called for further explanation. The greatest tribute I can pay to her memory is to try to perform this task in the year of 1984. In doing so, I shall address three problems: first, Soviet totalitarianism; second, the emergence and dissemination of totalitarianism and totalitarian political practices in the so-called "Third World"; and third, the decline of totalitarian movements in Western Europe without the disappearance of certain factors enumerated by Arendt as contributions to the "origins" of totalitarianism.

I.

No redefinition of the notion "totalitarianism" makes Arendt's ideal type obsolete. The way a social system emerges is, and remains, indicative of the whole character of this particular social system. The genesis discloses more about a system than does any period of "normalization." Normalization is the final product of genesis. The mark of genesis remains stamped on its product. In fact, genesis is the hidden substrate of normalization. Stalinism has remained the secret clue to contemporary Soviet totalitarianism, and it is in this sense that denizens of the Soviet world still live under the shadow of Stalin. All attempts to abstract the present from this genesis and display the latter as something gone and surpassed, fail to come to grips with the fundamental systemic features of the Soviet Union today. However, certain distinct, genetic features have not sprung from totalitarianism *per se*, rather from the particular process of *totalization*. Up until World War II, Stalinism had been the period in which the construction blocks for the new society were produced and fitted together. Both the *Führer-principle* and *waves of indiscriminate repression* on a mass scale functioned as vehicles of totalization. Both became obsolete once the systemic features of totalitarianism were sedimented. The Stalinist "revolution from above" had transformed human attitudes, cultural patterns, ways of thinking and acting to an extent required to ensure the smooth reproduction of the system. A return to the Führer-principle and waves of indiscriminate repression is not a likely possibility, though *not* because of any systemic change in the regime but because the regime already exists in a sedimented form. However, there can be little doubt that, were a legitimation crisis to emerge in the Soviet Union (hardly likely in the foreseeable future), both the Führer-principle and waves of indiscriminate mass repression would be revived again, as a result of the need for retotalization. The terroristic phase and form of totalitarianism has not been excluded from the systemic patterns as a result of its sedimentation. Terroristic totalitarianism has only become temporarily redundant, even counterproductive. In the event that the regime becomes confronted with prolonged and stubborn resistance, and in particular, armed resistance (as in Afghanistan), the machinery of wholesale terror would, again, be set in motion. Western analysts who have taken great pains to discover the evolutionary potentials, or even the manifest results of an essential, systemic reform of Soviet totalitarianism, are blinded by their own hopes. Needless to say, the substantial decrease, or disappearance, of waves of indiscriminate repression is an enormous relief to the subjects of totalitarian societies. Such sobering and gratifying events, however, should not be misread as evidence of "social progress" or "systemic change." The system can only go under in a manner similar to which it emerged.

Arendt made the important distinction between totalitarian movements and totalitarian rule (governments). I would add a second distinction to the list, that between totalitarian rule and totalitarian society. This differentiation does not involve evaluation. From a human point of view, totalitarian rule can be just as unbearable as a totalitarian society. Further, the distinction is relative. The tendency to totalize society is inherent in every totalitarian rule, but not all kinds of totalitarian rule aim at *complete* totalization. Totalitarian rule can restrict its objective to the political and ideological totalization of society. Among the three distinct types of totalitarian rule that emerged in Europe after World War I, fascism (Mussolinism) did not aim (at least not before the Salo Republic) at an over-all totalization of society, whereas both nazism and bolshevism did. However, the twelve years of the thousand-year Reich, as Arendt put it, did not suffice to accomplish the totalization of society. The only totalitarian society in this sense then is the Soviet type of society. I would not say that it is the only possible form to come, and some are already in the making, but it is the sole existing one that lends itself to comprehensive theoretical analysis.

The Soviet state was already totalitarian as early as 1921. What followed was the totalization of society by the totalitarian state. This was the unique achievement of the Stalinist "revolution from above." The end result was, and has remained, a completely new social system and completely new attitudes that ensure the maintenance of the system.

Totalitarian rule itself has to be defined in such a way that the definition should encompass *all kinds* of totalitarian rule irrespective of whether or not a society has been completely totalized. I call a rule totalitarian if a party is the *sovereign* of the state (the source of *all* powers) and if this sovereign *outlaws pluralism*. Since the party is the source of all powers, it is, by definition, the source of legislative power. Legislation is nothing but the expression of the will of this sovereign (the party leadership). If the party wills something, this will is by definition law (whether or not it takes the form of a law), and as a consequence, every contrary will is outlawed. Of course, pluralism subsists, although it is not legal. Whether a certain kind of pluralism is practically (never formally and legally) tolerated, depends on the will of the sovereign. Society is not completely totalized (although its rule already is) if the will of the sovereign is merely ideological and political in nature. Society is completely totalized if the will of the sovereign determines the whole socioeconomic structure of the society in question, thereby outlawing not only political and ideological but also socioeconomic alternatives. The attitudes that maintain totalitarian rule are political and ideological and, further, psychological and moral ones in conjunction with political action and ideological myths. The attitudes that serve to maintain a completed totalitarian society are, thus, all-encompassing. Arendt was unfortunately only too right when she described the ease with which attitudes can be reshaped into totalitarian, ideological, and political action patterns under specific social circumstances, though this insight also led her to the conclusion that Stalinist terror had been dysfunctional since 1934. In this, I believe, she was wrong. Since society had to be completely totalized in the Soviet Union (in accordance with the Bolshevik project), the *sum total* of the attitudes, and not just political and ideological ones, had to be reshaped. This is why the "Great Terror" was not at all "unnecessary" or superfluous from the aspect of the regime. Rather, it was precisely this period that accomplished the totalization of society. The "Khrushchev-intermezzo" was both an organic and an inorganic period in Soviet history. It was organic for it opened the path to an oligarchic rule far more adequate to a sedimented totalitarian society than the autocratic-charismatic rule of Stalin. At the same time it was inorganic and, moreover, self-contradictory, for it turned against, if only marginally and inconsistently, a period that had created the very system within which autocratic rule could be abandoned.

Arendt seems, further, to underestimate the *utilitarian motivations* operating during periods of totalization. On one level it is difficult to see how a person's interests could be served in any theatre in which the secret police are the stage managers. Yet the interest basis of a totalitarian regime can be illustrated in two distinct ways. First, if everyone is guilty of mass murder, everyone will have a *vested interest* in upholding the regime in whose name it was committed. Second, totalitarian rule implies in itself a *change of elite*, but the totalization of society is *the very process* in which a change of elite is effectuated on an unprecedentedly grand scale. This is how Stalin's rule is understood and even defended, especially by those who had benefitted from it personally or through their families, up until this day. The dissident Zinoviev is a good example here. His last interview (published in *Encounter*), an apology for Stalin coming from his otherwise resolute enemy, exposes without much ado that during the Great Terror, every corpse was a stepping stone for the careers of the living. Newcomers were hungry for position and power; the more the "old guard" was wiped out, the better their chances of gaining positions of power and moving to the top. Arendt was obviously right in emphasizing that in a totally atomized society, such as the Soviet Union under Stalin, class or group entity in any collective sense did not exist, or at least it could not be properly articulated. However, this in itself never diminished the basis for interest motivation. The interests of millions of human "atoms" had already been vested in the system during Stalin's lifetime, and thus it has remained ever since. Upward mobility, once made possible through brutal elite alterations, has disappeared with the advent of an ossified elite. I only have to add to this that in the Soviet satellite countries, where Stalinism proper had lasted only for a very short period, there was no time to transform human attitudes to the extent needed for the proper operation of a totalitarian society. The attitudes sufficient for political and ideological totalization were, unfortunately, not found wanting. But the moment the terror declined, legitimation crises set in, and no East European society has been properly legitimized since. In fact, totalitarianism collapsed in Hungary, Czechoslovakia, and Poland, and has been completely or partially restored solely by an occupying army and its proxies.

Soviet society, as it now stands in the Soviet Union, conclusively corroborates Arendt's main thesis. It represents a distinct type of *modern* society. Totalitarianism has turned out to be the motive force and the intrinsic essence of a new kind of modernity. Without going into a detailed analysis of Soviet societies and repeating views I have argued at length elsewhere,[1] I mention only one of its outstanding features. N. Luhmann has pointed out—to my mind correctly—that in contradistinction to premodern-stratified societies, modern society is increasingly functionalist in character. Whereas in premodern societies the performance of specific functions was allocated to the position occupied by human groups on the scale of stratification, in modernity the reverse takes place: it is the performance of specific functions that allocates persons to specific social strata. Yet, and this has escaped Luhmann's attention, in the liberal-democratic type of modernity neither political nor social action evolves solely from, and crystallizes solely around, the performance of a function. In spite of an increasing tendency toward corporatism in certain Western-type democracies, both political parties and social movements recruit their constituencies along transfunctional issues. No constituency is constituted solely along functional lines. Thus, the existence of civic liberties and the forms of political and social organizations and the kinds of action patterns ensuing therefrom strongly counterbalance systemic constraints. Yet due to the complete lack of civic liberties and political-social pluralism, Soviet society—and it alone—has realized the functionalist tendencies embedded in modernity in full. The only action possible in the Soviet society is the performance of a function. Stratification is exclusively functional, and moreover, transfunctional action is outlawed. This means that in Soviet society system integration and social integration merge into one. More precisely, the absence of any normative basis of doctrines in support of the system has also become a systemic function, namely, the function of the sovereign. Ideology, in the sense of an alternative interpretation of the doctrine, is outlawed. However, although the doctrine still cements the system as a point of reference and the source of legitimation, it has lost momentum since the sedimentation of the system. As Zaslavsky has pointed out, the word *communism* has become empty, sometimes an object of derision; the overarching propaganda image and the only point of reference for "creeds" is the so-called "Soviet way of life."[2] Yet pluralism, though outlawed, still exists in marginalized, privatized niches (for instance, religious devotion and practices). But such *intermundia* cannot counterbalance the sweeping preponderance of the system, at least not in the Soviet Union. This is why people not integrated into the system are viewed as mad and readily transferred to mental asylums. In a world where there is no social integration, only system integration, such people must appear mad. In my view, the coalescence of system integration and social integration must eventually lead to a deficit in moral motivation and to neuroses on a scale that could undermine the reproducibility of society. Lack of moral motivation is not identical with the irrational, shame-regulated morality that dominated the period of totalization. The latter is now in retreat.

The other intrinsically modern feature of the Soviet system, not unconnected with the former, is its *industrializing impetus*. Soviet society is not only modern, it is also "modernizing." It is quite irrelevant in this respect how good or bad the performance of Soviet industry may be. Even if it is true that industrial production for household and private consumption cannot be compared to the performance of the military-industrial complex, it would be utterly ridiculous to term the greatest, or perhaps the second greatest, military power in the world an "underdeveloped" society. If one type of modernity can be characterized by the triad "capitalism, democracy, industrialization," the other type corresponds to the triad of "functionalism, totalitarianism, industrialization." Needless to say, I would not wish to suggest by this that there are no other types of societal organization, nor that there is any necessity in these combinations. Rather, I have only sought to specify the basic constituents of the Soviet model of modernity.

Terroristic types of totalitarianism may survive for a while (which is an unendurably long time for their victims), but measured with the yardstick of history, their longevity is generally limited. The permanence of a state of war always has limits. However, totalitarianism knows no temporal limits. Once sedimented and reproduced in accordance with functionalist patterns, a totalitarian society can continue to reproduce itself smoothly. Conflicts cannot be excluded, but the equilibrium can be restored without excessive efforts. Contemporary Soviet totalitarianism, which has left its revolutionary birth-pangs behind, is an entirely conservative society, a legitimized and, at least for the time being, a well-functioning one. Unfortunately, all hopes of a near collapse of this social structure seem as misguided as hopes for its eventual thoroughgoing social reform. This does not, of course, exclude *changes within the framework* of the existing structure, for no society can be completely static. Here, a few comments on dissidents as the social locus of opposition within Soviet society are called for. My point of reference is the dissident movement in the Soviet Union, but my statements are, at least in part, relevant for other East European dissident groups and movements, excepting *Solidarity*.

In the Soviet Union, dissidence has become a *vocation,* an orientation that has absolutely nothing to do with the career paths followed by the caste or elite of "professional revolutionaries." "Vocation" signifies the opposite of "function." The group of dissidents does not constitute a nucleus of any emergent anti-Soviet revolutionary movement; rather, it is the nucleus of *"society"* as such. In a totalitarian world where only system-integration is left, where action is nothing but the performance of a function, dissidents provide a niche for a *social integration* that is *not* system integration. This facilitates the performance of *transfunctional actions* of various kinds. Soviet society confirms the paradox that the outlawed sphere is the only one that can legitimately be called "public."

Accordingly, if there are citizens left among subjects, they are dissidents by vocation. There is no need to speak about the content of the dissenting ideas, as they represent all possible colors of the rainbow. The main point is that the very existence of such movements provides a barrier, not against totalitarian ideas that may indeed set foot behind this barrier, but against a complete system integration. Nor are the different shades so terribly important in themselves, for several distinct versions of liberalism, democracy, and authentically socialist discourses, all conducted within this outlawed public sphere, provide a counterbalance against the expansion of the political limbo that might prove fatal in the case of a sudden collapse of the regime and a resultant power vacuum. "The flourishing of art" in which Hannah Arendt rested her hope belongs to a bygone past, and its flowers now grow in a foreign soil. Totalitarianism was only shaken for a moment, if at all. However, a change in the attitude of a few is still discernible and, moreover, this changed attitude will continue to reproduce itself as long as it is not wiped out by brute force.

II.

Colonizing imperialism is, according to Arendt, one of the major roots of, and preludes to, totalitarianism. Due to rapid decolonization after World War II and to the growing national self-identity and nationalism of the middle classes in the vast region we refer to as the "Third World," "race thinking," this poisonous fruit of imperialism, is in retreat. Needless to say, racism still holds one of the most powerful appeals to the social cluster that Arendt calls the "mob," even though it had lost momentum among the "masses." Or to put it more cautiously, racism has to be clad in presentable garments, political, religious, or national, in order to mobilize a considerable proportion of the masses. With the exception of South-Africa, no publicly racist state has remained, notwithstanding the continued existence of several *de facto* racist societies. As a consequence, of the three original types of totalitarianism (the Nazi, the Bolshevik, and the Fascist), the Nazi one does seem to be inimitable. The ideology of the dominating race is unlikely to reemerge, even more to spread. Simultaneously, however, a kind of covert racism has gained momentum within other types of totalitarianism. It has been often pointed out that antisemitism, conspicuously absent from fascism and bolshevism before World War II, has rapidly increased in the Soviet Union in the last four decades, as has a strong anti-Russian and, at the same time, Russian racism (both are not simply identical with nationalism). Official antisemitism can partially be explained by a constant and renewing need for scapegoats. But there is an additional explanation. I mentioned earlier that with the sedimentation of the totalitarian system and the closure of the period of mass repression, the constant and unbroken flow of the process called a "change of elite" had been thwarted, and the path leading to upward mobility jammed. Racist scapegoating draws the attention of dissatisfied contenders to the "disproportionately high" percentage of the members of certain nations or ethnic groups in lucrative positions. Ideology and factual truth can, of course, be miles apart. Despite the *numerus clausus* applied to Jews in all tertiary educational institutions (and *numerus nullus* in case of sensitive government jobs) in the USSR, Russians in particular are made to believe that they remain on the lower rungs of career ladders because of Jews. Similarly, Ukrainians firmly believe in the "Russification" of all leading positions, while Russians claim that they are constantly discriminated against. In Sudan, racism makes its appearance in the guise of a religious ideology. The costumes may vary, but the costumes are constantly there, for this reason I believe an *undisguised,* Nazi-type racism is very unlikely to reemerge.

In contrast to Nazism, both the Bolshevik and the Fascist types of totalitarianism have proved to be imitable, and both of them have gained momentum in the Third World. The liberation of the colonies has brought very little liberty for the populace of this immense region of the world, and colonizing imperialism is far from being an innocent party in this outcome. It is too easy a line of defense to assert with ill-conceived self-righteousness that the totalitarian dictators in contemporary Third-World countries are of indigenous origin, some of them openly hostile to the West. Hannah Arendt's point holds true in this respect as well. Totalitarianism has nothing to do with traditional dictatorship; it is not the product of backwardness or underdevelopment; it is intrinsically *modern,* often the consequence of a deeply problematic development. Imperialist colonizers have expanded the world market on the one hand and prompted modern industrialization on the other. However, instead of implanting the seeds of Western liberalism or democracy, with very few exceptions they ruled the colonies with proto-totalitarian political practices. Now the chickens have come home to roost. Indigenous Third-World totalitarian rulers learned the practice of power from Europe and not from their own traditions, and their power base is not the "people deep down on the social hierarchy" but the power-hungry and greedy middle classes created by the capitalist world market and industrialization.

I do not wish to assert that all instances of dictatorship in the Third World are totalitarian in character or even close to this pattern. There are traditional models of dictatorship among them, and not just in Latin America. In this region, as the Chilean scholar Jorge Tapia-Valdez argues, a new kind of "institutionalized militarism" has gained momentum, a phenomenon that can be identified in Asia as well. (Chile and Indonesia would be the major examples.) Institutionalized militarism is certainly not totalitarianism proper, but it creates certain typically totalitarian institutions and uses certain totalitarian practices. At the same time, in some Third-World countries traditional monarchies have survived, while in others a certain kind of liberalism has taken root. However, to deny the gaining momentum of totalitarianism would be wishful thinking.

I have distinguished between "Fascist" and "Bolshevik" types of totalitarianism. Sometimes the two contest each other, while at other times they merge, even with great ease. Two reasons can be identified: First, what Arendt called "class thinking" is in decline in a way similar to, although not to the same extent as, "race thinking." Nationalism (or pan-nationalism) is subsequently substituted for orthodox class thinking. Even indigenous "Third-Worldism" (and not its European and utterly inauthentic version) is a pan-nationalist thinking of a kind. Now pan-nationalism was the ideological, organizing center of (Mussolinist) fascism, though, paradoxically, Lenin's doctrine of anti-imperialism likewise inspires a certain type of pan-nationalism. Second, the *social basis* of both kinds of totalitarianism is roughly identical (middle classes, the huge mass of university students, the mob), and the only difference is that of political affiliation. However, despite a possible merger, the distinction between Fascist and Bolshevik types of totalitarianism is fairly clear. In the case of fascism, the rule (the government) is totalitarian, but society is only politically and ideologically totalized, and the totalizing ideology is nationalist or pan-nationalist. In the case of bolshevism, the totalitarian ruler and the ruling party unleashes a wholesale and complete totalization of society, and the ideology of totalization includes "class thinking." The actual extent of repressions and the extent of terror felt by the populace are not dependent on the Bolshevik or Fascist character of the particular totalitarian regime but on other factors. However, both Fascist and Bolshevik versions share to a certain extent what can be called "the totalitarian imaginary."

There is always something new under the sun. Third-World totalitarianism has added two novel features to those of their European ancestors: antimodernization on the one hand, and a religious ideology as an instrument of totalization on the other hand. The first antimodernizing instance of totalitarianism was, surprisingly, a *totalitarian movement within a totalitarian society:* the Maoist cultural revolution. The second case was Kampuchea under Pol Pot, and the third is Iran under Khomeiny. The first two instances were based on class thinking, elevated to a far more exclusive and pathologically exaggerated degree than usually evidenced among totalitarian societies, rules, and movements in the Third World. The third case emerged from a religious doctrine. Up until the cultural revolution, all totalitarian societies and states were, in principle, industrializing-modernizing; therefore, this new phenomenon confronts us with a puzzle. I have already insisted in the wake of Arendt that totalitarianism is an intrinsically modern phenomenon. How can this assertion be valid if movements, practices, and rules mobilizing the whole paraphernalia of totalitarianism now turn against modernization? How can the thesis be upheld if an emerging totalitarian rule focuses on a premodern doctrine, for example, the Shiite-

Moslem religious doctrine used as a tool for Khomeiny's terroristic totalization is a premodern type of imaginary, in contrast to nationalism, pan-nationalism, class and race thinking? As far as modernization is concerned, the mystery is not so deep as it seems at first glance. Anti-industrialization has been a decisive trend in European ideological modernity right from the beginning. The romantic generation of intellectuals who jumped headlong into the radicalism of totalitarian movements in the second and third decades of our century had a very strong antimodernizing bias. As Arendt has pointed out, they have embraced the new barbarians because they alone are able to rescue "us" (that is, the "integral" or "authentic" man) from Western civilization. It proved rather difficult for them to reconcile their longings with the actual modernizing fervor of totalitarianism, and, in fact, they often became deeply disillusioned. The utterly misguided sympathetic reaction of certain Western radicals to the cultural revolution, to Pol Pot or the Khomeiny-dominated outcome of the Iranian revolution, their reluctance to face mass murder, pogroms and, in the case of Kampuchea, genuine genocide, can be accounted for, although not excused, by their adherence to a romantic antimodernizing modernism. As for the movements and regimes themselves, and more important than the fact that Pol Pot studied in Paris and Mao called himself a student of Marx, is the undeniable fact that they understood themselves to be a *conscious reaction* to the Western (Soviet or American) industrializing-modernizing patterns and their concomitant "decadent" features, while retaining totalitarian practices. (In Mao's case this was obviously a reaction to the Soviet type of industrialization, while in Pol Pot's and Khomeiny's cases it was a reaction to the American version.)

One puzzle still remains, that of the place of religious doctrine within such a modern compound. Up until now, "synthetically made" modern myths of totalitarianism have claimed exclusivity and have not seemed prepared to share the imaginaries of traditional religious myths. Yet Khomeiny's Iran is still comprehensible in Arendt's terms, for the Ayatollah's brand of Islam can be conceived as a new pan-religious movement, one that, if organized on the basis of a totalitarian state, can far more easily totalize *the whole of society* than can any kind of nationalism or pan-nationalism. The latter are normally vehicles of politico-ideological totalization. They are, as such vehicles, sufficient to shape the attitudes that are necessary to keep a political-ideological totalitarianism running, but they do not and cannot alone provide the kind of doctrinal diet people must live on for a considerable time in order to change all their social attitudes, down to their most elementary everyday routines. Put bluntly, nationalism (pan-nationalism included) does not constitute a *way of life,* molded after the pattern of a new totalitarian society. Yet a religious doctrine interpreted by a charismatic totalitarian Fuehrer could be as perfect a diet for the eventual change of all behavioral patterns as the class thinking of Western origin had been in its Stalinist interpretation. Of course, it is a distinct possibility, even probability, that the Iranian brand of totalitarianism will fail before the time necessary for a complete totalization lapses. Arendt once made the reasonable guess that only countries of sufficiently large size can embark on the totalitarian venture with any chance of success. This prognosis turned out to be incorrect, and it will suffice here to point to the example of Albania. Totalitarian rule is not dependent either on size or on time, but any complete and all-encompassing totalization of society does take time. The more diverse the political factors that have to be considered, the shakier all long-term political predictions turn out to be; therefore, I shall not venture into prognoses concerning the viability or nonviability of a religiously founded totalitarian system or the longevity of Third-World totalitarianism in general. I only stress that the phenomenon exists and it has to be understood by use of the same theoretical tools, analytic and historicist, that were once shaped by Hannah Arendt, calmly, objectively, but never *sine ira et studio.*

III.

While shifting their main thrust to the Third World, totalitarian movements have abated in Western, Central, and Southern Europe. Sporadically one can still find totalitarian parties, but they do not command movements, but rather cater to specific interest groups and subclasses. The detotalization process of the most influential Communist Party of the Western world, the P.C.I., has been spectacular. The totalitarian psychology, mentality, and ethos survive in marginal groups rather than in mass movements, in particular in the underworld of international terrorism and national right-wing Fascist terrorism. Masses no longer rally around charismatic Fuehrers to seek salvation in a superhuman will. De Gaulle was a charismatic leader, but not of the totalitarian kind. He was no Fuehrer, and following him was at least rationally motivated (based on his actual rescuing of a nation); as a result, many people became disappointed in him simply because their interests had not been satisfied by him. These well-known facts only serve to buttress one of my initial statements: certain decisive factors enumerated by Arendt, among those comprising the origins of totalitarianism, can contribute to the emergence of social tendencies quite different from, occasionally diametrically opposed to, totalitarianism. Let me recall some of Arendt's tenets: a disillusionment with parliamentarism, including traditional political parties; the substitution of certain grand issues for the pursuit of well-defined collective (class, group) interests; the withering away of classes; and the emergence of a "classless" society of a kind. In my view, these tendencies, far from having disappeared since World War II, have rather gained momentum without giving rise to any new kind of neo-totalitarianism. What they have given rise to is a new type of social movement.

As far as disillusionment with parliamentarism is concerned, Arendt made one exception: Great Britain. In 1984, the exceptions are rather the historical newcomers to the parliamentary system: Spain and Greece and to some extent Italy, where all parties, except the neo-Fascist MSI, define themselves *against* the background of a fatal Fascist past. (*Formally,* not even Stalinist Greek communism is an exception here.) The disillusionment with parliamentarism can be strongly detected in France, West Germany, and Great Britain. In present-day France, no party except the dwindling Communist Party has a tradition. In Great Britain, the emergence of the liberal-social-democratic alliance, irrespective of how it might fare electorally, challenges the traditional two-party system, whereas the traditional background of conservatism has given ground under Thatcher to a more ideologically oriented rather than pragmatically circumscribed right-wing politics. In West Germany, the success of the Green Party has divided social democracy, whereas a new brand of nationalism has superimposed itself across party- and class-lines on merely interest motivated objectives. Although Western societies have not become classless (least of all Britain, the traditional class society par excellence in Europe) and class affiliation still expresses itself in voting patterns, cross (that is, ideologically motivated) issues have moved to the forefront of contestation. These issues are carried by social movements that increasingly dominate the scene of the European political theatre.

In times gone by, big demonstrations were organized by parties, and the biggest ones were organized by totalitarian parties that still held sway over a social imaginary. However, the biggest demonstrations of the last decades have not been organized by parties at all. The sweeping movement of 1968 in France took the Communist Party by surprise; communists did not even understand how they might capitalize on the movement. Even if totalitarian fringe groups participated in the events, they were relegated to the sidelines. More recently, almost a million demonstrators marched on the streets of Paris in defense of private education. Although all right-wing political parties (Le Pen's neo-Fascist party included) were conspicuously present, the demonstration was not organized or orchestrated by them. Similarly, certain totalitarian groups regularly participate in the enormous peace rallies in Germany and Great Britain, but they neither organize nor dominate them.

In pinpointing these new phenomena, I must stress that I am not engaged in gathering material for a refutation of Arendt's theory. Rather, at first glance, the contrary is the case. Arendt, herself a prodigy of a romantic generation, was far from happy with soulless parliamentary politicking. Rather, her ideal type of democracy was shaped by the image of the ancient city-state, while later, the old American township and the conciliar system spawned by the Hungarian Revolution of 1956 suited both her theory and temperament far better. I am speaking in her spirit if, regarding recent changes in the European political theatre, I strike a cautiously optimistic chord: instead of the passivity of atomized masses, we see a rather active populace ready to fight out issues directly by circumventing the channels of representation. On the other hand, Arendt regarded mass movements *per se* with a not unfounded suspicion. Movements often fail to encourage discourse. If issues are carried by a crowd *with one single voice*, differences in opinion cannot be articulated and particular groups cannot stand for the complex network of their interests. What Arendt called "the mass," is still the subject of mass movements, even if the mob is absent or relegated to the background. This is why optimism must be subdued, though not completely abandoned.

In conclusion, I should like to touch briefly upon certain misconceptions concerning the internal cohesion of totalitarianism. There is a widespread view that whereas traditional dictatorships frequently collapse from internal causes, totalitarianism, once established, never does. I have already mentioned Hungary, Czechoslovakia, and Poland as conclusive evidence to the contrary. As long as totalitarian rules totalize society only ideologically and politically, the system can as easily collapse from internal causes as any traditional dictatorship. Moreover, as long as a particular society is not completely totalized (the totalization of attitudes included), the collapse of the regime from internal causes is equally possible. I would rather argue that it is precisely during the process of the complete totalization of society that a collapse like this is most likely to occur. The complete totalization of a society requires a very long period of time, during which anything can happen. (And in any case, the Soviet type of totalitarianism is the only example of complete totalization; religiously based totalitarianism could perhaps be the second.) If nationalism is a strong imaginary institution in a totalitarian society, external threats decrease rather than increase the chances of collapse. Soviet totalitarianism was ultimately cemented in the Great Patriotic War. Taking into consideration both this and my firm conviction that the collapse of Soviet totalitarianism could not occur through any gradual change, but only by a predictably cruel revolution, I repeat that external threat decreases rather than increases the chances of such a collapse. No ruling totalitarian oligarchy could be shaken by the fear of an external threat (to be what they are is simply a condition of existence for them); the populace would rather be pushed into rallying around the oligarchic leaders in defence of the imperial might or the mythologized "national pride" of their country. Further, attempts at undermining the economy of a totalitarian society never weakens the totalitarian character of a Soviet type of society; it can only unleash waves of repression in them. If people starve to death, this is indeed their problem and not a factor of, say, the government's "electoral chances." Although totalitarian oligarchies, as all governments, prefer to satisfy the elementary needs of their populations, they will not alter a single cog of their system even if they cannot satisfy those needs, but raise sham objectives, select new scapegoats, or increase oppression instead. The Soviet leaders are no longer "free" agents of an arbitrary policy, not even in the sense that Khrushchev had been. They are themselves caught in the web of systemic imperatives. They are unscrupulous and cynically lucid as to the *modus operandi* of their regime and its requirements. But they are no longer infernal, in the sense that Stalin (and his entourage) was evil incarnate. Nor have they any hidden wisdom on their side. Therefore, the never-ending attempts by Sovietologists to fathom the secrets of a possible future leader are but academic exercises.

I have drafted this paper as a new preface to the imaginary re-edition of *The Origins of Totalitarianism*. Some of Arendt's prognoses in 1966 proved wrong. I hope that some of my prognoses will prove equally wrong. It is with this hope that I can look forward to a further preface to *The Origins of Totalitarianism*, in the next millennium.

Notes

1. In *Dictatorship Over Needs* (London, Blackwell, 1982), Ferenc Feher, Gyorgy Markus and myself have sought to give a comprehensive analysis of the dynamics of Soviet societies.
2. Victor Zaslavsky, *The Neo-Stalinist State*, M.E. Sharpe-The Harvester Press, New York-Brighton, 1982.

Alain Touraine

16. Social Movements, Revolution and Democracy*

The Idea of Progress

Emancipation

In the modern Western tradition, *social movements, democracy* and *revolution* were at first not separated. The notion of social movements, with emphasis on *social,* did not even exist. Movements were political, and there was no difference between revolution and democracy. Revolution was destruction of an Ancien Régime, privileges, or a foreign domination. Democracy was the political expression of the general idea of progress, the triumph of reason. The American Revolution was by nature democratic, even if it was to a certain extent aristocratic, and was considered the result of a voluntary mobilization of the people. In a parallel way, Simon Bolivar considered himself to be serving universal democratic values through his long military campaigns and his attempts to create a unified Latin America. During the French Revolution, the three ideas were less integrated: 1789 remains a symbol of democracy; the Jacobin period is defined as revolutionary, while the Sans-Culotte and even more the Bras-Nus were perceived as social movements that could endanger the political revolution as well as defend it. Still, a very long tradition was created, which proclaimed that the three notions should not be separated because they are three aspects of the same general value—progress. Social movements were defined as progressive, as forces of liberation of the future from the chains of the past; democracy was the open society as opposed to the closed communities; and revolution was the triumph of reason over irrational interests and creeds. This was still Tocqueville's view in the 1840s, although he was worried by the progressive separation of the three forces.

Crisis of the Model

It is true that the identification of these three progressive forces didn't last much longer than the overthrow of Anciens Régimes and colonial dominations.

---

*From *Graduate Faculty Philosophy Journal,* vol. 10, no. 2, Summer, 1985.

The notions of progress, accepted by widely different political and social forces, were quickly reinterpreted in even more different ways. Capitalists were more interested in free enterprise than in public liberties and in political freedom more than in the free organization of social movements. Democracy became the way of organizing a limited political system, and social movements were largely identified with the idea of revolution, that is, with forces and goals that had been eliminated from the political system.

On a wider scale, democracy increasingly came to be identified with dominant countries, while the rest of the world had only to choose between a dependent participation—through nondemocratic process—in the democratic world or revolutionary struggles for independence and progress. At this point, the unity of the three notions broke down and was replaced by an opposition between two alliances: on one side, the alliance of social movements and revolution; on the other side, the alliance of democracy and bourgeoisie. Moreover, after the rupture of the old social order, the issue becomes one of the organization of an industrial society. Industrial conflict becomes more important than the opposition between tradition and modernity.

From Progress to Industrial Conflict

The Role of the Labor Movement

The first and most important aspect of the rupture of the "progressive" movement, which agglomerated revolution, democracy, and social movements into the general image of progress, is the formation of the *labor movement.* If we give a precise definition of this notion, it cannot be identified with unionism, in all its aspects, and much less with industrial relations. Even if union activities have economic aims and try to increase the political influence of workers, what we call the labor movement is primarily the agent in a social conflict concerning the control and appropriation of industrial production. Inasmuch as unions are a form of organized action to obtain collective goods—a definition that corresponds to what has been called market or business unionism—they are no more than the sellers of any other commodity either democratic or revolutionary. But the role of this type of unionism rapidly declined when the labor market began to be dominated by the influence of the unions themselves, by oligopolistic strategies, and by state intervention. Then a second meaning of unionism became more important, a political one: its capacity to exert influence on economic and social policies. Charles Tilly, analyzing the determinants of the frequency of strikes in France, attributes major importance to the changes in the political influence of the unions and, in influential books published on western European unions, C. Crouch, A. Pizzorno, and J. D. Reynaud defend a similar view, which inherits some of the main themes of the old British idea of industrial democracy.

But labor laws and collective agreements were more the results of strong, sometimes revolutionary, pressures from outside the political system than of an internal extension of political democracy. This pressure and revolt is what we call the labor movement. The important fact is that it is not defined in terms of political participation or exclusion, but in nonpolitical terms, in terms of social conflict and in most cases, including that of the United States, of class conflict. The labor movement stems from a direct conflict between employers and wage earners *in the factory,* especially about the conditions of work. More precisely, this conflict appears to be directly linked with the destruction of workers' occupational autonomy by the so-called rationalization that has been sometimes symbolized by the names Taylor and Ford and more accurately by the wage systems that link payment with output and productivity. It reaches its most acute forms in mass manufacturing industries where the directly productive indigenous jobs are replaced by unskilled and semiskilled jobs, not only on assembly lines but in most forms of production. Before this central stage of industrial organization, workers were more autonomous and defined their interest by the labor market, in bargaining as well as in radical terms. After it, they are incorporated into organizations where it is no longer possible to oppose their skill and autonomy to a management-dominated system of production, and they are subjected to a hierarchized administrative organization, to a *Herrschaftsverband,* to use a Weberian expression which is rightly used by Dahrendorf to describe the new situation and the limited political conflict it creates.

It is tempting to say that the labor movement, defined as agent of a structural conflict about the social use of technological resources, is by nature revolutionary because it is involved in a basic conflict with management and produces antimanagement, anticapitalist, and socialist ideology. Therefore, one level of union action, the economic one, should be considered to be autonomous, while the political level of action is oriented by democratic goals, and the direct class conflict by a revolutionary ideology. Such a view has been widely accepted, and the main discussions have been concentrated on the relative importance of each of these levels. It is important to discuss this view because it implies an image of the relations between social movements and political action that is debatable.

The definition we use of the labor movement as such puts the emphasis on concrete labor relations, on the destruction by management of workers' control of their own production. It defines it in a social rather than a political way. If this social protest is easily accepted and dealt with by political institutions, it takes on reformist or democratic expressions. On the other hand, if the political system is closed and authoritarian, social protest, being rejected, challenges the political institutions and becomes revolutionary. S. M. Lipset has given, most recently in his presidential address to APSA, an elaborate demonstration of this type of correlation.

The moderate A.F. of L., the revolutionary syndicalists, and the democratic radical leaders of the U.A.W. and the social democratic unions of northwestern Europe have shared over a long period of time the experience of the growth of mass-manufacturing industries, as well as the idea of the central importance of job-centered class conflict. This conflict does not determine political action by itself. Not only do its political expressions depend on the situation of the labor market and of political institutions, but it is unable to propose a model of social and economic transformation. It is defined by a conflict and cannot go beyond the ideological expressions of this conflict: the factory to the workers and workers' self-management. This class-oriented labor movement accepts its subordination to political action—in many cases to populist coalitions and in some cases to working class parties. But it is still defined in a Leninist way by the discontinuity between trade-unionism and political action, between the class *an sich* and the class *für sich*. The labor movement defends the workers and criticizes the irrationality, selfishness, and waste that characterize, according to its views, the industrial system. But to achieve rational use of technological resources, state intervention is required either to suppress the power or to limit it. In most cases, this intervention is conceived as a direct effect of mass mobilization, open conflict, and even general strike. This political role of the labor movement has been considered by revolutionary parties as fundamental, and economic action as limited "Trade-Unionism," but the importance of the labor movement for our analysis derives, on the contrary, from the fact that both roles proclaim the autonomy of social movements in relation to all forms of political action, democratic or revolutionary. The nature of the labor movement must therefore be defined by the association of two main features: it is an independent and central social movement, but its area of action is limited to the problems of production so that it is subordinated to political action; but the counterpart of this subordination is that its political pressure comes from outside the political system itself and supposes some degree of violence and rupture. The proof of this is that when unions participate too completely in the political system, a counter-labor movement appears, for example, in the well-known British case where shop-stewards, wildcat strikes, and wage drift are elements of a counter-labor movement that opposes the bargaining orientation of the Union leaders. The labor movement represents a first attempt—although only a partial one—of autonomization of the area of action of social movements. It separates workers' antimanagement unions from a political anticapitalist program. The first element is present everywhere at a given stage of industrial production; the second appears only in some economic and political conditions. For example, the first element is as present in Polish and Brazilian factories today as it was in Detroit in the thirties. However, in each country it takes different political forms. It is not always anticapitalist and prosocialist, but it always uses the same methods of opposition to management.

While previous social movements, from peasants' revolts in the seventeenth century to craftsmen's and tenants' protests during the fourteenth through nineteenth centuries, were directly political, pressing the state to control food prices and minimum wages and rebelling against heavier taxes, the labor movement is more social than political, even if it maintains some links with political action and recognizes its own subordination to it. The autonomy of the labor movement as a social movement is greatest when the class consciousness, which expresses the destruction of workers' autonomy by management, is sharpest. On the other hand, revolutionary orientation is stronger when unemployment and low wages are more important problems than poor working conditions and harsh "exploitation" in the factory.

A Limited Political System

The distance between the labor movement and democracy increases in two different situations. In some European countries, like France, the political and ideological mobilization of a "progressive" middle-class was more important than the autonomous action of unions. As a result, a part of social movements became directly subordinated to political parties, while another part of them refused to participate in the internal conflicts of the bourgeoisie and became antiparliamentary in a right-wing or in a left-wing way. The case of countries where the political system has a high capacity for integration or cooptation, but is not organized along class lines is different. In very different forms, this is the case of many American countries ranging from the United States to Colombia and Mexico. These political systems do not fight organized social movements; rather, they maintain or eliminate from the political system itself large parts of the population by segregation or more violent rejection. They function with a low degree of political participation and combine political cooptation and state violence. On the other hand, where parties are organized on class lines and where the political system remains open, the distance between democratic institutions and social movements is more limited, as was the case in Britain, during long periods of German history, or in Chile and Argentina.

Revolutions Abroad

To the separation between social movement and democratic institutions introduced mainly by the labor movement during the nineteenth century, the twentieth century added a growing disjunction between social movements and revolution and a sharp separation between democracy and revolution at the global level. Revolutionary movements in our century are decreasingly anticapitalist and increasingly anti-imperialist and anti-colonialist. This transformation has been made visible by the displacement of revolutionary movements from industrial to nonindustrial, from central to peripheral countries. This transformation, highly visible after the Soviet Revolution, had even more important effects after the Second World War. This was a consequence of the dramatic effect of colonial wars in Asia and Africa, of the growing role of multinational corporations, and of the direct intervention of foreign powers in the political life of many Third-World nations from Central and South America to Eastern Europe, and including Afghanistan, Angola, and Lebanon. Some analysts, like Lenin, linked imperialism with a reformist workers' aristocracy; others opposed the capacity of democratic regimes to institutionalize social conflicts to the necessity for social movements to resist the domination of authoritarian regimes by revolutionary methods. For both groups, the idea of democracy and the idea of revolution seem to correspond more frequently to different regions of the world.

Thus, the political and ideological evolution of the nineteenth and part of the twentieth centuries appears to be dominated by a progressive separation of these three notions. They are no longer agglomerated into an integrated evolutionist and modernist view of social life and social problems.

The Leftist Intellectuals

The intellectuals, to a large extent, participated in the decomposition of the old progressive ideology nourished by the Enlightenment, the American and French Revolutions. Few of them identify themselves with social movements, because these are generally anti-intellectual in a populist way. A larger number became the ideologists of democratic institutions and identified themselves with general principles more than with social forces or concrete problems. A large literary and artistic production contributed with an active neo-Kantian philosophical school in defining democracy by its essence more than by its functions.

A somewhat smaller but much more influential group of intellectuals identified themselves with revolution. Intellectuals feel at home with a revolutionary thinking that analyzes a system of domination, and concludes by asserting the impossibility of internal changes and the necessity of opposing the natural laws of revolution against the organized resistance of vested interests. Revolution must be scientific and gives power to science against capital. The role of the revolutionary intellectuals was especially important in the Communist movement, but Western anarchists and Russian nihilists are extreme examples of these scientific and revolutionary intellectuals.

The Unifying Ideology

However, in some parts of the Western world, intellectuals, instead of identifying themselves with either social movements, democracy, or revolution, tried to react against their growing separation. They tried to reunify them, not on a political but on an ideological level, and to reintroduce the idea that social movements reinforce and enlarge democratic institutions through revolutionary actions. The *more* democratic institutions, revolutionary national liberation movements, and labor movements were drifting apart, the *more* intellectuals proclaimed the unity of these forces of social and political transformation. For more than a century, the idea was expressed that class struggle, national liberation and cultural modernization are parts of the same general confrontation between future and past, life and death. From the end of the seventeenth century until the mid-nineteenth, with expressions of varying intensity from one country to another or from one decade to another, an increasingly powerful ideology—or better, myth, in a strict sense—was created to reunify progressively differentiated and even conflicting forces. This creative myth proclaimed the identity of liberties and liberation, of political democracy and the labor movement, and even of cultural liberation and political or national liberation.

These proclamations sometimes took shape in a moderate and reformist way: the Fabians and the Webbs in particular introduced the notion of industrial democracy that was used in a progressively more limited sense by the advocates of industrial relations systems. In Latin America, many intellectuals and political individuals became Terceristas, trying to find an intermediary path between dependent capitalism and revolutionary class struggle by a combination of State intervention and social reforms.

Sometimes, on the other hand, the myth expressed itself in a radical way. Here the French intellectuals together with some Third World intellectuals played a central role. From Anatole France to André Gide, from André Malraux to Jean-Paul Sartre, a long French tradition considered the revolutionary regimes, socialist, communist, and eventually Third World nationalist, as agents of transformation of a limited bourgeois freedom into a wider, more concrete and popular democracy.

Many interpretations can be given to the lasting and often blind efforts of many intellectuals to reject all testimonies to the despotic or totalitarian aspects of Stalinism and of many nationalist regimes, and to defend the "popular" character of the Stalinist policy or of the Chinese Cultural Revolution. The key fact is the existence of an autonomous stream of Leftist intellectuals clearly separated from revolutionary intellectuals, defenders of public liberties in their own countries, and most of the time attacked as "bourgeois intellectuals" by authoritarian post-revolutionary regimes. They tried to react against the growing separation of social movements, democracy and revolution. First they supported a new alliance between democracy and social movement, as Rooseveltian liberals did at the time of the birth of the C.I.O. and as French intellectuals did after the violent demonstrations of the Extreme-Right in 1934 and as did agents of formation of the Popular Front. In most countries, at the time Hitler was coming to power a Leftist orientation of this kind was based on a strongly anti-fascist orientation.

After the Second World War, when the cold war and then rapid economic growth reinforced right-wing governments, a new generation of intellectuals, finally conscious of the non-popular character of the Stalinist Regime—supporters of the Hungarian Revolution as well as the Polish October, and later of the Prague spring—found in the Third World liberation movement a new expression of both popular and revolutionary forces with which western liberals were to ally themselves in order to fight anti-democratic, imperialist, and racist forces in their own country.

Today it is commonplace to say that the nature of the Vietnam, Cambodian or Cuban Regimes demonstrates that these liberal-radical intellectuals were confused and politically ignorant, if not dishonest. Such a judgment is not acceptable because it identifies two groups that are different from each other, whereas it is precisely their progressive separation that is the central focus of this intellectual history.

The Revolutionary Populists

On one side, some intellectuals identified themselves with what they considered as anti-bureaucratic and anti-authoritarian revolutionary movements. They opposed Stalinism in the name of Trotski and Mao for the sake of the revival of a true socialist revolution. That led them to blindly support the Chinese Cultural Revolution and many extreme forms of political and ideological control in the Third World, and in their own countries to create or develop a new old Left, doctrinarian and opposed to the autonomy of the new social or counter-cultural movements. These fundamentalist revolutionaries were non-violent in France, half-violent in the United States, often violent in Japan, Germany, and Italy.

Intellectuals and New Social Movements

On the other side, the reference to Third World national and social movements was for other groups the way to discover or to create new social movements in their own countries. This tendency was much more visible in the United States and in France than in Japan, Germany, and Italy during the late Sixties. It became predominant in most countries during the late Seventies. Progressively, this new New Left became more and more anti-revolutionary and libertarian. It opposed the identification of social movements with state power. In a situation where social movements were weak, where democratic institutions were more clearly linked with the maintenance and legitimation of economic and political privileges at the world level than with the institutionalization of new demands and protests, they proclaimed the necessity of making political institutions more representative by organizing new social forces that should be represented and, at the same time, the necessity of breaking with a revolutionary type of action, that is, with the idea that a violent transformation of state power commands the formation of social movements and is a political prerequisite for social transformations.

These three types of intellectuals—supporters of communist and nationalist regimes, populist revolutionaries, and libertarians—were not entirely separate from each other when a major crisis was occurring, like the French colonial war in Algeria, the U.S. war in Vietnam, and the French, American, or Mexican '68. Nevertheless, they were always very distant from each other. Ideologically, Jean-Paul Sartre contributed more than anyone else in leading the search for the union of revolutionary movements and democratic values. Supporter of the May '68 movement and of all anticolonial campaigns, he was for a few years the figurehead of the Maoist movement, but never stopped describing himself as a petty bourgeois, a definition that includes the defense of personal and public liberties. When he died, the large crowd that accompanied him to the cemetery was conscious of the end of his dramatic effort to maintain the unity of actions and ideas that were more and more visibly contradictory.

The Critical Intellectuals

Other intellectuals were earlier convinced of the impossibility of an integration of so clearly divergent forces, but they tried to maintain the unity of social movements, democracy, and revolution no longer in a positive, affirmative way, like Sartre, but in a negative and critical way. They proclaimed that all societies, liberal as well as post-revolutionary, are dominated by absolute powers, that every aspect of social and cultural organization should be read as a sign of this logic of absolute domination. Thus, democracy is a lie, social movements are impossible, and revolution is nothing but the general destruction of social and democratic movements, which can exist only as critique and rejection of domination, alienation, and manipulation.

This view, which rejected all links with organized social or political movements, became in some countries the specific ideology of deceived revolutionary intellectuals and students. In France, this extreme determinism leading to the conclusion that all value-oriented collective actions are illusory, meaningless, or dangerous, maintained, after the downfall of the '68 hopes, a predominant influence. Many intellectuals and students accepted wholeheartedly the Althusserian idea that class struggle is a humanistic and confusing concept and that Marxism should be understood as a scientific discovery of the internal mechanism of a total domination that explains itself from the realm of production to the realm of reproduction. This idea was translated into a sociological vocabulary by Pierre Bourdieu. At the same time, in Latin America, the same view led revolutionary intellectuals to break with class action and mass movements and to rely only on guerillas to destroy a system of political and economic domination whose only real strength lies in support by American imperialism. In Venezuela, Peru, and to a certain extent in Uruguay with the Tupamaros, these guerrilleros acted in conformity with the ideas of a courageous former student of Althusser, Régis Débray.

Divergences

Both in the Western industrial countries and in Latin America, these three orientations drifted farther apart. In the United States and Europe, the new Old Left, Trotskyist, Maoist, and pro-Soviet movements opposed the new radicals, linked to new cultural and social movements, while some critical intellectuals were predicting the end of the integrated radical view by proclaiming, after Marcuse, the impossibility of social movements and revolutionary changes. In Latin America, after the failure of the guerillas and the death of Che, some revolutionary groups, from Nicaragua to Peru (and for a short time in Argentina), gave priority to revolutionary military action; while other groups, both liberal-radical and Christian, were organizing new grass-root, antiauthoritarian, and often communitarian movements. This division, this decomposition of radical ideology, indicates the end of a highly influential intellectual movement that tried to reconstruct the unity between social movements, democracy, and revolution. This movement had been progressively destroyed by the institutionalization of the power of the bourgeoisie, the conflict between political institutions and the labor movement and the growing identification of democratic countries with imperialist world-wide domination.

From Revolution to Democracy

The End of the Revolutions

The most direct result of this division of the leftist intellectuals at the end of the seventies is the decline of revolutionary ideologies. The era of the revolutions is coming to an end. Perhaps this is because Anciens Régimes have simply been destroyed everywhere and because many more people suffer from the domination of modernizing authoritarian regimes than from traditionalist conservative elites. Already at the beginning of the twentieth century, the Mexican Revolution was the reaction of middle classes, peasants, and industrial workers, not against traditional landowners, but against the rapid development of an agrarian and industrial capitalism dominated by foreign financial groups and oriented by the *cientificos* and their positivist and modernizing ideology. In Iran, the Khomeinist fundamentalist revolution put an end not to a traditionalist power but to a white revolution headed by the Pahlavis and foreign capitalists. In Poland, Solidarnośč, as a social, democratic, and national movement, is fighting the rule of the Communist Party that defines itself as an agent of modernization, and that destroyed what was, to a certain extent, an Ancien Régime.

Even in Western countries, the major protest movements now oppose an excess of voluntaristic transformation, not a lack of change. The revolutionary and progressive ideology opposed the open society to the closed community, the general rules of the state to the particularistic interests and values of landlords and priests. Now the concentration of power is so great, economic domination, political power, and cultural influence so often concentrated in the same hands—in societies where the control of information and communication is more central than the ownership of factories—that protest movements primarily oppose this concentration. At the same time, these movements often defend traditional or new communities and want to restore or create open institutions and a diversified, "mestiza," social life. Not everyone will agree that these protests constitute new social movements, but it is clear that they reject the idea of revolution because it opens the way to the absolute power of the state. They are not counterrevolutionary, but antirevolutionary, as much as the people who fought in Spain against the Napoleonian army that raised the flag of the French Revolution, or as much as the Polish or Czech workers opposed armies that covered their tanks with the flag of the revolutionary workers' movement.

The Triumph of the Liberals

Intellectually, the reaction against the transformation of social movements into totalitarian states provoked a strong backlash of liberal ideologies. Because France was the country where the influence of the Leftist intellectuals had been strongest and where a large number of them had supported Communist Parties, this country experienced the most brutal transformation of its intellectual life. Still, a comparable evolution took place in the United States. In a highly symbolic way, two former friends, Sartre and Aron, who had been separated by the conflict between democracy and revolution, met again in Paris shortly before Sartre's death to support the Boat People jointly. Unlike Sartre, Raymond Aron lived long enough to be convinced that at last his defense of democratic institutions and his attacks against the "opium of the intellectuals" were accepted by the Left as much as the Right wing, and that revolutionary ideology was rejected by almost everyone, including Sartre's followers. At a less dramatic level, when ministers of the now governing Socialist Party in France tried to mobilize Leftist intellectuals for the defense of the government, they received negative responses, and many well-known intellectuals preferred to campaign for Solidarnoŝĉ rather than for a socialist government.

The Search for Democracy

At a more intellectual level, the most visible transformation is the new importance and autonomy given to political categories and most of all to democracy. That is why Hannah Arendt's thinking is so influential today. After a long period during which democratic institutions were criticized in the name of a "real democracy" or even of a "people's democracy," so that the process of representation was said to be unimportant compared to the triumph of class or national interests, the greatest importance was given again to legal and institutional procedures, and more simply to the free formation and expression of interests, ideas, and reform movements.

Many Western intellectuals became more interested in studying the transformation of social and national movements into authoritarian or totalitarian regimes than in speaking on behalf of groups whose demands were rejected by political institutions. Even within the Women's Movement, if a revolutionary component was mobilized by the resistance of legal and political institutions to birth control methods and abortion, this component and the efforts to include the Women's Movement in the classical revolutionary tradition rapidly lost their importance and were superceded by quite different but not necessarily more moderate tendencies. It seems today that the idea of democracy has triumphed, at least in the Western world, while democracy, social movement and revolution have disappeared from the communist world and are weakened and in crisis in the Third World.

After long years of dictatorship, Brazilian, Argentinian, Uruguayan, and Chilean people have agreed to consider democracy and not revolution as their first and foremost political goal. In a parallel way, historians no longer accept the idea that social movements were just preparatory stages of revolutions, for example, that there was a continuity from 1789 to 1793, or that the Russian labor movement was just a preparatory stage of the Bolshevik Revolution.

Social Movements and Democracy

A New Principle of Unification?

It is rather easy to accept this idea of the end of revolutions, even easier to observe the crisis of the scientist and evolutionist views, on which revolutionary powers were built. But is it necessary to conclude from this critical observation that the decline of the revolutionary model leads to the triumph of the opposite political model, the democratic one; or is it possible to return to our main observation about the labor movement and to introduce the hypothesis that we are entering a period or a type of society in which social movements are increasingly independent of their political expressions? Thus, the decline of the revolutionary model would give the central role to social movements and not to institutional arrangements.

There is little doubt that today in the Western world the antirevolutionary attitude is so strong that any reference to social movements appears as an indirect and confusing way of maintaining some aspects of the crumbling and rejected revolutionary model. Even the idea that political action represents social groups appears to be linked to the ideology of "real democracy" as opposed to "bourgeois democracy." On the other hand, in Western countries most analysts insist on the autonomy of political institutions, on the importance of the balance of power, even when they criticize what they consider an excess of autonomy in the process of selection of political leaders or what they consider the paralysis that can be induced by an extreme separation of power. At a deeper level, the very notion of social movement is often rejected as actually being part of the revolutionary model or is transformed, especially in the United States, into demands that are dealt with by democratic institutions in the same manner as is any pressure for change from interest groups or reform movements.

New Social Movements

In spite of the strength of the intellectual current that emphasizes the central role of democracy and rejects both social movements and revolution as relying on the same integrative authoritarian and paralyzing image of social and political processes, consider defending a different perspective, observing the shortcomings of a "pure democratic view," and introducing the idea of the central role of social movements as basic conditions of a democratic political life.

The first critique to be presented of a purely liberal or institutional view of democracy is that it is as unable to recognize the formation of new social movements as the parliamentary republics or monarchies of the past century were unable to understand the birth of the labor movement. These new protest movements were borne farther from the political system than the labor movement because they did not attack the division of labor or forms of economic organization, but rather its values. In their simplest form, they do not criticize the social use of progress, but progress itself. Sometimes this is done in a neo-traditionalist way, but most of the time, beyond this crisis of industrial values, norms, and forms of social organization, appears the defense of the consumer and more essentially of the cultural actor. This is the individual who tries to keep or regain control over his own cultural orientation and behavior against large organizations that have the capacity to produce, diffuse, and impose languages and information. Most importantly, they produce representations of nature, of the social and historical reality, of the individual, of some collective personality or of the body itself.

The very fact that these social movements are now so weak that their influence is more diffuse than organized underlines the high degree of independence of these movements from political institutions and from the state, while political life deals progressively more with the formation of economic policies.

Social movements deal with problems and protests that were actually excluded from public life and considered to be private. They deal with health and sex, information and communication, life and death. At present, all these problems seem farther removed from political choices than labor problems. The most general expression of these movements is the Women's Movement, which is at the same time the farthest from the revolutionary model. Beyond the traditional theme of equality, which presupposes the idea that gender differences should be suppressed and that gender itself should become in most instances a meaningless attribute, or even beyond the rupture with multifold male domination and the call for a specific and autonomous feminine culture, it introduces new goals for protest movements. Traditionally, they defended production against reproduction, creation and change against socialization and control, and concretely, men against women. Now, against a growing concentration of power and a penetration of the most powerful decision centers into the field of not only economic but also cultural behavior, protest concentrates not on the transformation and conquest of the state, but on the defense of the individual, interpersonal relations, small groups and minorities, in opposition to any central power. Women are transforming or trying to transform what was inferior status—their "private" culture—into a force of opposition against a progressively instrumental and productivist type of culture and against the extension of the forms or areas of domination. The general notion of a minority itself indicates that social movements look for a limited, almost negative relation to the political system. To identify a social movement with the majority is to identify it with a democratic force. To defend minorities, implies limiting the scope of political intervention, rejecting the idea that everything is political, and protecting a nonpolitical but public territory that represents a concept of *Öffentlichkeit* different both from the bourgeois one and the socialist or trade-unionist one.

Representativity

But it is not sufficient to recognize the formation of new social movements independent of political parties and processes. We must recognize that in the past and probably in the future, the strength of democratic institutions themselves lies in their capacity to transform social conflicts into institutionalized rules of social relations and that they are strong inasmuch as they are representative. Democratic institutions are firm where industrial class conflicts have been strong and have been recognized as a central element of a chiefly autonomous civil society. Where social classes have limited autonomy, where the state and not the bourgeoisie is the main agent of industrialization, and when the working class is replaced by urban uprooted masses, democracy is weak.

It is too pessimistic a view to say that democracy exists only when political power is limited and when the central state is weak. Such a situation can very well lead to the absolute domination of local autocrats or expressive leaders. It is similarly insufficient to rely on extremely favorable economic conditions to maintain democratic institutions because the existence of large surpluses to be distributed does not lead directly to a wider access to power by a larger number of people. Democracy means representation, as the founders of modern democracies, especially in America, clearly expressed it. Doesn't that mean that democracy requires not only representative institutions but also—and more basically—*representable* social actors, that is, social actors who are defined, organized, and able to act independently of their political representation or influence?

If the weakness of democracy in the first category of developing countries, mainly in Asia, derives from the fact that an autocratic state makes the creation of representative institutions impossible, in many other countries, especially in Latin America and Africa, its main weakness derives from the fact that social actors are created by the state, that trade unions are not only controlled but organized by the state—as has been or is the case in Mexico, Brazil, and during the first Peronist period, in Argentina.

Our democracies are still strong because they have been able to transform the demands of the labor movement into labor laws and rules of industrial relations. However, at the same time, they are becoming weaker as they lose their capacity to transform social movements into political forces. Political institutions, when they are no longer representative, when they no longer find institutional channels and solutions to social conflicts, lose their legitimacy. They appear to be pragmatic rules that are, like the courts, more useful to the richest and the best informed. And we must recognize that their representativity is more difficult to achieve today precisely because the definition of the new social movements is less directly political, because the distance between culture and politics is wider than the distance between working conditions and law.

Conclusions

The transformations that have occurred in the relations between social movements, democracy, and revolution have led from the unification of the three forces within an integrated evolutionist image of progress to an increasingly greater separation of civil society and its social movements from the political system and the state. The labor movement proclaimed the autonomy and the central role of social movements, but it still maintained its own subordination to political action—sometimes through democratic processes, sometimes through revolutionary methods. The new social and cultural movements create a wider gap between social protest and political action. In many countries, the problems of economic development and national independence are the most urgent ones. In these countries, social movements are increasingly dominated or destroyed, while protests, conflicts, and initiatives are concentrated around the control of the state. In other countries, social and cultural movements go so far as to completely reject the state while accepting the risk of unwillingly reinforcing the position of a foreign state, although they condemn it even more strongly than their own.

1. The political system and democratic institutions can be strengthened by such a situation because they can act as a go-between, trying to combine the demands of social movements and the priorities of the state; but they can, on the other hand, lose contact with both and be considered a simple political market favoring the most powerful lobbies and opposing innovation.

2. The most visible consequence of this evolution is that social movements and revolutions are progressively more distant from each other. The revolutionary image of social movements is declining or is already dead. At the same time, the distance between democracy and revolution is becoming so wide that the two notions appear to be contradictory. Who still believes that the revolutionary action of a social movement creates democracy when revolutions destroy the social agents that have helped prepare them and have given birth to authoritarian regimes, and when the strongest democratic movement of recent years is fighting a regime in Poland that calls itself a People's Republic?

3. This view of transformation is opposed to neo-liberal thought, which is quite typically reinforced by the decline of the revolutionary model. It can be suggested that the political debate will be increasingly defined by the opposition between those who look for political expression in the new social movements and those who accept incorporation of progressively more democratic institutions into the state apparatus, the subordination of their representative functions to the defense of the national state, its international interests or its economic policy.

4. Our democracies never seemed stronger than in the present period of crisis of the revolutionary model and of weakness, in a period of economic crisis and declining expectation, of the new social movements. But democracies are weakened because their institutions do not recognize the priority and autonomy of social movements and the necessity of becoming more representative. The future of democratic institutions rests on the autonomous organization of new social movements. The definition of new actors and new conflicts demands the invention of new forms of negotiations and compromises.

Bertram Schefold

*17. Toward a New Economic Style in Our Society?**

In Western Europe, and in particular in West Germany, the last decade has been marked by an economic crisis accompanied by important changes in the structure of industry and by social and political transformations. The end of the slump is not yet in sight; there is a feeling of uncertainty and pessimism regarding the future such as has not reigned before in the post-war period. The experience of the United States seems to be different. Post-war growth was less spectacular, there was a different economic cycle and the boom that has begun is raising expectations. In this paper I want to speak about possible and desirable future transformations of the economic system. These transformations apply as well to other countries at a comparable level of development, but for the purposes of this paper I shall limit myself to the example of Germany. I do this because it is the country best known to me and, more importantly, because I believe that the German experience may be paradigmatic: the transformations that affect all Western nations are more clearly visible if they are accentuated by a break in the economic development.

Up to the early 1970s, post-war growth in Germany was characterized by a number of interrelated factors: the need for new equipment made possible the installation of modern technology, the opening of new markets and the establishment of the Common Market created new outlets and allowed business to benefit from increasing returns to scale and other advantages of mass production. The period from 1948 to 1974 was one of almost continuous growth, starting with unprecedented high growth rates of more than 10 percent *per annum;* it was interrupted only by minor recessions. The social basis for this development was provided by a work force impoverished by the war, disillusioned by the preceding political tragedy, and prepared to put all its hope to work for material improvements. New large and united trade unions agreed to preserve industrial peace on the understanding that real wages rose with productivity and thereby not only helped to absorb the growing product but also helped to stimulate the introduction of labor-saving machinery. Throughout this period, demand ex-

---

*From *Graduate Faculty Philosophy Journal*, Summer, 1985.

ceeded the combined growth of the domestic labor force and of productivity so that many millions of workers from Eastern Europe, refugees from Eastern Germany, and later guest workers from Mediterranean countries could be taken in. On this basis, social security and old age pensions were increased at a rate exceeding that of the national product. Yet the true dynamic of this development derived not from home consumption and investment, nor from the state, but from the growth of exports that induced domestic growth through multiplier and accelerator effects; the size of the market favored the introduction of advanced techniques in a circle of cumulative causation (Kaldor 1966).

This period came to an end in the early seventies. I do not propose to assess in this paper the relative importance of the various factors that led to this discontinuity. The disruption of the international monetary system and the rise in the price of oil were obvious influences; shifts in the exchange rate and the "technological gap" were among the fundamental causes. If one looks only at macroeconomic indicators, the discontinuity does not appear to be that great; some have suggested (without attempting an explanation) that growth continued steadily well into the late seventies, but following a linear and not an exponential trend. According to this view, the annual increment was roughly the same in each year; it was only expressed in terms of a lower and lower rate of growth because the national product itself was rising. The slowdown in the rate of growth of productivity—of which there has been a great deal of talk lately—similarly seems to lose its importance if a different perspective is chosen. The alleged decline may to some extent be a macroeconomic mirage that has to do more with unhelpful measuring concepts than with an underlying change in the trend of technological evolution (DIW 1980/81).

Nevertheless, I believe that the widespread feeling of a crisis is correct almost in the classical Greek literal sense of a juridical decision to be taken in order to resolve a conflict. The cycle of post-war growth in Germany has run its course on the basis of the exploitation of a number of related technologies; the growth of the corresponding outputs and institutions was adapted to this path of development. Now we are near saturation levels for many consumer durables, for cars and roads, house building, and so on. Germany is not leading in important technological areas (computers and space, for example), and it has become difficult to reshape the systems of social security, education, and so forth according to the new conditions.

On the other hand, there are indications that it will become necessary to change the path of economic development whatever happens to the endogenous dynamic of accumulation. While the "limits to growth" with the exhaustion of materials seemed only a remote threat in the later sixties, the energy crisis was concrete and upsetting. A different quality of environmental problems has now been reached in Germany, where air pollution is threatening to destroy major parts of the forests within ten to fifteen years. The successes of advanced industrialization are increasingly being questioned (Illich 1975). State action is counterproductive (Jänicke 1979). The sciences seem to lose some of their authority, alternative methods are much in demand (especially in medicine), and even beyond the intergenerational conflict, changes in the work ethic have been noticed (Strümpel 1977).

A continuation of the economic development of the post-war period would presuppose that a solution to all these problems can be found. A reform of the existing framework is necessary to provide a perspective for material growth, for securing its technological basis, for an efficient organization of the work process, with adequate provision of transfer payments, with a functioning national economic strategy to limit and abate pollution, and last but not least, with a social reorientation toward the task of an accelerated development.

Let me call this option the "hard" path. The alternative possibility is more vague: less emphasis on industrial growth, more leisure time to pursue domestic activities, more redistribution and less efficiency, more money to cultivate landscapes and less to construct motorways, and so on. Let us call this the "soft" path.

It may seem strange for an economist to assert that there exists such a bifurcation. The task of a theoretical economist is to formulate causal theories that the applied economist uses to predict the future—one, that is, the most likely, future. But how can we be free to make a decision regarding the character of future economic development? Are not the broad outlines of any future development determined by present conditions, which are in turn anchored in the material conditions of reproduction?

But the fact is that economic predictions are often quite wrong. We do not need the uncertainty principle of quantum mechanics to know that we cannot know the future—even if we had adequate theories—because we do not know the present with sufficient accuracy. The oracles of classical antiquity did not predict the future but, by their ambiguity, helped to clarify the nature of a decision to be taken. "If you cross the Halys, you will destroy a great empire," King Kroisos was told, and indeed, by crossing the Halys, he destroyed one, his own, for he was defeated. We want to know the character of the options open to us. That there is, in given historical instances, some kind of social choice open to us seems obvious precisely because the present presents contradictory aspects. It is at any rate unreasonable to deny the possibility of social choice for anyone who wishes to act politically.

Be it truth or mythology, it is a common belief among German economists that the economic institutions chosen by the Federal Republic in 1948 were chosen deliberately in order to attempt a reconstruction of the economy by means of competitive capitalism. There were strong tendencies toward democratic socialism comparable to British labor party policies. Instead, a so-called "Social Market Economy" was adopted, which was meant to be a compromise between a competitive market economy to raise efficiency and a system of social redistribution and control to promote equity. The experience of totalitarianism under the Nazi regime and Stalinism led to a revival of the doctrine of laissez-faire, but not without limits to be set by an economic constitution. The state was to be made responsible for a generous system of social security for those not able for reasons of age, lack of employment, and so on to stand up to the competitive pressures. The state was also thought to be responsible—within limits—for counteracting the business cycle and, especially, for the preservation of free competition (Müller-Armack 1966). And in all instances (except in the fight against monopoly), the action of the state was successful for a quarter of a century.

This "Social Market Economy" was called a *Wirtschaftsstil* or, translated literally, "economic style"—a somewhat unusual concept, at least in English, which needs an explanation. Economists had long before distinguished stages of economic development according to the material basis of production, such as the stage of hunting, of nomads, of agriculture, and finally of manufacturing. Today, economic systems are mainly distinguished according to forms and objectives of decision making: market economies are opposed to centrally planned economies with various intermediate combinations. The Marxian "mode of production" combines both aspects ("forms of production" and "productive relations").

The economic style may, at least in my view, be used, however, for a further differentiation that adds, to the criteria already mentioned, social values and institutional factors in order to characterize the style of an economy in a particular country. The feudal mode of production was compatible with quite different styles in the art of the Middle Ages, such as the Italian and the German gothic. Similarly, the modern economic system of capitalism can take on different forms as economic styles. If we compare, for instance, Great Britain and West Germany in the post-war period, we note that apart from material differences regarding the degree of modernization of technologies, there are also functional ones: the economy of Great Britain is dominated by one financial center with interests that are often opposed to those of the exporting industries, while the banking system of West Germany has helped industry to pursue a mercantilist policy for exporting commodities. British growth was conditioned by shrinking external markets due to the progressive loss of the empire and the necessity to stimulate demand by means of expansionary fiscal policies, which resulted in the well-known political business cycle of "stop and go" (Shonfield 1965). We observe that attitudes to competition, to work and wage bargaining, to social security and the welfare state all allow parallel distinctions that, taken together, create the impression of a characteristic "unity" of the style with which each country manages its own affairs in its own way (Schefold 1981).

I am not claiming that an economic style is free of contradictions. On the contrary, the style characterizes a unity of conflicting interests that are made compatible according to traditional ways of finding compromises in democratic and other decision-making processes. The vast majority of informed economists in the last century would have regarded the combination of capitalist industry with mechanisms of redistribution in a welfare state as an explosive mixture, yet some balance between the opposing requirements of efficiency and equity has been found in all Western states. The balance may be somewhat precarious, and it shifts through time in each nation, but the compromise may yet prove to be more stable than pure Victorian liberalism.

In 1932 Arthur Spiethoff presented a long list of criteria for the characterization of economic styles, grouped under five headings (Spiethoff 1932). He mentioned technological characteristics such as are used in the discussion of economic stages and the "economic constitution" that encompasses the distribution of property, income, work, and so on. Into this latter category fall the distinctions used in modern discussions about economic systems. It is therefore characteristic for the economic styles that, in addition, emphasis was placed on, first, social values (individual motivation, altruism, religious motives for action, innovative spirit, and so forth); second, social constitution (social bonds based on family and tradition, contract or legal duties, similar differentiation regarding the origins and functions of the division of labor); and third, economic dynamics (stagnant or growing society with steady or cyclical growth).

Following this line of investigation, we can observe characteristic differences in the economic styles of economies based on the same system. For instance, the slave-holding society of Athenian democracy in the fifth century B.C. was based on equal rights of citizens with—in principle—moderate ownership of land, few slaves, and economic decision making through political processes in the popular assembly. The democratic state helped to organize commerce (in particular of grains), employment (construction, military campaigns, and religious ceremonies), jurisdiction, and provision for the poor. The democracy thus represented a collective planning institution that complemented the economy of exchange in the market and, to some extent, the autarkic and self-sufficient domestic economy of the citizens on their landholdings. This economic style was, with all its implications for political conduct and its roots in the constitution of society, fundamentally different from that of imperial Rome, although this, too, was a slave-holding system with democratic origins. The writings of Aristotle and Plato are full of references to the conflicts that arose within Athenian democracy and to the forms in which compromises were worked out in order to preserve the organic whole of the state when it was being strained, among other things, by a growing inequality in the system of land ownership and some private merchant capital accumulation (Rostovtzeff 1972; Polanyi 1977).

Many other examples could be given to make the concept of economic style more precise as a complement of that of an economic system. In particular, I would like to draw attention to the fact that we observe a growing differentiation of the economic styles of various centrally planned economies in the East. The question to be addressed in this paper is whether the economic and social crisis in the West is indicative of a change in the economic style, and which direction this might take.

As an economist, I should first like to stress that I do not see any reason from the point of view of pure economic logic why a break in development should occur. The obstacles to a Keynesian policy of reflation are primarily institutional. The principal objective of a policy of employment is not to raise wages but to redistribute income by means of creating new employment. On the one hand, the overall level of demand must be sufficient to stimulate the expansion of industry, including new technologies. On the other hand, the competitive forces must be sufficiently strong to exert a downward pressure on prices, to eliminate inefficient equipment and, as far as the labor force is concerned, to keep wages low in backward areas that are not benefitting from the external effects of centers of industrial development. Under such circumstances, a restructuring of industries can take place in conditions of near full employment. But actions to protect wages and maintain high prices frustrate the process of restructuring and lead to inflation that has to be fought by means of monetary policy, and this in turn will make it difficult for the government to raise the level of demand. Moreover, the growth of the government sector, which has been going on to a large extent independently of the necessity to foster employment, has made it politically difficult to allow for a further expansion as a countercyclical measure. To pursue nothing but an effective Keynesian policy of employment thus requires a certain degree of altruism on the part of employed workers and, if it is to be sustained in the face of international competition, a high degree of mobility. The process of investment will not pick up unless an entrepreneurial spirit is alive and there are the institutional opportunities to motivate it. Finally, the growth of the government sector, which is appropriate during a slump, ought to be reversible during a boom. Since these and other necessary conditions for a consistent Keynesian policy are hardly ever fulfilled, it is not surprising that the ruling elites opt for laissez-faire policies that, by restricting demand, are to some extent successful in fighting inflation because they eliminate backward firms and weaken trade union bargaining power.

The policies designed to maintain the economic style of post-war growth are thus bound to be harsh, and it is doubtful whether they can be effective. There is no automatic mechanism that would cause investment to pick up promptly in the absence of external incentives. Moreover, there is the danger that the slackening of growth in a given country will help other countries take the technological lead. The failure to modernize is a cumulative process, too. That the social consensus for growth is a necessary factor for the promotion of growth policies, in a sense, results in an inversion of the materialistic interpretation of history: The development of the political superstructure is a limiting condition for the development of the technological basis.

However, an increasing number of people do not seem to wish the economic style of the post-war era to continue unchanged. And in fact, at least a qualitative change in the process of economic growth has to take place in order to stop the process of destruction of natural resources and the biological foundations of life. The parallel transformation of social structures has been interpreted as the "colonization of the life sphere." In the same way as the relentless pursuit of capitalist and imperialist goals has gradually, by force and through economic incentives, colonized all parts of the globe and is still gradually assimilating traditional societies into the ways of life of the advanced industrial societies, an "internal" colonization of personal lives is taking place (Ulrich 1983).

This has many dimensions. The predominance of technical rationality, complemented by an increasing professional specialization, the replacement of domestic production by the consumption of commodities and paid services, the increase of governmental interference, and the extension of state transfers have gradually reduced the sphere of personal life, based on interchange according to reciprocity within the world of a traditional culture. There has always been a shifting balance in the relations between the personal sphere, the domain of the market, and that of the state. The feeling is now, right or wrong, that the personal ("private") sphere is receding.

All three levels were, with changing importance, present in almost all known societies. It can be said, for example, that rights are determined according to status (which may be egalitarian) in the personal sphere, according to contract in that of the market, and according to the hierarchy of command in organizations with centralized decision making. Parallel distinctions can be made for exchange as gift and countergift, exchange of commodity against money or commanded delivery. Further distinctions can be made regarding the system of redistribution, the system of decision making (consensus, vote, dictatorship, and so forth). It is a characteristic mistake of modern economists, ever since the German historical school has fallen into oblivion, to overlook—at any rate to underestimate—the importance of traditional forms of the division of labor, of communication and exchange within the "life sphere." For instance, Adam Smith argued that the function of the division of labor was to raise efficiency. We all know that the division of labor among workers (but also among machines, among industries, and among nations) helps to raise productivity. But in antiquity the division of labor—or rather, of work—was commonly interpreted to have a different purpose: to allow greater perfection in the manufacture of goods. Good food or beautiful artifacts were to be improved by means of greater specialization; quality, not quantity, was what mattered. Another function of the division of labor also has been noticed. It is, paradoxically, a bond in society if specialization—for example, of different members of a clan according to their status—makes it necessary for all the members of the clan to be present because their tasks are complementary. Such a sharing of work does not presuppose a hierarchy of command nor does it require special skills that could not be acquired by anyone; it may be there only to increase the feeling of mutual dependence (Mead 1955). Of course, the division of labor can also become an instrument of domination by means of the principle *"divide et impera."*

The division of labor provides only one concrete example of how modern thinking can blind one to forms of rationality that are not utilitarian and how institutions can change their character according to the economic system in which they are used. Some advocates of a soft path of economic development thus seek forms of production that would be better adapted to natural requirements and that would at the same time lead to the enlargement of the life sphere. It had already been part of the Marxian program to liberate work from economic constraints that, in capitalism, took the form of alienated labor. When Marx realized that necessary labor, that is, labor required for the production of necessary subsistence, would remain geared to industrial methods of production for an indefinite time and was therefore not likely to become free and creative, he shifted the emphasis and spoke of a realm of freedom based on the quantitative reduction of necessary labor time: now it was not the "liberation of work" itself but the shortening of labor hours that was supposed to provide the opportunity to liberate the abilities of each human individual to realize his or her potential for self-fulfillment.

Of those accepting the significance of the Marxian tradition, Hannah Arendt was one of the most original in criticizing this conception. She pointed to the emptiness of the so-called "realm of freedom" in which everything seems willful, arbitrary, and without fundamental purpose and contrasted it with "natural" laboring for reproduction in which the daily fatigue arising from the need to provide a living changes with the satisfaction concerning completion of a necessary task according to a biological rhythm. Today, more and more people seem to feel the need to do their own work, not for the sake of artificial creations but in the context of fashioning a good life in a community of friends. At the same time, investigations show that fewer people seem to feel that work done within the industrial sector could provide such satisfaction.

Here the representatives of soft technology offer possibilities for a decentralized production based on smaller units of production and consumption. With the continued increase of productivity in the industrial sector and its quantitative expansion limited to the slackening growth of demand, with the requirement to save resources and the increase of foreign competition due to the spreading of modern technology to new industrializing countries, technological unemployment is bound to grow. The proposal, therefore, is to integrate a growing number of people who cannot be employed by the industrial sector of the economy in a so-called "dual" sector where productivity is lower, where there is less money to be earned, but where jobs give more immediate satisfaction and greater independence.

This assumes that technological unemployment will not be eliminated completely by the reduction of labor time alone. There are indeed a couple of arguments indicating that the shortening of the work week to absorb the redundant labor force is not likely to happen to the necessary extent for a variety of reasons: in particular the cost of transition, various difficulties with the social security system, and the unfavorable composition of skills. If we accept this argument, it is clear that there inevitably will be, for a decade and probably longer, a growing section of the population that is bound to be unemployed and that must somehow be reintegrated into the society. On the other hand, there is also a growing section of those who refuse integration in the conventional system. There is at least the possibility that a tolerable balance between a small but growing "dual" sector of people wishing to stay outside the economy as we know it and those inside may be struck.

I will now turn to a consideration of the conditions necessary for such a coexistence to function satisfactorily. (There can be no doubt that a certain dualism already has developed, that it would be difficult to suppress it, and that the coexistence now is very strained.) The dual sector would have to develop its own form of life or, as I say with some hesitation, its own culture. If greater scope is to be given to noneconomic forms of rationality to integrate society, cultural bonds must arise based on what is supposed to be the fundamental *raison d'être* of the new counterculture: the development of forms of production that are less destructive of nature. In a wider sense, not only agriculture and the landscape are concerned, but also health care and many social services. But a culture does not develop because a government has ordered it or because it has been postulated by a philosopher. If we therefore leave the culture of the dual sector to those living in it and assume that they are conscious of their role, we realize that they live in a contradictory situation for they are very much dependent on the industrial system that they want to try to overcome. It is inconceivable that their methods of production will be as productive as those of industry—otherwise industry would adopt them. Their standard of life will therefore be below average in terms of industrial commodities, and even then they will most probably require a subsidy in order to survive. Such a subsidy could take various forms. According to the most liberal conception, it could consist of a negative income tax. A negative income tax would ensure a minimum income for everyone. The payment one would receive if one had no other income would gradually be reduced if one earned money; beyond a certain threshold the negative income tax would be converted into a positive, progressive ordinary income tax. People would thus be free not to work at all without the stigma of being unemployed, if they chose to do so and were content with a low income. They could better their condition either by means of ordinary work or by contributing to such a dual sector. They could help in a home for destitutes in the city or they could live in an agricultural commune in the countryside.

However, the subsidy would probably to some extent have to be geared to the usefulness of the tasks undertaken. The rapid transformation of rational ways of production with the progress of industry calls for more and more compensating activities, which range from the care for landscapes that are being abandoned by modernized farming to the reintegration of minorities, which can no longer be achieved by ordinary social workers. The point is that the subsidy to be paid need not—and in many cases should not—have the character of a wage or salary.

Whatever the form of subsidy, the usefulness of the dual sector must in the long run be both established and recognized by the conventional strata of society. The recognition would have to be based on the respect for the sacrifices and the concerns of those within the sector.

Such a complementarity would by no means be new, whether we think of old monastic orders or of the financing of art by the bourgeoisie in the nineteenth century. The bourgeois adored art and was prepared to pay for it, even if he preferred his son to enter his business rather than to risk his reputation by attempting a dubious career as an artist. That art depended on the generosity of citizens, not only within the family but beyond, was only too obvious for the artist himself. The symbiosis worked because both sides felt that life was richer for art's existence, and the understanding of this relationship was based on cultural forces. In each case, the culture corresponded to an economic style, as is most obvious if we think of the coexistence of different orders of society in medieval times, where the church had profound influence not only on the leisure time of the merchant but even on his conduct in his business itself.

There are many reasons why one can doubt the emergence of such a dual sector. However, if it is to emerge and if it is to coexist peacefully and successfully with industry, traditional services, and the state, some compromise based on mutual understanding must be found. Industry and the state would have to accept limits to their expansion and to look for ways to adapt their own processes to natural requirements.

The necessity to formulate compromises, according to established political procedures and without abrupt changes, characterizes all economic styles, and in particular the Social Market Economy. It does not have to be conceived as a perfectly harmonious paradise. For instance, the endogenous business fluctuations of the capitalist economy would persist on the soft path although they would be tempered not only by the state but by the dual sector as well, which would be less market-oriented by definition. On the other hand, it is clear that the sectors could not be as sharply demarcated in practice as they are in theory; there would be many intermediate professions and occupations. Accordingly, the two economic styles (the "hard" and the "soft" paths) might appear diffuse and ill-defined; they do not just represent different compromises within themselves (between the efficiency of the market, the redistribution of the state and the noneconomic principles governing the family and the cooperative sector), but they are also likely to generate "intermediate" forms of production. The images of both scenarios can nevertheless be rendered clearer by means of analytical methods.

I came across these concepts first in the context of a large research project on the "Social Compatibility of Alternative Energy Systems for the Development of Industrial Societies," which is directed by professor K. M. Meyer-Abich in Essen and myself (Meyer-Abich/Schefold 1981). The project involves a rigorous numerical description of two scenarios for the future energy supply systems of the Federal Republic of Germany in terms of the gradual substitution of fossil fuels. The amount of fossil fuels consumed is the same in both scenarios. The first shows a gradual increase of the supply of nuclear power, the second of technologies to save energy (in particular in heating) and to use solar power directly (biomass, hydro-electricity, and so on). The exact elaboration of these scenarios is a huge task, involving an explicit description of the technologies used, an analysis of their costs to individual users as well as to society, the impact of the corresponding investment programs, the dynamic of the economy, and social institutions.

In this context, the question of social compatibility can be posed by asking, for instance, which adaptations of the legal system would be required either to safeguard a vast system of nuclear power production with breeders and reprocessing plants (Weinberg 1972; Rossnagel 1983) or to enforce the saving of energy even where this cannot be done by cheap methods. One may then also ask which changes of social values and attitudes might favor the transition to one or the other energy system; in this context, the concept of economic style was introduced. The task of designing the future economic style was compared to that of the paleontologist who wants to find out what the mammoth looked like. He can use the bones of a dead mammoth and his knowledge about the trunks of elephants for his reconstruction. We have the numerical constructions of the energy scenarios with associated numerical characterizations of the economy as the bones, and various historical societies served as our living elephants to illustrate our vision of the future.

It is a peculiar but not an exclusive characteristic of the energy system that it is vital to the economy and that the potential technologies that can be used for the supply and the use of energy services present a wide range of variations such that it becomes possible to distinguish, with some caution, technologies that would be more suitable for development according to a "hard" or "soft" path. Since the same is true for some other sectors, it can be shown how the different paths of development have distinctive technological roots corresponding to different social and economic frameworks.

The reader will probably expect me to end with an appeal to work toward the soft path as the realization of a new economic style. But I am too much of an economist to be able to do so without adding two substantial qualifications.

The first concerns the economic feasibility of such a process of economic growth in the international context. The growth of the productivity of labor on the soft path would by definition be lower and thus puts any economy choosing it at a disadvantage in international competition in the long run. I have therefore emphasized the dualist nature of the concept. As long as there are no international agreements to reorient the strategies of all advanced industrialized nations, no single economy can opt out without suffering the grave consequences of losing external competitiveness. I have therefore emphasized the necessity for the *industrial* sector of an economy to continue to foster technological progress, and I have only proposed to limit the size of that sector by letting employment shrink within it (as it already does to some extent) as productivity grows. Costs of production of industrially produced and internationally traded commodities and wages of workers in industry could thus follow international trends. But the transfers to be paid to a dual sector would still constitute a burden that must not substantially exceed that of the welfare payments of other countries. Some computer-based estimates of quantitative relationships as extensions of the scenarios have been made. They indicate that the cost of a negative income tax would be of the same order of magnitude as unemployment benefits.

The second objection concerns the political will not only to tolerate the existent tendencies toward a dualist development but to actively encourage them. Dualist forms of development in less industrialized countries have presented formidable problems and tensions. Moreover, I feel that it is the prevailing mood, at least in Germany, that everybody should be given the same opportunity to participate with his or her work in nonindustrial activities not only by having the option to choose between alternative forms of employment, but even within a chosen career. In practice, this can only mean that people prefer to stay within ordinary employment and to increase their share of free time by reducing working hours, and to use their free time more meaningfully not only for activities of consumption or earning more money by having a second job but by doing one's "own work" domestically, or in services for the community. I suppose that the ideals of the "soft" path and its corresponding economic style will emerge only in extremely reduced form if this mood prevails: On the one hand we shall then lack the example of full dedication to the many tasks that cannot be performed well by either the commodity producing subsystem of the market or the bureaucracized subsystem of the state. On the other hand, limits to the potential reduction of labor time are clearly visible, given economic aspirations, the strength of competition, and the existing system of social security. We seem to be lacking the generosity to tolerate the dual sector as well as the people who would really be prepared to take up the corresponding tasks and sacrifices. The likely outcome is a "compromise of compromises," but that is the subject for another investigation.

References

Arendt, H. "Vom Sinn der Arbeit." *Technologie und Politik 10*. Rowalt: Hamburg, 1978: 64-174.

DIW (Deutsches Institut für Wirtschaftsforschung). *Wochenberichte* 48/80, 14/81, 22/81.

Illich, I. *Selbstbegrenzung. Eine politische Kritik der Technik.* Reinbeck, 1975.

Jänicke, M. *Wie das Industriesystem von seinen Mißständen profitiert.* Opladen, 1979.

Kaldor, N. *Causes of the Slow Rate of Economic Growth in the United Kingdom.* Cambridge, 1966.

Mead, M. *Cultural Patterns and Technical Change.* New York, 1955.

Meyer-Abich, K. M. and Schefold, B. *Wie möchten wir in Zukunft leben?* München, 1981.

Müller-Armack, A. *Wirtschaftslenkung und Wirtschaftspolitik.* Freiburg, 1966.

Polanyi, K. *The Livelihood of Man.* New York, 1977.

Rossnagel, A. *Bedroht die Kernenergie unsere Freiheit?* München, 1983.

Rostovtzeff, M. *The Social and Economic History of the Hellenistic World.* Oxford, 1972.

Schefold, B. "Die Relevanz der Cambridge-Theorie für die ordnungspolitische Diskussion, Vortrag auf der Jahrestagung 1980 des Vereins für Sozialpolitik in Nürnberg." In *Zukunftsprobleme der Sozialen Marktwirtschaft.* Berlin, 1981, 689-715.

Shonfield, A. *Modern Capitalism.* Oxford, 1965.

Spiethoff, A. "Die allgemeine Volkswirtschaftslehre als geschichtliche Theorie, Die Wirtschaftsstile." In *Schmollers Jahrbuch* 1932 (Festschrift für Werner Sombart), 891-924.

Strümpel, B. *Die Krise des Wohlstands.* Stuttgart, Berlin, 1977.

Ulrich, P. "Sozialökonomische Entwicklungsperspektiven aus dem Blickwinkel der Lebenswelt." *Schweizerische Zeitschrift für B.B. Volkswirtschaftslehre,* III, 1983, 237-59.

Weinberg, A. *Social Institutions and Nuclear Energy.* Science, 1977 (1972).

Reinhart Koselleck

18. Time and Revolutionary Language*

In discussing time and language, especially historical time and revolutionary language, I will try to throw some light on a throng of interconnected problems. I will deal with concepts and key words of the political language as they pass through the temporal focal point of the French Revolution.

Abstractly speaking, it is possible to define the relation between words and the subject matter to which they refer by four relations: First, the subject matter remains the same, and the words remain the same; second, the subject matter changes, but the words that signify these matters remain the same; third, the signifying words change, but the subject matter remains the same; fourth and finally, both of them change. Historically speaking, one might guess that the last case is the usual one. Everything changes, the subject matter and the conceptions. That is true, but is in some way commonplace and does not help us to analyze the relation between revolutionary concepts and historical time. Institutions and their concepts have been changing at different rates since the end of the eighteenth century.

My thesis is that many concepts of the political language are subjected to a process of temporalization that changes their former meanings more or less fundamentally. Moreover, new words arise with a meaning temporalized from their initial employment. In other words, the comparatively static meanings of Aristotelian political terminology lose their weight, and its concepts become dynamic. They indicate and, at the same time, produce the new experience of political and social life of so-called modern times.

To prove this thesis of temporalization, I will proceed in two steps. First, I will show how it is possible to analyze a nonexistent thing such as time; how it is possible to analyze temporalization in the semantic fields. Second, I will elucidate the function of these modern concepts in the pragmatic field of their political employment.

Let us begin with a very simple statement. During the French Revolution, "time" became one of the key words of political language. Hundreds of

---

*From *Graduate Faculty Philosophy Journal*, vol. 9, no. 3 (Fall 1983).

combinations—like *Zeitgeist*—developed. Originally these meanings had a legal and moral sense. In the German language there are more than 100 combinations of "time" with other words, which before the eighteenth century were moral or legal combinations related to legal discourse or moral reflection. Since the end of the eighteenth century, however, the new combinations have had a historical or political sense. Therefore, as Clausewitz said, "time" would become one of the most misused words in the world. Almost no one could express himself politically, socially, and constitutionally without accepting the challenge that inhabited the word "time." This key word inspired the rest of the political vocabulary and language. There was no central category of political theory or social program that did not depend upon this indicator of change. No one could argue without hinting at this change that took place everywhere. Every argument had to be legitimated by the course of "time"; special legitimations needed to be linked with a general recourse to "time."

But this statement is not very striking. Why should one not be pressed to use this fundamental word in times of revolutionary changes? Therefore, it seems more fruitful to discover the temporal meaning of concepts that are not necessarily connected with this fundamental word.

As we all know, historical time is a difficult thing to convey; it depends on a spatial connotation and can be expressed in metaphorical terms only. There is one possibility, however, of adducing historical time from our sources. This purpose is served by two anthropological categories that are suited for deducing a notion of time from written sources. I am talking about the dimension of experience and the horizon of expectation. There is no historical act that is not based on the experiences and expectations of those involved in it. To this extent, we have a pair of metahistorical categories that set out the condition of potential history. Both these categories are excellently suited for discussing historical time, for past and future are joined together in the presence of both experience and expectation. These categories are also suited for discovering historical time in empirical research, since through their content, they guide the concrete agents of social and political movement. I will give you a simple example: The experience of the execution of Charles I opened up Turgot's horizon of expectation when he insisted that Louis XVI should introduce reforms so that he might be spared the same fate. Turgot warned his king, but to no avail. However, a temporal connection between the past English and the coming French Revolution could now be experienced and explored, and this connection pointed beyond mere chronology. The relation between experience and expectation is not solely a relation along a chronological line. Rather, the space of expectation and experience is somehow "fused" in the present status. Thus, we possess all three dimensions of time in these two categories. Through the medium of certain experiences and certain expectations, concrete history is thus produced.

I cannot analyze in detail the interplay of experience and expectation on this occasion. But this much seems clear: both temporal extensions are dependent on each other in very different ways. In experience, historical knowledge is stored that cannot be transformed seamlessly into expectation. You cannot deduce immediately from your experience to expectation. If that were possible, history would always repeat itself. Just as with memory and hope, the two dimensions are different in status. This is the point of a political joke from Russia:

> "On the horizon, we can see Communism," Khrushchev remarked in a speech. Someone interrupted and asked, "Comrade Khrushchev, what is a horizon?" "Look it up in the dictionary," Nikita Sergejewitch replied. Back home, the inquisitive fellow found the following definition: "Horizon, an imaginary line which separates the earth from the sky and which moves away when approached."

That which is expected in the future, is apparently limited in a way different from that which has been experienced in the past. Expectations that one may be entertaining can be superseded, but experiences one has had are collected. The dimension of experience and the horizon of expectation therefore cannot be related to each other in a static way. They constitute a temporal difference in the here and now, joining the past and future in an asymmetrical manner. This means that we have found a characteristic of historical time that simultaneously demonstrates its variability.

My historical thesis is that, in modern time, the difference between experience and expectation has steadily increased. To be more exact, modern time has only been conceived as such since expectations have departed from all previous experiences. "Progress" has become the key word to indicate this growing divergence toward an open future. Since the eighteenth century, the political and social vocabulary has changed completely. Political and social concepts now have an internal temporal structure that indicates that since the eighteenth century the respective weights of experience and of expectation have shifted in favor of the latter. Insofar as this has occurred, one might speak of a revolutionary language—necessarily replete with utopian elements.

From Aristotle to the Age of Enlightenment, the concepts of political language have served primarily to collect experiences and develop them theoretically. The notions so obtained, such as monarchy, aristocracy, democracy, and their declining varieties, were sufficient for conclusions to be drawn for the future from past experiences comprehended in this way. And this is true despite changing social structures; that is, we have the same words, but changing subject matters. From this state of affairs one might deduce a certain structural homogeneity in history until the Enlightenment. What could be expected from the future could be derived directly from previous experience. Since the Age of Enlightenment, this view has changed radically. Let us look at the ancient general term *res publica* under which specific forms of rule were listed. During the Age of Enlightenment, all types of constitution were forced into a choice between two alternatives: On the one hand, there was the republic, everything else was despotism. The decisive aspect of these antonyms lies in their temporalization. All constitutions were given a temporal indicator. The path of history led away from the tyranny of the past toward the republic of the future. The notion of republic, originally laden with experiences, became a concept of expectation.

This change in perspective can be demonstrated by taking Kant as an example. For him, the republic was a historical objective that could be deduced from practical reason. In anticipation of this future, he used the new expression "republicanism." Republicanism indicated a principle of historical movement whose promotion was a political and moral imperative. Republicanism was a concept of movement that achieved for political action what progress promised to achieve for history in general. It served to anticipate the forthcoming historical movement in theory and to influence it in practice. The temporal difference between the forms of rule previously experienced and the constitution to be expected and intended was conceptualized in this term. Out of the present constitutions, Kant chose the desirable elements and pointed in the direction of a constitutional republic with its division of power. In this way he hoped to render unnecessary the monarchic and democratic elements he defined as despotic.

There arose a long series of new words ending with *-ism*. They, too, extrapolated from various perspectives in order to indicate historical movement and to legitimate political decisions.

Soon after Kant, the young Friedrich Schlegel substituted "democratism" for "republicanism." With Kant he conceded that the goal of true democracy was to abolish all personal domination, and this could be accomplished only in an indefinite future. So democratism became a term of indefinite progress. Thus, the traditional constitutional notions such as "republic" or "democracy," which circumscribed possible states, were transformed by the suffix *ism* into notions of movement. The general function of these notions of movement was no longer merely a theoretical one, but primarily a practical one, calling for political action.

Shortly thereafter, "liberalism" became one of the new temporal alternatives that differentiated all political and social life according to past and future. To use Heinrich Heine's definition: "The liberal party is the one which determines the political character of today while the so-called servile party still acts essentially in the mood of the Middle Ages. Liberalism progresses at the same rate as time itself or liberalism has slackened as much as the past endures in the present."

Socialism and communism followed in claiming a sequential future for themselves. As Marx said: "To us, communism is not a state which shall be created, it is not an ideal to which reality has to be adapted [a statement directed against Kant's moral position], we call communism the real movement that transforms the present-day status. The conditions of this movement result from the new, existing premises." This was to become the new form of historical proof.

Therefore, temporalization not only changed the old notions of Aristotelian categories, it helped at the same time to establish new ones that found their common temporal denominator in the suffix *ism*. Considered from a temporal angle, all these categories have something in common. At the time these concepts were developed, they had no experiential content. Whereas the Aristotelian notions of constitution were directed at the finite possibilities of political organization so that one could be deduced from another, the new concepts of movement were meant to open up a new future. The lesser their experiential content, the greater the expectations they created—this could be described as the short formula for the new type of political and historical concept. So we have found two characteristics of revolutionary concepts. First, they are terms of compensation in favor of an unknown future. Second, in every one of these newly coined notions we find a continuing transition period between past and future.

Further, their corresponding antonyms, like "aristocratism," "monarchism," "conservatism," or "servilism," serve a special temporal function. The elements of these constitutions and the behavior of their representatives are ascribed to the past on the constructed time-axis. Consequently, the conservatives themselves did not accept the designation "conservatism" by their opponents until fairly late, for they did not like the term because of its temporal pressure or compulsion toward the past.

So far we have spoken about neologisms. But there exist many terms that, while the terms themselves remain, change their temporal meanings. Even if they once had certain implications, now they cannot escape the drain of historic temporalization. For instance, the term *revolution* loses its circular meaning indicating either the regular recurrence of constitutions or the turning points of epochs. Since the French Revolution and industrialization, the term *revolution* has also come to imply an open future. So it became possible for Jacob Burckhardt to define the French Revolution as the first period of our revolutionary era. Since the beginning of the nineteenth century, revolution—like crisis—has indicated the process of permanent change accelerated by war or civil war.

Similarly, *emancipation* loses its old meaning as a single legal declaration of majority, repeatable from generation to generation. The legal institution is lost in the temporal wake of irreversible proceedings that should guide the human race toward ever increasing self-determination. To quote a German academic (circa 1848): "which extension of the concept is by no means accidental or arbitrary, but necessarily founded on the essence of mankind and its way of development. Therefore emancipation practically became the most important notion, especially the center of all constitutional questions of our time."

The corresponding notion of "dictatorship" taken from the language of Roman Law is affected by a similar adjustment to the historical process. The former meaning of dictatorship implied the restoration of the old order within a limited period of time. With Napoleon I, this task underwent a fundamental change. From then on, it became a historical challenge for dictatorship to transform the social conditions and the political institutions or to introduce new codes.

Dictatorship with its corresponding notions of movement, "Caesarism," and "Bonapartism," as well as the dictatorship of the proletariat, fit into the same scheme. It is in this sense that Konstantin Frantz applied the term to Napoleon III. Here dictatorship was no longer exceptional, as in the ancient republics. It became, as Frantz said, a new type of dictatorship, corresponding to conditions never before experienced in history. The ancient limited and delegated dictatorship became the modern sovereign dictatorship, which legitimated itself in historical time.

The uniqueness of the new situation is proven by a similar extension of this notion from the political and legal fields to the social field—as we have already noted for "revolution" and "emancipation." It is in this sense that Lorenz v. Stein spoke of Napoleon's "social dictatorship." As for Napoleon III, he added: "Dictatorship is no institute, but a historical consequence. It is no dictatorship, if it is installed; it must generate itself." Dictatorship gains the same self-referential connotations that are typical of the leading temporal terms such as evolution, progress, history, or time itself. The self-generating dictatorship already provides its own historical legitimation.

It is in this dimension that the political and pragmatical function of these terms is implied. All our notions aim at an irreversible process that imposes responsibility on the actors while simultaneously relieving them of it because the self-generation of the promised future is included in the notion. This means that these notions gain a diachronic thrust from which all participants in the political discourse draw their impetus.

All the cited notions of movement—a series that could easily be expanded—carry with them the temporal coefficients of change. Therefore, they are apt to be organized according to the three temporal dimensions. Either they correspond to the signified phenomena or they provoke the phenomena to which they refer or they react to pre-existing phenomena. Expressed in another way, these three dimensions can be given completely different weights, oriented more toward the present, the future, or the past. Like the historical circumstances to which they refer, the notions themselves have an inherent temporal structure.

So our anthropological premise can be verified semantically. Modern revolutionary time is characterized by the fact that the difference between experience and expectation has increased. Of course, the elements of experience and of expectation exchange positions to the extent that the projected systems are being realized; that has occurred for liberalism, partly for democratism and socialism, not for communism. But the temporal tension that was once created has left its mark on our political and social language to this day. The new concepts of movement served to reorganize the masses, released from the system of estates, under the banner of new slogans. In this respect they also had a slogan-forming effect in that they could be instrumental in creating parties. General concepts of a high degree of abstraction were needed to coordinate heterogeneous interests. At the same time, the content of these concepts had to be emotionalized in order to mobilize the mass of the voters. This led to a tension between the instrumental use of the concepts and their potential meaning. The central challenge had always to change existing conditions, that is, initially to redefine them; but this was possible only by an anticipation of a future lacking actual experience.

This temporal structure of our notions leads us to two closely connected findings, which characterize our times in a particular way. Political and social concepts are becoming the navigational instruments of historical movement. Not only do they indicate or record given facts, but they are themselves becoming factors in the formation of consciousness and the control of behavior. Thus, they are factors in all those changes that have affected bourgeois society since the eighteenth century. And only in the course of this temporalization has it become possible for political opponents to incriminate each other as ideologists. In a certain way *Ideologiekritik* constitutes ideology. The whole function of social and political language has been altered by this critical technique. Unmasking the enemy as an ideologist has become a linguistic weapon in political conflicts.

First, until the middle of the eighteenth century, language had been stratified along the lines of the estates. The political language had been a prerogative of the nobility, the lawyers, and scholars. The units of life and action remained relatively closed. Even the permeability of the estates did not remove their boundaries. In the feudal world we find complementary layers of languages. This changed slowly with the disruption of the estates. The lexicographer Adelung had already realized that the language of "high society," of the sciences and arts, would change much faster than the dialects of the common man, which had persisted more or less for thousands of years. Even if this comparison was not correct, Adelung was already using the new temporal coefficient of change in order to describe the different linguistic zones. But the restraints would soon be shifted.

The number of participants in the political discourse learning the political terminology, especially its catchwords, increased remarkably. The speech of the educated bourgeoisie began to dominate even the political communication of the nobility. Moreover, in the course of events, the lower classes learned to articulate themselves politically. Therefore, a struggle of concepts had been inflamed, a struggle that was immediately fought out in France during the Great Revolution.

In the Prussian administrative language, we find a struggle between the concepts of "class" or "estate." An example of this conflict of concepts can be seen in what occurs after the introduction of the liberal agrarian market in Prussia.

At that time the nobility of the old estates reacted against being called "owners" (*Besitzer*)—owners of their estates. They insisted on the title "*noble* estates." Nevertheless, the chancellor who introduced the reforms always referred to them by the locution "to the owners of the land," indicating thereby that the ground is not a *noble* ground but one that might be sought by any bourgeois or even a peasant. The liberal market, then, changed the connotation of the estates, but the owners of the noble estates kept their political right to install judges where they ruled and to head the police; that is, the old feudal functions remained. Only the market became open. Thus, the change in the name estate toward that of "owner" was a political struggle concerning the legal status that dominated the decades of the reform. This type of change in denomination indicates a change toward a hope for the future. This battle of words indicated the fight against feudal rights to change the one-time landlords into landowners who could equally be nobility or bourgeoisie.

The more people were reached and involved in the political discourse, the more urgent became the need for control of the language. This challenge, too, introduced a mutation into the temporal structure of our notions. It was typical for traditional concepts to collect and organize *past* experiences and subsume them under one term. For modern political terminology, it is typical that this relationship be reversed. To be exact, a lot of modern concepts are preconceptions (*Vorgriffe*). They anticipate the future. They are founded on the experience of the shrinkage of experiences. For old experiences were no longer applicable to the changing conditions occurring in the course of industrialization and politicization. The acceleration of change increasingly devaluated most of the previous experiences. Therefore, new expectations have to be created and nurtured. For moral, economical, technical, or political reasons, they formulate goals, promising to fulfill desires that past history was not able to satisfy. Such a semantic development paralleled the results of the French and the Industrial Revolutions. If the decomposed feudal society was to be reorganized at all in the local communities and factories, in the clubs, parties, unions, and companies, then this necessitated precepts of the future. The political and social bearing of such preconceptions could be measured in terms of their ability to transcend the contemporary experience.

For example, the new situation called for organization. This term itself originated from that very situation. Therefore, a concept was made possible that combined planning, prognosis, political action, and social institutions.

Second, the art of criticizing a political opponent specifically as an ideologist could only now be developed. Theories, notions, attitudes, programs, or habits that are classified as ideological obviously have to be distinguished from phenomena that might be defined as errors, lies, or prejudices. Lies can be uncovered, errors may be eliminated, prejudices may be overcome. The refutation of an opponent works through criteria presumably acceptable to both opponents.

Even the art of unmasking, as demonstrated by the great French moralists, flourished on the weak grounds of commonly shared human misery.

The reduction of an opponent to an ideologist proceeds along different lines. It remains at a distance from the misery it is trying to unmask. For this type of criticism, there exists a historical precondition, the growing generality of those key concepts needed to assimilate modern experiences. It is typical of modern, everyday life that the visible relation between words and their designated social and political subject matter disappears. In particular, the technical and industrial conditions of daily experience are no longer accessible to experience. Therefore many notions have become more abstract in order to make comprehensible the rising complexity of the economic, technical, social, and political structures. This, however, imposes a semantic burden on the daily use of language.

The more general the notions are, the more parties can make use of them. They become slogans. Liberties in the form of privileges can be claimed only by their owner, liberty itself by everybody. Thus, competition develops for the correct interpretation, even more, the correct usage of these notions. For example, "democracy" has become a universal and exclusive constitutional term claimed by every country and every party in a different way.

The very same notions became bearers of different interests, inclinations, experiences, and expectations. This leads to techniques of exclusion designed to prevent the competitor from using the same word for different ends.

In this situation, temporalization offered a questionable remedy: One would place the various opponents or enemies on a moving time-axis in order to refute them as ideologists. This critical approach to styling an enemy as an ideologist is derived from the temporalization of our concepts—parallel to historicism. This approach is comparable to a historical short circuit. Even the present will be unfolded by notions of temporal movement. The criticism of ideology leaves political discourse with the burden of the sequence of time. By asking about the relationship of "earlier" and "later," especially of "too early" and "too late," one can decode attitudes as ideological. Even if someone argues rationally or consistently, it becomes possible to attribute to him a false consciousness. His insights and notions become relative through their temporal classification and are thus proved to be ideological.

Very often criticism using such temporal concepts defers the burden of proof to the future. For this reason, the opponent is left in a double bind. The historical time scale by which he is measured is a floating one. On the one hand, his present position is declared historically conditioned; all his prejudices are unresolvable. On the other hand, the same position might be considered utopian in a future that might never be attained. Third, the same position might be located in the past as surpassed and obsolete. As soon as future criteria of desirability enter into the judgment, it becomes impossible to reject empirically the suspicion of ideology.

In summary, the designation—or destination—of our contemporary history has not lost the characteristics of a transitional time: transitional time, not in the Christian sense, but in the sense of a revolutionary period with an open future. Infallible criteria of modern time are the concepts of motion and motionalized concepts—indicating social and political change and at the same time, influencing thought, manners, and habits by operating as linguistic factors in the formation of consciousness and indeed in the critique of that same consciousness as ideological.

Notes on Contributors

KARL-OTTO APEL (Professor of Philosophy, University of Frankfurt, West Germany), author of *Towards a Transformation of Philosophy; Analytic Philosophy of Language and the 'Geisteswissenschaften'; Charles Peirce: From Pragmatism to Pragmaticism; Die Idee der Sprache in der Tradition des Humanismus: von Dante bis Vico; Die Erklären—Verstehen Kontroverse in transzendentalpragmatischer Sicht; Sprachpragmatik und Philosophie;* co-author of *Funkkolleg praktische Philosophie und Ethik* (5 vols.).

VINCENT DESCOMBES (Professor of French, Johns Hopkins University, Baltimore), author of *Modern French Philosophy; Objects of All Sorts: A Philosophical Grammar; Le Platonisme; L'inconscient malgré lui.*

AGNES HELLER (Hannah Arendt Professor of Philosophy and Political Science, Graduate Faculty, New School for Social Research, New York), author of *The Theory of Needs in Marx; A Theory of History; Everyday Life; Radical Philosophy; The Man of the Renaissance; Dictatorship Over Needs* (co-author); *The Power of Shame; Beyond Justice; General Ethics.*

MICHEL HENRY (Professor of Philosophy, University of Montpellier, France), author of *The Essence of Manifestation; Philosophy and Phenomenology of the Body; Marx, A Philosophy of Human Reality; Généalogie de la psychanalyse: Le commencement perdu; La Barbarie; Voir l'invisible: sur Kandinsky.*

HANS JONAS (Alvin Johnson Professor Emeritus of Philosophy, Graduate Faculty, New School for Social Research, New York), author of *The Gnostic Religion; The Phenomenon of Life; Philosophical Essays: From Ancient Creed to Technological Man; On Faith, Reason, and Responsibility; The Imperative of Responsibility; Zwischen Nichts und Ewigkeit; Augustin und das paulinische Freiheitsproblem; Organismus und Freiheit; Macht oder Ohnmacht der Subjektivität?; Technik, Medizin und Ethik; Der Gottesbegriff nach Auschwitz.*

REINHART KOSELLECK (Professor of History, University of Bielefeld, West Germany), author of *Kritik und Krise; Preussen zwischen Reform und Revolution; Das Zeitalter der europäischen Revolution 1780–1848; Föderale Strukturen in der deutschen Geschichte; Futures Past: On the Semantics of Historical Time.*

JÜRGEN LINK (Professor of German Literature, Ruhr-Universität Bochum, West Germany), author of *Artistische Form und ästhetischer Sinn in Platens Lyrik; Die Struktur des literarischen Symbols; Biedermeier und Ästhetizismus; Die Struktur des Symbols in der Sprache des Journalismus; Moderne Kollektivsymbolik; Elementare Literatur und generative Diskursanalyse;* co-editor of the journal *kultuRRevolution*.

JEAN-FRANÇOIS LYOTARD (Professor of Philosophy, University of Paris-Vincennes at St. Denis, France), author of *The Post-Modern Condition: A Report on Knowledge; Driftworks; Just Gaming; The Différend: Phrases in Dispute; Peregrinations: The Law, the Form, the Event; La phénoménologie; Discours, Figure; Dérive à partir de Marx et Freud; Des dispositifs pulsionnels; Economie libidinale; Les transformateurs Duchamp; Instructions païennes; Rudiments païens; Récits tremblants* (co-author); *La partie de peinture* (co-author); *La constitution du temps par la couleur dans les oeuvres récentes d'Albert Aymé; Daniel Buren, les couleurs, les formes* (co-author); *La pittura del segreto nell'epoca postmoderna, Baruchello; L'assassinat de l'éxperience par la peinture, Monory; Le postmoderne expliqué aux enfants; L'enthousiasme: la critique kantienne de l'histoire; Que peindre? Adami, Arakawa, Buren; Heidegger et "les juifs"*.

WILLIAM J. RICHARDSON (Professor of Philosophy, Boston College), author of *Heidegger: Through Phenomenology to Thought; Lacan and Language: A Reader's Guide to the Écrits* (co-author).

MANFRED RIEDEL (Professor of Philosophy, Erlangen University, West Germany), author of *Between Tradition and Revolution; The Hegelian Transformation of Political Philosophy; Theorie und Praxis im Denken Hegels; Metaphysik und Metapolitik: Studien zu Aristoteles und zur politischen Sprache der neuzeitlichen Philosophie; Erklären oder Verstehen? Zur Theorie und Geschichte der hermeneutischen Wissenschaften; Lineamenti di etica comunicativa. Elementi e principi di una teoria del discorso morale; Norm und Werturteil: Grundprobleme der Ethik*.

STANLEY ROSEN (Evan Pugh Professor of Philosophy, Pennsylvania State University), author of *Plato's Symposium; G.W.F. Hegel: An Introduction to the Science of Wisdom; The Limits of Analysis; Plato's Sophist: The Drama of Original and Image; Nihilism; Hermeneutics as Politics*.

BERTRAM SCHEFOLD (Professor of Economics, Frankfurt University, West Germany), author of *Theorie der Kuppelproduktion; Nachworte zu P. Sraffa; Arbeit ohne Umweltzerstörung* (co-author); *Wie möchten wir in der Zukunft leben?* (co-author); *Die Grenzen der Atomwirtschaft* (co-author).

REINER SCHÜRMANN (Professor of Philosophy, Graduate Faculty, New School for Social Research, New York), author of *Meister Eckhart: Mystic and Philosopher; Les Origines; Heidegger on Being and Acting: From Principles to Anarchy.*

THOMAS SEEBOHM (Professor of Philosophy, University of Mainz, West Germany), author of *Continental Philosophy in America; Kant and Phenomenology; Die Bedingung der Möglichkeit der Transzendentalphilosophie; Zur Kritik der hermeneutischen Vernunft; Ratio und Charisma.*

LUDWIG SIEP (Professor of Philosophy, University of Münster, W. Germany), author of *Hegels Fichtekritik und die Wissenschaftslehre von 1804; Anerkennung als Prinzip der praktischen Philosophie.*

ROBERT SPAEMANN (Professor of Philosophy, University of Munich, West Germany), author of *Der Ursprung der Soziologie aus dem Geist der Restauration; Reflexion und Spontaneität: Studien über Fenelon; Einsprüche; Zur Kritik der politischen Utopie; Rousseau, Bürger ohne Vaterland: Von der Polis zur Natur; Die Frage Wozu?* (co-author); *Moralische Grundbegriffe; Philosophische Essays; Das Natürliche und das Vernünftige.*

ALAIN TOURAINE (Director of the Center for the Study of Social Movements, Ecole des Hautes Etudes en Sciences Sociales, Paris, France), author of *The Academic System in American Society; The Post-Industrial Society: Classes, Conflicts, and Culture in the Programmed Society; The Voice and the Eye: The Analysis of Social Movements; May-Movement: Revolt and Reform; La Conscience ouvrière; Sociologie de l'action; Lettres à une étudiante; La Société invisible; Les travailleurs et les changements techniques; Les Sociétés dépendentes; Vie et mort du Chili populaire; Au-delà de la crise; Un désir d'histoire; Lutte étudiante; Mort d'une gauche; Le Pays contre l'Etat; Pour la sociologie; La Prophétie anti-nucléaire; L'Après-socialisme; Solidarité: Analyse d'un mouvement.*

BERNHARD WALDENFELS (Professor of Philosophy, University of Bochum, West Germany), author of *Das sokratische Fragen; Das Zwischenreich des Dialogs; Der Spielraum des Verhaltens; Phänomenologie in Frankreich; In den Netzen der Lebenswelt; Ordnung im Zwielicht.*

ROBERT PAUL WOLFF (Professor of Philosophy, University of Massachusetts at Amherst), author of *Kant's Theory of Mental Activity; A Critique of Pure Tolerance* (co-author); *Philosophy: A Modern Encounter; Understanding Marx: A Reconstruction and Critique of "Capital"; Understanding Rawls: A Reconstruction and Critique of "A Theory of Justice."*